LEFT BEHIND IN NAZI VIENNA

LEFT BEHIND IN NAZI VIENNA

Letters of a Jewish Family Caught in the Holocaust, 1939–1941

Edited and translated by
H. Pierre Secher

McFarland & Company, Inc., Publishers
Jefferson, North Carolina, and London

LIBRARY OF CONGRESS CATALOGUING-IN-PUBLICATION DATA

Left behind in Nazi Vienna : letters of a Jewish family caught in
the Holocaust, 1939–1941 / edited and translated by H. Pierre
Secher.

    p.   cm.
Includes index.

ISBN 0-7864-1864-8 (softcover : 50# alkaline paper) ∞

   1. Secher family—Correspondence.   2. Jews—Austria—
Vienna—Correspondence.   3. Jews—United States—
Correspondence.   4. Holocaust, Jewish (1939–1945)—Austria—
Vienna—Personal narratives.   5. Jews—Persecutions—Austria—
Vienna.   I. Secher, H. Pierre, 1924–
DS135.A93S4255 2004
940.53'18'092243613—dc22

                     2004017523

British Library cataloguing data are available

On the cover: the Secher and Schab family in 1923; family documents

Manufactured in the United States of America

*McFarland & Company, Inc., Publishers
  Box 611, Jefferson, North Carolina 28640
   www.mcfarlandpub.com*

To my wife, Lucy,
whose love and understanding
kept this project going

Contents

Preface

I first discovered the letters reproduced here in English translation on the occasion of my mother's death, in 1994, as we were emptying her small apartment on New York's West 74th Street. She was 95 years old and had lived at that address since my father's death in 1953. As soon as I began casually perusing the letters it became obvious that here was opened up to me a period in the life of our family that had been lived with great intensity by my father and mother, but which had almost completely vanished from my consciousness by the time I reached adulthood. The letters from Vienna, still in excellent condition though a bit frayed at the edges, movingly described how five elderly, close relatives—two grandmothers, two aunts and an uncle—were trying to cope with ever worsening conditions for Jews under Nazi rule as World War II approached. The letters from New York, all written by my father, on the other hand, tried to maintain an upbeat tone designed to assure those who had been left behind that no stone was being left unturned in trying to bring about their successful emigration to America. At the same time Father's letters also represented a rather minute record of the experiences that gradually unfolded in our quest to make this new country our home. But most important was the light these letters threw on the stringent requirements of the U.S. immigration laws—laws that were most responsible for leaving untold thousands caught in the net of persecution and eventual extermination by the Nazis, and that also sealed the fate of those five individuals in Vienna.

My lifelong profession as an academic and research scholar enabled me immediately to recognize the historical, documentary value of this correspondence; my thoughts also turned to my closest family members, and how important it would be for them to gain some firsthand knowledge into those years of striving in New York and the sufferings of those whom

1

we had to leave behind in Vienna. It was obvious that these letters needed to be translated into English. Before translation could begin, they had to be preserved effectively to withstand constant handling during the translation process.

Initially I did not think of myself as the person who would do the translating. Having begun to read the letters I found myself in such an emotional turmoil—the images they evoked of my happy childhood, contrasted with the misery of those individuals who had been instrumental in making it so happy—that I seriously considered looking for someone who would do the job for suitable remuneration. I actually talked to two or three individuals whose German was impeccable but who were not sufficiently acquainted with the Viennese-Jewish idiom to understand the nuances of expressions that were woven into this familial discourse. So I finally had to face the fact that I alone would have to bear the burden of translating nearly 400 letters.

I began gradually, translating slowly and in no particular order as I engaged in the process of preservation, chiefly by securing each page in an acid-proof see-through envelope. I concentrated first on the letters from Vienna written by my two aunts, Marie and Ella. They were handwritten in ink on fragile, airmail stationery, mainly in the Latin-style cursive as opposed to the Gothic script known as Kurrent used by my maternal grandmother. That the writing was easily readable and without maudlin sentimentality graphically reflects their simple patience, endurance, even heroism. Their hopes, fears and forebodings are recorded in clear, factual, sometimes even terse sentences without recourse to embellishment. My father, by contrast, in his letters tried to provide insightful, occasionally humorous commentaries on his family's adjustment to life in New York besides reporting on the progress of the immigration status of the Viennese relatives. He wanted to inform as well as entertain them, so that they could forget, if only for a short time, the bitterness of their surroundings. From their answers it is apparent that this was also the spirit in which they received his letters.

As I delved deeper into the letters I began to see many stylistic repetitions but rarely any grammatical deficiencies. Any editing therefore needed to concentrate chiefly on excising references to persons and places whose role in the family or whose eventual fate was not really pertinent to the story that needed to be told: the deliberate grinding down of an aging, unwanted population group through gradual deprivation of shelter, food and other resources. My father's letters, on the other hand, required little if any editing. Typed single-space on both sides of 8 × 11 stationery, they had been composed with great style and chock-full of useful information. It was upon reading Father's letters that I realized that above all they represented a remarkable record of family loyalty, my father's willingness to devote his life to helping his family and his shock when he realized at the end of two years that all had been for naught.

For this book I selected the most poignant letters, those that would bear additional witness and serve as a memorial to a terrible period in recent history. A long and arduous effort spanning almost nine years led me to the current selections. It took at least four of those years for me to develop the thick emotional skin needed to translate the warm, familiar, loving phraseology of the correspondents into idiomatic English; I kept only all those Yiddish phrases that had been part and parcel of our Viennese-Jewish culture then.

I presented this collection to the McWherter Library of the University of Memphis because there was a dearth in our region of original material dealing with this period of history. Both undergraduate and graduate students should be able to profit from these letters, either as teaching aids or as source material for scholarly work.

I shall be forever grateful for the assistance rendered me by the McWherter Library in bringing this project to conclusion. Dr. Les Pourciau, the former director of the library, invited me to use available office space as well as equipment to move my work along and his successor Dr. Sylverna Ford, dean of libraries, most graciously continued this informal arrangement. But without the constant encouragement, interest and willingness by Tom Mendina, assistant to the dean, to act as my sounding board as well as a source of sound advice as both an expert and a friend, I am not sure that this manuscript would ever have made it to publication; I thank him especially for that. Others helpful in keeping this project alive were Ms. Judy Broy, the indefatigable secretary of our Friends of the Library, who was always there when needed most. Ms. Nancy Thomas of computer systems provided me with invaluable help in fighting the computer devils and Dr. John Evans from the very beginning steered me away from "linear" thinking when it came to working with computers. Last but not least I must thank Ed Frank, "keeper of the shrine" as curator of special collections at the McWherter Library, who aided me in the preservation of the original letters and who will be their guardian now that they have been made part of the holdings there. Again, I thank them all. My cousins the Wittons and Sussmans in Sydney, the Schicks and Kuplers in San Francisco, and the Schabs in New York, and Haifa, all direct descendants of the two grandmothers, provided steady moral support, especially at times when my enthusiasm began to flag. My daughter Josie Ballin's help was invaluable in compiling the index.

Most importantly, these letters are a memorial to my father, who devoted every day of his life from our arrival in New York in November 1939 to the day of the Pearl Harbor bombing to getting his loved ones out from under the clutches of Nazism. He typed one, sometimes two letters every week and spent most of his free time during the week looking for ways to expedite the immigration of his family and friends. With one exception—a niece who had already escaped to England and finally arrived here long after the war was over—he was unsuccessful in his quest. His overall failure contributed to his death at 57 in 1953. But the message he leaves for his descendants is priceless—his loyalty and devotion to the family will echo through the ages.

Introduction

In 1938, when Hitler annexed Austria, making it part of his Greater German Reich, approximately 185,000 Jews lived in Vienna. Unlike their fellow Jews in Germany proper, they had only a short time in which to make plans to emigrate. The development and application of racially discriminatory policies in Germany took nearly five years to come to full fruition. In Austria the ruthless attempts at exclusion of the Jewish population from both social and economic institutions took barely five months. By the time of the *Reichskristallnacht* on November 9th of that year, it was clear even to the most optimistic Jew living in Vienna that emigration was the only way out. Yet less than a year later the outbreak of World War II in September '39 reduced the opportunities for escape to one single country: the United States of America. However, in the 1920s that country had set up barriers to emigration that enabled only a miniscule minority to gain entrance during this time of crisis. My father, my mother and myself were among these lucky ones.

On October 29, 1939, we bade farewell to the city in which we had been born and raised. The awareness of having to separate ourselves, for an indeterminate period of time and possibly forever, from those in our family whom we loved most struck us with unavoidable force. My father's 78-year-old mother, Fanny (Grossmutter) Secher (b. Handel), his sister Marie, 56, and her husband Emil Kupler, 62, my mother's mother Regina (*Omi*) Schab (b. Braun), 80, and her daughter Ella, 50, unavoidably had to be left behind. The prospects for getting them out of Nazi Germany and into the USA depended entirely on our ability to obtain the necessary guarantees for their admission to the U.S. The guarantees—in the form of legally executed "affidavits"—would assure the American authorities that these individuals would never become a burden to the American taxpayer.

That was not considered to be too difficult in their cases. Marie and Emil's son Otto and his wife Stella had arrived in New York two months ahead of us, and together with my father could be depended on, once everyone had a job, to provide the required support for their immediate family. Similarly, one of Grandmother Schab's five sons, William, and his family had also gained entrance to the States and were in such settled circumstances that there could be no question concerning his ability to care for his mother and sister. There was only one obstacle to surmount: Visas were issued by the U.S. consulates based strictly on the date of registration by the petitioner, regardless of whether the affidavit of guarantee had already been deposited at the consulate.

In March 1938, the month of Austria's annexation, few people knew about the registration requirement other than those whose relatives in America had already told them about the intricacies of the U.S. immigration process. But by July of that year the word had gotten around and mobs of people, including my father, began to line up at the U.S. consulate in Vienna. This "early" registration left him and his family with the prospect of qualifying under the immigration quotas sometime within 12 to 18 months. He went to repeat the process for his mother, his sister and her husband, as well as his mother-in-law and sister-in-law, sometime later that year, probably in September of '38. The consequences of this decision are reflected in the letters written by my father in New York to the family members in Vienna and their replies over the period of November '39 to December '41. Anyone registered during or after September of 1938 would have to figure on at least a two-year waiting period before receiving a summons to appear for the medical exam required prior to the issuance of the visa. The situation was aggravated by the fact that my Grossmutter Secher, as well as my Aunt Marie and her husband, my Uncle Emil—unlike Omi Schab and my Aunt Ella—had not been born in Austria. That fact made them subject to the lower quotas for immigrants from Eastern European countries (quotas created deliberately under the immigration laws then prevailing) and would not qualify them for entry into the U.S. for years to come. Exceptions could be made if the guarantors were blood relatives who had established residence with well-paying jobs, or had acquired U.S. citizenship.

Exodus

On September 1st, 1939, the day Hitler announced his "retaliatory" strike into Poland, followed by declarations of war from England and

France, we received the notification to present ourselves on October 10th at the U.S. Consulate for the issuance of the emigration visa to America. With that stamp in our passports we could now book passage on a ship to America. The earliest ship available was the Italian liner *Saturnia*, scheduled to leave on November 2nd from Triest for New York. We were fortunate to obtain places, because the demand for the ship's tickets came not only from refugees fleeing Nazi persecution, but also from vacationing Americans eager to get out of a Europe dangerously close to an all-out war.

The six weeks beginning with the issuance of the visa to the actual date of our departure were hectic, filled with packing and other preparations. At that time we were still able to ship two crates filled with household goods and sentimental family paraphernalia, to be stored in New York until such time as we again had a place of our own. However, about four days prior to our scheduled departure from Vienna, an unexpected jolt was delivered to our nervous system. Father received a summons mailed out by the Jewish Community Organization for Vienna (*Jüdische Kultusgemeinde*, JKG) ordering him and his family to proceed within a few days to the Nord Bahnhof railroad terminal, carrying only hand luggage, for transportation to Poland where the family would be "resettled!" Adolf Eichmann, who had descended on Vienna a few weeks earlier, was making good on his promise to the führer of making all German cities *Judenrein*, i.e., cleansed of all Jews. Father immediately went to the JKG to show them the U.S. visa stamped in our passports—recently also decorated with a J for "Jew"—and only that fact protected us from deportation and the uncertain fate awaiting those chosen for this special treatment. It was also the first inkling we had of what was in store for the people we left behind. It reinforced my father's determination to leave nothing undone in trying to get our family out of there as quickly as possible.

In the early evening of October 30th, 1939, the end of a cool but still sunny fall day found us standing in the large departure hall of the Südbahnhof southern railroad terminal ready to board the overnight train to Trieste. The platform was crowded with civilian travelers, and military contingents marching in formation to the tune of such stirring songs as "On the heath there blooms a pretty blue flower and its name is Erika." An air of victory was unmistakable when the troops that bellowed out the girl's name so loud as to make the rafters ring were received with applause and hurrahs by many of the civilian travelers. The Jews—a group of probably not more than fifty, counting both those who were leaving and the family members accompanying them—tried to appear as inconspicuous as possible, but shuddered inwardly at this emotional display. It more than

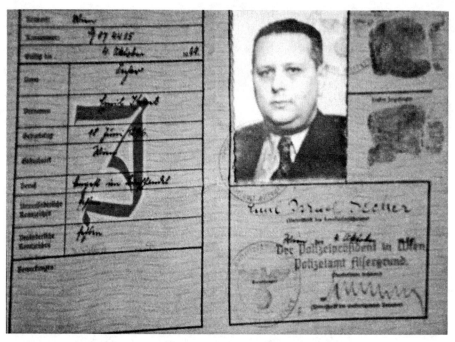

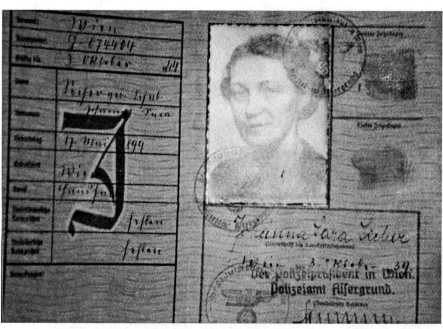

ID cards required of all Jews.

emphasized that for us this parting farewell was likely much more serious than an *Auf Wiedersehen* (till we see each other again), and we won-
dered if we would meet anytime in the near future. Neither one of the
two grandmothers had been permitted to accompany us to the station.
Uncle Emil Kupler stayed with Grossmutter and *Tante* (Aunt) Ella with
Omi. Only Marie was there, to impart to her brother some last instructions concerning her son Otto and his wife Stella, who had only recently
landed in New York. Two or three very close friends had also come, and
Father reassured them that immediately after our arrival he would set in
motion whatever was necessary to help them follow us soon. All of them
were still shaken by the news of the impending deportations to Poland.
None of them knew how and when this would affect them.

After we boarded the train and it started moving, my father broke
down badly. I remember it because I had never seen him cry, and I believe
Mother asked me to leave the compartment. We were alone in this compartment—not many people traveled to Italy at that time of the year—
and maybe by design all our fellow refugees were also in that same railroad
car, each in separate compartments, though not sleepers as I had hoped.
Traveling by sleeper took second place only to an airplane in my fertile
teenage imagination. I had to be satisfied with comfortably upholstered
benches. In general my feelings were hardly those of my parents. A fabulous adventure was awaiting me: on a great ocean liner we'd sail to America, the "Land of Unlimited Possibilities" as it was still known abroad.
On the way through the Mediterranean Sea we'd stop and see a part of
the world that had always figured large in my imagination: Greece, Italy,
Dalmatia, the Balearic Islands, Portugal, even Africa, and of course
Gibraltar. The Azores island group would be our last port in European
waters. That was the advantage of sailing to America on a cruise ship
whose course had been charted long before the beginning of the war. Now
it had to serve both rescue and entertainment purposes. No fifteen-year-
old could be immune to the travel temptations that were spread out before
me, and my excitement at the possibilities continued after we had set foot
on American soil. For this boy the past was dead and the present here to
enjoy.

The world of those who were left standing on the station platform
also took on a different hue. The departure of the three Sechers brought
a sense of finality to the remaining five members of our immediate family. They knew instinctively that time was running out for them and their
only hope of ever leaving the Nazi horror rested with Emil, their brother,
son-in-law and friend. He had shown in many previous situations that he
could be depended on to fulfill his obligations. He was well known for

his loyalty to family and friends, dependability to his employer, discipline in his personal habits, and correctness in his behavior toward others.

In general our trip to America was uneventful. Only one incident stands out in my memory, apart from the wonderful exotic impressions that awaited us at every port of call. On the journey to Trieste to board the ship we had to cross the German-Italian border. There our train was delayed to make way for an Italian troop train that pulled alongside us. The young soldiers immediately began to shout while making threatening or obscene gestures. The Jewish passengers from Vienna had crowded around their compartment windows, breathing just a little easier now that Germany was behind them. They immediately recoiled, interpreting these gestures as obvious signs of the newly aroused Italian anti–Semitism. That is until my father suddenly recognized the shouts as *A bas la Germania!* ("Down with Germany!"). He so informed his fellow passengers and immediately a rain of chocolates, fruits, sausages, pastry, etc., began to shower on the young Italians whose surprise was clearly visible at this arm's length distance. The train then began to move and the atmosphere on the railroad car carrying the Jewish refugees became perceptibly more relaxed and louder.

NEW YORK, NEW YORK

When, nearly three weeks later, our ship docked in New York, early in the morning of an unusually balmy day in November 1939, Mother and I were standing on deck, totally in awe at the sight of the Statue of Liberty gradually emerging from the lifting fog. Father, who had been up even earlier so as not to miss this long-expected sight, was already at his usual place in one of the ship's public rooms, writing his weekly report to the relatives whom we had left behind only a few weeks ago. From the day we had boarded our ship, Father had spent every available opportunity chronicling our extensive sea voyage, first through the Mediterranean and then across the Atlantic, for the benefit of the family members remaining in Vienna. It was a habit he would continue after our arrival, even as the pressures of settling down, finding a job and assuming responsibility for unaccustomed household duties began to bear down on him and his family.

None of his letters written from November 1939 until the end of that year have been preserved. They perished along with their recipients. What we know about them comes from the replies our relatives sent in which they refer to the soothing effect of father's entertaining descriptions, which helped them to face the loneliness and progressive grimness of their existence. Father preserved these letters from Vienna, mailed between November 1939 and November 1941. Later he combined them with the carbons of the letters he began typing on his German Triumph typewriter on January 8, 1940, a practice he continued until December 8, 1941, when as a result of the attack on Pearl Harbor and the ensuing declaration of war all postal traffic was halted. My mother died at the age of 95, in March of 1994, and my wife and I found these letters while cleaning out her apartment. They had been carefully wrapped in some protective material, and stored inside a small, bright red American Tourister suitcase by my mother. It had been forty years since Father's death and more than fifty-five years since the letters had been written.

The original intent of his letters was to cheer up the family members who were still in Vienna, and to keep them informed of all the steps being taken to facilitate their escape from Nazi domination as quickly as possible. From the day we had left, Father had no illusions about what awaited his loved ones in Vienna, and he knew that time was of the essence. Two people in Vienna were the main contributors to this correspondence: his sister Marie Kupler and his sister-in-law Ella Schab; Omi Schab also wrote to us frequently. Grossmutter Secher could write German only with great difficulty since she read and wrote in Yiddish, though her spoken German was quite good. She restricted herself to short scribbled notes in German—so that mother and I could also read them—but they were almost illegible to anyone but father, who cherished them all the more knowing the effort she had to put into them. His brother-in-law Emil Kupler rarely added anything to the letters, but the important role he played in keeping these four women alive shone clearly through many of their letters.

At the time of our departure, the two grandmothers, together with the last remaining members of their families, were still living in moderately comfortable circumstances. Omi Schab occupied the same apartment in which she had raised eight children and into which she and her husband had moved nearly fifty years ago. It was a large, friendly place fronting the street, with an orangery where she raised flowers and green plants, facing a very sunny backyard. There was inside plumbing, and a large kitchen with a gas stove on which hot water still had to be heated since there was no bathroom. That was not unusual even in large apartments in that district, and there were always public baths available for a more thorough weekly cleansing. One of these was the Römerbad, where one could choose from three types (or classes) of baths, showers, steam, bathtub, etc., depending on one's pocketbook or inclination. The flat consisted

of two very large bedrooms, one of which had become Ella's personal
property, so to speak. She had furnished it elegantly, according to her
taste, with a grand piano, an intricately carved wood sofa bed, pictures
painted in oil and bookcases topped with small sculptures, and of course,
a marble washstand that held a very beautiful porcelain water carafe and
washbasin. There was heavy carpeting, with matching plush curtains that
framed two tall and wide windows. A tall wood burning brown tile stove
completed this picture of more or less Victorian elegance. The rest of the
flat was similarly furnished with heavy wooden pieces, credenzas, an over-
sized dining table, large ottomans and club chairs. It also boasted an enormous green tile stove built into the corner of the dining room which,
when heated to capacity, would give enough warmth for the dining room
and the bedrooms adjoining it on each side. There were also anterooms,
a lengthy cabinet and a sleeping chamber for the maid. The cabinet had
been Felix's (the youngest brother) habitat until he too escaped early in
'39. The flat had been a place where the family gathered to celebrate grandparents' birthdays and some religious holidays, and where any one of the
grandchildren was always welcome to spend the night or pass a cozy, win-
try afternoon visiting Omi over hot cocoa *mit Schlag* (whipped cream) and
a piece of pastry. Mother and I spent two weeks prior to our departure
sleeping there since we no longer had a permanent residence. Father stayed
at his sister Marie's place, practically around the corner from Omi. Marie's
flat was not as imposing as Omi's but it had a very large corner bedroom,
a large sitting room, and an equally large kitchen—somewhat of a rarity
then. Most of the daily routine took place in the kitchen, with Marie usually presiding from a raised chair behind the large kitchen table. Grandmother Secher occupied two tiny rooms and a kitchen two floors up from
Marie. She spent most of her time downstairs, gossiping with Marie and
the neighbors. She had raised her family in what was now Marie's place,
but had later moved upstairs to make room for Marie's children.

   These two flats had been the central poles of our lives when we still
had our own place, but they became even more so after we were forced
to move from our home early in 1939. At the time of our leave-taking the
question of housing for the two grandmothers did not loom very large.
Though many Jews had already been displaced under duress from their
homes, these, like our own, had been fairly new places equipped with modern conveniences such as bathrooms, telephones, etc., and were located in
more desirable neighborhoods. The question of what the two grandmothers would do if they too were forced to move had not been broached, or if
it had, it was dismissed as something beyond anyone's control. In any case,
the family thought that by the time it became a problem, our presence in

America would enable us to expedite their immigration. Therefore, any other housing arrangement in the meantime would be of a very temporary nature. As far as money was concerned, some precautions had been taken to guard against any hardships until such time as the immigration process became fully operative. For Omi Schab and Ella, the situation was made somewhat easier by the fact that there were only two of them, and at least two of the brothers had left cash for Ella before they left the country. Ella had a savings account, which hopefully would last until she and her mother would be able to leave, too. Once brother Willy was settled in New York money could also be transferred via Deutsche Bank. However, it was feared that such action might leave Willy open to blackmail by the Nazi authorities, who could refuse to give permission for Omi's and Ella's exit from Germany unless large sums (in U.S. dollars) were paid into German accounts. Ella's letters consequently were very chary about mentioning Willy's name in connection with money. Grossmutter Secher, her daughter Marie and her husband Emil were in a much less favorable financial position. Grandmother Secher had a small pension, which presumably would continue to be paid. Marie and Emil technically had nothing other than whatever cash her brother would be able to leave her. Once we reached the U.S. my father, together with their son Otto, would send money regularly assuming he and Otto could find jobs immediately. Father had also made arrangements with some very old and good friends of his, Heinrich and Helly Beck, to lend money to his sister, which would be reimbursed as soon as they reached the U.S. This couple also expected to be able to immigrate to the U.S. within less than a year. If worst came to worst Father had instructed Marie to appeal to the Jewish Community Organization (*Jüdische Kultusgemeinde*) to be included on their welfare rolls. Eventually, it was hoped, Father would be able to reimburse the JKG as well.

In short, we firmly believed, even as rumors of further restrictive policies against the Jew began to circulate, that before the situation worsened appreciably the five remaining relatives would be well out of reach of Nazi policies designed to remove Jews from their homes. Also, now that the Polish Campaign had been successfully completed by the German armies there was much less concern in Vienna about the Jews. The openly physical effrontery expressed against the Jews had largely subsided. Jews were no longer subject to calumny, insults or even physical assaults on the street, as they had been so often from the time of the Anschluss (the German annexation of Austria) almost until the spring of 1939. The regime had taken its anti–Jewish policies out of the hands of the mob, and wanted the world to know that it was now observing strict "legality"

in its actions designed to remove Jews from the German social fabric.
Those who were able to would be permitted to emigrate after paying some
compensation to the German people whom they had "deprived for so long
of the fruits of their honest labor." That was the purpose of the *Reichs-
fluchtsteuer* (National Escape Tax) levied on emigrating Jews proportion-
ate to the wealth they had accumulated. Those who could not or would
not escape would eventually be resettled, most likely in Poland. But by
October '39 that too was only a vague goal that had not yet been formulated in detail. Nobody thought that it would apply to old people, and
people assumed that if it ever came about, younger ones would be called
first.

"Normalcy"

A deceptive aura of "normalcy" characterized the situation of those
who had been left behind, despite the fact that, technically, Hitler's Germany was formally at war with the British Empire and France. The successful campaign in Poland had ended in that country's division between
the Soviet Union and Germany. This was Stalin's reward for giving Hitler
a free hand in Eastern Europe after agreeing to the stunning Hitler-Stalin
pact that preceded the formal beginning of the war, on September 1, 1939.
Since Mussolini had chosen to stay out of the war, at least for the time
being, the Jews remaining in Germany had good reason to believe that
an escape route would be available to them for a considerable period of
time. There simply was no room for pessimism: everyone knew that a Nazi
regime unchecked by any external considerations would not hesitate to
rid itself of the Jews, one way or another. The Jews built upon any hope,
including the firm knowledge that individuals outside the German sphere
of influence were doing their utmost to accelerate the process of emigration. Given Hitler's military victory over Poland in the fall of '39, which
followed diplomatic successes ending in the annexation of Austria in '38
and the absorption of Czechoslovakia in early '39, it was not unreason-
able to believe that the quietness on the Western Front, the so-called
Sitzkrieg, would also prove amenable to a peaceful solution.

Thus, in the letters from Vienna, there was not yet any urgency with
respect to the emigration of the five family members. What did slowly
creep into their correspondence was the recognition that sooner or later
they would have to vacate their respective, comfortable apartments—in
exchange for what, they knew not. By the spring of 1940 the Nazi policies directed toward the expulsion of the Jews had only gradually begun

to take shape. They were to be "resettled" in Poland—the place Jews allegedly came from originally—and, with their labor, forced to contribute to the German war effort. What was not clear to those affected was when, how and who would go first. We know now that neither did the Nazi bureaucracy know, or for that matter care, how this would be accomplished. They were satisfied to have the process put into motion by the Jewish Community Organization, the JKG, which was charged with the task of initial selection, and ultimately with informing those selected of the date set for their departure. Judging from the letters written by both Marie and Ella during 1940, there did not seem to be any rhyme or reason behind the selection of individuals marked for deportation. The process was not accomplished very speedily; quite possibly the JKG was deliberately dragging its feet. Some individuals were being sent away to Poland, to the large Polish ghettos, probably in Lodz, Warsaw and other provincial cities. Since there was no real plan of resettlement those ghettos became more and more crowded, until their existence no longer became sustainable in German eyes and a more "permanent solution" had to be sought. It was only when this "Final Solution" was eventually decided on, at the well-known conference at Wannsee in January of 1942, that the deportation also accelerated from Vienna and other German–controlled cities. Sometimes overlooked is the fact that the Wannsee Conference was convened within one month of America's entrance into the war. The deportation and murder of Ella, Omi, Marie and Emil all took place in the second half of 1942.

The primary goal of the Nazi authorities in 1940 was to remove Jews from all outlying residential districts in Vienna, forcing them to gather in the second district, the Leopoldstadt. It was known colloquially as the Mazzoth Island, because it had always housed the large majority of Jews in Vienna, but only a few city blocks in the second district were to be reserved for Jews. Consequently, when Ella and Marie embarked on their search for new quarters, they were severely limited in their choices. They could only move in with another Jewish family that had been given permission to share its space with other Jewish lodgers. Again it is unclear how and by whom such permission was given. Undoubtedly, influence, connections, and other factors within the JKG were important in obtaining permission to remain in one's flat on the condition of sharing it with other Jews. Apart from that, "market" forces and personal preferences more or less determined who moved in with whom.

Marie Kupler, her husband Emil and Grossmutter Secher were forced to vacate their flat before the Schab family remnant, Ella and her mother, our Omi, were forced from theirs. That was an extraordinary piece of luck since it enabled Grossmutter Secher to move in temporarily with Omi and

Ella. In one of the more humorous passages Ella describes the warm relationship between the two great-grandmothers, or the two "Sarahs" as she
preferred to call them, an obvious reference to the Nazi edict that required
all Jewish females to adopt "Sarah," (all Jewish males were to adopt
"Israel") as their middle name. Marie and Emil found a room not too far
from their original abode, in the Lessinggasse, in a flat they shared with
two other families. It provided warmth and at least an easy access to the
WC and the shared kitchen. Gradually everyone adjusted to the changed
circumstances—but always there was the unspoken proviso that it was
only temporary, until they could join their loved ones in America. Ella
and her mother finally ran out of extensions, but in early May were able
to find a fairly acceptable room on the same street, Taborstrasse, a few
blocks away. Marie's husband helped with the move, but both women—
Ella, 52, and Omi, 80—lost much of their strength in the process of being
forced from their home. Only their belief in an impending notification
from the U.S. consulate, instructing them to present themselves for the
medical examination required prior to the issuance of a visa, helped them
to get through this period.

The differences between the two aunts who remained behind in
Vienna could not have been greater, whether in looks, background or
demeanor. Marie was physically well-endowed, formidable in her appearance, energetic, and not easily intimidated—whether by creditors who
infrequently came wanting to "attach" some piece of property to secure it
for a loan on which Emil, her husband, had defaulted, or by policemen
coming to deliver a warning due to a complaint lodged against Emil for
some minor infraction, such as making too much noise after closing hours
at the local pub. If everything else failed she usually turned to her brother
Emil, my father, for help, which he never refused. Since his brother-in-
law had no regular employment and worked only sporadically my father
contributed to Marie's household—which also included Grossmutter—
whenever his own resources permitted.

Marie had little use for sophisticated entertainment, preferring the
sanctity of her kitchen, where she ruled unopposed, though she did endure
occasional grumbling by her mother about Marie's unwillingness to keep
kosher just for her. To be sure, there was a separate shelf for Grossmutter's
dishes, but not surprisingly other dishes occasionally got mixed up with
them, much to Grossmutter's chagrin. Marie had two children, Irma and
Otto. Irma had made a good marriage and lived happily in one of the better residential districts, raising Marie's only grandchild, Heinzi. Her son
Otto was in his early twenties, and still lived at home when I, still a small
boy, got to know him. He worked as a traveling salesman whenever he

Amtsbeſtätigung.

Der Jude _____ Emil S_oher _____
geboren am __18. Juni 1890__ in _____ Wien _____, in Wien, II. Bez.,
_____ Vereins- _____ Gaſſe / Straße / Platz Nr. __15/c__ wohnhaft,
hat heute hier angezeigt, daß er zuſätzlich den Vornamen Israel annehme.

Er wurde belehrt, daß er überdies die Anzeige bei der Bezirkshauptmannſchaft ſeines Wohn-
ſitzes zu erſtalten habe.

Unterſchrift des Beamten:

Amtsbeſtätigung.

Die Jüdin _____ Johanna S_oher geb. Schab _____
geboren am __17. Mai 1893__ in _____ Wien _____, in Wien. II. Bez.
_____ Obere Donau- _____ Gaſſe / Straße / Platz Nr. __9/14__ wohnhaft
hat heute hier angezeigt, daß ſie zuſätzlich den Vornamen Sara annehme.

Sie wurde belehrt, daß ſie überdies die Anzeige bei der Bezirkshauptmannſchaft ihres Wohn-
ſitzes zu erſtatten habe.

Unterſchrift des Beamten:

In 1939 all Jews were required to adopt the name Israel or Sara as a middle name; this is the official receipt showing that they had done so.

had the opportunity, which in the depression-rife economy was not always easy and thus added to his mother's worries. He was deeply involved in sports, especially swimming and skiing, in both of which he took great pleasure in improving my skills. He was quite attractive and could always be found in the company of a good-looking female. He was engaged to a girl, Stella, admired for her poise, beauty, intelligence and a socially well-placed family background. When Hitler annexed Austria they did not hesitate long. They married, registered at the American consulate sometime in June '38 and soon after escaped to Switzerland, there to wait their turn on the American immigration quota. They waited, interned in the rather prison-like atmosphere of a Swiss camp for Jewish refugees from Germany, until August '39, when it was their lucky turn to leave Europe, on a Dutch liner. His sister Irma, with her husband and five-year-old son, escaped on a rickety ship that rafted down the Danube and eventually landed in Palestine. Their father, Emil, had been a successful cattle and horse dealer before the war. During the war he supplied the cavalry with horses and was himself a dashing cavalry man, as can be seen in photographs in which he sports a very curled black mustache and carries a glistening saber. When I knew him the mustache had long since been clipped to short stubble on his upper lip, which together with his weatherbeaten, wrinkled face, made him look not much different from many other Austrians at that time, including the most infamous of them all. His favorite entertainment remained the horse races, where despite his earlier career working with horses, he usually picked more losers than winners.

These then were the five individuals we left behind in Vienna that fall of 1939: Omi (Regina Schab), Grossmutter (Fanny Secher), Ella (aunt) Schab, Marie (aunt) née Secher, and her husband Emil (uncle) Kupler. What emerges almost immediately from the beginning of the correspondence between them and my father in '39–'40 is the gradual closeness developing between the remaining members of the two families. Neither of my two grandmothers, the two aunts, nor my Uncle Emil ever visited in each other's homes, as far as I can remember. Yet as soon as Father's letters began to arrive, even during the long voyage to the States, both aunts hurried to each other's flats in order to read them together.

Of the five persons who contributed to this correspondence, only Grossmutter Secher died a natural death. I found her death certificate among Father's documents long after I had started translating the letters. The *Israelitische Kultusgemeinde* (IKG, Jewish Community Organization) informed my father of her death on May 6, 1946. She had died on November 29, 1941, of cardiac arrest at age 81. Her last weeks were spent in the

From left: Emil Kupler (1877–1942?), his wife Marie Kupler (1884–1942?; both perished in Auschwitz), grandmother Fannie Secher (1862–1941; she died in Vienna), Irma Gutter (née Kupler) and her husband Benno—ca. 1926, at an excursion in Grinzing, a suburb of Vienna.

only remaining Jewish Old Age Facility at II. Malzgasse 7. Her daughter Marie, with husband Emil Kupler, must still have been able to attend her funeral at the Jewish cemetery where she was buried next to her husband Abraham. The information mailed to my father gave her exact burial site as *Zentralfriedhof I. Tor, Gruppe 49-18-77a.* I was able to visit this site in the summer of 1957 during my tenure as Fulbright Professor at the University of Vienna, shortly after the birth of my daughter Margaret in that same city. Father died 16 years later in New York, on the same day of the month as his mother.

Omi Schab was deported to Theresienstadt on July 11th, 1942. She was number 696 in a group of 1000 that left Vienna in only the third transport for that destination. Omi died there two weeks later, on July 27th, 1942, at age 82.

Regina Schab (née Braun), maternal grandmother, known as Omi. Born January 29, 1859, she died on July 27, 1942, at KZ Theresienstadt, shortly after her arrival.

The information on Omi's death was obtained from "*Totenbuch There-sienstadt*" *vol. I Deportierte aus Österreich*, published by *Jüdisches Komitee für Theresienstadt*, Vienna, 1971. No other name of family members or friends mentioned in the letters was listed in that or any other sources.

None of the individuals still in Vienna—friends, acquaintances or relatives—mentioned in these letters were able to escape the deportation program that was initiated by the Nazis in October 1939 and carried out relentlessly until the end of the war. Their names have not turned up in any of the files allegedly so carefully kept by the authorities charged with its execution. Consequently, it must be assumed that they fell victim to the ultimate fate reserved for those who were deported first to the ghettos of Lodz, Warsaw, etc., and subsequently to Auschwitz and similar camps: extermination and cremation. No information was ever recorded as to the destination of my aunts Ella and Marie, or Marie's husband, Emil Kupler.

My parents' closest friend was Dr. Robert Lakner, a highly qualified chemical engineer. In the summer of 1938 he obtained a Shanghai visa for U.S.$10.00, with which he managed to get out of Vienna, eventually jump-ing ship in Singapore. He expected to have his mother Emma and sister Hansi follow him once he had resumed his career at one of the rubber plan-tations in Malaysia. He and my father hoped to bring them to the U.S. first, where their son and brother would join them. It was not to be. They were deported, together with Heinrich and Helly Beck, equally close friends of my parents, for whom every effort to obtain affidavits required for immi-gration to the United States failed. All those who had shared flats from 1940 onward with either Omi Schab or Grossmutter Secher in the *Juden-Häuser*, the ghettoized areas of the II District, were deported and never heard from again. Their names are recorded in the greetings that father regularly sent to them in his letters to the loved ones he had left behind.

Of my mother's five brothers, Ernst, his wife, Melanie, and daugh-ter, Lisl, escaped in 1939 and settled in Sydney, Australia. His bachelor brother Felix joined him there later. Willie, his wife Ada, daughter Franzi and son Friedl escaped to Switzerland and later to England, and arrived in the U.S. in September 1939. The oldest brother, Rudi, together with his wife, Jerta, and son, Otto, floated down the Danube on a leaky raft to the Black Sea, where they boarded a decrepit ship that just barely made it to Palestine, also in the summer of 1938. Another brother, Victor, and his wife Hedwig (known as Hedi) escaped to Riga, Latvia, where they were brutally murdered during the German invasion of the Soviet Union. Their only daughter, Hannah, with her husband Emil Witton, both barely 19 and she pregnant, reached Sydney in early 1939, where she gave birth to the first grandchild born after the emigration to the Schab family. Only one immediate member of the Secher family was able to make it to the U.S. thanks to the efforts of my father, and even she had to wait until the war had been over for a year. That person was my cousin Olly Epstein, who had escaped to England shortly after the Anschluss. Her sister Elly, who escaped to Switzerland at the same time, was interned there. Thanks to her sister and my father acting as sponsors, she was able to enter the U.S. in the late '40s. Their parents, Adolph and Malvine (Emilie?) Epstein escaped to Riga, Latvia, from where they hoped to later reach the U.S. They too were brutally murdered in the excesses that followed the German invasion of the Soviet Union. Adolph Epstein and Victor Schab met in Riga, and for a while were able to send food parcels to the grandmothers in Vienna. The names of these individuals, as well as some more distantly related, always recur in the letters written by my father in the context of his efforts to obtain guarantors for their immigration to the U.S. The name of one other person among my parents' friends needs to be singled out for separate mention: Mrs. Wally Nagler, whose son Hans, age 9, was sent to England with one of the *Kindertransports* in 1939. I tutored Hans in English for several months prior to his departure. When the war started, his mother was no longer able to correspond with him, but this was remedied as soon as we arrived in the U.S., and until America entered the war their correspondence was carried on via our address in New York. Frau Nagler also never made it to England, or to anywhere else. Another individual, not a family member but in a close relationship with one, was Hans Samec, Olly's fiancé at the time. Several months after Olly had reached England, Hans, thanks to the issuance of a Shanghai visa, was able to sail to the Philippines and start a temporary existence there, but only until both he and Olly could reach America and get married. They also corresponded through my father, and the young man especially made it a point to stay in touch with his future in-laws in Riga. Hans and Olly never were able to proceed with their wedding plans. Hans was in Manila when it fell to the Japanese and he was never heard from again. Some very touching letters from Hans to Olly's parents have been preserved.

As the news from Europe concerning the situation of Jews worsened, Father intensified his self-imposed efforts as "rescuer," yet without tangible success. Throughout 1940 and 1941 various repressive measures with criminal penalties against Jews were taking effect. Among them were prohibitions against Jews using public transportation, using the services of a barber, owning a typewriter, and keeping furs or woolen clothing. The wearing of a yellow Jewish star became mandatory. Much of this was reported in New York by the Yiddish press, rather than the daily English-language newspapers. In one of his letters in the spring of 1941

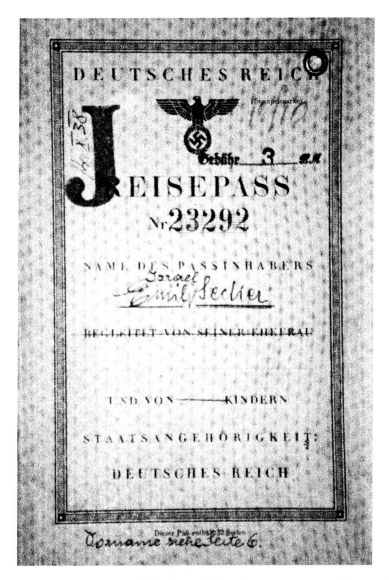

German passports were required to have a "J" for Jew stamped onto them beginning in late 1938.

Father wrote of Mother's new habit of buying a Yiddish newspaper and taking it to work, where some of her co-workers spoke and read Yiddish and did the translating. Though the effect of this information took an obvious emotional toll of my parents, I do not recall that it ever spilled over into their conversations with me. I was very busy with school and extracurricular activities of all kinds, doubly so because I was also pursuing my goal of becoming an absolutely Americanized teenager. Only sixty years later, upon going through the letters, did I realize how carefully Father avoided the subject with me. Though he would write rather mockingly to the family in Vienna about my efforts to "conceal" my European origins, he never confronted me either seriously or jokingly on that subject. Most likely it became a matter of pride for him that his only son was able to grow to manhood more or less unencumbered by some of the sordid news that made the rounds among the refugee families.

Sometime in March of '41 all able-bodied German Jews became part of the national labor pool and had to accept work anywhere regardless of age, experience, or lack thereof. For anyone under sixty that amounted to forced labor in a concentration camp, or assignment to some menial job locally, such as scullery maid in a public eating place, street cleaner, or any other undesirable activity in which the Germans could use the manpower. Father's sister Marie guardedly expressed her concern about this possibility, since it would mean having to leave Grossmutter alone during the day without anyone to care for her. By some stroke of luck she was never called, but her husband Emil did receive such a call. The letters never reveal what job he had to perform, although they say that he had to leave the house early in the morning and returned late at night. Marie had to provide food for him out of the short ration available to her, but according to her he received some remuneration, though she never indicated how much or where he worked. She looked upon his working as a means of avoiding deportation to Poland, for a while at least. That, together with evidence of affidavits on file at the U.S. consulate, and, hopefully, the ability to show that passage to the States would be paid, might postpone the deportation process.

However, in April '41 Ella wrote that they were now required to provide not just evidence that their passage would be paid for, but also the name of the ship, the date of departure, and the cabin number in order to convince the authorities that they were leaving Germany. That was an obvious impossibility, and Father told Ella that shipping lines did not disclose such information, even for first class bookings, so far ahead of schedule. But Father was indefatigable. After queuing up at the offices of the Joint Distribution Committee (JOINT) at 6AM for several days, he heard a rumor that the JOINT had a direct line to the applicable Jewish organizations in Germany. These would be informed as soon as money for the passage of any individual had been paid in New York. The Jewish organizations then would do the actual booking with the ship companies. Once these Jewish committees had obtained bookings, the JOINT would provide payment on their orders. All of this turned out to be empty speculation. First of all the ship companies in New York did not sell any tickets for specific departure dates from Lisbon, the only remaining open port. Secondly, trying to reserve space for the earliest date available, so-called open booking, turned out to be impossible because of overcrowding that lasted for most of the next year. Furthermore, applicants were warned that booking passage that far ahead was no guarantee that they would obtain an American visa.

One organization representing the interests of immigrants in the U.S. publicized a suggestion to "centralize the booking process and disseminate widely any further information to those willing *to sacrifice their last remaining resources*, initiate a form of price control, possibly by chartering their own ships, plus financing of ship tickets through loans to wage earners, etc."

The fact was that everyone was trying their utmost, in every possible way, yet the local aid organizations in New York knew nothing certain or positive. Against this background, the 1941 Passover holiday was approaching. Father refused all invitations from our sponsors to join them for the Seder despite their often-expressed sympathy regarding the fate of the family members still waiting to join us. He wrote that people should not be bothered with one's own misery all the time. He felt that, despite their kindness, they couldn't really empathize with what they themselves had not experienced. Most importantly, he somehow was beginning to sense that time was running out, and that consequently, he could not spare even a minute for activities that did not pertain directly to moving those in Vienna closer to the goal he had promised them. As he wrote very explicitly to his sister:

> You must believe us, when I say we simply cannot spare the time for social visits. Our life here does not give us one minute of which we can say it belongs only to us. I told you once before, we have more money to spare than time. That reminds me of an aphorism I read somewhere long ago: whoever has no money can always borrow it or receive it as a gift, but a person who has run out of time has no recourse at all.

Shortly after Passover in 1941, a silence of nearly two months was broken with letters from Vienna that had been mailed at least four weeks prior. During those two months, both Emil and Hansi, according to their letters, worried every hour, every day about what could explain this long silence. Every newspaper story, every radio report was received with trembling and alarm. They stood endlessly in lines at the various aid organizations, such as the HIAS, or the JOINT. Early in the morning either

Father or Mother went there to stand with people they did not know, but whose terrified expressions were only too familiar from the days in Vienna, when they had hurried from one meeting to the next, hearing much talk but no real information. But the letters showed that the five family members who had been left behind were at least still at their last abodes, and still alive.

Nevertheless, the news was not generally good. Without a doubt the deportations were accelerating, and good friends as well as distant relatives had already been notified to present themselves on certain dates, ready to leave. Father read that the mother and sister of his best friend, Robert Lakner, had already left. That news really shook him, since on the same day he received a letter from Robert, now in Singapore, asking Father to let him know anything at all about his family in Vienna. "I find it difficult to give him such sad news without any details," he wrote to his sister-in-law. "Who told you, Ella, that they had to leave, where did you find it out, were you or anyone else able to talk to them prior to their departure, or did they write to you?"

And still Father would not send any letter without some positive, uplifting or entertaining tidbits. He did after all accept one invitation to a Seder, from a family who was not related to our sponsors. The woman and her husband, Fanny and Sam Carrol, were of approximately the same age as my parents. Father had last met Fanny as a young girl, twenty-five years earlier, when she and her parents had turned up in Vienna on their way to America and had stayed for some time with his mother. He told us quite frankly that the chief reason we went there was so that he could talk to her about his mother, and then write Grossmutter in detail about the Seder. He later described it as a "food orgy," and I can testify to that. He wrote with obvious relish about the "Americanized" Jewish holiday dishes, compared them to the ones his mother used to make, and even asked her what ingredients she used that made them taste not only better, but also different than the ones Fanny had served. He then segued into a praise of New York department stores and their offerings during the Passover holidays. He was amazed at Macy's colossal display of kosher food for the occasion.

Most bakeries and groceries were actually closed for the whole period, and he proudly wrote to Grossmutter that "we did not eat one piece of bread all during those eight days, not that it would have been possible: bread is simply unavailable!" I would hardly have made the same claim, and my excuse undoubtedly would have been that nobody forced me to eat only Matzoh in Vienna.

The Atlantic & Pacific Food Market, better known as the A&P, also

caught Emil's attention, and in his descriptions of its cornucopia of tropical fruit, mountains of fresh vegetables, and counters of tastefully displayed meat, fish and poultry available in all seasons were almost lyrical.
"I believe my dear ones, that Europe could live on what remains untouched
and uneaten. And yet," he notes, "the cost of living here is not as reasonable as it was in Europe, considering the magnitude of goods available. I
am an old conversion man—and am teased a lot on that account by my
friends—because I can show them that over there in untroubled times one
could obtain everything cheaper despite a lot of it having been imported."

Father did not hesitate to write about such things, even though he
knew about the scarcity of food and other goods prevailing in Europe.
He knew, and he mentioned it on occasion to us, that our people in Vienna
wanted to know that we were well off in America, and that it eased their
pain when they could revel in such information. The letters they wrote
in response to his fulsome descriptions of life in New York proved him
right. They literally shared our improved circumstances vicariously, and
voiced their appreciation of every bit of news about their American relatives, most of whom they had never met. Father never failed to mention
some of the small and not-so-small family and business worries of our
sponsors, who owned a very popular cafeteria in Jersey City. Their two
teenage daughters were often discussed in father's letters; they were
between the ages of 16 and 18, when boyfriends came to play an increas-
ingly important role in their lives. This gave rise to demands for even more
"freedom" than American daughters already could claim. Father was fascinated by their lack of interest in world events, or at least their ability
to ignore them. Of course they spoke only English, and they had no desire
to learn any foreign tongue, least of all the Yiddish of their fathers. I guess
that he envied them their carefree attitudes, and was wise enough to realize that this made for a happier existence than the one he and others like
him were experiencing, which may explain why he never imposed his sorrows and anxieties directly on his son. The relatives in New Jersey also
had a son, a young dentist, who was among the first men drafted for military service. With obvious pride Father wrote about the "smart looking"
First Lieutenant and his duties at the Army base in Fort Dix. To Father's
everlasting disappointment his own son was not able to pass the rather
haphazardly applied physical requirements for military service over a year
later, forcing me to complete the process of Americanization as a student
working my way through college in the Midwest.

Another factor had entered the bureaucratic process governing the
immigration laws during the early spring of 1941. Most of the affidavits
issued by sponsors in 1940 would lose their validity after a year if no visa

had been issued. Thus they had to be renewed, or supplementary guarantees had to be obtained, showing that the sponsor's ability to care for
his charges under any circumstances had endured unimpaired. This procedure involved the usual mountain of paperwork, and was a task that
only lawyers could accomplish successfully. Fortunately, Isaac Safirstein
and his wife Hannah Handel, both lawyers, could be counted on to work
on these matters, no matter their cost in time and money. They had been
instrumental in arranging our passage to America, and they were still
doing everything humanly possible to help those who remained behind.
Documents had to be collected, photographed, notarized and mailed to
the U.S. consulate in Vienna. Mother's brother, William Schab, had arrived
only a few weeks ahead of us in New York, and was continuing his enter-
prising career in the rare book business. He had immediately taken on
the responsibility as sponsor for Omi and Ella. This largely involved handling their affidavits, which needed renewal, having been granted back in
1939, soon after Willy's arrival in America. Several times during 1940 Ella
and Omi thought they were about to be issued visas, but both internal
obstacles and international events intervened, and postponements became
almost routine. Among the obstacles were the frequent temporary clo-
sures of the U.S. consulate in Vienna, ostensibly to catch up with the backlog of immigration applications. Sometime in May '41 some movement
in the consular working process appeared to develop. Father was deluged
with entreaties from individuals in Vienna who he barely knew, begging
him to contact even their most distant relatives here in the hope of per-
suading them to act as sponsors. Some of these requests came via Ella,
and it was obvious that Father had acquired a reputation as someone who
would at least pass on the burdensome information. He did just that,
almost to the limits of his physical ability. He could never really get away
from worrying about his own—our closest relatives, for whom he had
been able to do anything, or at best, next to nothing. Still, he drew a line
beyond which he absolutely refused to go: he would not ask our original
sponsors for help involving anyone other than Grossmutter, Marie and
Emil.

These sponsors, Herman and Isidor Handel, nephews of Grossmutter Secher, had extended their generosity to other members of their families. Father wanted to be sure that their affidavits for father's three people
would not be called into question because of financial inadequacies when
the time came to appear at the U.S. consulate. Father's nephew Otto, the
son of Emil and Marie, was married to a woman named Stella. When
Stella insisted that her mother in Switzerland and her sister and brother,
who were already in Argentina, should be brought over with the help of

our sponsors, Father was adamant. The sponsors were not to be burdened with guarantees for anyone else until Grossmutter and Otto's parents had safely arrived in New York. This "veto power" of Father's for a while made for bad blood between him and Stella, but in the end she understood. He knew that there was still a long wait ahead, due to their qualifying only under the crowded Eastern European immigration quotas. But the longer we resided in the States and the better our own financial situation became, the better their chances became to qualify, as immediate family members, under the preferred quota.

Suddenly there surfaced encouraging news that the quotas for Poland, Czechoslovakia and Hungary were not being used to their full capacity due to the war and occupation by the German armies. There was now hope that Otto's parents and Grossmutter could be expected to escape Europe within a foreseeable time frame. This news came around the time of my parents' 20th wedding anniversary, in May 1941, and was received by them as a proper reason for celebration. I turned 17 that same month, and was more interested in practicing smoking the pipe I had managed to persuade my cousin Otto to give me as a present. Otto was now foreman in a pipe factory, and his wife Stella, a professional hair stylist, well established in a local barbershop and beauty parlor, treated him to a "real American" haircut.

Omi and Ella were already making preparations for their departure sometime in July or shortly thereafter. As native Austrians, all they had to watch for was how close the American consulate was to reaching the registration number they had been assigned in the late summer of 1938. Father also kept on top of the situation, writing continuously to the Jewish Community organization in Vienna and to other aid committees to make sure that the pertinent files did not get lost somewhere in the shuffle. Willy had filed all supplementary affidavits and had made sure that the provisions for transfer of money for Omi and Ella's passage were in place. Father was so sure of their arrival within a short time that, in one of his letters written during May, he explained to them how to find one's way along the streets and avenues in Manhattan, so they would not get lost after their arrival.

Our hopes further ripened as the summer of 1941 began. The soon-expected arrival of at least two of our five relatives remaining behind in Vienna meant that we had to make more concrete plans. We were now in our second summer, and we had all become acclimatized. We no longer moved in an unfamiliar city and were no longer afraid of getting lost when traveling long distances by subway, and thus we began to look forward to spending lazy Sundays at the New York beaches. Father celebrated his first full year at the same job, a job that he liked and one in which he was well-appreciated by his boss, Mr. Kraus. He was rewarded with an invitation to join Kraus for a drink during lunch, and as a bonus was given a ten-dollar bill. "A raise would have been better!" Father wrote home, but he enjoyed it nevertheless. The mail between Vienna and New York took on pre-war character: some airmail letters arrived within 12 days. Father was overjoyed, and his letters showed it, in spite of his receiving bad news about living conditions, and some family unpleasantness involving a distant relative that had plagued Ella. Nothing mattered anymore except to count down the months or even only weeks until at least part of the immediate family would be able to embrace each other again.

On June 22, Hitler's armies invaded the Soviet Union, and all U.S. consulates were immediately closed for an indefinite period of time. When they reopened in July, there was a new set of regulations governing immigration to the U.S. Effective July 1st, the U.S. State Department issued revised rules for immigration that were, of course, relevant only to European Jews. The significance of these new rules was that all effort and progress up to that date had been for naught. Each immigrant applicant had to again undertake the lengthy and convoluted process of applying for a visa from the beginning.

As might be expected, this news was a terrifying blow to Father, and to all who found themselves in the same situation. Though Father did not try to conceal his feelings in his letters to the family in Vienna, he insisted that help would be on the way, and predicted that the embassy in Berlin would take over work that was until then done in the consulates. He certainly did not skip a weekly letter—on the contrary, his letters became longer, and always included some New York vignette. There was the shoeshine boy who sang himself into religious rapture with spirituals while polishing shoes to a lustrous gloss, or the policeman who pirouetted gracefully while directing heavy traffic, and even a gangster shoot-out at the corner of 42nd Street and Fifth Avenue. He included the smallest items if he thought they might interest someone on the other end of the correspondence. Ella, my favorite aunt, had once assumed the task of raising the level of my musical awareness by taking me to concerts and operas. With understandable regret, she had already noticed in Vienna my growing fascination with American jazz. She now learned that her nephew had finally developed an interest in classical music, and actually went to hear free concerts at the open-air Lewison Stadium, not too far from where we lived, with some friends. He could occasionally be heard whistling the theme of Schubert's Unfinished Symphony, though not always in tune, her brother-in-law reported with obvious glee.

Father did not ignore the invasion of the Soviet Union. Somehow he linked it to the abnormally hot weather, which eventually abated. Every war is followed by some kind of peace, he opined, and then we could all once again embrace each other. Have courage, he counseled again and again. On the occasion of Grossmutter's and Marie's birthdays in July, he sent them a minute description of the birthday cake that would await them here, and described the specifically American manner in which birthdays are celebrated. He transmitted good wishes from Palestine, business successes from Australia and love letters from the Philippines to those who would be most affected by the good news. He even apologized to Ella for the lateness of his birthday wishes for her, since he had expected to deliver them in person upon her arrival! "Fate has indeed put all of us to a severe test," he wrote, "but we shall not concede defeat and we shall not lose either our hope or our courage. Think of it simply as a postponement and not a cancellation."

Though the outlook for escape remained dim for the family members in Vienna, the family in New York was beginning to experience the rewards of hard work in a rising economy stimulated both by the impending war and the sloughing off the effects of the Depression. The entire family was working full time, and were thus able to save money and plan for the future. In August of '41 Father happily wrote to Vienna that we were about to rent our "own" three-room apartment, with "cross-ventilation," of course. Otto and his wife Stella were also able to strike out on their own and move into a rented studio apartment. The apartments were still in Washington Heights—ours on 157th Street off Broadway, only two blocks from the Museum of the Hispanic Society at 155th and Broadway, and theirs on Fort Washington Avenue in a newly built art deco–type apartment house close to the George Washington Bridge.

Our lives were beginning to take on the semblance of normalcy, a condition described by Father in minute detail to the loved ones still left behind. All of us spent weekends at the city beaches, and even Father took a vacation after Labor Day, most of which he spent exploring the beaches when he wasn't busy at his typewriter. Only Mother took a real vacation, in a small resort in the Hudson valley, after a short period in a convalescence home not far from the city. Her state of health had deteriorated rapidly after the disappointing news in July and, since she now belonged to a union—ILGW, the International Ladies Garment Workers Union— she was able to take sick leave for treatment of a thyroid condition, which eventually required that gland's partial removal. During Mother's absence we moved into our new apartment, took delivery of two crates stocked with mementos and household goods that had been in storage since our arrival, and decorated the flat in preparation for her return. After we moved in and started unpacking the crates, Father delighted in telling Marie and the others how every piece, no matter how simple or trivial, reminded us of them. He was particularly happy about his collection of nearly 20 photo albums filled with family pictures. These soon began to draw visitors also from Vienna, for whom the pictures represented a look at the past, albeit through the other end of the telescope.

All of these happenings Father lovingly related to Grossmutter, Omi, Ella, Marie and Emil. Their letters of September '41 showed that they received this news with great enthusiasm, and it was obvious that it helped them cling to the hope of leaving their misery behind and joining us soon in our new abode. They did not mention that as of September 1, they had been ordered to wear the yellow star. If we knew it from other sources, I do not recall it ever being the subject of conversation among the family. Father did inquire how they could possibly shop for necessities in the single hour a day permitted to them. There was no letup in his quest to somehow find a way out for them. He heard rumors of the availability of visas to Cuba, only to learn that such a visa sold for $250.00 per person, plus a deposit of $500.00 which allegedly would be returned upon leaving Cuba. In addition, a bank guarantee of $1,500.00 was required, though such a guarantee could be secured for $150.00. "To this must be added, obviously the cost of transportation. And then where are you? In a place with a terrible tropical climate and still four days distant by ship from New York," he commented in anguish. Yet he immediately softened this bleak picture with the comforting thought that at least "we would be able to go there and visit with you." At no point did he dismiss this plan, in spite of the immense costs. Undoubtedly he believed that if it were truly an available option, he would somehow beg, borrow or steal the money. But when he read about and saw individuals who had just arrived on the *Navemar*—a Spanish merchant ship with regular space for 15 passengers that had accommodated 1,100 Jewish refugees for 68 days at sea—he dropped the whole idea. Passengers on that "ship from Hell" had paid as much as $500.00 as a deposit, plus $1,000.00 to be allowed on the ship. Father felt he could not encourage Grossmutter to undertake such a trying trip.

In the end, all that was left were the letters expressing everyone's hopes for a better future. They are the legacy by which these individuals and all others like them will be remembered by those who take the time to learn what happened during those bitter years.

New York Letters, 1940

New York, January 8th, 1940

My dearest, beloved mother, dear Marie and Emil!

Finally—the mail which we longed for so eagerly, arrived yesterday, it was from December 12th, 1939, not quite as fast as the last one, this one took almost four weeks; a bit long for airmail. Irma too, has written, as well as Heinrich/Helly who wrote us an especially nice letter. I hope that in the meantime you've received our continued and detailed mail, which we send regularly every week, sometimes a day later or a day sooner, depending on the schedule of the "Clipper," the airplane flying from New York to Lisbon. Due to the stormy, generally bad weather during this season they do not keep regular schedules either way. To this has to be added the censorship that checks all letters coming from you but most likely also those addressed to you, and that surely accounts for the long delays. I mention all that in order to calm your anxiety in that respect. We write to you regularly and will continue to do so in the future no matter what.

Much as we enjoyed hearing from you—and special thanks to you, mother, for your dear lines—the content of your letter was not designed to calm our anxiety. There is first of all the matter of your apartment. I had hoped you would write: "We're moving on such and such a date, to this address, the flat, or rather the room looks like that etc." Unfortunately nothing like that, on the contrary, still the same uncertainty, still the same tiresome search for a roof over your head, queuing for hours at the Housing Office, and all this without success. Soon it will be time also for our loved ones in the Taborstrasse to move. I can only repeat what I already mentioned in my last letter: I put my trust in God and our lucky star—otherwise I am completely powerless and cannot help in any way.

There is not much that is new about us here. Actually we're almost fully caught up in our day to day routines; no longer do we crane our necks to look at the skyscrapers, the densest traffic hardly matters to us— not even the abundance of food titillates our appetites, and the wonderful freedom prevailing here we accept already as a matter of course. We grumble when we have to wait 10 minutes for a subway train upon returning home from a visit at 2AM, and we really get mad when on icy days there is usually not enough sand on the sidewalks. I believe, judging from these attitudes, that the moment will not be far when we'll actually feel like natives, rather than someone on vacation who, complete with camera and street map, strolls along the streets of the city. However, there is one thing lacking to make all this truly routine—and that is your presence. You, my beloved mother with whom, of an evening, I could always schmooze a little in Yiddish, you who often had an appropriate comment that would clear up even complicated matters, you with more knowledge of life than even a learned scholar could command, we miss all of you and we miss you more, the more we talk about you. And talking about you we do a lot. You folks in the Vereinsgasse and Taborstrasse—you must suffer from a lot of hiccups unfortunately mostly during the night, awakened from a deep sleep no doubt, because that is the time we talk about you, when the family here gets together in the evening, usually between 9 and 11P, which is about 3–5A your time.

During the recent period without any mail arriving from you all relatives here shared our anxiety. Every letter from you is read by them with great interest and concern, especially by Jonas to whom I bring them usually around noon; due to his job we never see him in the evening, he doesn't come home until 2A, except on Thursdays. Hannah as always acts as our guardian angel, very much concerned about our physical and mental well-being. When she comes home from the office in the evening she puts on an apron and works in the household. Starting at 9P out-of-town guests and locals continue to come and go, every one is made to feel welcome and treated to their generous hospitality.

Emil Secher (ca. 1950) wrote all letters from New York.

But Hannah is also a very able attorney. Only recently I had this corroborated by an old acquaintance of mine from Vienna, for me a very proud and satisfying occasion. Hannah won that case and then asked that we at least permit her to buy a bed for Herbert since she considered the one provided for him by our landlords very inadequate. Well, it is not exactly a "bed of roses" but neither is it all that bad! Only with great difficulty did I persuade her to postpone this generous gift until our life had become more settled.

You see, I had not mentioned to you when talking about a "daily routine," which is after all, precisely what makes one's life so very livable, that it did not yet include a real job for the both of us or, what would be preferable, for me alone—these uncertain, temporary jobs are not exactly right for restarting one's new existence. I recognize that this is difficult, very difficult. But it'll happen with the Lord's help, I am sure. Don't you worry your heads about this, not even one bit. *Above all remember this*: it is impossible to go hungry here! Of course we want more, most of all, our own small flat, but you'll see it too will happen!

Last week we also received a very detailed letter from Olly that brought us much joy as do of course all news from our relatives now so widely scattered across the globe. She is doing relatively well, is still on her old job, she worries only about Hans, she hadn't heard yet that he was able to get out. My good old friend Güns has also written from Brussels. We're in touch now with almost all our beloved family members and friends, with the exception of Ernst Schab in Australia and Dr. Lakner. I fear very much that the latter has been interned in a camp. Occasionally I get together with my old friend Emil Offner, he always inquires about all of you, but especially about you, mother, and he sends you his best regards. Irma and Benno [in Palestine] are doing quite well, thank God, but their anxiety over you, their inability to help makes them very bitter. Who can understand this better than I do!

I have very little contact with Adolf Handel. He is financially very well off, but his family gives him some trouble; his mother-in-law has cancer and is not given any hope to recover. Julius I have not met so far—he doesn't seem to care much for family relations.

What you wrote us about Bernard made us very happy. Please give our best regards to his wife. On the other hand, we are very saddened about Sigmund and Frieda. When will we finally be able to get some news from them? We read in the local press that Russia opens the borders for those who can show that they have relatives in the Russo-Polish region who are willing to act as their guarantors. Obviously this is not a solution but at least it is something. Do you see Sigmund's wife occasionally?

Please give her my best regards. Do you, Marie, visit sometimes with Regine and Dora? Please do it and comfort them. They must not lose their nerve and they'll have to come here as healthy persons. The same goes for you, my dearest ones, I must impress that on you, no matter how difficult it may be for you. Remember at all times that you have people here who care and worry about and who will never leave you in the lurch, come what may. Please tell Mr. Streit he must have just a little more patience. The affidavit is in the process of being drawn up. Besides, the later it is ready the longer its validity.

Please remember us to all our friends and acquaintances and I kiss and embrace all of you but especially you my dearest, beloved mother, your Emil.

#2

New York, February 8th, 1940

My dearest good mother, All my loved ones!

Hansi enclosed a few lines to my last letter of February 4th, which did not meet with my approval at all. It was the result of a mood caused by her illness—from which thank God, she has now fully recovered—which made her complain about our fate in a totally unjustifiable manner. She has even less cause to do that, since her situation here, first in comparison with our last months in Vienna, and secondly, unlike that of thousands of emigrants here who have neither a job nor sometimes even a roof over their head, can only be called princely, given the loving way in which our local relatives i.e. those who guaranteed our affidavits, care about us financially as well as emotionally.

I make allowance for her only in view of the intense homesickness, the longing to be reunited here with you, that I certainly share with her, coupled with that feeling of powerlessness to speed up the process of your being able to join us.

I and many others are certainly strongly attached to the old homeland, the place where one was born, experienced one's youth with all its beautiful and unforgettable memories, spent in fact half one's adult life—and I despise those individuals who, immediately after the first day of landing here, dive head on into America, adopt a 100% American attitude, can barely remember having once lived on the other side, pretend to having forgotten the German language—actually they never really knew it well just the way they barely know English and will probably never

speak it correctly. Only now they imitate the Americans in a dozen trivial and superficial ways: usually those range from the obnoxious gum chewing to resting their legs on the table!

Neither do I appreciate those of us here who continuously bewail the
loss of the Kahlenberg, the Heurigen, and Coffee house life in general,
the Café Victoria in particular, Viennese trolley cars (not because they ran
better, but because they had such a beautiful red color), Ankerbrot, or
bread crumbs because only with real Viennese ones can Wiener Schnitzel
be fully appreciated! On the other hand nobody criticizes the water
because not even the most fanatic fans of the Viennese Mountain spring
water can find any fault with it. And so forth, with one triviality succeeding
the other. I won't even mention the fact that most of the things whose
loss is being bewailed here were no longer made available to us with an
absolute finality, and that we did not voluntarily give up our way of life
over there. But in Hansi's case I cannot forgive her that she complains to
you of all people, you Marie, you Ella and you Mama who need comfort
and sympathy a hundred times more than we do. She is making the mistake made by so many who are slowly beginning to forget what and how
it really happened over there. Is it not possible for them to keep their memories alive, do they have to be shaken up every day? Do I have to remind
Hansi of Ella's day from the time early in the morning when you open
your eyes and start removing all blackout curtains to that time late in the
evening when you are permitted to close them for a short while? What
you Marie and Ella have to go through on just an ordinary day –and I
only think of those so-called "ordinary" ones? Did Hansi consider that
when you hold her letter with its unjustifiable lament in your hands, you
my dear ones in the Taborstrasse would no longer be in your old, comfortable flat? That to this day we are ignorant of exactly where you have
moved, and what those four walls look like where you will live for hopefully not too long a time prior to your departure for America? That we
are still without news how the move went for you in the Vereinsgasse to
the Lessinggasse? How do you like it there, how do you manage to suffer
through the terrible cold? Do you have enough to eat and whether the
Jewish Community Organization still can feed you? What do you do for
money, how do you manage with what you have, how do you budget, and
in general how much do you spend in one day, how much do you need to
live, what rent do you have to pay in these newly commandeered flats?
And so on and so forth—all these are questions on whose answer we are
waiting with great longing for more than three weeks—that is how long
we've been without mail from you. While you are burdened with all these
worries, most of which I am convinced you conceal from us, how should

you muster up the understanding for the variety of nonsense in our existing routine, maybe even provide us with comfort and sympathy? They call me a fanatic here, but unfortunately that is not so—were I one indeed, I should have to climb up somewhere and yell it all out to the world....

Of course, Hansi has to work hard, she gets up at 6AM, toils for at least eight hours at a factory bench, rides in the crowded subway pressed together like herrings for the 1½ hours roundtrip—but let her tell you herself how many "emigrants" can be found among the 800+ employees, many of whom are older than Hansi and surely have seen better days on the other side. How others envy her for this job because it is not easy to find work these days. Also, if she were not relieved of any worries about the boy, she could hardly take on that job in the first place. We hope that she will not always have to work, that this is only a temporary arrangement and that not too far down the road we'll be able to afford a modest, small flat once our earning power increases. So please don't take her complaints too seriously—anyway her mood has changed by now and she is her old happy self again.

My dearest mother, for you I have greetings from Jakob Fingermann whom I met here. Also, from his mother, who is here with him and had a very good trip across the ocean. You my dear Emil will be glad to hear that your old "friend" from the KG, Mr. Haber, is also here and now is exactly the same kind of nonentity as the rest of us, who whines at the door of the Refugee Aid Committee the same way that once thousands of us did in front of his door at the KG; all of those who recognize and remember him from Vienna revile and hiss when he appears.

How is it going with you, dearest mother? What about your cough and your nose? Please drop by at Dr. Schnardt's and tell him I'd really appreciate it were he to send me a few lines about your condition that you could enclose in your letter, unless one of you could write me about it. I beg of you dear Marie and dear Emil to be patient and understanding with mother in every respect. Everyone has his little faults and everyone suffers bitterly and equally under the same sad and difficult conditions.

The terrible cold here has somewhat lessened, weather is mild and the sky has a southern blueness. I hope that you too, by the time these lines reach you will be able to feel at least a trace of spring.

Last week, the wife of my former boss in Vienna, Mrs. Epstein came for a visit to Willy's when we were there, too. Have I written you already that she had accepted a job as maid in a household not far from New York and is quite satisfied with her lot? She too has seen better days and in Vienna kept a stable of horses! When she has her "day off" she usually comes to New York and sometimes drops by our house.

We're in touch with Dr. Weil, [MD former family physician in V.] though less in a personal way. He is very busy, spends eight hours daily learning English, since he is due to take his Language Exam in April, a requirement prior to qualifying for his license to practice medicine. Has he written to you, Mama as he promised us at one time? You too dearest Mama must give us an exact report on your health. Not only we but also Dr. Weil, are very concerned about you in this respect. And how are you dear Ella? As always most conscientious, courageous and brave? Your reward will not fail to appear, I guarantee you! Once you all are over here, you shall only have to rest your hands in your lap and we shall take over the task of caring for you.

What do the others write? Do you get regular news from Irma? And what from Victor, Ernst and Rudi? It's been some time since we've heard from them. Victor, we hope to be able to greet here in the not too distant future. What's with Heinrich and Helly? From them too, we lack any news. Where do they stand with their examination? When will we finally receive from them that much longed for telegram? Last evening we phoned Irene and the others. They too haven't heard anything for weeks from over there. Give both of them a hug from us and convey our best regards to Helly's mother. Have mother and daughter Lakner left already? Even though we've written to them several times and had you pass on to them news from us we've not heard from them to this day. Do you visit at Dora and/or Regine's or do they come to see you frequently? Hannah and I recently wrote both of them a very detailed letter. When will we finally get some good news from them? Marie maybe you can drop by sometime at Mrs. K. and find out what's new at the firm. From there too I have no news. Give everyone there our best regards, also all our dear friends, such as Herr Erdheim, the Streit Family (are they already in possession of the affidavit?), the Ball family, etc. Dear Ella give my special regards to dear Frieda. A few personal lines from her would please us enormously. How is Frieda Laufer faring? Is she in touch with her children? How do matters stand with Edith? What's with Victor? Do the Braun-girls visit you often and how are they doing? Dr. Weil, too has inquired about them, especially Mimi and we talked a lot about them. How is Frau Dr. W.? And what about all the other dear ladies of the old "Gin-Rummy Circle?" Are you all busy playing? And what about our dear, good Rosa? None of those mentioned or not mentioned here are missing in our thoughts, which are often and intensely with them. Please give them our best and most heartfelt regards. Surely we do not need to mention Mama Neumann [mother-in-law of Victor] separately in our letters. Our letters are meant for her as well as for all of you. As far as we are concerned she belongs to our closest family.

I shall close now and my dearest, good mother I embrace you most tenderly. My thoughts are always with you and I know, actually feel that you're always thinking of me and the others, wishing us only the best; that we also wish for you, but most importantly good health, much courage and a heart full of hope. The rest will take care of itself. You too, all my other loved ones keep on writing, be truthful about everything, keep nothing that concerns you from us everything interests us. I embrace all of you most tenderly and accept my best regards, your Emil

P.S. I am writing this letter as I did the one from February 4th with one extra copy so that I can send one by air and the other one by surface mail. Please write me the time difference in their arrival.

#3

New York, February 18th, 1940

My dearest good mother, all my dear ones!

Otto sent yesterday a few lines to his mother-in-law in Switzerland, asking her to mail them on to you. He did this because the "REX" left yesterday for Europe and he hopes that you might get news sooner from us than by airmail which lately doesn't seem to be working at all—not to mention that postage is insanely high. At the head of that letter he wrote that I already had a "job." And I too, mentioned it in a few words. I do not know which one of those letters will reach you first, but just to be sure I also mention it again here at the beginning since I know how you have worried—unnecessarily—about that. This is an enterprise that produces rather cheap leather goods, e.g. belts and similar things; it has ca. 200 employees. I get paid $15.00 a week. How this will work out I cannot say now, as I've only been there hardly a week. In any case I am happy since we are now both working. Hansi and I now actually have an income and we may even be able to save some. If this turns out to be permanent, we shall soon start looking for a modest flat to rent. In that way we can slowly prepare matters for your arrival. I obtained this job through our revered Safirstein who just like all our other relatives does not leave a stone unturned to help us.

If there is anything that mars our newly found contentment, it is our continuous anxiety concerning your well-being, our endless longing for you, my dearest mother. The more so since it is more than 14 days—after your short note of January 9th—that we've had any news from you. Otto Donath recently wrote me a short note that put my mind at ease about you but it is already out of date. I did O. Donath an injustice when I complained not having heard from him since his arrival here. He is not in NY but in Freeport where he has a job as a housepainter, and his wife works as a household help for strangers. He'll be in NY sometime soon and I'm looking forward to seeing him then.

Yesterday I received a letter from Elly. She is happy to be no longer in St. Gallen, but lives now with her beloved Leo in the refugee camp at Diepoldsau. On the other hand, I do not have from Olly (in London) or her parents in Riga a line in a long time. I hope to have an affidavit for Olly very soon. But we do receive quite a lot of mail from our loved ones in distant lands and that gives us the greatest joy. Thus we got a very detailed letter from our friends the Roths. Irma and Benno also write us fully and of course they suffer the same pain we do: our all-consuming longing for you! They are doing OK, Benno has kept his job, even got a raise, and Heinzi (Zvi) is healthy and happy. Hermine's daughter Trudi arrived in P. from London; Hermine is very unhappy in London, but we've known her as slightly hysterical already in Vienna, she ought to be happy with her fate that is the envy of hundreds of thousands! She too will eventually be united with her husband and the rest of the family—she ought to learn from you to bear her lot with patience and courage. I was really happy to receive a very detailed letter from Hans in Manila; when I read his lines and look at that postage stamp from Manila, I can't get over the fact that this young man for whom I had given up all hope, was lucky enough to get away. On his trip he met our friend Dr. Lakner who is the owner of a beautiful new car. Hans, subsidized by the Committee in M. is having a great time. But he doubts that he will stay very long there, the conditions are not conducive to settling there and the climate is awful, he says. Eventually he hopes to be able to come to Australia. The Philippines are not a country where he would want anyone of his family, including Olly to join him. In any case he appears to be a very ambitious young man and can be expected to stay afloat.

There is nothing much to report about us, through my many detailed letters you are pretty well informed how we spend our days. My "cruising around days" in this gigantic New York, which I know now like the inside of my pocket, are now at an end since at long last I have an occupation. All I can say is: Thank God! Now I can no longer serve you as the local reporter with all of his impressions about this city—but you already know enough about New York, anyway. For new impressions I should rally travel somewhere else. You should know, dearest mother, that I've almost gone through the heavy soles of the new shoes I bought just prior to our departure and the second pair is also almost at that stage. Of course you know me and I've already had them soled wonderfully by a local cobbler.

After some wonderfully warm spring weather last week we suddenly, last Tuesday were hit by one of those terrible blizzards, snowstorms—you cannot possibly imagine how terrible these American snowstorms are. It snowed so hard for 48 hours you might have thought a white wall actually fell from the sky—in fact the storm raged in such a way you were unable to set foot on the street. All surface traffic stopped and it is lucky that 80% of NY's transportation is below ground—still even today there is a meter high snow covering the streets. The snow removal efforts are enormous—every 200 steps the machines create 10m high snow mountains from which cranes lift loads onto trucks that dump it somewhere. Nevertheless the streets are a sea of mud now in which one can easily sink in because during the day we have again beautiful sunshine that thaws the snow masses, only to have them freeze again during the night which creates almost impassable ice in the morning. This is when our high over shoes really are handy—nobody seems to have this kind here, and American women look with envy at Hansi's and sometimes ask where she got them. Those who wear them are mostly "refugees" like us. So you see there are things that Americans do not have—in fact there are quite a number of those. You cannot possibly imagine how badly, the average American is dressed. In this respect we're quite poorly informed over there. That is undoubtedly the fault of American movies. Fact is well dressed men can be seen here too only in the movies! Everybody here comments admiringly on my beautiful "Sphinx" or "Phoenix" ties with their distinguished colors, and I've given away quite a few of them. Only recently I met someone at the "Jewish Council" who told me that he supplements his support money by the sale of his European ties and has made as much as $20.00 that way. If anyone of our friends is planning to come over here he should not fail to bring along quite a bunch of beautiful ties.

Without really wishing to do so I've started to "schmooze" again. That happens because as soon as I sit at my typewriter, I imagine I am talking to you dearest mother as well to all the others individually. When with the Lord's help I shall one day have all of you sitting right here in front of me I shall have nothing to tell you but you of course will have a lot to tell me. In the meantime I would be only too happy if I had detailed and positive news from you. What's with you in the Taborstrasse? No longer Taborstrasse? So where? And how did it go with the moving?

Were you able to postpone it after all? We're terribly concerned about that and are devastated by our powerlessness in this respect. I asked you in the Taborstrasse and you in the Lessinggasse, about so many things in my last letters, I really do not want to repeat this, hoping that you did get our mail and will answer it so that our pain will not be so hard to bear.

Something else: in my various letters I've always asked about our dear relatives, friends and acquaintances and sent them my greetings. Even though I know about her, I often think of Mrs. Uhrmacher and believe that I did miss inquiring about her. Did she too lose her flat? Is she even still in Vienna? If yes, does she visit with you, mother? In any case give her my best regards. I embrace you my dearest mother and all you my beloved ones, I kiss you many times and remain your Emil

P.S. Just now came a letter from Olly and she writes that she is doing well. She wrote you a letter but sent it first to Elly so she can add to it before she mails it to you. But Elly writes that she does not have your address and will try to get it from uncle Josef. Maybe you can write her a postcard, Marie. Address: Elly Epstein Emigrantcamp, Diepoldsau, Switzerland. Do not forget to give my best regards to those with whom you share the flat: Mr. Hacker and Family Tragholz. What gives with Heinrich and Helly? From them too, we lack any news and not only we but also their relatives here are concerned; the latter have called us several times recently about that. Mrs. Bredhoff, Heinrich's friend has written us a few lines since she too hasn't heard from them and thought I would knew more. Please, Ella, do me the favor to get in touch with them, give them our best regards and tell them we are anxiously waiting for their arrival. What about Regine and Dora? From them Hannah hasn't heard anything and neither have we. If only we could get the good news from them! And now at last greetings to all our dear friends, relatives, acquaintances, I won't mention all by name this time. Today (Sunday) we're invited for coffee at Mr. Eston—formerly Essig.

#4

New York, March 3rd, 1940

My dearest Beloved, dearest Mama and Ella,

My dear Mother, my dear sister, dear Emil!

Before I turn to you first of all, Mama Schab, in order to give you a real scolding, I want to acknowledge your dear letters, as follows: from you Marie, January 24th & February 1st; and from you Ella, January 25th & February 2nd. As usual these so fervently longed for letters, after a three week long pause, have brought us much joy yet, at the same time, also much unhappiness because of the hopeless mood which we can read from your lines and even more so between your lines. We beg of you, fervently, for God's sake do not let yourself go and lose hope. You must hold out, no matter how difficult it is for you, and be assured that we shall not fail, in fact will do anything at all to draw nearer to the point in time when we all can be united again. As far as the Affidavit for you, Ella, and Mama is concerned we have all the necessary documents from Willy in our possession. The affidavit itself has been set up in a most professional manner together with a preference petition that has been sent to Washington, and will be sent registered to the Consulate in Vienna with a copy for you. There is at present no absolute hurry for the Affidavit, since regardless of preference it will take some time till they get to it. Important is that we have the necessary supporting documents from Willy and this was hard work but was accomplished by Hansi all by herself. Not that Willy resisted in any way, on the contrary, but it involved a number of errands, correspondences etc. and you know how much W. dislikes that sort of thing, since in his life here as it did in Europe, lack of time is always an important factor. Only today Hannah informed us that one or the other matter still has not been taken care of, e.g. she still does not have the number of his First Papers, etc. Nevertheless its been done.

Now as for you, my dear ones in the Lessinggasse, you my dear mother, you Marie and you Emil, matters stand as follows: Hansi and I have already received our notification to appear on March 7th at the City Hall in order to receive our First Papers. That makes us almost half citizens since these papers have the same weight as a passport, entitling us to travel all over the world—even to Europe—which is something that U.S. citizens are prohibited from doing (the government is concerned that something might happen to its citizens, e.g. while crossing the ocean), as long as we return within a period of six months. But that also gives us the right to provide guarantees (affidavits) for our next of kin, the more so that we both are holding down jobs. I have already submitted a petition for preference for you, my dearest mother, and Otto has done the same for Marie and Emil. Unfortunately this applies only to preferences <u>within</u> the quota and not outside of it. The latter is possible only for parents whose children are already U.S. citizens. On the other hand, requirements for preference for parents demand only proof of a job and not the amount earned. Nevertheless, both Isidor and Herman have, without any prodding on my part, already told me that if a larger subsidy is necessary they will of course provide that. I just don't want to send off the affidavit too soon, but you can count on the fact mother, that as surely as you will be helped, as surely will these affidavits be ready for you and Marie and Emil.

So I beg of you most urgently, have courage, be patient; and in this context let me compliment you dearest mother, since according to all unanimous reports, orally and in writing, you are considered to be the bravest of them all! Dear Marie, just look upon this entire period as just temporary and the more beautiful and cleaner will things be here for you.

And now let me turn to you, my dear Mama Schab, you who are seriously hurting us with your unbroken silence; the more so as we're not aware of having done anything wrong, having written to you always and regularly. And writing to you is far from an onerous duty, on the contrary, we can hardly await this hour in which we can talk to you—even when we are not writing, our thoughts are constantly with each one of you: whether it is on the job, or on the subway to and from work, or in our conversations with others. Hansi has been working already for two months, except for a short interruption of three weeks from December 24th to January 15th and therefore has not as much time as I did prior to my job. Furthermore she was sick with a slight case of grippe that kept her in bed and for that reason was unable to write any detailed reports that anyway could only have been a repetition of mine. Besides she has since then written repeatedly and in great detail to you personally, which letters should have reached you by now. The same is true about our most heartfelt birthday wishes, whose late arrival made us very unhappy since we mailed them already on January 8, and the same for that equally detailed letter from Willy. Also, concerning him and his family, you will have to come to terms with their reluctance to write letters. I know this is cheap advice I am tendering. Fact is, for twenty years I could not get used to certain of his peculiarities—yet in this case: they too are always with you in their thoughts, always talk about you—only to bring themselves to writing a letter, that they seem to be able to accomplish only with great difficulty. They are not the only ones in this respect: many here say they simply cannot get themselves to write. That Friedl finally brought himself to write was mainly Hansi's doing and, let's admit it, Herbert is no different. I have to postpone mailing of letters for 2 or 3 days until I can persuade that little bum to add a few lines to it, not to mention that for days I don't even get to see him. Dearest Mama, "Take it Easy" to cite a favorite American expression that we get to hear up to 50x a day, so please don't make us suffer for it.

As I already wrote recently, we're now both working that is I am for nearly 3 weeks. I am not dissatisfied with my job; on the contrary, it just takes getting used to. I have there the opportunity to learn a great deal since I am being used almost in the whole enterprise. This is the beginning of the season—which is why I was being hired in the first place—

and I make a lot of "overtime"—usually I do not get home before 8:30P. And then we still do some "homework": Hansi makes some bracelets for a small business while I do some bookkeeping for that same place. You can see we're taking a short cut to becoming rich. Still we're not dissatisfied and together we're making ca. $35.00, even 40.00 sometimes, a week. That is ca. AS800.00 a month. But one should not convert. Even for our present situation that isn't bad if only I would be the sole earner of that income and not both of us.

Dearest mother, during the past week I received a detailed letter from Epstein in Riga. He too would like to be able to come over here and I have already contacted his relatives in Washington. Last week I also visited Frances Ball and found Donath there as well. I also met there Herr Schall and at least 10 other folk from the old neighborhood Vereinsgasse-Volkertplatz-Café Lenger—they even played cards and talked a lot about Vienna and the good old days; you especially, dear Emil were mentioned a lot. Herr Schall also told me that his wife still had difficulties with the affidavit. Many thanks to Mr. and Mrs. Streit for their greetings sent through you, dear Marie. I am sorry from the bottom of my heart that they were made to give up their apartment. How did this happen so suddenly? Wasn't this a j. [Jewish] house? I am getting together with Eston soon and will tell him everything. There was something else I wanted to tell the two mothers for a long time already, only I have always forgotten: all your pictures and memorabilia that you had sent here with Otto are here in good condition and will surely decorate your rooms when with the Lords help you'll soon be with us ... Dearest Ella we shall put the Braun girls too, on our short list. The saying here is: to find a job is very difficult, but this day to find still another sponsor for an affidavit is even more difficult ... How are Heinrich and Helly? Has she recovered from the recent malaise? Tell them not to lose heart; they are relatively speaking not worse off and we're counting on their early arrival ... I embrace and kiss all of you and especially you my proud brother-in-law who so far hasn't presented us with even one line, your Emil

Special thanks to you my dearest mother for your sweet personal lines they warm my heart.

#5

New York, March 17th, 1940

My dearest, good, mother, All my loved ones!

This time I, and all of us are feeling quite desperate since we've had no acknowledgement of any of my detailed reports that I've mailed to you weekly since January 8th.

I hear that you mother have complained to Mrs. Bock in a letter of February 20th, that you're completely without news from us. I hope you're all smart enough to realize that under no circumstances will I let you without news and that I shall write again and again. Furthermore, the British, on the Bermuda Islands, where all flights stop prior to the "big hop," simply take down all mail designated for Germany for censorship and pass it only after weeks have gone by! Since this was repeated despite American protests, there will be, according to today's newspaper, no more stops in Bermuda (which is British territory), beginning with the end of March; instead they will fly directly from here to Lisbon via the Azores. Obviously the delay caused by the British censors becomes even longer when you add the censorship by the German authorities. Nevertheless I hope that you must, by now, be in receipt of a major part of our mail sent since beginning of January. But no matter what, please be always assured that we will never forget to write—and most important that nothing untoward has happened or is happening to us. Besides what could possibly happen to us in this country?! Even your fear, dearest mother, with respect to an accident, which I remember still from Vienna, is totally without basis, given the conditions prevailing here. Even though traffic here is fifty times denser than in Vienna during the height of the summer season, a traffic accident here is extremely rare if not in fact impossible. First of all, nobody can jump on or off a trolley car. On all public transport media, whether underground or above ground, all doors close and open automatically—and only after the train, trolley, bus or metro has come to a full stop. That is so even though people here have less time than we did over there. There is in this gigantic metropolis of New York not one single street which does not have a traffic light at every street crossing, all of which function automatically without any traffic police man present. There are dozens more installations and preventive measures that reduce the chances of a traffic accident to a minimum. I really have to add to this that the automobile drivers her are incredibly disciplined. When a car drives along a street in the middle of the night, without another car or pedestrian in sight, and the traffic light turns red, he will stop immediately regardless of how fast he was driving at the time—and even though no policeman is in sight! The pedestrian is less disciplined and frequently crosses the street even when he shouldn't. He can do that without the risk of a penalty—but of course, at his own risk. This seems to be in keeping with the spirit of democracy, which says that every one is free to lead his own life as he pleases. However, I, and those who are with me, always stop at the crosswalks and only proceed when the light turns green. So have no fear concerning us, mother! If only we could be as assured for even the fraction of a second concerning your well being as you can be about ours. By the way, for reasons of security I mail my letters to you already since the middle of February in duplicate, i.e. the original by air to you and another one via Mrs. Zelinka in Switzerland. Even though the latter are not sent by air, by now you should have received those letters sent first to Mrs. Z. in Lucerne. Hansi always wrote in great detail, too— only she uses ink rather then the typewriter, and only once; but I always typed on the copy that Hansi has written by hand on the original airmail letter. Thus if you received the letter sent via Switzerland earlier, please do not feel hurt, especially you all in the Taborstrasse if you miss an enclosure from Hansi or Herbert. *You can't really ask them to write their letters twice.* Besides the last time I reversed the process and sent the original with Hansi's added note via Lucerne.

There is not much to tell about us, mostly the same and I can only repeat that we're doing well, that I started on a job about four weeks ago with which I am fairly happy, that Hansi, too is working and both of us also have a small job on the side—so you might say we're on our way to riches in the shortest possible time! Details about our jobs, especially mine, I wrote you in my letter of March 10th.

Last week we received our First Papers, one could say we're almost half way to citizenship. With these in hand I immediately applied to Washington to have you, dearest mother put on the preferred quota. Unfortunately that does not mean outside the quota, because that privilege is reserved only to citizens. So just be patient, my dearest ones, soon we'll see each other. Since the matter of the affidavit from Willy did not seem to be moving forward, we've simply turned it over to our other lawyer cousin Hannah who pursues this most energetically, especially the procuring of certain still missing documents. She already conferred with Willy about these and with her he cannot hide behind excuses of "lack of time today, he'll get to it tomorrow" etc.—on the contrary, with her he is most charming and obliging and she is actually enthusiastic about him. So please just be patient, worrying about the affidavit should be the last thing for all of you in the Lessinggasse and Taborstrasse! The affidavits will be yours, even if we have to dig them out of the earth. You will also get them in time, as a matter of fact much too early, i.e. I mean earlier than you can expect to be called given your high registration number at the consulate. Because even with the preferred quota we must expect to be kept waiting for several months.

In the matter of Epstein, I have corresponded with his guarantor in Washington even though E. told me it was hopeless—he had written to him for the past half year and received no answer. Only now Mr. Schutzman wrote me "he is in the happy situation where he can again act as a guarantor, having put his accounts in order after serving as guarantor for 20 affidavits." Thus he will renew E's expired affidavit. It was in any case a very nice letter and I have immediately forwarded it to E., urging him to write to Schutzman again. I just want to mention again that Willy has drawn up affidavits for you as well as for Victor. That was done not without difficulty because one consulate is in Vienna and the other one in Riga. If all of you were responsible to just one consulate that might not have been possible, Hannah cautioned, but in this case there should not be any objections. Should there be any difficulties we will find stronger supplementary guarantees for Victor. Once the affidavits are ready for mailing we will inform him by telegram.

You cannot imagine what an enormous correspondence I am engaged in with all our relatives, friends, etc., all about affidavits, ship tickets, etc. I use every free moment for that, on some Sundays I am up to ten hours at the typewriter, and never mind the expense connected with this correspondence. Yet when I see only the smallest success as a result of this correspondence then this is my greatest reward.

Herbert continues to do real well. As I am writing this letter a heavy snowfall is blanketing the city, even though we're only three days away from spring.

But this too will pass and you too will have warmer weather and the sun, which does not differentiate will warm you as well as all the others. Farewell all my loved ones, one after the other, but especially you my dearest mother, I embrace and kiss you all most fervently, your Emil

Emil, you too, should write some time!

Please give our best regards to Mama Neumann, also to your fellow house mates in the Lessinggasse the Tragholz couple, Herr Hacker, and all our dear relatives, loved ones, friends, too many to name them all one by one, but we think of you all continuously and with love.

What gives with Helly and Heinrich? When shall we finally be able to greet them here? In the meantime I have written together with Hannah to Dora and Regine separately. Have they heard more from Frieda and from where?

#6

New York, April 7th, 1940

My dear ones, dearest mother, Mama, Ella, Marie and Emil!

That we received your news up to and including March 8th, I indicated briefly in my last letter to you. Today I can also acknowledge your dear letter of March 20th, written by you, my dearest sister Marie. We're overjoyed that out of the many letters we wrote between January 1st and 28th, you at least received that of January 28th. Beginning with January 1st, we did not omit one single Sunday on which we didn't write you a detailed letter—and we can only hope that gradually, one by one you will receive them all. As I've told you many times, since the middle of February all my letters left here in duplicates, i.e. the original per airmail and its copy via Mrs. Z. Since American mail planes no longer fly over Bermuda where the British confiscated all mail addressed to Germany, we can assume that, if you haven't already, you'll receive my mail twice in a very short time. Otto too writes his letters with copies, the original goes by airmail, the copy to his mother-in-law in Switzerland, so now we have three paths that lead to you. Something's got to work now and from now on you can rely on receiving news from us regularly.

Also, we've mailed the affidavits for you Mama and Ella, as well as those for Victor/Hedy, all registered directly to Victor, so that he can send them on, registered anew, to the U.S. consul in Vienna, with a copy mailed separately to you. Believe me it was a difficult piece of work and the lion's share of responsibility for its success goes to Hansi who kept urging W. continuously, often rode late at night to him for another signature, or some other necessary document. Hannah, in turn put the whole matter in the required form, obtained the Photocopies, Notarizations, book experts, etc. Hansi is going to write you about all this separately. And as I wrote to you in the Lessinggasse so often before, for you too, everything is being prepared, although—it pains me to say this—there is no real hurry about that. Just be assured that you aren't going to stay there one second more than necessary and that the affidavits will arrive in time. On the contrary as I wrote so often, we are using every opportunity, looking for every piece of information that could accelerate your arrival here. I trust that all of you in the Lessinggasse und Taborstrasse will come here together; for you my dear mother I will order on the ship very special kosher meals which according to Marie Ringel, a recent arrival, are really excellent. If the affidavits are sent too early there's always the danger that they expire or become invalid and then one hast o start all over again. The reason we sent the affidavits for Mama Schab and Ella now is that it is already the turn for Victor's registration number and much of the documentation for him is also necessary for your affidavits and so we prepared everything in duplicate. Nevertheless we shall prepare the affidavits for you, Mother, Marie and Emil within a short time, all of them generously supported by Herman and Isidor (although Hannah says that affidavits for parents need not have such supplementary subsidies, since all of us are already "major money makers"!) I do know how happy one is when that piece of paper is already in one's possession even though it doesn't mean that one can depart immediately.

My dearest good mother, again and again I hear with great joy, from our good Marie by letter, but also in person from recent arrivals, how smart and reasonable you are, that Toi, toi, toi you look good and have made good friends with your new house mates. It is also wonderful that our lovely, dearest Ella, admired by all of us, is so concerned about you, visits you frequently, brings you sweet things and, more importantly, good news about us; for that I thank her a thousand times. But you in turn must promise not to make life difficult for her or the others when the mail, for reasons that I've explained above, does not always reach you regularly.

Very soon now we shall have Passover. One is reminded here of it on every corner, in the newspapers, advertisements on the street and in the subway, even in big neon lights that now appear, high as a house in Hebrew letters, in certain Jewish quarters of the city and they all say their Matzot are the best anywhere. Our landlords here have already asked Hansi to cook only with goose fat during those 8 days and not to bring any bread home. They also invited us to their Seder and Mrs. Gartenberg offered to cook for us during these eight days; but of course we'll be with Jonas Handel at that time.

The holidays, as beautiful as they are celebrated here, always make me terribly sad. Not just that you are unable to join us, but that you are suffering and are in want. Day and night I keep thinking how I could let you share in this colossal abundance, and were it only with the tiniest bit. I already wrote you that Herman and his wife sent us a basket with fruits. In order to keep the many oranges and grapefruits from turning bad, we squeezed them and made "juice" which Americans just love and drink at every meal—even I have gotten used to it. And you my dear mother are happy when someone takes pity on you and brings you one single orange! And still, I beg of you and all of you my dear ones, do not despair, and keep up your courage and patience. The good times will and must come for you as well!

I have sent some money to Adolf Epstein and he will pass it on to you. Also my friend Güns [in Belgium] has offered to send you something and I encouraged him to do that, since in this way he can pay back a small debt he owes me. Otherwise we are well satisfied—though there is less work now on the job for Hansi but also for me. In my factory the season hasn't really started yet, but will again in May at the earliest. I already wrote you that I have a small part time job that earns me a few dollars. My dearest Marie, I've written you so often about everything—but unfortunately those letters are still missing. Please turn to my good friend Heinrich; I am sure he can lend you up to a RM100.00. He is such a good and dear person and promised on the day of our departure that if you need anything to come to him without any qualms. I shall only hope that his resources have not shrunk, in the meantime. We were deeply depressed by the news that the Viennese consulate is again closed until July and that hit Helly/Heinrich particularly hard. We were counting so much on their arrival here within a short time. All our relatives here are so concerned about these two whom they know only through us. It is so hard to give comfort, and I can imagine their feelings only too well, nevertheless, I cannot repeat it too often: in the name of heaven do not despair, have courage and patience. As surely as you all will be helped we shall most certainly embrace them here. Please give them our very best regards, and if Hansi and I are still envious of Hellie for anything at all it is the fact that she can stay just a little bit longer with her dear mother. This week we got a lot of mail, from Ernst alone a five-page letter, his first one from Australia to us since we arrived here. It probably has the same content as ... [*Letter ends here*]

#7

New York, April 21st, 1940

My dearest beloved, good mother, Dearest sister Marie and my dear
  brother-in-law Emil!

We were overjoyed this time by your news, specifically your letters Marie, of March 28th and April 1st (latter with a postscript of April 2nd). We were immensely happy to read your added lines my dearest mother, and that you dear Emil honored us with your detailed lines, after such a long time, not to mention the fact of their happy tone, really amounted to a feast for us. We are glad that after the months long wait you too are receiving our mail in big heaps. You can read them at your leisure and it will help pass the time even though much of their content is long out of date. Not much of importance has changed here in the last months other than the fact that I am now employed, not just once but twice (I already wrote you that I have another job on the side), and that all of us are in good health and wish only to hear the same about you, if at least we cannot hear anything else more pleasurable. Much of your news really shocks us, even if it is only a line or even one word, thus when Mrs. P.[Prdszly] brought you an orange and what a feast that was for you, or that on the occasion of Purim you didn't even have an evening meal. I have written you repeatedly, I speculate day and night how we can send you foodstuff in some form. Money does not enter into the calculation. I recently wrote Epstein and also sent him some money and he in turn informed me that he has already submitted an application to ship you a larger package for the holidays and was hopeful it would work. Now I learn from you that it didn't. I am glad that at least Güns could send you something, even though it was only very little. In the meantime I wrote him again and hope he'll be able to send some more, though according to the latest reports in the newspapers, things aren't going very well over there, either. When I see, not what we have here in abundance, but what we just discard or waste carelessly in the course of one day, my heart breaks thinking of you. Whatever we put in our mouth knowing that these are things you've been doing without for so long, fruits you probably don't even remember how they taste, it makes us think of you and no longer agrees with us! But how does that help you, anyway! Tomorrow is Passover and there is a hustle and bustle everywhere, everyone is in a pre-holiday mood, as if this were a national holiday. We already have a tiff with our relatives over this holiday. Jonas who is still not fully recovered from his serious illness of last year, went to see his specialist doctor who was shocked over his high blood pressure and prescribed a strict diet for him. But he is a patient very much like my father-in-law of blessed memory, and you too, my dear sister: he doesn't keep his diet! His wife and Hannah decided therefore not to have a Seder this year with all its tempting goodies. We agreed instead to be the guests of Safirsteins at one of those world famous Jewish restaurants on the so-called Eastside to celebrate an outstanding Seder meal and service there. This is the way it is done here: publicly, lots of guests, great splendor, with many a millionaire present with his wife all decked out in the latest fashion. But Jonas learned of this plan and he became very upset with all of us. He would not hear of not having a Seder in his house. That's the way it always was and that's the way it should continue to be, he says. Just between us, we're really glad about that. First of all we're not really in the mood to spend such an evening in grand toilette, etc. we also feel hurt every time we see Safirstein spend good money for such useless things, because within the blinking of an eye 15.00 to

20.00 dollars are gone to the devil and that is an amount that the three of us live on for one week including rent. Moreover, I know that they are not doing too well themselves. Their law practice is suffering and two lawyers who had rented space from him in their offices in Chamber Street had to leave; so now he is stuck with the large rent for his office in a sky-scraper that rents exclusively to lawyers. Nevertheless, Safirstein is always in a good mood, he is somewhat of a happy-go-lucky type, in contrast to Hannah, who is a real Handel: very thrifty. By the way, yesterday Safirstein made a gift to Herbert of two very beautiful summer shirts and a white leather belt, and to me he gave a beautiful tie. At other times he brings gifts to Hansi, Otto and Stella. But we too pay attention to him and fre-quently bring some small things. For the second Seder we're invited at Fanny's house and that too was fought by Jonas over the phone for an hour but in the end he had to give in. He absolutely wanted us to spend both Seders with him. Our landlady, Mrs. Gartenberg also feels offended that we had to decline her invitation, she already tried to make our mouths water with her announcements of how well she would prepare the Gefilte-Fish. So you can see, my dear ones and especially you my good mother, no need to worry about us—if only we could have such joyful thoughts about you as you can have about us!

The news about Sigmund shocked us all, especially Jonas. All our sympathy goes out to Irma his poor wife and I ask you, dear Marie to express to her our special condolences and comfort her as far as this is possible. Safirstein who is of the same age and used to be his school mate, will try to convince Adolf Handel, who had always been very close to Sig-mund, to do something for his wife; his hopes are not very high however, since Adolf whom nobody likes, is callous and a very tough nut to crack. If anyone has influence it is Safirstein who gives him legal advice. We abstain from importuning the other Handels for her, since not only have they already guaranteed 10 affidavits, they most recently provided one for a nephew who is currently in a KZ in France; besides we have their solid promise to provide support affidavits for ours in case that is needed for you all. That includes also Olly unless she prefers to go to Manila. Please ask Irma all the exact data and mail them to me. By the way have you heard anything about Bernhard? Relatives of Safirstein recently wrote from Belgium. Hannah also wrote to Josef Handel in B. maybe there'll be some reference to Bernhard in their reply. How is his wife, Lotte? Be sure to give her too, our best regards.

There is not much other news. Weather is still miserable not fit for man or beast. Cold, rain almost daily, sometimes even snow; it looks as if it does not want change to summer. On May 11th he World's Fair will be reopened and everywhere one can see preparations for that grand open-ing. Otto was able to see it shortly after he arrived here last year, but when we came it was already closed.

I am glad to learn that you Emil have the chance to earn a few Marks. I thank you for caring about our mother, especially so that she doesn't have to suffer too much from the cold. When you and all the others will come over here with God's help we shall make your life just wonderful. You will not be asked to lift one finger and from morning till night all you'll do is take walks.

Have you, dear Marie talked to my friend Heinrich? You know he promised me that he would not leave you in the lurch and help you with up to RM100.00. I am not sure whether he can still do that, he may be short himself, but maybe he can still remember his pledge. He knows that I will repay him.

We hope to see Helly and her dear husband here very soon and even if it takes a little longer than expected, they must not lose courage. Also they mustn't worry about anything. Once they arrive here we shall all take care of them. For this time I must close, and I send you my dearest good mother and all my other loved ones, fervent embraces and kisses, as ever your Emil

---

#8

New York, May?, 1940 [Fragment]:

...to return. People here are often disappointed in that regard, espe-cially those who, having finally found a job, immediately begin to work out that they now have enough to see them through for such and such a length of time, to save so and so much, to be able to buy this and that, etc. And from one day to the next they're back to where they started. This is the reason why 90 percent of the refugees are dissatisfied, even those who had put up with the most terrible things in Europe. Otto's friend Adler is a prime example: Although he is earning, and even quite well, and this since the first week after his arrival, he feels inconsolably unhappy and is always wondering how he can return, even illegally! He misses the Vereinsgasse and the Blumauergasse and things weren't really all that bad and he never noticed any food shortages, etc.

But as far as the Streit family's point is concerned, one has to agree with them. Older people who have hardly any chance of earning money here and who have no family to look after them might as well stay put, as long as their existence there is not threatened and they still have a few mark to keep their heads above water for a time. But of course not, if there is another deportation to Poland or something similar. It is true that no one will starve here, the Committee sees to that. However one might have to put up with being sent by the Committee to any one of those virtually identical, monotonous small or medium-sized towns in the American Mid-West or even South, the majority of whose inhabitants are Negroes. I have heard that from people I know who have been sent to places like that and are quite desperate. And many, of them run away, giving up the support they were receiving and come back here to this vast city of New York in the hope of being able to make a modest amount of money after all.

But to come back to Hansi and her not having written lately: she will soon be writing in detail to Helly and Heinrich and they can both rest assured that not a single day passes without Hansi talking to me about those two delightful people. Yesterday, Saturday, Hansi had such a long-ing for Helly and Heinrich that at about 6P she suddenly decided to take the almost one hour trip on the subway to see the Becks in the Bronx. Unfortunately I couldn't go along, as I have to work on my second job on Saturday afternoons. They just wouldn't let Hansi leave. She only got back home after midnight and told me so many lovely things about those people who are really having a hard time, especially Mama Beck, who, although—touch wood—is in the best of health, has only the one pas-sionate wish, namely to be able soon to hold Heinrich and Helly in her arms. By the way, today, Sunday, I'm intending to go and see Frau Bredhoff and will write to Heinrich later on about my visit.

We were absolutely delighted to receive your news, Marie dear, about Regine and Frieda. Dora made no mention of it in her long letter of April 19th to Hannah, but the good news was already there in your letter of the 23rd. You can see how right I've been up till now with my words of encour-agement! And now when they are almost at the finishing line, is definitely not the time to lose hope. Everything must and will turn out right! They will probably still have to face many difficulties, but that is, above all, to one purpose and one goal! You can hardly imagine what a happy mood this news has brought to everyone here. We are expecting them to arrive here latest by the end of June. Hannah is already discussing the details of their accommodation: the intention is to take a larger apartment which has become vacant in the same building, so as not o have to share with other people. But those are our happy worries. They must do their best to see that everything over there goes according to plan. Hannah and I consider that everything that Dora wrote in her letter about Frieda and Shanghai has now definitely been overtaken by events. They must also do their best to ensure that their traveling expenses are borne by the KG. Ella dear, I have another small request of you: I recently received a very nice, long letter from Dr. Anny Abelis. Anny Abelis reminds me a lot of you. She too has so much responsibility resting on her shoulders now, whereas in the past she didn't have to worry about a thing. Apart from giving her our warmest regards, please tell her that I am giving slow-moving Otto no rest. Unfortunately the affidavit arrangements have failed because of one sponsor. Now Otto and his sister Lisl are going to issue the affidavit for the two of them. It should be ready to be sent off very shortly. In any case I intend to see that it is. I hope that Frau Abelis has recovered from her illness in the meantime. And now I come back to you, dear family, and especially to you, sister dearest. Everything you have told us in your last few letters has brought us joy, except for what you write about yourself. We are quite depressed to hear that, besides your mental suffering, you are also not really in the best of health. And it only makes it worse for us that we are powerless to help and that from so far away we can only try to console you. Perhaps it would after all be a good idea for you to take baths and quite lengthy, strong ones. And spare no expense. Before the end of the coming week we are going to send a trial transfer of money via the bank, as Otto has already mentioned a number of times in his letters.

Once more, dear Emil, I have heard nothing from you for quite some time now and, in complaining to you about it, I would like to tell you that I miss you very much and that you are a fine chap who deserves a better fate in life. But I don't have to urge you to have courage and patience. For you, too, will see better times and you will experience a happy and more carefree old age, your children and I too will see to that. I've even spied out a Kaffeehaus for you, in which you will feel right at home, amongst cronies. Sometimes I get a bit tired of the Americans and their smart ways and when I feel like some real Viennese company, with people like you, I sometimes go there. I know it's not always easy for you with the two women, even if they too are to be commiserated with. And they should realize how fortunate they are to have you around. By the way, I've been meaning to ask you this for a long time: Did you have any success with the medal bonus? Here you will again be a member of the Jewish Frontline Soldiers' Association, who are also established here and organize many social functions.

And now, Mother dearest and all my dear family, I send you my most loving hugs and kisses and please give our warmest regards to all our dear relatives, friends and acquaintances, Your Emil

#9

New York, May 12th 1940

My dearest, sweetest only mother,

All my loved ones in the Lessinggase and Taborstrasse! This week we didn't receive any mail from you but we do not want to be discontent, given that we received so much and good news from you last week. Hopefully the next European mail will again bring good news from you, most importantly that you're all healthy and that Mama Schab's move is happily completed. Today is Mother's Day, which is celebrated here with typical American hoopla—it is after all an American invention and to do "business" is at the top of the list. I hope not only you, mother but all the other dear mothers and grandmothers will not think the worse of me when I say that in my case there is no need to be reminded of love for one's mother! Such a reminder is necessary only for bad and uncaring children and I am sure I can speak for all your children, mother, Marie, and Mama Schab when I say that they've all been good all the time. For us each day is Mother's Day, more than ever our thoughts are with you and we only have one burning wish to be reunited with you!

And just as we do on each of the three hundred sixty-five days of the year we wish you today and as always everything good and beautiful and that all your wishes should be met as soon as possible.

For this week I have a small piece of news for you: actually it isn't news anymore, since I've kept it to myself for almost three weeks; mainly because at first it was only temporary, a sort of test run. Well, I no longer work in the belt factory, but have been employed by a small but very well thought of book dealer, actually more of an art/antique dealer, my same "line" as in Vienna. This is a small success of my campaign carried on for five months among all local book dealers. My new boss is not a local how-ever, but an emigrant of an earlier arrival date than ours. He inquired about me at Willy Schab as well as at Ranschburg both of whom I always listed as references, and then offered me the position. My pay is not much higher than my previous one—but let's face it, this is really different! First of all I'm now working in one of the most exclusive, elegant areas of the city, no longer in the factory district. My work is no longer paid by the hour, which meant, in the last few weeks when the season was slackening off, that I hardly made any money at all. Most of all I am enjoying the work and soon I hope there'll be an improvement in my salary, too. In any case I have a steady weekly income, rather than the "paper" income of my last job where the actual pay was a lot less. Among the tens of thousand of immigrants, I am now one of the few who has a so-called white-collar job; most of the university graduates among us refugees, former doctors, lawyers, civil servants etc. etc. generally work in factories, some even as dishwashers. Many of them find jobs now in the many restaurants of the newly opened '39 World's Fair. My office is only a three-minute walk from that famous and beautiful Central Park where I usually spend my lunchtime.

Until now I had to get up at 6A in order to be at work at 8A, now I do not start before 10A and business closes at 6A, with one hour break at lunch. Who could ask for anything more? Maybe more pay, but with God's help that too, will happen.

Herbert had birthday last Wednesday, celebrated jointly with our 19th wedding anniversary, and as much as we tried to keep this a secret from our relatives here—we wanted to avoid any unnecessary attention and besides that boy has already received so many things from them— Hannah did not forget. After all she knows all our data from the documents she prepared for the affidavits. She promptly arrived with a fabulous radio, the kind Herbert had wanted for a long time. It has all kinds of technical specialties, one can listen to the hundreds of domestic station as well as those in other countries—it is not very big and can be taken along almost anywhere. From the relatives in Jersey he received a real classy sport vest with a little note that said in English: "Who told me about your birthday? A little birdie did, etc. etc." We were really wondering how those relatives in Jersey knew about his birthday—no doubt Hannah had something to do with it, though she energetically denies that.

Dear Mama Schab, the matter with Mama Neumann's relatives in Milwaukee I would pursue only too gladly, but the data you sent give almost no clue. You write their name used to be "Löwy" and is now "Louis." That is most likely incorrect. You are writing the name the way it is pronounced here; more likely they are called "Lewis" now, as are most whose name used to be "Löwy." But the name "Lewis" is as frequent as was "Löwy" over there. New York has five telephone books one for each district and each of these books is as big as the whole Viennese telephone directory. In every one of them the name "Lewis" takes up more than 10 pages, with several hundred on each page. Of course Milwaukee is much smaller than New York, with only ca. half a million inhabitants—but there too one will find hundreds even thousands of "Lewis!" So how can anyone find out anything like that, especially since in the U.S.—as is well known—there is no mandatory individual registration? Here if you need to know the address of a friend or acquaintance you have to consult a detective agency—that is not a joke! In their advertisements, detective bureaus always list first that they can find residential addresses. I would even do that were it not such a common name and the other identifying data so vague. Maybe you can send me more leads....

Felix' letter of which you sent us a copy we passed on to Willy. I was deeply moved by his lines. Nobody or only a few will be able to understand him as I do. He suffers from the same longing as I do and that feeling of powerlessness to be unable to help as quickly as possible something we all want to do. Felix too, cannot get over the fact that he had to leave his beloved mother and sister behind, but it is just this pain that gives each of us the urge not to leave you in the lurch as we did and to do our utmost now to bring about a happy reunion.

We are all here still under the impact of the most recent events. Will they affect our mail to you and from you? That is our first thought. Otherwise we know as little about things as do those in the warring states. The reports from all sides that one reads or hears only help to confuse us more.

Last week we had a few wonderful spring days; I enjoyed the lilacs in bloom in Central Park also the horse drawn carriages on rubber wheels cruising through the park and led by very dignified looking coachmen in gray top hats. Yes that too is possible in New York, a pleasure reserved only for the very rich! Today it is again rather gloomy and windy. I shall close for today and embrace you my beloved mother, and also all my other loved ones, but wishing again all mothers, grandmothers and great-grandmothers only the best, remaining with more greetings and kisses for all our dear relatives, friends and acquaintances, your Emil

---

#10

New York, May 26, 1940

My dearest, good sister! The sweet but also so very sad letter you mailed to my home address arrived and I already acknowledged it briefly in my last letter. It brought me a lot of grief yet at the same time showed me I had not been wrong in suspecting that all of you had other matters bothering you and consequently I urged you to write me about everything, without holding back anything. I believe that no one among all your loved ones is as capable as I am to empathize with you, to understand what you're going through, since I was the one who had stayed until the very last and then had to leave you behind. Even though I was actually the only one who had the forethought of registering all of you I chide myself for having done this so late, every hour of the day. And yet, my dearest Marie, apart from that feeling of euphoria that flooded through me when stepping on American soil, for us emigrants it is not the greatest of luck, maybe not even the smallest one, to live here and get used to our new home country. Maybe this is true for people whose nature is different from our family and my own in particular—people who are made of sterner stuff—it will never be that for me, now or in the future. I often ask myself: what's the use? Why did I yearn so much for that hour in which I could leave you and our country—and there is really only one answer to that: Herbert. That I'd be feeling that way I already knew in Vienna, when everything suddenly seemed to be working and our departure was no longer in question—I literally had to drag myself to the train with my last ounce of energy, instead of going there joyously with a springy step.

I beg of you, my dear Marie, do not misunderstand me, I am not ungrateful to God and the fate He had planned for me. I realize that every one considers me really lucky, envies me our salvation at the eleventh hour, the fact that I and those I love most dearly could actually make it over here—our truly wonderful relatives who gave us such a reception and continue to look out for us—I didn't have to go hungry, on the contrary, we both found work, and I am now working in a great job that makes use of my original professional training. When I now think of the fate of all those hundreds of thousand of people in Norway, in Holland, in Denmark and lately also in Belgium, that of my old friend Güns who notified me just prior to it happening there, that he had to return the watch I sent him because he could not raise the money to pay the custom duty—and now he like thousands of others is wandering about only God knows where in Belgium—then even I have to admit to myself that I am lucky! I tell that to myself but also to Hansi who feels just as unhappy as I do with the difference however, that she is able to express her unhappiness by writing to you and her mother, which makes me very mad yet I can understand her. I feel badly about it because I know that neither you nor any of the others will understand us, no more so than we could understand those who similarly complained to us while we were still over there with you, but above all because you are burdened by an immense and immediate sorrow, that makes it impossible for you to feel our own pain which is clearly of secondary importance.

In this regard, Otto and Stella are of a happier disposition mainly because they did not have to live through that difficult year 1938-39, that year which for any one who experienced it engraved itself inextinguishably into his heart and soul; I envy them for that, but am actually glad that this is the way it is. After all what should still tie them to that land over there, other than their longing for you? Otto especially did not have a happy youth, overshadowed as it was by the First World War, and even afterwards not much good happened to him. We talk a lot about you, discuss many things, and Otto says that you too, won't find much happiness here and maybe he is right. We who are older feel our unhappiness twice over. We are not happy in this foreign country and carry a longing in our heart for something that has been irrevocably lost and will never come again.

And as far as the present situation is concerned, we have a little more distance and perspectives than you do, so when we talk about you we tell ourselves that relatively speaking, you're lucky to be still in Vienna. How much more horrible would it be, were we to think of you somewhere in the emigration, even in Switzerland or worse in Belgium where so many of our relatives and acquaintances now reside.

There is one more matter, my dearest, good Marie: I can read between your lines that our dear mother with her little peculiarities is really testing your already taut nerves to the utmost. Please do not take it too hard and make a tragedy of it. Can't you, too, recognize how very unhappy this poor old woman is—for which she finds some release, just as old people generally do, by taking it out on those closest to her? And I beg of you,

Otto Kupler (1910–1983), son of Emil and Marie. This picture was taken ca. 1938, shortly before his escape to Switzerland.

think of me a little bit when it gets too much for you, how I must feel, being so far away from the people I love most, knowing that something is not all right, yet I cannot help the way I used to by simply coming over from the Alserbachstrasse in order to make peace between you! I shall also write a few lines to mother on that subject and you must promise to read them to her.

Also, my dear good Marie, please go to a decent doctor, have him examine you thoroughly and possibly prescribe a more radical cure. Mother will certainly give you something if that is necessary, in any case we shall for the time being send monthly $10.00 for which you will receive ca. RM60.00. Later, God willing that everything works OK and you receive this money without any difficulties, we'll send a larger amount. But you simply must do something for yourself!

I have recently also mailed a petition to the KG of which I sent you a copy. Has something resulted from that? If not, Emil has to go there and push! I would like to ask Dora to go with you to Dr. Schnardt and then send me an exact report, the way she did about mother which calmed me a great deal, and for which I thank her with all my heart. She should do me this small favor for you before she comes over here and then can possibly tell me about it in person. Again my dearest Marie, be smart, and don't take your little differences with mother so tragically—even though I can understand you only too well. We are all of us, after all, only poor, pitiable human beings and have our faults. Once it is irrevocably too late, then every bad word said to our loved ones or to our fellow men in general, burns inextinguishable. How much I would like to make unsaid every mean word directed at you, mother or Emil in a moment of thoughtlessness or ill humor—how happy and comforted on the other hand, does it make one feel to know that you've done something good for any one of your loved ones in the past!

My dearest Marie, I have let you look more into my inner thoughts than I really wanted to, or as I usually do in my letters to you. Not that my letters were not true or exaggerated, I simply tried always to give you only what is concrete, maybe a little entertaining so you can forget for a moment your own misery and foremost because I know how much you enjoy learning that we are doing real well here. So please do not tell mother and the others about my having poured out my heart to you this time. I too feel a little bit relieved for having done that. For you my dear Marie, I can only repeat what I've said so often before: watch out for your health, have a little more patience and courage! You are all of you heroes—so please remain so until we meet with success, until you're released from all your sorrows! I embrace you and kiss you, your faithful brother Emil

P.S. Otto has moved to another lodging not too far from here and we see each other daily. We too thought about moving, possibly share a flat with them, but postponed this in view of the uncertain situation abroad.

#11

New York, May 26th, 1940 *[Ed.: This is the 2nd letter with same date]*
My beloved dear mother,

All my dear ones in the Lessinggasse & Taborstrasse!
This time we only have a post card from Mama to acknowledge, in which she advises us of her successful move. Nothing else arrived, but we shall not be immodest, during the last few weeks all of you wrote frequently and in detail. I know Marie that letter writing robs you of much of your time, especially in view of your ill health, and also costs you a good deal of money, after all you write not only us but also to Irma, Mrs. Bock, Epstein and many others you want to stay in touch with. The same is true of Mama Schab who in addition to the move, has to stay in touch with continents. On the other hand we are still awaiting some more news from Regine and Dora. I already acknowledged their telegram in my last letter and acted immediately concerning the ship tickets which have been paid in full, telegraphed again etc. We are listening with bated breath and pounding heartbeat to the news from Europe and only hope most fervently that the three of them will succeed in making it over here. This week I received a very detailed and interesting letter from Irma. She described for us the Seder festivities with Heinzi and how that boy of theirs is really thriving. Otherwise they suffer from the same pain in their heart, the intense longing for you. She writes that she is continuously engaged in sending you news and hopes that at least some of it reaches you. Please you need not worry about her at all if the mail doesn't always arrives on time. Conversely we're calming her about you and we comfort each other that everything will end well. Eventually we most surely will be able to hold you all in our arms. Do not lose courage no matter what may come!

As we told you once before we had been looking for a flat but postponed this project again. The situation here is much too uncertain, especially in view of the latest European events; these do influence the economy here since several markets in Europe are now lost, such as Belgium, Holland, Denmark, even those in England and France are at risk. We would have to furnish everything from the bottom up which would be quite an expense. We do not want spend all our cash since that is reserved foremost for you. Hansi works only two days a week and some times just one.

In order to make up for that she is trying something new: she helps out at a ladies' tailor in the Bronx, mainly alterations, but also a few made to order clothes. It is important that Hansi, even though she knows dressmaking very well, gains the necessary experience here should she want to open up her own shop for alterations later in our neighborhood. Here everyone has dresses altered, mainly because the big department stores where dresses can be had very cheaply—for $2.00 one can get a passable dress—do not make sure that they also fit well. So many go to these alteration shops—mainly run by refugees—in order to have them made over so that they fit right. But all that too, requires some experience with local practices and that is exactly what Hansi is after. Most importantly she learns that way tailoring according to the American style, which means, quick, quick, quick and don't bother to do everything precise and exact the way we were used to on the other side. Hansi is simply amazed how finished products are delivered: threads are everywhere; nothing is pressed and everything is sewn with large stitches. Yes, the average American woman is dressed only for show—and that mainly for those who must be nearsighted. You can't come too close and look. To all of that is added a lot of color, on the cheeks, the lips, flashy red nails, and on the head a crazy little hat—equally meshuggene shoes with open toes, in the summer without stockings but the toes now colored most exotically, all this under a cloud of perfume creating a total picture that is absolutely amazing. Much must be said for the American woman, she is physically always very well groomed, even if she is only a poor factory girl. This is due to a very advanced housing culture—there simply isn't a flat without a bathroom!

Unfortunately, Hansi's so-called experimental job is far up in the Bronx, the round trip takes nearly two hours by subway; she doesn't get home at night before 8PM. She likes what she is doing, but hopes that her job in the artificial flower factory will start again soon. About myself and my new occupation I already wrote in my last letter. I can only add that I am still quite satisfied, but would be even more so if the pay were a little more. But that too will happen, eventually. Of course that too depends very much on the international situation. Current events influence this business a great deal.

Please, dear Marie, tell Mrs. Weissberg I talked to Hannah and the address she asked for is Wadsworth Avenue 7. It'll remain that over the summer months. Should anything change I'll inform Mrs. W. directly or through you. It is enough when she writes once a month. Let me know Marie when she has written so I can notify Hannah, letters do get lost especially if they're not sent by airmail.

During the past week we've had a number of hot days and I perspired a lot. But it is bearable. On days like these one consumes a lot of iced drinks and above all fruit ice. Here too, shops selling ices move into empty storefronts during the summer. Here too you can see little carts on the street, with the difference—after all this is America—here they are regular little autos but with the same bells only louder, so that they can be heard all the way up to the 30th floor of the office skyscrapers. One more thing is different and that is the quality of the ice even though it costs only 5 cents (ca 25 Groschen) and is served in hermetically closed cups making it very sanitary and with a little wooden spoon plus napkin. But it is ice cream and not the fruity, sorbet type we used to get at the Italians. Oh, how I must think of you and the good ice we got at Fredrizzi across the street, I used to bring up the cones with ice sometimes helped by Heinzi and we all gathered around including you dearest mother and attacked the ice. Is this still available? Do you drink at least every once in a while a Raspberry Soda? Oh, better not think about it. I received a very nice letter from Irma Handel. Please thank her in my name and tell her that whoever turns to me in his need, I shall try to help in so far that is possible given my limited power. It hurts me to say this to Irma it is useless to do anything for her since she only registered in July 1939. I had assumed she had done that much earlier. But she mustn't lose her courage. In a few months I shall again try and I hope meet with success. It makes no sense to ask people for an affidavit, which becomes invalid after a short time and the whole procedure has to be repeated. Usually people then do not want to renew just like those relatives of Epstein's. I already wrote you that I managed to get a new affidavit for Olly and if everything goes well we can expect her here in 2–3 months.

About Herbert I can relate that he too now earns some money. From 6:30A to 8A he delivers breakfast rolls for a local bakery in ca. 15 apartment buildings. This is not such a difficult task here since all these buildings have elevators. Then he comes home, takes a shower, dresses in his school clothes picks up his books and is again a "student."

Now I embrace you all, especially you my dear mother, your Emil.

#12

New York, June 2nd 1940

My beloved Mother, My beloved in the Lessinggasse & Taborstrasse (in the new one at last)!

In our letter to the Taborstrasse of 26th May and mailed on 28th I was able to add a few quick lines to Ella in which I acknowledged your letters of 13 May (Marie) and 12/13 May from Mama. Our joy is great to

receive these dear and detailed news especially about Mama-Ella's having a little place to live with which they can be at least half-way satisfied.
I hope by now you have gradually put things in order, so you can rest a
bit, especially you dear Ella, and not just from the physical exertions. Your
nerves too, will relax, now that you no longer have this worry, which has
occupied you for more than six months. Even though there is nothing we
could do to help, we too, feel as if a great burden has been lifted from our
shoulders. It really calmed us down to learn that brother-in-law Emil was
of such great assistance to you—and you expressed your appreciation certainly in the most generous manner, I was told. Even if it isn't meant that
way, his two ladies who are, after all in charge of managing the declin-
ing reserves keep Emil on very short rations; he surely enjoyed it. I do
thank you as well, and so does Otto from the bottom of our hearts. Once
you're settled in and have caught up in other ways with your new situation, please write us in detail what your new place looks like. Do you have
telephone? Be sure to let us know the number if you do, one never knows.
At last, Marie, you made the effort and went to see the doctor. Dora wrote
me about it and that has reassured me. Please write, Marie whether the
injections are successful. I hope that with the arrival of the warmer season, these rheumatic pains will disappear completely. Please thank Dr.
Schnardt for his care in my name as well and if there is anything I can
do for him he should not hesitate to ask me. The news about you mother
dear, are the high point of my life here, so far from you, and they make
it easier to tolerate all the other difficulties here and hope for a better
future.

    We received a very detailed letter from Dora and I much thank her
for her efforts concerning all of you.

    Her reports about your state of health have made us happy and reas-
sured us. Her visits to Mama-Ella, despite all her big problems, is very
kind, and we just want to experience that hour when she, Regine and
Frieda will be here and we'll be able to express our thanks not just in
words. Unfortunately we have not yet heard about Fr.'s return home and
about the examination at the U.S. consulate which we've been anticipating for so long. But that too will happen with the Lord's help. We're
confident that the ship connection with Italy will be maintained, despite
a variety of rumors, at least via American ships. In response to the
telegram, which, we assumed was sent by Dora via the Italian Shipping
Line, and not via the Jewish Community Organization we immediately
gave instructions to reserve the ship tickets. I am sorry that we had to
answer the telegram itself in a negative way—but this should not worry
her. Her arrival here will on that account not be delayed by even one hour,

which might have been the case if the KG had to make decision on that score. On the other hand, the fact that the crates have not yet arrived here, we cannot understand. The amount demanded by the Parisi Shipping Company was mailed months ago, practically on the same day his bill arrived. About 14 days ago Hannah airmailed a duplicate of that check to Triest, since her bank in fact discovered that the first check had not yet arrived. No payment of additional fees was required. It can be assumed that the crates are already on the high seas, probably on a freighter and that usually takes 3–4 weeks. Hannah wanted to go to the Italian line yesterday in order to have the tickets transferred to an American line, in case the Italian lines stop sailing. I haven't seen her since then, but this should be possible without any difficulty. We do not really understand why the KG in its telegram insisted so determinedly that the tickets had to be paid into an Italian line. We would have booked on an American line in the first place. As I mentioned above we assumed most assuredly that Dora sent that telegram herself via the Italian line. We therefore speculated that that Fr. was already home, and a ticket had already been prepared for him by the KG; we further assumed that the examination of Dora and Regine at the U.S. consulate depended on providing proof of payment for their tickets, the same way it was done when we left. The trouble is that there is no fast direct connection now that the private exchange of telegrams has been stopped. We also assume that Miss W. already has her notification from the American consulate that her affidavit has arrived. Did you give her Hannah's message I sent you in my last letter? If she is really so kind to help you out, please let us know. Otherwise we shall do what Otto and I already mentioned earlier. We only postponed it for a while when you, Marie told us of the kind proposal made by Regine's sister. Please give her as well as Dora our best regards and tell them they must persevere no matter what happens.

I am glad to hear that the KG has not forgotten you altogether, but would like to know whether the subsidy, however small, is at least sent regularly. Maybe this will be the case this time, in view of my direct petition.

We received a very nice letters from Hansi Lakner and her mother. Please tell them, dear Ella—via postcard if you do not have a phone— that we continue our efforts on behalf of their affidavits. I visited with the guarantor for Robert, concerning mother Lakner's affidavit. She was very friendly but pointed out to me that she had already received a warning from Washington because of her many affidavits. She already told the same thing to Emmy Lakner. I then insisted, without becoming pushy, and she actually gave me some fairly specific promises. A few days later

I received a postcard from her in which she urgently asked me for the address of Emmy, which had gotten lost. We had agreed earlier that if prospects would again appear positive she should pursue the matter of Emmy. (Personally I rather hope that both of them will be able to come directly from Shanghai and from Singapore on the *Conte Rosso* on June 14th and that would make the whole matter of the affidavits moot. But I don't want to mention this to either one of the other sponsors or to anyone else because that would make them relax in their efforts.) And I do not want that under any circumstances! It would be best, dear Ella, if you copy the lines I put in parenthesis literally and send both of them our best regards. Once we know more, we shall write to them directly.

This time I've written less about us, but responded to other dear persons in that letter really meant for you. There is precious little to say about ourselves. We are healthy and feel good physically in every respect. Only Hansi moans all the time, she is getting too fat. I shall try to take a few pictures with my camera, though it is difficult to get the right film size here. Weather was agreeably cool all week long which for me mans it was wonderful. I tell myself this is already June, so the great heat with which the "natives" threaten us can last only 2–3 months. Our Jonas started his summer vacation this week—just one week, there are no four-week vacations—and he can rest from his really hard work. Recently I went for a walk with him in the evening. I continue to be satisfied with my "job" and only hope they are with me. This job frequently brings me together with Willy and Ada who are doing very well, have received your letter and send their best regards. They promised me they would write. Haven't heard from Dr. Weil for some time, but I do not want to disturb him during this time when he is studying hard for his exams.

What do you hear from Heinrich and Helly? We spoke recently with a couple, which registered on September 10, 1938, and arrived here about a fortnight ago. They were the last ones prior to the closing of the consulate. We hope to talk to them again soon. Whatever happens it will always be possible to find a way to sail over here, and the newspapers assure us that the American ship lines will maintain their schedules. Have H & H visited you in your new flat? We hope to have them both here real soon. We greet and embrace them with all our heart.

Now, once again I turn to you, dear mother. Please continue to be smart and give me happiness. If the weather permits it, go often for a walk with Marie, and don't save your money, d'you hear? Treat yourself and the others to the few good things that are still available. I greet and kiss you with all my love; and just as faithfully I embrace all of you in the Taborstrasse and Lessinggasse! Greetings to all our dear relatives, friends and acquaintances, especially Mama Neumann, the Braun girls, our dear Frieda, also Laufer Frieda, we much enjoyed her greetings. We hope she is in touch with all her children and gets only good news from them. I greet and thank our dear Mrs. P. [Prdszly], who doesn't seem to abandon you, dearest mother something I will never forget her; I greet all your housemates and simultaneous card partners of Emil, and remain always thinking of you, your Emil. P.S. The returned pictures, Marie, did arrive.

#13

New York, June 16th 1940

My dearest, much beloved mother,

Dearest Marie and Emil, Dearest Mama and dearest Ella!

I already acknowledged briefly your many and detailed letters in my postscript to my letter of June 9th. These letters were a bright moment in this otherwise so sad week. Last week we received Mama and Ella's letter, also the one directed to Herbert. We thank you for your good and detailed report. You dearest Marie skipped one this time. Wouldn't it be possible that one week you'll write, Marie, and Ella or Mama the other time? One of you could write a short note that the other one would include in her report and you could carry this to the one who is writing that week. Only one of you should always report in detail and that way we'd be always kept up to date about what everyone is doing—and you of course would be saving on postage. Here I am making plans for your mail when it is quite possible, we fear that the mail, which has been functioning so well lately, may be stopped altogether. That immediately has its effect on our disposition and mood. For one half week we enjoy the mail we received, keep reading and re-reading it, sometimes Hansi even asks for your letter in the morning so she can read it while riding to work. Otto and I carry on a steady fight over your letters, dearest Marie, and at Handels we usually stand in line for them! We know exactly when the Clipper arrives—that means there'll be mail the following day. Fact is that Otto comes home earlier from work; consequently he can get to Handels ahead of me and pick up your letters there. However since I need to be at my new place of work only at 10AM I usually go there in the morning—but I am not always lucky since the mail sometimes gets there only in the afternoon. Nevertheless I reserve for myself the right to the "Registration and Administration" of all arriving mail! So if anyone needs to look into one of your earlier letters then he has to come to me and ask very politely for my permission! Well, and then the rest of the week is spent in joyous expectation of the next batch of mail! We wish for nothing else so fervently than that this condition at least will prevail. Because you must believe us, as long as we know you to be there and are not able to have you here there is no life for us. The past week with all its events has made us absolutely sick and in view of our suffering friends Helly and Heinrich, as well as Regine Dora, Frieda, we just sat there wailing. Do not say we are looking for sympathy in view of the misfortune of others, but what person can still exult over his life when for seven months he trembles over the fate of others, shares every phase of their misery, yet always waiting for the sense of relief that will come only with a message that they've already received the notification for the examination at the U.S. consulate, that their passage has been booked, that they have embarked, just as we did not so long ago, on their voyage over here—and now everything is gone, or at least moved even farther into the future.

You my dearest mother, all of you must know how we long for you and that our whole existence here is designed only to achieve a reunion with you. Your time will come and this war too, will have an end, no war has lasted forever and then you'll be able to come over here in peace or we may even come and get you ourselves. But these people, Regine, Helly and all the others who thought themselves so near to their goal, have suffered so much to come even this far—and now it is all for naught. This time we cannot even comfort you, don't even want to, because we're ashamed to speak to them of courage, hope and patience, yet all our feelings are with them. I cannot believe that there is no longer any way to come over here and I must implore all of you do not be affected by these new circumstances. Do not, for heaven's sake, let yourself go! There will, there must be a way! The same also applies to you my beloved ones. I beg of you do not give up; continue to be courageous and full of hope. Think of us for whom you are life itself! We shall be definitely reunited again.

You wrote you wanted to know something about my job. I work in a small store for rare & antique books on 57th street, a very good location where most art and antique dealers can be found; that is also true of Madison Avenue where Willy has his shop, quite close to us. Our office is on the 6th floor, so it isn't a just a street vendor's place. Business is done mainly via correspondence, mainly with hundreds of private and public libraries all over the country. I am the only employee except for a Negro who does the heavy work—packaging, moving books—and I am frequently all by myself since my boss is mainly on the road. But I too, am frequently away, usually in the famous New York Public Library to search for bibliographical information, check records on valuable old books, their provenance, descriptions, information for cataloguing etc. Of course my greatest handicap is still the language. I must write business letters in English—but that is not the way it was over there, where we figured even if it is not completely correct they'll understand! Here I have to make our offers in English, accept orders, fill out the shipping manifests, etc. also handle orders by telephone, actually perfectly normal tasks but everything, everything in English! And of course I don't want to disgrace myself, want to have everything look just perfect, just as if I were a Native American! For example, when the phone rings—and here the phone rings very often—with calls from Baltimore, Washington, San Francisco—I get nervous, have to pull all my five senses together (because frequently and with pleasure they are concentrating on you) in order to understand everything exactly and reply correctly, just so there is no mistake and misunderstanding. This is the difficulty for me in contrast to the others who are engaged in factory work. They are busy at the assembly line or the drill press or whatever and they do not have to meet demands on their language skills. The small amount necessary for the daily routine or the technical expressions of their line of work they're able to acquire very quickly. That is especially and most admirably true of Hansi. You must believe me when I say that in the evening on coming home I am totally worn out even though my work is physically by far not as demanding as that of the factory worker. But it is all right—I learn a lot. Most importantly I'm gaining some insight into American business practices, its general mechanics and that is what I've really wanted. It is certainly worthwhile to be able to fill out correctly an American freight manifest, deal with a variety of government offices, communicate verbally and correctly on the telephone with a book dealer in Milwaukee where, by the way, English sounds quite differently from that spoken here. Here we say they "murder" English, and they on the other hand, accuse New Yorkers of speaking English very poorly. I should mention in this connection that all of us—not to mention Herbert, of course—including Hansi speak a very passable English. To watch, rather to listen to Hansi do her shopping in the grocery store is truly amazing. I still lack the technical expression for that undertaking. Otto speaks quite fluently, which means that due to his arrival here one month ahead of us, his conversational skills were also better than mine. He is very ambitious, reads only English newspapers and is particularly crazy about the radio, which is of course very useful for learning the language.

I am also enclosing a few photos so you won't worry about how we look. Hansi looks very American, the same is true of Herbert—unfortunately I still look more than just well fed! One thing you can see on my pictures that I really wanted to hide: I've gotten quite gray!

Please Taborstrasse do not fight with Lessinggasse over these pictures! Next time I shall send more copies. But for the time being you will just have to share them with each other. Please Ella, tell Heinrich concerning my postscript in my last letter—sent directly to Helly—that unfortunately I've been unable to achieve something with the shipping company Tice & Lynch because the English consulate does not issue any "Navy-Certificates" for goods originating in Italy anymore. But it is not hopeless, only right now nothing is definite. In any case I sent a letter to the shipping agency Merzario in Genoa and we'll see what he says. Here is another favor I must ask of you, Ella. Please call Anny Abelis who wrote me a very lovely, long letter and tell her that the affidavit sponsored by Lisl Margulies was mailed registered about a week ago and she should have received it in the meantime. Even though this is a result of my intervention I am far from satisfied because it should have happened much sooner. But she too must not be discouraged. I send my greetings to both these ladies, as do Hansi and Herbert and will write to them directly very soon.

My dearest, good mother, the best comes last—talking to you. How are you and are you still so chic, and a model to the others in your courageous behavior? Do you take frequent walks with Marie? Now it must be getting warm on your side too, judging from the temperatures over here.

Do you like our looks on the pictures? Can you recognize Hannah? Hard work, worries etc. have left their traces despite her age of only 38 years. Unfortunately Jonas is ill again, last week he had some very heavy asthma attacks at night and the doctor had to be called. June is not a good month for those suffering from asthma but we hope it'll get better soon. Actually he had rallied already quite well.

I must tell you dear Marie that Otto and Stella will send pictures the next time. They were supposed to be with us on that Sunday when the picture were taken but went swimming instead with Morris, Hannah's brother.

Now I must close again with the ardent wish that these lines just like the previous ones land happily in your hands! I embrace you my dearest mother, as well as Mama-Ella and Marie-Emil, with kisses, your Emil. Received another card from Olly. She's changed jobs but otherwise is doing well and can hardly wait to come to us.

#14

New York, June 23rd 1940

My much beloved, good mother,

All My Beloved ones in Taborstrasse & Lessinggasse!

My first thoughts are for you my dear, good Marie! As I sit here at 11AM and am writing to you, where it is now 5PM.

I can feel it; you're sitting unhappily contemplating your birthday today so far from your beloved children and amidst these so very sad circumstances. You too, Marie must feel it how we are with you in our thoughts, not just now and that we would gladly make any imaginable sacrifice to be able to bring you over here, as well as mother and Emil. Just carry on you and the others and you can be sure that we shall see each other again in this life and under happier circumstances.

This time the mail did not bring us anything but we still hope to receive a sign of life from you that we longingly look forward to during this week. We are convinced that the new reorganization in France will bring about not only an improved postal service but also the possibility of a departure for overseas. I want to take this opportunity to mention our efforts to establish a connection with a Japanese line, for Regine-Dora-Friedrich. It is said that the connection to reach the U.S. via Russia is open as far as Wladivostok and from there one can reach San Francisco by way of the Japanese lines. Allegedly some emigrants have already taken this route and I am curious to learn when they'll be arriving here. However these will not come from Vienna but from Sweden, etc. Should we learn something positive we shall immediately inform you, so that you can pass it on to Heinrich/Helly. Is it true that in Vienna the transit visa through Russia is available without any difficulty?

Olly wrote us a very detailed letter last week. She has changed jobs and lives now with the happy expectation to see us again soon. She had thoughtlessly failed to have her quota registration number transferred immediately after her arrival in London so now it may take months for her turn. My reproaches for that she accepts as fully justified. She sends her best regards to all of you and especially to you my dearest, good mother.

Concerning our affidavits for Victor and Hedy but also for Mama/Ella, which we sent on April 7th direct to Victor, we had been worried for the longest time. We reproached ourselves for not having sent yours directly to you instead of via that roundabout way to Riga. But you knew there was this meeting of unhappy circumstances, most of all the fact that mail to Vienna appeared to function so poorly; you kept sending us your desperate requests for news, then began the war in Norway just after the documents had been mailed to Victor, which stopped the whole ship traffic on the Baltic Seas. So when we also heard rumors on June 19th about riots in Riga, we just went ahead sent a telegram to Victor. Can you imagine, we received immediately a telegraphic reply as follows: "Documents arrived. All in good health." So he actually received our telegram simultaneously with the documents! What a coincidence! We are happy and assume that in the meantime Mama/Ella have also received their papers from Victor.

We shall now begin slowly with the drawing up of your papers, my dear ones in the Lessinggasse in order to be able to mail them sometime in September. We hope that after that point in time they will no longer become invalid prior to your coming over.

There isn't much more to report about us. Herbert received his report card with quite satisfactory results and will be promoted to the 7th term. His best showing was in Mathematics (90%) but please don't think badly therefore about Americans! Now we worry what he should be doing over the summer. Just to be sure he got himself a work permit from his school, a requirement if you're not yet 18, and he will look around for a suitable job. But we're not forcing him to do anything and if he wants to spend the vacation at the beaches we have no objection. For the time being the weather is—I almost said Thank God—not for bathing. After a very short, intense hot spell it is again quite cool, rainy and windy. Hansi is working as I have written several times already in a ladies tailor shop since the artificial flower production has stopped for a few weeks. For myself, I can tell you that my boss gave me a raise of $2½. When I asked him whether he had made a mistake he answered very short with "no" after which we shook hands. So he must have been at least halfway satisfied with me. My dear ones it is real luck to have a job around here that is not cancelled in the summer. This is true of almost all our friends here. Unfortunately also of Otto, though he wisely looked around in time for a substitute and found one, the Lord is praised. And still, we are not satisfied; our thoughts are constantly with you, from early morning till late at night. Many a night I cannot get to sleep, thinking of you my dearest good mother. How are you and what are you doing just at this time? Can you bear it to be without this or that, something that you'd like to eat but cannot obtain, and something that is absolutely necessary? How is it generally with the food supply? Apart from the fact that it is summer now, there should be lots of foodstuffs coming in from the occupied territories. Do you at least get something sweet now and then? Does Miss W. provide some of the support she so graciously offered? If not please let us know. It is after all quite possible that she made that promise in view of Regine's imminent departure which would have eased her burden somewhat. But now with their departure postponed it is quite possible that she herself is short. By the way in one of last letters I included the address she wanted and I repeat it here: ... Should she change her address we shall let you know. For a short while, dearest mother, I was quite satisfied about your state of health, as well as that of Marie and Mama Schab thanks to Dora's favorable bulletin. Is that still valid? Are you still so smart looking in every way? Are you taking a lot of walks? I hope and wish it from the bottom of my heart!

June 24th 1940

I've gotten into the habit of waiting always for just another Clipper, before I send my weekly letter and this time as so often before I was again rewarded! Many thanks for your dear letter of June 6th, and the postcard of June 11th as well as your letter, dear Ella, from June 11th.

Unfortunately we see that you're again not receiving our mail regularly. But I hope that after the armistice [with France] things will improve. We are so sorry to hear Marie that your injections still do not provide the expected relief, but maybe the effect will come later. I am grateful to Helly for her kindness to our mother. But it pains me that the moment so longingly awaited by her and Heinrich—a moment which Hansi and I talked about and imagined innumerable times is always being postponed. But we are certain it is only a postponement! By the way, I sent an airmail letter to the shipping agent Merzario, since the local one, in view of Italy's entrance into the war and the consequent impossibility of obtaining the necessary "Navy certificate" from the English consulate here, refused to intervene. I can't really say he "refused" but he said we'd just have to wait. Nevertheless I wrote to the Genoa agent and we'll just have to see what he answers. Maybe it will be possible now after the armistice, to transfer the crates to Lisbon from where an American liner can take over. Just tell them please, those crates should be the least of their worries. Helly also should not mind that Hansi didn't write in greater detail until now. In the meantime she received my detailed letter with Hansi's long postscript. Hansi, apart from the fact that she simply doesn't have the time, cannot sit down and write. I have on that account a difficult time with her, usually I have to hold back my weekly letter for a few days before I can get her to add a few lines. But the fact is that she is the one who continuously talks and thinks about you.

Dearest Ella, your letter I have already passed on to Ada. I am happy to know that they too, write you more often which last not least is due to our and specifically Hansi's efforts. We'll do whatever we can for the Braun girls; in the meantime give them our best regards. Marie writes how nice everything is in your flat and how much she likes to visit with you and how kind you are to her. It is good to know that in these difficult times you can at least find a little solace and comfort with each other. I close for today and I embrace you my dearest mother, I kiss and greet you as well as Mama/Ella and Marie/Emil most fervently, your Emil

Did you, dearest Marie receives our telegram? To all our dear relatives and friends our best regards.

#15

New York, July 3rd 1940

My dearly beloved mother, My dear loved ones!

This time I am interrupting my regular schedule of writing Sunday; first of all it just wasn't possible as we used all of that day for packing and besides the mail from Europe usually arrives on Monday so that I wanted to read your replies in which case I could refer to them in my letter. Unfortunately there was no mail from you and we're again beginning to get anxious. Is there going to be a repeat of the period between January and March when postal service just wasn't working right or is it now just a minor interruption? May the good Lord just make it the latter because just as it is for you so is it for us the most important event here. As I mentioned above we were packing all day Sunday because we were moving on Monday! As we've mentioned repeatedly in our letters we've been contemplating for quite some time to change our accommodations. We couldn't make a quick decision like Otto because of all our possessions plus odds and ends, you know the size of it (Otto has a lot less of that stuff and consequently is much more mobile than we); furthermore we were debating whether we shouldn't try to rent a small flat of our own. That latter option we dropped for the time being. First of all these flats are quite expensive. A suitable two room flat—here they call it three room apartment because the kitchen counts as a room—in any fairly decent neighborhood rents for about $45.00 including the usual conveniences. To this has to be added $200–250 for furnishing the basics since we obviously do not have anything along these lines. However we want to abstain from dipping into our reserves, which are designed primarily for you; also the situation here as a consequence of the European events, regrettable as it is, has become very uncertain. Nobody knows what will happen from one day to the next, the campaign for the presidential election is about to start and unless Roosevelt is elected for a third time, which is highly improbable, one will have to expect a thoroughgoing overhaul of the existing system. Already a new law has been passed requiring the registration of all aliens something that has never happened in this country; even our fingerprints are being taken. Well, I'm sure you'll understand my reservations to assume the responsibility for major expenditures. On the other hand it has become quite necessary to change our domicile. True we had a nice room and we had all the usual conveniences one finds and even expects here, but for the three of us it was rather too small. During the winter it was still bearable but now that the heat waves have started it became quite unbearable. We have therefore rented another room, almost twice as large as the old one, naturally with all possible conveniences: built-in bathroom (the apartment has two bathrooms), separate use of the kitchen, Frigidaire, elevator, an excellent location with a very partial view of the Hudson (this is called "River View" around here) etc. It is only three minutes distant from Riverside Drive, the finest and most famous street in New York, in other words just around the corner! The room itself is a corner room with two large windows on both sides of the corner. This is a fact very much in demand here, always emphasized in the For Rent notices in the newspapers: "cross-ventilation." That means counter current and I'm sure you think its odd for a flat to advertise that there is a "draft"—which in Europe reduces its attraction but does here exactly the opposite. But how necessary it is here in the summer to have a "draft" you will surely see once you get here, with the Lord's help. The room costs $8.00 per week an enormous sum by Viennese standards and not exactly cheap for here; but if you include all the conveniences, hot and cold running water all the time, gas, electricity and central heating, then it is not so bad. So you can imagine that Monday was a strenuous day, although I must admit to my everlasting shame that I didn't participate in the actual move since I had to be at my "business." However Hansi had a free day and she got great support from Otto whose job starts now at 4PM and lasts till 11PM. But then I did spend half the night unpacking and squaring things away. You know me, every drawer has to be lined with paper and held down with thumbtacks etc. We now live a little farther from the Handels, about a 15 min. walk from us. When we visit them we walk along the Riverside, which runs into Haven Avenue. I am writing this letter not at home but in my "office"—my "boss" is on a trip so I can permit myself to take care of my private correspondence—so don't worry about Hansi's not writing a few lines. Tomorrow is a very big holiday, "Independence Day" this is the day on which 270 years ago [sic] the American people declared their independence—Hansi is not working and she promised me she'd write to you.

Herbert too has found a job, as a messenger boy in an enterprise that supplies such boys to businesses. It is a very common occupation for college-boys in the summer. He works daily 4–5 hours, boys of his age cannot work more, at least not officially. Last week he earned over $7.00 and you can imagine how happy he is about that. The job is not even very strenuous since he rides almost everywhere, and in the tall office building are elevators all the way up to highest floors! A school mate of his told him about this opportunity, he had done it during last summer. It still isn't very hot here—that much-feared heat has not yet arrived... [*Letter ends here*]

#16

New York, July 14th 1940

My dearest, good mother, all you loved ones at Taborstrasse & Lessing-gasse!

I hope that these lines also reach you in time, just like all the other letters we mailed in the past few weeks, and that you my dearest mother punctually received our birthday wishes. Everything good and lovely should descend for you from heaven, but also for all the other suffering and unhappy people, most of all your solid health, so that you can steadfastly hold out through whatever you have to endure prior to our happy reunion, especially a Wiedersehen with all of us, because joy and happiness sometimes make one more vulnerable than the greatest sorrow. So, mother, health and a long life with happiness! But you know that God only helps those who help themselves, so that is your first duty to yourself. Watch carefully over you, don't deny yourself anything in so far that is possible, do not save and treat yourself now and then. All those around you are doing their best, primarily Marie and Emil and all those others— we received such a nice, lovely letter from Helly in which she writes a lot about you and Mama Schab, and neither does Dora fail to send regular & detailed reports about you mothers, grandmothers and great grandmothers, Ella too, reports about you and it truly moves me that these folks who are so busy themselves, whose sorrows are so large now, are still able to feel the pain of others and are able to provide comfort and understanding of which they too need so much. So again my dearest good mother look after yourself, celebrate your birthday with joy for you and the others, as far as that is possible under the present conditions, think of us in the absolute knowledge that especially on this day everyone's thoughts here are with you, with the most fervent and most faithful love!

Last week we sent you RM100.00 via telegram, since we still do not know whether Mrs. W. is able to provide you with a regular, monthly assistance, considering her limited means, even though her willingness to help is great and obviously well meant. But if she can really do it and wants to, please accept it without compunction. I have no idea right now how we can repay her, but maybe with God's help we'll achieve riches some day so we can reward her a hundredfold.

In the meantime she'll have to be satisfied with our humble thanks and the assurance that we'll be happy to do her any favor, such as visiting her relative Hannah as often as she wants us to in order to convey greetings to her. We did this the last time very promptly, and are even more willing now that we know what a nice person she is and a visit with that lovely lady is a real pleasure. She must write us any time she wants us to see her, or even better, let us know through you dear Marie and this way she can save the very high airmail fee.

My dear Ella, I have gotten in touch with Willy, and not satisfied with just his verbal agreement, I right away walked with him to the bank and in my presence he telegraphed RM250.00. Don't misunderstand me he did it gladly, and thank God he can also afford it. My offer to participate with $10.00 he refused politely, but whatever we keep in reserve for you, no matter how modest, does not get lost. Hansi has opened a special account for that. There isn't much to report about us. Until Thursday we had a fiendish heat wave, which was finally, broken by a gigantic, one is tempted to say a truly American thunderstorm! When I went to the subway at about 6PM it was beginning to get dark and an incredibly hot whirlwind almost took my breath away. When I exited 20 minutes later it was into an Egyptian blackness, streetlights were on as were car and bus lights, even though it was only 6:45PM (daylight saving time). I just managed to run quickly to our house where to my joy I found Herbert and then a thunderstorm began of a kind I've never before experienced. Lightning followed lightning, and the thunder wanted to prove that He could still do it better than all those artificial imitators on the various war fronts in Europe. All this accompanied by a whirling storm that made me fear for the skyscrapers downtown. After a few hours it was gone and succeeded by a wonderful cooling down that made it possible for Hansi and me to take a short walk at ca. 12 midnight. The cool freshness lasts till today despite the dazzling sunshine.

Last Sunday we went swimming for the first time at Orchard Beach.

That was a hard trip, more than three hours on several subways and buses; you can imagine what I mean if I tell you that the next day the newspapers wrote that on the Orchard Beach alone there were over 500.000 people! A total of 2 million people visited all of the New York beaches that's almost a third of the population. But in comparison with the traffic on a summer's Sunday in Vienna to the beach Gänsehäufel the traffic here proceeded much more smoothly. Still, these immense masses populating these gigantic ocean beaches had a depressing effect on me for which not even the wonderful coolness was sufficient compensation—not even bathing in the salty waters or walking in the finest sand for miles along the beach. But on weekdays it must really be wonderful here and when Hansi can stop with the alteration job at the tailor's, which hopefully she'll be able to do soon, then she can come out here oftener with Herbert. For the rest we're not doing anything much and you probably won't believe me when I tell you that since our arrival we've been hardly more than 3x to the movies. We've even been told that in New York there is now a World's Fair, a repetition of the one of last year but that too is something we've only heard about. We have neither the time nor the desire for all that but shall make up for it when all of you dear ones will be here with us.

Last week Dr. Weil and spouse visited with the Handels. He used the occasion to examine Jonas very thoroughly but could only confirm what other physicians diagnosed previously: Asthma. Dr. W. even dissuaded Jonas to travel anywhere just now, something he had planned, at least not until the illness had improved some. We hope that this will be the case real soon. Dr. Weil didn't seem to be doing very well himself: he is very unhappy and inclined to serious depressions. He has a very difficult time with the language and even though he took the exam earlier this month, he is sure he didn't pass. The results will be announced much later directly from Albany. It is indeed bitter, that a 56 yr old individual, a physician has to start all over again, and even if he reaches that point— how and from where is he going to be able to establish a practice? A person is only capable of feeling his current misery and quickly forgets his past one. When I pointed out his even more unfortunate colleagues who were left behind, he stated simply, if he had known all this prior to his departure from Vienna, he'd rather have stayed. He has a married daughter in New Zealand whom he originally intended to join—but of course that is now out of the question.

I shall again close for now. I kiss and embrace you my dearest mother and birthday child and wish you again everything good from the bottom of my heart. I embrace you, dearest Mama, Marie, Ella, Emil, I greet all our dear friends, specifically Heinrich and Helly whose letter brought us much joy and which we shall answer separately. Your Emil

---

#17

New York, July 29th 1940

My much beloved mother,

All my dear ones in the Taborstrasse & Lessinggasse!

Your dear letters of July 2nd and 9th, also one from Mama/Ella of 9th I already acknowledged briefly in my letter of last week; we are glad that our pictures made you so happy. The whole series you wanted will reach you with the next mail. Your added lines, dearest mother made me especially glad. However, for now do not have a large picture made of me; I shall send you one from here. Otto took a picture of myself just for you but it didn't turn out well. And as for my birthday—there was no big celebration in the Waldorf-Astoria, but all my loved ones here congratulated me most warmly. Hansi was too busy to bake a cake but she did buy a very excellent one and on Sunday before my birthday we had such a wonderful Backhendl [Viennese version of Southern Fried chicken] everyone said it must have come from grandmother. From Herbert I received a half dozen "Anklets" that are socks reaching only to the ankles and especially in the summer make for very comfortable wear.

Our half stockings for gentlemen of which I bought a lot in Vienna thinking that suspenders for ordinary socks would be quite shocking in America are practically unknown here. The "real" American wears only the most ordinary socks in the most conspicuous or impossible color combinations either held up by a suspender or, when without one, then rolled down to the shoes. I noticed this kind of fashion on Otto almost immediately once we got off the ship, and when I questioned him, whether he is meschugge, he just shrugged and said that's the American way. So with the above mentioned "anklets" you do not need to roll them down, and since Herbert knew how much I've wanted some he got me that half-dozen. I didn't write you initially, my dearest mother, about the cake and the Backhendl because I was ashamed to mention this in view of your approaching birthday, also that of Marie and Ella, without being able to do anything for you; even you are not in a position to buy something nutritious, not to mention sweets for yourselves.

Sometime ago when the Bohrer family came for a visit they promised to look around to find something for Herbert on a farm that would get him out of New York in the burning summer heat, make it possible to earn a little money as well as see some more of America; it is known that New York is almost anything but not "America"! We'd forgotten about that, also in the meantime Herbert had found a small job as I told you earlier. Last week we received four postcards from Helene saying she found something for Herbert on a farm in Otisville not far from Middletown where they live. Herbert of course still cherishes a very romantic notion of life on an American farm obtained from wild west movies he saw in Vienna: he rides on a black horse across the prairie dressed as a cowboy with a large sombrero on his head, swinging a lasso in one hand and in the other a highly accurate rifle: his goal is to reach the next Indian village where the inhabitants undoubtedly are already waiting for him with a solid breakfast, since Herbert's appetite after such a taxing morning ride is considerable. Given these fantasies my sweet son could not be detained and his enthusiasm for this job was boundless. This will also give him the opportunity to travel alone on the railroad and pretend to be a world traveler. So last Wednesday, unmercifully teased by myself he bade us farewell to see "the world" on his own. Saying good-bye to the Safirsteins netted him also a money gift as well as a wonderful, real cowboy sweater—it is so colorful that should he be espied high on his horse by a herd of buffaloes, they'd surely stampede to get away!

So far we received only one card from him announcing his arrival there. Well we shall see what comes of this—just in case he should decide to return, something we rather expect, we daily make up the bed for him.

Friday we had a very nice visitor that gave us much pleasure: Helly's nephew, Bruno Löhner. Please tell Helly that Bruno has grown into a smart looking, tall young man in whom I'd never have recognized the little boy in the sailor suit I remembered. He is a real gum chewing American who is just now taking his vacation. A very nice uncle, a most decent sort, invited him here for two weeks all expenses paid. Only his most fervent wish, to move completely to New York has not yet been met. Bruno lives with his parents in the South, in Augusta, state of Georgia, a 28 hours RR ride away. This compares approximately to the distance Vienna-London. The poor guy is not too happy down there; he is fascinated by New York. If he could live here permanently he could make contact with people in the film business, he has already written a few screenplays. I don't want to be indiscreet and I hope I am not making a mistake if I suspect that that there is also a small flame involved who pulls him to New York. About his parents he says they manage to make a living as best they can. They were even offered a small business by the Committee but didn't succeed at it, mostly because it was in a bad section of town, chiefly populated by Negroes, but also due to his total lack of knowledge of the language. It should hardly be necessary to mention that our conversation was mostly about Heinrich/Helly and that we all hope to see them here within the foreseeable future.

I wrote to Marie Ringel—but I really didn't expect anything different from her. At the time I begged her to write you a few lines about our meeting, told her she can send them to me and I would pass them on so she could save the expensive airmail postage. Nothing! Not even a one-cent postcard did she send us. And after Hansi and I gave her such a wonderful, loving reception! She and her family belong to that category of humanity, for whom Vienna and Europe with all the unfortunate people they had left behind simply sank into the ocean, the moment they themselves had reached safety. Please, dear Ella, be so kind and tell Hansi Lakner that we are completely distraught over her last letter in which she writes that the Bachners/Ellington/Finders here still have not done anything. To be sure the Bachners appear to be very nice people but with respect to getting anything done on a matter of importance, absolutely the most boring and slowest individuals one can imagine. I have not been able to talk to her cousin Finder during the nine months we've been here. In fact she really screwed things up for me with Mrs. Wolff. When at one time I talked with that lady she said that Mrs. Finder on a previous visit had emphasized how well off she (Finder) was and that she could have guaranteed the affidavit herself for Hansi Lakner, etc. etc. Nevertheless I shall again try to get in touch with Mrs. Bachner and also Mrs. Eisler; from the latter I hope to get at least something for Hansi L. From Robert we haven't had any communication for months. He has not answered two airmail letters that must have reached him within 7 days. I find this peculiar since he must know that through us he has the best connection with his mother. We send our best regards to Hansi and Mama Lakner and as soon as we'll learn anything positive we shall write them in detail. One other small favor, dearest Ella. Please tell Mrs. Vally Nagler that we have received her letter and immediately sent it on to little Hans. As soon as we have news from him we shall immediately pass it on to her.

As you can tell from the change in my typing I am finishing this letter in my office today on August 1st. I am really having a good time now that my "Boss" is on vacation, but it's only for a week. As does all of New York during this season I am taking it a little "easy." Day before yesterday we had after a heat wave that lasted 14 days the hottest July 30th since 1872. The heat even crowds out Europe from the first page of the newspaper and the statistics are truly fantastic: the hottest day since Adam and Eve, since the discovery of America, how many tons of ice cream are being consumed, how many people went swimming on this or that beach etc. etc. I can only repeat, it isn't all that bad and there are worse things that must be borne. One gets used to it just like with the other *tzores.* This morning it cooled off completely without any thunderstorm and we have wonderful sunshine.

This letter is mailed again 4 days later after I began it in the hope of getting mail from you and again I didn't wait in vain. I thank you dearest mother for the lines you added and your good, fervent wishes. We're happy to hear from your letter of July 15th that you're all well. Victor wrote me what he had sent you: 1½ kg butter, 1/2kg cheese 1/2kg ham, 2 cans of sweet condensed milk, 1/2kg coffee, also some tea, 1/2kg cookies, and 2 cans of chocolate. He writes that he will send something again in 3 weeks, but I am afraid the change in the situation in Riga will make that impossible. But I shall be happy if you and Mama/Ella receive at least this one package. You mother will then be able to have a good birthday.

I am going to close now, my dearest ones. Please give Helly/Heinrich our best regards and tell them that we've been wanting to visit with Heinrich's mother for the longest time but always postponed it on account of the heat: riding the subway in this heat during rush hour is a pain invented by the devil! We thank Helly and Heinrich that they care so much, especially Helly for you grandmothers. I wrote to Victor that he should send them too, as well as Regine one package each. But I am afraid it may no longer be possible. It hurts us so much; it is like a dire fate that we seem to be incapable of doing something positive for our loved ones and friends, no matter how small! I am enclosing a picture of Hannah for Dora, as she, H. asked me to do. Our most sincere thanks go to Miss W. for not forgetting you. I conveyed her greetings to Hannah and when H. writes to her the next time she will acknowledge that. Did you receive our wire transfer from the Bank? In any case we're glad that Miss W. also helps you out, because you can imagine we're not doing all so well ourselves right now and therefore have to leave you to the kindness of others. But as soon as it is possible again we shall not only help you but also shall not forget those who've been so good to you. And now many, many regard and kiss for you my dear mother and all you other beloved ones. And give our regards also to you housemates in the Taborstrasse & Lessinggasse. Your Emil. You'll have to excuse Hansi; I am mailing this letter from here, downtown; Hansi will write you separately.

#18

A fragment of a page dated August 1940 ["page 1 is missing"]

...Recently I received a very detailed letter from Victor. However, it is dated June 12th, which means it is already outdated by his telegram of June 19th. In that telegram he acknowledges the receipt of the documents for the affidavit, while in the letter he is still unhappy about the absence of these papers. Among other things he writes that he is able to send a food parcel every 2–3 weeks, via department store and he asked me whether I want him to do that for you, mother, as well as Marie/Emil. Of course I immediately agreed to have this arranged. I shall wire together with Otto the necessary amounts for this undertaking. These will be the same shipments now mailed to Mama Schab. But this letter is dated June 12th, which is prior to the changes that have taken place in Latvia and I can only hope that this will still work. Please dearest Ella, when you write Victor, convey to him that I wrote you about this arrangement as well as to him. It is possible, after all, that he gets my letter and the money later than you get this one, the mail there is obviously in a miserable condition as I could already see from my mailing of the affidavit documents. He should in any case arrange the shipments to my mother and Marie/Emil the money will definitely reach him. He writes that his money is very tight, the more so because he doesn't know how much longer he will have to stay there. I am also awaiting anxiously some news about Miss Weissberg. Should she not be able to help, we shall have to think of another way. In any case don't let your feelings be hurt, mother dear if you have to contribute something. Always let me know how much, because Otto and myself already calculate everything in. How are you my beloved mother? And how about the rest of you? We're always with you in spirit and longingly nurture only one wish: that you all remain healthy and that we can embrace you soon. I close this time and most fervently embrace you mother, Mama, Marie/Emil and Ella Your Emil

Many loving greetings for Regine, Dora, Heinrich and Helly. I stopped by recently at a Greek Line that reportedly is running and docks at Genoa. They promised me more information in a few days on whether ships are sailing and when.

#19

New York, August 4th, 1940

My dear, good, mother,

All dear ones in Taborstrasse & Lessinggasse!

Until now no letter has arrived from you—but don't think I am blaming you. All of you are writing very good and often; we wouldn't mind at all if in order to save postage either Taborstrasse or Lessinggasse were to write in alternate weeks with one always reporting on the other one who doesn't happen to be writing that week. The Clipper arrives today, Sunday, and we hope that it will bring news from you again.

As far as newsworthy events of this week are concerned, we can report that Mr. Herbert Secher has returned from his Farming adventure! Even Family Bohrer wrote that they had acted somewhat prematurely. First of all those farmers who wanted help were not J. as we all had assumed and of whom there are quite a few in that area. What was also decisive for Herbert, they weren't going to pay him, either! On the other hand they demanded a lot of work, starting at 5AM. Though I am quite certain that Herbert is just not destined to make his fortune in agriculture, even for some one who might have felt more at home in a rustic locale this would not have been easy—to jump, without any prior experience and in the middle of the hottest summer, into heavy work in the fields. Herbert is after all a typical child of the city. He told us how already after a few days he longed for the asphalt of New York City. Before he came home he spent two days with the Bohrers all of whom send their best regards. Herbert went back to his job as messenger boy where he was received with open arms and is again earning his pocket money. He is happy as a lark and prefers to view American farm work and cowboy life from the comfort of an air-conditioned movie theatre.

Yesterday we received from Olly a detailed letter. Given her situation, all things considered, she feels fine but is still waiting longingly for the notification from the consulate. I wrote you already once before that she missed transferring her papers in time from the U.S. consulate in Vienna to the one in London—and that is why she has to wait so long. I would love to see her getting out from there and are hoping to have her here in the fall. She always asks in detail about every one of you and sends her best regards to all of you and especially to you, dearest mother.

As I wrote you in my last letter, Hannah went to visit her parents in Jamesburg where she found her father, Jonas, rather weak but still in more or less satisfactory condition. Her mother will come home this week and Jonas will remain there a bit longer.

From Marie Ringel I received a postcard in which she writes among other things: "...Even though I got sick soon after my arrival here in Hamilton and had to stay in bed for six weeks, I wrote two airmail letters to Mr. Stanger, as well as many other cards and letters and have already received answers to some. I also wrote to your sister Marie, though not by airmail, because the postage of 30 cents is a little too high for my personal correspondence. I am doing here quite well, so far, we are living together with Schigo and it is really quite nice ... etc." Please Marie pass this news on to her relatives.

Have you, my dear ones already received Victor's first food parcel? Unfortunately I fear it may also be the last one for the time being! Please write us whether you continue to receive mail regularly from Victor even after the upheaval in Riga. Also the wire transfer of ca. RM100.00 should have reached you by now, together with the one from Willy for ca. RM250.00. By the way, Willy and Ada have gone to the country for a vacation and they promised me to write you in detail from there. I don't know whether they wrote you about Franzi's difficulties in the matter of the school; her choice of partner did not turn out to be a very happy one (apparently a morphine addict). The matter has been referred to Safirstein who hopefully will bring it to a satisfactory conclusion. But please do not mention this in our letters, if they haven't written you about it themselves.

You recall that I had a part-time job with a small producer of costume jewelry. This job I haven't had for some time now since that manufacturer went nebbish mechule. Some of his customers didn't pay up. This person too, I led to Safirstein-Handel; from the honorarium they received for their successful conclusion of this case, they bought me a beautiful silk short for the summer, and gave Hansi a wonderful light summer dress. Those two absolutely believe they have to share their honorarium with us—even though the life of a lawyer is a very difficult one. First of all they only work on consignment. Thus a lawyer may work for months and not see one red cent if he cannot bring the case to a successful conclusion. What's more there are an immense number of lawyers about, the competition is fierce and the practices not always of the kind that can be justified with the reputation of the law. Not exactly the right profession for decent people, I've reproached both of them. I don't mean they are not decent people but they should've opted for another career; of course they loved the law too much for that. Real lucky in that respect is Morris, Hannah's younger brother who, only 29 years old after many difficult examinations and in tough competition with thousands of applicants managed to obtain a position with the government with a beginning salary of $3,600.00. He is now with the Supreme Court and can look forward to a brilliant career. He is regarded as an outstanding legal theoretician. The law here is probably one of the toughest professions since every one of the 48 states has its separate laws and regulations. For example it is interesting that the death penalty does not exist in every state, and where it does it is not always executed by electric chair! But as a practicing attorney Morris, who is a bit of an eccentric, probably would not have succeeded anyway. He is almost of the same age as Otto and they became friends easily.

My dearest good mother, tomorrow is your birthday and be assured, on that day I, as well as all of us will be continuously with you in our thoughts. We shall make a feast of this day here, celebrate, as it deserves, drink a little glass of wine to your health and well-being. Again we wish you from the bottom of our hearts everything loving and good and especially a happy and speedy Wiedersehen!

For a change we're very satisfied with the weather. Have I already told you that it is the custom here in the summer to spend evening on the roofs, which are always flat and sometimes decorated with greenery and even potted palms? Especially the big skyscrapers sport elegant bars with music and dance—these exist instead of the usual European coffeehouse gardens, which over here do not exist at all.

Well, for today I've gossiped long enough with you; I close, kissing and embracing you my dearest mother, as well as all the others in the Taborstrasse & Lessinggasse most fervently, your Emil. Please give my best regards to Heinrich-Helly, also to Regine and Dora, none of whom we can forget, to Mama Neumann and all the rest of our dear relatives, friends, acquaintances and those you share your house with in the Taborstrasse and Lessinggasse.

#20

New York, August 14th 1940

My dearest, good mother, dearest Marie, Emil,

Dearest Mama and Ella! Yesterday we received your dear and wonderfully detailed letters of July 22nd & 23rd, which were the cause of much joy among us. We were happy to see that the mail is working and hope it'll continue to do so. We're also glad that the matter with the wire transfer went all right and assume that in the meantime you've come into possession of the money. Did you have any expenses and how much? Hopefully you're also in possession of the care packages from Victor, which, however, I fear may also be the last one—at least for the time being. Even though we're not overly worried about Victor—there is really no reason for that, after all—we would like to have some news from him again.

His last letter is dated July 22nd and, from what I can tell, in Riga they had inkling of what was about to happen. Your supposition, dear Ella, that it cannot be easy for Willy to send you the few marks necessary for your support is quite correct, but one doesn't want to tell this to one's close relatives and rather tries everything possible to protect them in their troubles. Even though the order went under his name, the largest part came from all relatives that could be reached for that purpose. But please don't mention any of this in your communications to him, I'm sure he wouldn't like my having revealed this to you. On the other hand, it isn't exactly a secret that we're not lying on a bed of roses here, we're emigrants who made it over here with only the bare necessities on our bodies and the struggle for existence here is very, very difficult. If we manage to squeeze out something from the little we have in order to support our relatives abroad then this is our most basic duty, which doesn't make us either millionaires, the way some naïve persons over there seem to think, nor are we to be pitied for taking our last bite from our mouths as you do, dearest Ella. So please don't worry about that any more, enjoy the small benefits of this assistance for your daily life.

I shall still go and see the Becks this evening (Saturday) in order to talk to them about the matters pertaining to Heinrich/Helly. Even though the external circumstances surrounding their notification—finally—from the U.S. consulate have changed from the ones we originally envisaged, we're still happy about it; it is at least a glimmer of hope and has brought them closer to their goal.

I've heard that the ship tickets can be paid in RM as far as the Pacific Ocean and in $ only from Shanghai (or is it Vladivostok?) to San Francisco. The price is relatively speaking not so high—ca. $180.00 per person—i.e. less than the price over the Atlantic—to which must be added, of course, the trip from S.F. to N.Y. ca. $80.00. I believe however that even this amount can be collected if everyone contributes his small share, and that includes us, too. According to your last report Ella, Heinrich/Helly are somewhat bitter concerning the behavior of the relatives here. That is understandable but not really justified. Unfortunately none of them is doing particularly well, with the possible exception of Mr. Gang, and therefore unable to shoulder the whole costs. I don't know too much about Oscar but it cannot be assumed that in Gloversville his lot is any better than that of all other immigrants here. Maybe Heinrich/Helly feel hurt about their relatives writing little or nothing at all. This is not due to any indifference, I am sure, but mainly the result of their feelings of powerlessness to help or even merely to offer comfort. Mama Beck of course, but also the others get in touch with us if they haven't heard from abroad for some time. Foremost, Mrs. Grete, who recently was successful in finding the necessary sources for the ship tickets. That events turned in such a way to make the money unreachable is a great misfortune. Now I want to get in touch again with Mrs. Grete and through her bring B. and possibly Mrs. Redlich again into the circle of sponsors.

I usually write a postcard to Mrs. B. about every two months in which I inform her about Heinrich/Helly. It is in their interest that we do not lose touch with her. When she didn't answer me immediately the last time, I wrote her a second time, approximately in June, and I am including their answer, so that Heinrich/Helly can see that this lady has not forgotten them and surely will help.

I see from your letter that the shipping agent Merzario did receive my letter after all. I did not yet receive an answer from him. Heinrich should write him either directly or via the Viennese shipping agent that under no circumstances must he auction off his crates—if that involves any expenses I shall assume them and give him my address (c/o Handel). I shall also write to him again from here. Unfortunately these shipping agents do not seem to care about answering these letters. That goes for Parisi as well who, in the matter of Regine-Dora, has received from us not only money but also innumerable letters. Dora too, should write via her Viennese shipping agent to Parisi that he must not under any circumstances auction off her goods. First of all he already received money on account and if that should prove insufficient he should get in touch with us.

Concerning traveling via Russia: Regina-Dora need not worry about the costs of the trip. What's important is that they should reach that stage soon—and that all <u>three</u> of them can appear for the examination at the U.S. Consulate. But it is difficult to argue with them if only the two of them are called.

Now my dearest Ella, I need to ask you for a small favor: Enclosed you will find two communications addressed to me in the matter of Hansi Lakner. I cannot do more at the moment but hope that in the meantime she has gotten the notification from the U.S. consulate. We shall write to all of them, Heinrich/Helly, Regine/Dora, Lakner's mother and Hansi directly but in the meantime our best regards go to all of them.

Now I turn to you my beloved mother: We were very happy with the news reaching us from all sides as well as from yourself. I see from all that how strong you are and that you carry the burden of fate quietly and remain full of hope. The good Lord will reward you. From you Marie we should like to have some better news about your state of health. Have the mud baths proved useful? Do you have any opportunity to sunbathe? Last Sunday we got together with Otto, not at the ocean but at a "pool" similar to our open air, municipal pools in Vienna, except there are no beautiful lawns and shady spots. These facilities here show an absolutely incredible cleanliness and neatness, that goes so far it is even prohibited to bring any food and drink. We didn't know that, had some wonderful delicacies prepared but our faces showed great disappointment when, prior to admission we had to empty our beach bags of all food items. So we remained a short time in this very beautiful pool eventually our hunger drove us to collect our good food, which was returned to us as we left he facility.

I've told you that for two weeks I was all by myself in the office since my boss was traveling, making the rounds of clients. Now he is back and was so satisfied with my conduct of office management that he plans to leave for another two weeks on August 27th. Everything would really be great, if only the salary would be a little more! I hope that in the Fall I'll get a raise. Right now there is hardly any business and frankly he is doing me a favor by keeping me on instead of dismissing me and closing the office temporarily, as is done by many stores here.

In September your affidavits will be mailed to you, my dear ones, mine as your son for you mother and Otto's for you, Marie-Emil. If with the Lord's help we shall have finally reached that stage and it should become necessary to obtain further support affidavits you will of course receive this from our relatives.

Jonas is still out there in Jamesburg and is recuperating real well according to Hannah who visited him there last week. They than you for your concern… *[Page ends here]*

#21

New York, August 19th 1940

My much beloved, little mother,

All you my dear ones in Lessinggasse & Taborstrasse!

This time according to the news, the Clipper was forced to land again on Bermuda due to a fuel shortage with the result that lbs.1500 were seized. I am beginning to believe the British are doing this on the Bermuda

Isle because they are getting bored and need something to read to pass the time! When we receive our mail a few days later, the envelopes show, peacefully next to one another, the seal marks of both the British and the German censorship. Anyway, this time there was nothing for us. But in a few days we hope to get your letters, which surely will arrive with the next Clipper.

We're now in the middle of the high season of the summer and my trained eye recognizes immediately its impact on the traffic as well as on the daily routine around here. Though the extent of the traffic would still make a very large impression on you it is far from what is normal in other seasons of the year. On a Saturday afternoon, "downtown" (this is what they call the City or the Business District here) is deserted and hardly recognizable. This strikes me as very unusual since I am used to glancing out the window now and then and enjoy watching the gigantic traffic out there. From the time of Independence Day (July 4th, the biggest holiday) till Labor Day (September 2nd also a big holiday) all banks close on Saturday, so do the factories, even the big department stores such as Macy's, Bloomingdale's, and a dozen others all of which are ten or twenty times the size of "Gerngross" in Vienna. Macy's is allegedly the biggest department store in the world making Wertheimer's in Berlin a midget in comparison. In any case it seems truly peculiar that these stores are closed on Saturdays in the high summer season, a day in which retail stores on the other side usually earned most of their income for the whole week. On the other hand the innumerable food, butcher, fruit, candy (bonbon) stores are open late into the night both on weekdays and Sundays, and one can do one's shopping for the next day as late as 11PM. It is a custom to shop after returning from a visit or a walk, and one to which the emigrants have become quickly adjusted. These are the peculiarities of this land of unlimited opportunities—which in many respects, one discovers very soon are in reality quite limited.

After the fierce heat at the beginning of August we now have the most wonderfully clear and pleasant weather you can imagine. Not very hot, evenings are pleasantly cool, no humidity and always sunshine! This weather, too, at this time of the year is considered not normal and the newspapers are again full of: not since Adam and Eve, or not since Columbus, if you please has there been such a moderate August. The Americans even worry that these are signs of a possible end of the world. And their feelings are really hurt when out of sheer contrariness and malicious joy on my part I tell them that temperatures "over there" in the summer are a lot higher. They want to have all records for themselves, even the bad ones! But then they'll threaten me with September, and even Octo-

ber. But these are just rearguard actions and with those they can't bluff
me! In any case, my dearest mother there is not the slightest reason to
worry: we do not suffer in the least from the heat. We have many, many
more worries concerning other matter that one is powerless to do anything about and that indeed is our greatest sorrow. I think often about
Olly, she could've been here already a long time ago if only she had
attended to the transfer of her papers in time. Still, maybe we can see her
by late fall. I received again a letter from Elly. She is doing all right in a
manner of speaking and she is content. Again and again she asks me to
do something for her parents. It is difficult, very, very difficult. The relatives for whom they had made all kinds of sacrifices have left them in the
lurch in the most shameless way. I wrote to old Mrs. Weiss, not to mention dozens of letters addressed to Schutzmann and that person Bleicher,
I have phoned, sent telegrams all with the result that they sent Epstein a
telegram refusing any assistance. After that he sent me again another
telegram with a plea for help. We have pleaded with innumerable people
here, not too long ago Hansi thought she had found a well-to-do lady
who seemed agreeable to act as sponsor. But when she learned that the
people she would have to sponsor were in their early 60s, she reconsid-
ered. What are those people going to do here, she asked, what are they
going to live on? This is the constant and anxious query. The resources
of the Committee are pretty much exhausted and whenever a refugee
comes to them for help they mercilessly turn to the affidavit sponsor who
is legally bound to maintain the person he sponsored. Earlier, the council generously overlooked this and provided aid from their own resources.
Under these circumstances individuals are afraid to act as sponsors of an
affidavit since they actually would be called on to subsidize the person
they guaranteed. I will not and cannot ask the Handels for support for
the Epsteins, especially not as long Regine-Dora-Frieda are not here and
because of you as well. I may need their affidavits to support mine for you.
I am sure that once Olly gets here it will be possible to do something for
the parents. Unfortunately there hasn't been any mail from Riga, nothing from Victor either. Please write right away when you receive mail
from him. We haven't received any mail from Rudi and Irma, but nobody
is getting any mail from that region. On the other hand all reports from
there are very favorable and you needn't worry about them in the least.
We intend to send a telegram next week maybe with paid return message,
so that Rudi and Benno should get in touch with each other. One or the
other can reply to me and tell us how they are doing.

By the way, dearest mother were you happy with our telegram?
Unfortunately they would not accept a night letter, i.e. they would not

Herman Handel (left) and Frances Handel. The family owned and operated a very successful cafeteria on Journal Square in Jersey City.

guarantee its arrival on time and so I had to send a regular telegram, with only ten words but much more expensive.

As I mentioned at the end of my last letter, we've been in touch with Grete Brainin. She had been sick, as was her husband and they had problems with their 20-year-old son: first he got married and then he was held in England where aliens were put in internment camps. Mama Beck has gone to see Oscar who lives outside the city. We shall not fail to try anything, even though I cannot report in detail about the various phases.

Last week the first refugees arrived who had taken the Siberia-Japan route, however there was nobody from Vienna among them. For the most part they were persons who had already been in Sweden, Riga or similar places. There was a detailed report about them in our local German-speaking immigrant newspaper. I shall summarize some of this for Heinrich-Helly, Regine-Dora eventually, since it contains valuable, worthwhile information about fares, connections, etc. For now I shall cite only one passage and this is for your benefit dearest mother as well as that of Mama Schab:

There is a description of the trip from Moscow to Vladivostok by Trans-Siberian Railroad lasting 9 days, considered one of the more difficult parts of the journey when compared to the three-day crossing Vladivostok-Tsuruga (Japan), then by train from Tsuruga to Yokohama (12 Hours), from Yokohama to Seattle, U.S.A., north of San Francisco (14 days) and then the last stage, Seattle–New York 4 days travel in wonderfully comfortable Pullmans, or by autobus. This is what the report says about the 9 day trip through Siberia: "…I want to emphasize that old people, too, even 70–80 year old, provided they are healthy, can weather this trip without difficulty…" The one who reports about this trip is in fact a woman who traveled 3rd class, praises the comfort, 4 persons to a compartment, each one has a bed, food is plenty in the Russian manner, lots of tschaj. Strenuous is the monotony of the trip through the Russian steppes, but she writes, literally: "the joy over the approaching goal modifies the impressions of those plodding, dragging days on the train…" So you see, mother and Mama, do not fear, only keep your health—that is the most important thing. But even those faint of heart, Helly and Dora should heed this! No postponement just because the journey goes the other way around from what one is used to. If you're nervous the reporter recommends to take along Oropax—together with other medications of course—which will protect you against the uninterrupted, noisy activities of the Russian radio!

As you may already have noticed I failed to enclose the postcard from Mrs. Bredhoff (for Heinrich) as well as the letter for Hansi Lakner from George Bachner, because postage would have been too high. I'll enclose something now, and then again the next time.

Dearest, good Marie, Otto called and asked me to send you his best regards and kisses. He is once again very busy and makes a lot of money. For the next two weeks he again works at his old part-time job and since the weather is very pleasant, all of it is not very strenuous. But he just can't find any free time—but for the money one has to make sacrifices! Have you received the food package from Victor and our latest money transfer? How is Miss Weissberg? Should we once again visit her relative and bring her regards? We were there in July the last time and before that in June. Have you started your mud packs, Marie? Do they help? I know that you and Emil are really very determined individuals and would walk on foot all the way through Siberia to see your children again—but you have to be in good health, too! So please take good care of yourselves and for Pete's sake don't slack off! Now I must again tear myself away from you for this week, Hansi wants to add a few words. My most fervent greetings and kisses for you my beloved mother, Marie, Mama, Ella, Emil, greetings also to all our friends, relatives, acquaintances! Your Emil embraces all of you.

#22

New York, August 28th 1940

My much beloved mother, all my loved ones in the Taborstrasse & Lessinggasse!

This time I am a bit late. Last week arrived your letters of July 29th and August 5th (also from Mama/Ella with the same date) in which you complain about our silence. We knew that this could only be temporary, because we mail without fail every week our report to you, usually between Monday and Wednesday, and therefore waited for the next mail from you, which arrived indeed promptly yesterday (from August 11th, and from Mama-Ella dated August 14th). In it you acknowledge all three of our letters, those of July 14th, 21st, and 29th. This is the one thing that makes us happy, the smoothly functioning mail and wouldst God that it remains that way until such time as we can communicate orally and need no longer resort to writing. Many thanks for you good and detailed news. I especially thank you mother for the whole page that you wrote me and to all of us! How much you enjoyed all our birthday wishes. And how much better you liked this year than the past one. With the Lord's help we'll be able to celebrate it here next year.

Marie wrote how everybody brought you something, especially our Ella and also Helly; I thank them who have so many worries of their own that they still helped you to forget yours. We're glad to learn that Mama is busy preparing vegetable for canning so that it will be possible to save something for the winter. We, on the other hand, avert our gaze with pain from the windows of the food stores, chockfull with delicacies—I can never pass them without thinking of you.

Oh, what a country this is in which you can have anything, I mean anything nature produces, from the north pole to the south pole, fresh or preserved, a land, you'll be happy to know, dearest mother, where you can even get canned "Borscht," either with eggs or the way you always made it and the way I liked it best, as clear bouillon with just a pinch of garlic!

We were glad to learn that Emil has found some work, because that is already a good sign, on the other hand we were equally glad to hear he lost it again because we're sure the work was heavy and his help in the household is very much needed, since he relieves you that way, my dear

Marie. He mustn't worry about his pocket money, we will see to that. Regardless of the assistance rendered by Regine's sister whom we cannot thank enough for her understanding attitude; we shall again wire you something in September through the bank. Let us hope that in the meantime the unpleasant delay caused by the misspelled name (which was not our doing) has been cleared up and you're already in possession of that money. You too, Mama/Ella, should you need anything, just write us in time and we shall see to it that the relatives here will do their part.

We are glad to hear that you're keeping up your social contacts, lately visiting with the ladies at Mrs. Abelis. Hopefully they can use their affidavit soon. I contributed to make this possible thanks to my continuous "dunning," something I did not only because of my admiration of my fatherly friend Mr. Abelis of blessed memory, but also because of my love for both these ladies. Recently Margulies let me read their letter to Lisl Margulies. Give them as well as Hansi L. my best regards. I am also happy that you Ella spoke with the Ranschiers and found them all in such a gay mood. I hadn't heard from Mrs. Kaiser for nearly two months, except that she did receive an affidavit from Dr. Feith. But due to her late registration she cannot expect to come here for at least another year. Thanks to my present occupation I think often about all those people and especially Fritz when I copy his beautiful descriptions from his catalogues that serve my purpose here very well, indeed. Unfortunately I do not have enough of them here. A lot of my time is spent at the "Reference departments" of the New York Public Library, Columbia University, New York Academy of Medicine etc, etc. I copy for hours from the Sabin, Hain, Proctor, British Museum catalogues. And many times I'd love to ask Fritz about something. However, Otto Ranschburg is very nice and helps me to bridge the great deficiencies in my training as antiquarian. I am especially sorry now that on the other side I had so little opportunity to work with the bibliophile division of Gilhofer & Ranschburg, even though I always let it be known that this was a wish of mine. W. surely was to blame for this, who considered any interest in this department as an intrusion into company secrets, and consequently rejected any attempt as such. Here I meet daily with all those large and small antiquarian dealers whose names already made us sit up with respect in Vienna, as for example Emil Hirsch, Schatzki, Stechert, Brentano etc. not to mention those who were well known in Vienna, as were Willy and Otto, but also Reichner, etc. When we sometimes sit together, having a smoke at one of those dealers on the Madison Avenue, the business home of nearly all of them, I could believe I am back in Vienna, the way all transactions take place. The above-mentioned dealer groups buy up the books at Parke-Bernet where the best auctions are held almost weekly. Then the dealers auction the books off among themselves, which is accompanied usually by some good-natured fun.

Almost every week I get together with Sessler, rather with his right hand Miss Zahn from Philadelphia. "Sessler" that is another one of those names at whose mention in Vienna everybody stood at attention. In fact all of them are socially very comfortable, nice people. Now everything is rather quiet, in the rare book trade especially, between Independence Day and Labor Day. The order departments of the libraries are closed and the rare book dealers go on vacation. Beginning in September business starts up again. Fritz's heart would certainly beat quicker over here. If you see him again, dear Ella please give him my very best regards, also Hilde, dear Toni and all the rest.

Yesterday was a big day for us. My boss got married and we were invited to the reception in Riverdale one of the most beautiful suburbs of New York, reminiscent, for me, of the Hinterbrühl of course without its little hills. On this occasion I was able to dress up in my "tuxedo" (this is what they call our "smoking"). The reception was in form of a "garden party" and it was really very nice if you overlook the enormous amounts of food being consumed on this occasion. However it was also a little cool in the garden. You are not going to believe me when I tell you that we're actually freezing here! Today the heat was turned on in my office. That is the American way—as soon as it gets a little cooler everyone yells for more "steam heat."

I am again alone in the office, probably until September 13th, since my boss is on his "honeymoon" (wedding trip). Of course first to Washington, that is the custom here the way Venice was in Europe—no wedding trip can be without it.

I must apologize for inserting an English expression every now and then. I am sure you consider this silly the way I used to regard this in he beginning. But it just slips in and whenever we speak German among ourselves now the English expressions just come naturally as if there is not a good German word available, viz. "honeymoon."

Last week I visited Otto at his evening job. He looks really smart in his white uniform and cap. I made him serve me the most wonderful ice cream, which I enjoyed even more because I didn't have to pay for it. His job is really quite pleasant now that it is a bit cooler, and there aren't many crowds, so it is also quite a bit more varied. He is sorry that this job won't last long, but when they need him they'll ask him to come in again.

We received a post card today from Grete Brainin. She'll visit us Saturday to talk about Heinrich/Helly. We shall then report to you. Take

care of Helly and for God's sake do not let her give up. We hope most
fervently that Dora's last action at the KG met with success and we'll be
able to welcome all three of them here soon. We hope this for Hannah's
sake, who is worrying herself sick about Dora-Regine-Frieda. Jonas
returned well and relaxed from his vacation and is working again after an
absence of nearly three months and against the wishes of his children. All
of them and especially he are very moved by your concern over him an
send their best regards. Hannah will write a few lines again soon to mother
and Mama. And now I must close again for now. You my dearest mother
and you all my loved ones, I embrace and kiss you as ever your Emil

---

#23

New York September 1st 1940

My dearest, good mother,

All my dear ones in Taborstrasse & Lessinggasse!
Your dear and detailed letters of August 11th and 14th I acknowledged already in my last letter to you. For the present, we remained empty
handed this week, i.e. no Clipper has yet arrived. With today's date August
is past, as is the summer or at least the height of the heat. Fact is that for
the past few days we've had weather here of the kind we got over there
in late fall. Heavy fog covers New York and it drizzles continuously, the
air is actually drenched. The flats feel moist and so does the stationery.
The envelopes close by themselves without having to be made moist. Yesterday Hansi gave herself a wonderful hair wave using her fingers and a
new kind of liquid, known hereabouts as a "finger wave"—in the evening,
when Grete Brainin and spouse came to visit, her hair was a mess hanging downs in long strains! From the climatic point of view this is truly a
very peculiar country, this America. The worst season is the summer, with
its absolutely tropical climate. That is when you become aware that you're
living on the latitude of Naples. In no other country suffer people so much
from Rheumatism and/or Arthritis in the joints. But now there is some
protection against that, too. First of all everyone here wears the unavoidable undershirts summer and winter. At first I could not get used to them
but now I would not be found without them. The most whiners are not
to be found among us poor refugees but among the native Americans.
Anyway: now it is September and that means it cannot last much longer.
The fall, it is said is by far the most beautiful season, more so than the
spring on the other side.

My dearest ones: soon our holy days will be upon us—not that it is possible here to forget them. Already there are posters with the schedules of synagogue services, and big ads in the major newspapers, usually accompanied by a flattering photo of the chief cantor. He is shown in his full ornate finery and cited are press reviews, from leading Yiddish or English papers, praising the bell like quality of the voice of this or that chasan just like the critics of concerts and operas over there. Even though it is a little early please accept our most fervent wishes and that we may soon embrace you over here! And since I am wishing I do not want to forget you either my beloved brother-in-law, Emil on your soon to be birthday. May you spend the next 60 years in the same cool manner and in the best of health united here with us. You are indeed one of the bravest and to certify this you don't need any of the several decorations you received for bravery under fire! Be assured that this courage, this patience, this ability to endure will definitely be rewarded!

Tomorrow, 2nd of September is a big holiday here, the so-called Labor Day. So this together with Sunday is a double holiday, which we shall use to write all our relatives and friends strung out over the five continents. In view of Irma's coming birthday, Otto and I have drafted a 32-word telegram, which we shall send in 2–3 days. In it we ask her also to get in touch with Rudi who is only an hour and a half driving time by car from them, and with prepaid reply tell us how everyone there is doing. We shall then immediately report this to you. Don't you worry about them a bit, Marie, according to all the news they're doing very well there in Paraguay *[codeword for Palestine]*. The only reason you're without news from them is because of the enormous distance and the ships to Europe sail only rarely. Need we worry still about you, dearest Marie or can we hear something favorable for once about your health? What is the effect of the mud baths? Please tell us everything exactly! Be brave and courageous, my dearest sister, everything will turn out well, you'll see!

We want to write directly to Heinrich/Helly but do not know their new address. So I hope they won't feel bad if we use this letter to report to them. First of all: yesterday arrived Heinrich's postcard of July 12th with Helly's postscript. But its content appears to be out of date according to a later letter from Ella in which she wrote that the auction of the crates did not take place after all, due to my letter to the shipping firm Merzario. In the meantime I've written him again. Why in the name of heaven doesn't this man answer me? Heinrich should immediately arrange via a Viennese shipping firm that Merzario let me have his storage fees. I shall wire this to him, possibly for some time in advance, if there is no chance to send these crates now—but under no circumstances must he auction them off! He can correspond about this with a local shipping firm Tyce & Lynch, 21 Pearl Street if he does not want write to a private person or simply doesn't believe me!

As I mentioned earlier, Grete and husband visited us on Saturday evening to talk about Heinrich/Helly. There is no point to go into all that in great detail except to say that everything possible is being done. Above all, the $100.00 solicited earlier, is still intact and will be added to the sum needed. We hope that an official telegram can be sent within the next two weeks, stating that passage from a Japanese harbor to Seattle or San Francisco has been booked. After that, we'll send a telegram privately to Heinrich and that should be sufficient to guarantee their invitation for the medical examination at the U.S. consulate.

Grete looks very bad she has lost at least 20kg and is past a difficult thyroid operation leaving her with two ugly scars on her neck. They have a lot of worry with their son. He got married in England and consequently lost his preferred status on the immigration quota as the child of resident aliens. And that just shortly before he was supposed to leave on his trip over here! He only registered for the preferred quota a few months ago— so now he may have to wait years before he could be admitted again. All this is the more tragic in view of his internment and if he'd have had the American visa in his passport he could have left immediately. Mr. Brainin was also sick and so everyone has to carry his burden. Mama Beck visited her son Oscar and is expected to return tomorrow. Helly must not let herself go, under no circumstance must she give up hope, and she must muster some more patience. Please talk to her and help her straighten herself out, Give her our best regards, embrace her and Heinrich for us, also her mother and Mrs. Lola.

I hope my dear ones that by now you're in possession of the money. We are very sorry about this delay for which we are however not to blame. It must have been easily explained that "Kupfer" was only a mistaken spelling of "Kupler?"

How are Regine and Dora? There too we are awaiting with a sense of relief the news concerning Frieda. Once that has been taken care of, the two women can go about their business with the American consulate. They need not worry about their Passage. We thank Miss Weissberg that she takes such good care of them. Her latest greetings for her relative here we delivered promptly. To them too we send our very best regards!

In conclusion I arrive again at the best and that is you dearest mother, and want to talk to you just a little bit more. Again I want to thank you for your lines, only I beg of you do not write too much if it requires all your strength. If I can only see your handwriting I am happy and content. How do you do otherwise? How is your health? Do you take a walk now and then? You're making extended visits to Mama Schab and Regine who are all so extraordinarily kind to you. Pray for the best things for yourself dearest mother, during the holy days, as well as for all the others. I greet and kiss and embrace you, mother, Marie, Mama, Ella, Emil and all our dear friends and acquaintances, above all your house mates, Mrs. Neumann, Mr. & Mrs. Tragholz, your Emil

---

#24

New York, September 15th 1940

My dear, good mother, And all you dear ones!

This week we were overjoyed to receive a letter from Irma after nearly three months silence. The letter is so detailed and so interesting, that Otto will literally copy some passages for you. I am only sorry that we sent our telegram prior to the arrival of the letter. Too bad, if we had held this letter only a few days earlier in our hands we could have acknowledged it in our telegram. Whatever, it appears that everything is just fine with them and especially about Heinzi she writes much that is interesting and wonderful. All, or almost all Gutters are there and are doing quite well. Only Hermine and Rudi have not been in touch with them since June, and we'll try and get in touch with Hermine from here. Unfortunately Benno informed me of something that saddened me greatly. My good friend Alexander Hajek who left Vienna about the same time as we did, passed away in a sanitarium for the treatment of tuberculosis. He was also well acquainted with Vally Nagler and maybe Ella you can pass on this piece of sad news to her. You have her address. Benno and Irma are also corresponding with Rudi and family in Haifa and they too are doing quite well, thanks God. There is simply no reason for you to worry about all those there. Paraguay is very far, and totally isolated from Europe. Even with us the connection is very tenuous but we shall see to it that it is not cut off and we shall always write to you immediately when we hear from them. Furthermore they say that they are writing you continuously and I hope that by now you will have news from them.

From Alexander Güns, our old family friend, we received a letter last week, the first one since April and after I had already started a search through the Red Cross. He is well and living somewhere in the south of France, near the Spanish border. He is asking for an affidavit in order to be rescued from there. One would love to help but it is devilishly difficult and that depresses us even more.

From you we have had no news last week, but we're hoping for tomorrow, and if not then surely for the day after tomorrow. About all of you we just want to know that you're in good health and have not given up hope. Then we can bear everything else much more easily. You won't have to wait much longer for our affidavits. We just would prefer to know for certain that once we've mailed them these papers will be final and will not have to be renewed or supplemented some time later.

What else is news with you, my dear ones? How are you, how do you manage your daily life, how is your health? Do you have enough to eat; most importantly do you have sufficient money to support your needs? I know you're writing regularly and the mail must cost you a pretty penny. In general we can somehow conjure up a picture of how you're getting along—but we always want to know more about your life, because we do live our life here together with yours. Is every one of you able to muster a little understanding for the sorrows of the other one? Are you making this difficult enough existence more bearable for each other? You dearest mother are really good and wonderful according to all reports reaching me from everyone. It makes me very happy to hear that you're making visits at Mama Schab as well as Regine. I ask you to please continue to take good care of yourself and remain chic and smart looking. Only you, dear Marie still owe us an encouraging report concerning your health. Do you really still have to engage in much physical labor? How are the mud baths, soon there must be some beneficial effects. Now that the household has become so much smaller, oughtn't you to have some more free time in which you can rest? We also hear satisfactory news about you, Mama and Ella and hope that the shrinking of the household has brought you too some relief—especially with respect to your nerves. I have organized a small "informer" system since I am not always satisfied with what you tell me and so sometimes turn to others for verification.

We finally received news this week from that shipping agent Parisi and there is no need for Regine to worry about that anymore. There is absolutely no danger anymore of an auction! He writes that there is no way to transport the crates at present but he is sure that this will be once again possible. I should like to reach the same agreement with Heinrich's shipping agent Merzario—but he hasn't answered me yet. I repeat what I already advised Heinrich in my earlier letters to either communicate with M through a Vienna based shipper or tell M. to write me directly. Whatever storage fees he demands we can take care of from here. Concerning the booking of passage for Heinrich/Helly we've done everything possible and are confident that it will be arranged satisfactorily and soon.

Yesterday I did my duty with respect to the new legally required registration of all aliens and went to register. The procedure lasted about an hour with the collection of all kinds of data and in the end one had to be finger printed, first each individual finger and then the whole hand. But everything went very smoothly—the offices were kept open until 10P so that each and everyone could do his civic duty. As it turns out there are more than a million foreigners living in NY, some of them for more than 30 years or longer. Whether that is due to laziness or indifference is hard to say—fact is that many simply were never aware that they were "foreigners" here. Frankly there is really no difference in that respect. Every day the newspapers report about this never before registration of aliens and every time they emphasize that this is done for the benefit of foreigners and not, God forbid as a measure to penalize them. And in order to show in what good company all of us foreigners are, there are daily items and pictures relating to that new process: e.g. Greta Garbo or other world famous stars of stage and screen are pictured, as they are about to register! More than 70% of the Hollywood population are foreigners! Well known writers and scientists, "about whom we didn't even know that they are not citizens," writes a newspaper, "but we hope now that soon they will be citizens." There is another matter that that has become an intensely argued topic among the public: universal military service which has just been introduced, and which affects all men between the ages of 21–35. Married people are however, not included and so there are ca. 3,000 marriages recorded daily in New York alone! Yes, the men here do not like to serve in the military and many walk around with a button on their coat lapel that says: "No Conscription" that means no serving in the military. Here they prefer to play baseball and they do that with a passion that is simply incomprehensible to us. Soon our holy days will be upon us and there is hardly a place here that doesn't remind you of that. All of us wish you, my beloved ones everything good and lovely, solid health and a happy reunion very soon with those who are so dear to you. Do not lose your courage and your hope. With these fervent wishes I remain with kisses and embraces, my dearest mother, as ever your Emil.

#25

New York, September 29th 1940

My dearest good mother, Dearest Mama, Ella,

Dearest sister Marie and brother-in-law Emil!

Your dear letters of September 2nd and 11th as well as a letter from Mama and Ella I already acknowledged briefly in my last letter and can only repeat that they provided us with much joy. Best of thanks, dearest mother for your lines in which you celebrate heroically the anniversary of our departure despite your sorrow over the separation from your children and grandchildren. We too remember always that hour in which we bade such a sad farewell and our whole chronology starts with that hour. Only four more weeks until the first anniversary of the day we said goodbye and six weeks until the day a year ago, when we stepped on the soil of this country and began a new life. Generally we've adjusted quite well, better than thousands of others, and mainly due to our ability to join, relatively soon, the work rhythm that prevails here. Thanks to that fact we were spared the cruel side of this country and especially of this city, which pitilessly lets anyone fall by the wayside, who doesn't have the vigor and will to assert himself. Nevertheless I am tempted to say that this lack of pity is not altogether unjustified, because anyone with just a little desire to work can find a job. Of course you can't be choosy and must loose all the prejudices one has brought along from over there. It is true that there are 10 millions unemployed as has been reported so often on the other side—but these are not always the same 10 millions! Almost no occupation or line of work can be considered "steady" and each one has a period during the year of at least a few weeks when one is laid off. However, once the season starts in one or the other "line" then it frequently happens that there aren't enough workers available. On the other side, in earlier times when one had the misfortune of being forced to join the army of the unemployed he would almost be certain that for the next ten years or possibly even forever he could count on being part of that army. I do not want to generalize too much; here too there are plenty of people willing to work who find themselves without any income. One cannot always demand the self-denial shown by one of my acquaintances from Vienna, who was a highly successful lawyer there and at one time a very wealthy customer of Gilhofer & Ranschburg.

Now he sits at a machine in the same factory where our Otto works. I hesitated a long time before recommending him to S. so that he could find a place for him there. S., in turn was reluctant to place a professional colleague as a common laborer. But in the end it had to be done, the man could no longer pay his rent and stood in danger of being evicted. No one else could find anything more suitable for him—there were others besides S. who had tried. In the end the man was very happy and grateful judging from a Thank You note he sent to S. together with a small picture he had been able to save from his once large and valuable collection in Vienna. S. was actually very annoyed about that. Fact is that factory work is not really the worst that can happen to you. If I were a few years younger I would most certainly have tried my luck and remain in one of these "lines" of factory work. With some skill and ambition one can soon distinguish oneself from the mass and once you have reached the position of foreman—Otto is just about to be promoted to that job—a weekly wage of at least $25–30 is nearly certain. Owning a car is for any permanently employed worker a matter of course. Otto says that even at his place of work, which is really not very big by American standards, 30–40 cars belonging to workers there will be found parked in front of the building; some are even nicer than those driven by the bosses.

There are other ways too, which we have become accustomed to with some ease. For example Hansi can make herself understood in colloquial English in a way that doesn't cease to amaze me. I am stunned when I observe her "shopping" in the various stores of our neighborhood. She hardly misses any of the necessary technical terms and expressions of which in German I barely have an inkling myself! Especially when asking for certain cuts at the butcher's I am still at a loss—in either German or English.

But otherwise we never forget that our whole life here has only a temporary character and will remain so until all of you will be here. There doesn't exist for us another thought or a different desire. A few days ago Dr. Weil, MD, took his exam for the second time according to his wife who visited Hannah at her law office. This time he is more hopeful about having passed them. We had not heard from him for quite some time and that annoyed us a bit since we as well as the Handels have invited him several times and he, usually in the last minute, asked to be excused. His wife complained bitterly about him. He suffers from depressions and she is afraid to leave him alone. But he ought to be able to overcome this after all. He is not really all that old and if he is able to open his practice within 2 or 3 years he hasn't lost that much either. Especially in view of his future medical practice he should be able to get a grip on himself now. He is not without means and his daughter earns quite a good income here.

Last week we visited in Jersey where we spent a very nice afternoon mainly busy stuffing ourselves. All our relatives on the other side of the Hudson asked about you at length and send you their very best regards.

They complained a lot about business and it is true that both brothers, especially Isidor, the older, do not look very well. His wife, Dora, has recovered very well from her auto accident on New Years Eve, except for occasional headaches. They send best wishes for the New Year and hope that soon they will be able to welcome their "Auntie Feige" over here.

Today we'll go to Aunt Beck where I'll talk to Grete and her husband because that whole matter concerning Heinrich and Helly is just taking too long. By the way I finally received news from the shipping agent Merzario and I am about to write to him as well. He asks for $20.00 without any details what is covered by this amount. But neither does he threaten with auctioning off the crates or anything like that. I'll send him $10.00 for the time being and will ask for more details before I send the balance. Everything in a very friendly way, you understand. I just want to delay matters a bit. Yesterday came a very nice letter from Ernest Strassmann. He allegedly had heard from Richard that we're trying to do something for Heinrich. Even though he is not doing very well he offers his help within the few resources available to him. Maybe this will provide a little comfort to Heinrich and Helly as proof that they are not forgotten and that any of the previous failures are the result of the intervention by a higher power against which we are helpless, a fact that makes us too, very unhappy. We wish them all the best and they will soon be able to begin their departure from their most recent domicile. We send heartfelt greetings also for Helly's mother and Mrs. Lola.

Has Dora recuperated from her illness? How is Regine doing?

Does she have news from Frieda? What does she hear from the KG? It is up to them now, isn't it? … Hannah and all of us here are interested to learn more about when Dora's brother-in-law, Peter left and where he went. Hannah's thoughts and wishes circle only about what can be done for Regine-Dora-Frieda. It is her opinion that that if Peter could find a way, they too could follow that same route. We also thank Mrs. Weissberg for her greetings. I have visited with her cousin already four times, starting in June, and convey her regards even if Mrs. W. had not asked us directly.

The day before yesterday we received a telegram from Olly. In it she informs us that her registration papers finally arrived from the Viennese U.S. consulate and that she has already gotten notification from the London U.S. Consulate. She still lacks a few data, hence the telegram. I immediately got in touch with her sponsor and hope to be able to airmail the desired supplementary information in a few days. During the last few days the poor girl must have had quite some experiences.

Dearest, good Ella for you I always have something to do. But please don't be mad at me. A former colleague of mine, Schönfeld by name, who is at the same place as Olly, only not at liberty, wrote to tell me that he is well and healthy and wants me to send his mother greetings from him. Unfortunately he doesn't mention her address. I recall that she lived in Hietzing in the Hadikgasse I can't remember the number. I doubt that she still lives there but it is possible that Hilde Ranschler knows her address or, at least the number in the Hadikgasse. You can take care of all this by writing. Ask Hilde via a postcard. If she doesn't know anything maybe something can be learned from the KG. Pertinent data: Name: Mrs. Schönfeld. Unfortunately I do not know her first name. She and her daughter are single, ca. in her mid-forties, by profession Kindergärtnerin. She may even be employed by the KG. A year ago when I left they were still living in the Hadikgasse. In any case I thank you very much, Ella for doing this. Have you, dear Ella, informed yourself about when it might be your turn? I am confident that when you and Mama as well my people are notified there will be a direct way rather than the roundabout way via Siberia. Once again we are very depressed over the Japanese clouds though the Americans are much less bothered—they have that attitude of "we're No. 1 and they or anyone else had better not tangle with us!"

My dearest mother, I am glad that from time to time you're getting some assistance from the KG. Is this true of you, too Marie? Mama too should receive something! In fact what do you all live on? You're not writing anything about that. It is terrible that we cannot do anything for you from here!

How is your health, dearest Marie? Have the mud baths had some effect? I surely hope so! How is the weather over there? Here we have the most wonderful days, but we do freeze occasionally. That's no joke. It is bitter cold, especially at night. In many buildings central heating is already in operation. By the way, today I can write an hour longer without losing any time. Today ends the daylight-savings-time. So now I must once again tear myself away from you all. I beg of you my dearest, sweet mother take good care of yourself especially now that you are entering the cooler season, all of you must guard your health! I embrace my dearest mother, kiss all of you my dearest and beloved and remain with best regards for all our dear friends and acquaintances, your Emil

#26

New York October 3rd 1940

My most beloved mother, all you beloved people in Taborstrasse &
  Lessinggasse!

Today is Holy Day and even though one should not write on a day
like that, I cannot conceive of a better task, actually not a better way of
expressing my devotion to God than to write to you. I am of course not
working and have the added advantage that nothing is deducted from my
wage, much in contrast to those working in factories. Hansi is losing $5.60
for these two days she is taking off but she simply would not have it any
other way, refusing to stay on the job. At least she gets some rest for 4
days—Saturday is also an off day. She prepared a real Holy Day meal, a
carp done in the Polish manner, something for which she has already
reached celebrity status among our friends here. I shall not tell you about
our dinner today because I'd feel ashamed doing so. Otto and Stella will
be joining us as well. In the evening we're invited at the Handels.

We were practically inundated with holiday wishes in the mail today
from our relatives and American friends. You're included in everybody's
wishes; everyone wishes that in the coming new year we should be able
to embrace you! If only these wishes will be granted! Of course neither
did we forget our relatives and friends; Hannah already scolded us early
in the morning by phone for spending so much money on flowers for her
and her mother. Fact is that Americans value such attention, appreciate
such gifts and do themselves always observe such niceties and courtesies
of behavior. That is the way it should be because small tokens of consid-
eration maintain the friendship.

On the occasion of these holidays one can really observe how many
Jews there are in New York. Never before have I seen our section of Broadway done up in such a dignified, holiday mood. Normally one hardly ever
sees a closed store, not at night and not on holidays or Sundays. The businesses that close on Saturday are hardly noticeable. But today there is
holiday stillness on Broadway that is truly impressive. Last evening, ca.
10P we went as usual downstairs to do some shopping for the following
day only to discover after running up and down the street for nearly half
an hour that we could not even buy a bottle of milk. In the Bronx I am
told even the non–Jewish stores are closed on these holidays. Across the
street from us on 161st Street there is a very exclusive synagogue, and
while I am writing I glance over occasionally through the window. I see
a large number of very well dressed people in their holiday finest milling
about and that reminds me of some better times of our own. But there is

no reason to be sad you will come over and those times will come again for you!

The seats in the synagogue are very expensive, ca. $5.00–8.00. There are other areas in the city where they are cheaper; some can be had for only $1.00. If I'd had the time to go to the Jewish Council I would have gotten one for free. But believe me it really doesn't matter. Tomorrow I am sure they'll let me in somewhere, also on Yom Kippur and especially for the Memorial Service. In any case, my being able to talk to you via this letter is a true service! Next year, once you're here we shall catch up on everything.

This morning I already sent a telegram to Olly, telling her that the supplementary documents necessary for the completion of her affidavit were sent to me in the required form and I immediately airmailed them to her. I sent her the telegram so that the poor girl can at least quit worrying because it'll take at least 10 days for the letter to arrive there. She had practically bombarded me with telegrams and airmail letters. Let us hope that now everything will be all right and she can get away from that hell over there and we'll be able to welcome her here very soon. Coming back to Olly's parents, the Epsteins in Riga, it is unfortunate but I cannot risk going to Washington and accomplish nothing once there. In all probability Schutzmann and the rest of the relatives won't even want to see me. Those people appear to me as just that sort. The tip, for me to travel there, was given to Epstein by the old Mrs. Weiss,

Ollie Donat (née Epstein), daughter of Emil and Marie's sister Dora (d. 1918). She was the only close relative whose immigration to the U.S. Emil Secher was able to successfully sponsor. She arrived in New York in 1946, and later married Walter Donat, also from Vienna, with whom she had a daughter, Doris, who presented them with four grandchildren. The Schick family lives today in the Bay Area. Their great-grandparents, Adolf and Malvine Epstein (stepmother of Ollie), were murdered in Riga following the German invasion of the Baltic states.

the mother-in-law of Schutzmann. It's easy enough for her to give such tips. Shouldn't she have some influence of her own on her son-in-law, and if she cannot get to him what makes her think I can?! Those people have never found it worth their while to answer the many letters I wrote and the telegrams I sent to them. Just before I decided that I might go to Washington after all, I wrote again to Mrs. Weiss. But she didn't bother to answer. Under these circumstances it appears like a waste of time to sacrifice money and time. I hope that once Olly gets here she will do her bit to for her parents. For the time being no matter how hard it is they will have to be patient.

October 5th 1940

My dearest ones, I continue my letter today. The first holy days are past. We celebrated them very nicely, always thinking of you. On the first holy day Rosh Hashanah, Otto and Stella came to dinner and in the evening we ate supper with the Handels. Afterwards we rode out to Riverdale to the Liebermann family, good friends of Safirstein-Handel, about whom I've written you earlier, I believe. Mrs. Liebermann is a friend of Hannah's from their school days. We returned home very late at night. The weather was wonderful—the "Jewish" holiday weather is as well known here as it was over there!

No mail again for nearly two weeks and we're waiting for some with great longing. Surely you are all in good shape and healthy. That is always our greatest worry. How are you my darling mother? Don't you dare to fast on Yom Kippur! You don't eat exactly sumptuously during the rest of the year, either. And you dearest Marie, how is your health? Has there been some improvement? How about you Mama and Ella, what's doing with you? What are all of you doing about money? Write in time, it takes a long time before a money transfer takes place. We do not have anything ourselves at present, and shall have to alert all the relatives, left and right, to send you something and that takes time. So please do not be ashamed and write us in time about it. After all there isn't much other than that, we can do for you.

How are our dear relatives, friends and acquaintances? Regine-Dora, the Braun girls, none of whom we can forget, Mama Neumann, Laufer Frieda and the other Frieda? What about the Streit family and the Ball family? How are good, old Erdheim, and Mrs. Uhrmacher? Has she heard anything from her children? How is Mrs. Prdszly doing who never forgets you? And how is her family? What's with Willy Nördlingen? Last not least what's up with Heinrich/Helly? I've written earlier concerning the status of his matters and we're expecting an announcement from them with respect to the possibility of routing via Lisbon. Aunt Beck is not doing too well since she returned from her visit with her son but given her strong constitution should be up and about very soon. How is Rosa? Is she suffering from the current diet with her weak stomach? How are the ladies of the "Gin Rummy round table"? Do they all still have a little game now and then? To all of them whether we mentioned them or not we send our most heartfelt greetings. I kiss and embrace you my dearest mother as well as Marie, Emil, Mama Ella, your Emil

---

#27 [Excerpt]

...Today we had another very important event: Registration Day, i.e. registration for the draft, universal military service with the country at peace, for the first time in the history of America. No less than 16 million men came to register on one single day and everyone is full of admiration for the smooth organization making this possible. Otto too had a "sprig of flowers" on his hat—only here it isn't that but simply the draft card stuck in the hatband, proudly displayed as a sign that the wearer can be counted on to defend his country! I am almost a little envious of these young people here. In New York alone nearly 1½ million men registered.

#28

New York October 23rd, 1940

My beloved mother, all my dear ones!

I hope you've received all my last letters in which I thanked you for your detailed mail from September 23rd till September 30th. So far we haven't received anything for now, but we shall not demand the impossible, are satisfied if everything stays the way it is as far as the mail is concerned.

We have right now, my dearest ones, the most wonderful season of the year you can possibly imagine—just the kind of weather and temperatures I love the most. For two weeks a cloudless, azure blue sky with the most aromatic air one can imagine. Of course at night and in the early morning it is quite cold but during the day there is mild and agreeably warming sunshine. Now you can see how beautiful this New York really is: the glorious fall colors of Central Park framed by the skyscrapers provides an incomparable view which I enjoy more every day. I do mind however that all buildings, residential and office are already on central heating so one can only work or relax in shirtsleeves. The heating season begins automatically in early October regardless of how warm the sunshine keeps the outdoors.

Last week it was a year to the day since we, Hansi, Herbert and I went to the American consulate for our medical exam, etc. and I know for sure that you too remembered this day. This was the day we longed for during one and a half years of waiting—yet once it came and passed we realized that this meant a difficult farewell from all of you for a very long time. What followed was an uninterrupted giddiness even frenzy from which we did not emerge until we stepped on board the ship in Triest. It was only then that we became really aware how we had left you behind, hard-pressed, in bad trouble and misery. This awareness has not left us to this day and we shall not be happy and cheerful until the day we are again united with you. That during this whole time we have not been able to come any closer to this self-imposed goal depresses us immensely; still, all that will not take from us the hope of a Wiedersehen with you. If we only know that you are all in good health, are carrying on patiently, will not lose your courage and hope then everything is easier and more comforting for us and we can look into a better, brighter future. Once you're here with the Lord's help, then none of you will have to worry about the future. Together all of us will be able to lead a simple modest life, we shall all have a roof over our heads and neither you nor we need to be afraid to lack our daily bread. One can hold out and make an honest living here, it is not easy but I always have to think of the words that were addressed to us categorically immediately after our first arrival at the offices of the Jewish Council:" Nobody ever needs to starve to death here in this country!" And that is truly the case. Much appears very strange here, a lot is very peculiar, and with a lot of things one finds oneself in disagreement. That is due to certain prejudices the others and we have, but on the whole a beautiful and lovely country. Only one thing one can regret: if you weren't lucky enough to be born here, one ought to have come over here much earlier, already thirty years ago or at least after the war. After all it is not a simple matter to brainwash yourself of an existence spanning forty years and more: of early child hood, schooling, service in the war, of the home one had built later, the apartment in which one had invested all the love and care one could spare in the belief it would last forever. At first one tries to forget just as the good hearted American recommends while he pats you on the shoulder: "Forget about it!" A little later you just give up trying to forget and then suddenly you're actually afraid you might really forget! This remembrance is after all the only thing you can really call your own. With the language it is another odd matter. Almost without noticing one slips into an imperceptible mixture of German and English even if there still isn't any English word present. Somehow one begins to translate from the English into German. The sentence may be perfectly correct German yet it doesn't sound German. Here is an example: one refugee will ask a second one who hasn't been here quite as long as the first one: *Wie lieben Sie dieses Land?* Literally: How do you love (or like) this country? The correct German would obviously be: *"Wie gefällt es Ihnen hier?"* Literally: Does this country please you? Or even better how does this country strike you? Actually one would not pose this question at all in German. It was not customary for us to ask anyone how he liked Vienna or any other place. But here one asks the other refugee because one had gotten used to being asked the very same question by Americans within minutes after making their acquaintance: "How d'ya like this country, fella?"

These are observations I make of others and also of myself.

Somehow it saddens me that gradually one becomes alienated from the language for which one had developed such skillful sensitivity, almost feel it slipping away at the same time that I am still fighting for every correct English expression. Even if my knowledge of colloquial English is quite satisfactory, I am very well aware that when I want to express ideas, emotions, impressions, or relate certain events in a gripping and grammatically correct way I am far from doing this with any facility or without feeling inhibited—and then comes the realization that it may take years to reach that language dexterity, if indeed I can ever reach it.

October 23rd, 1940. Please do not be mad that I am taking my time in mailing my letters. Today, my dearest Marie arrived your dear letter of October 7th with the lines added by mother. Nothing from Mama Schab, I am sorry to say. Let me first of all express my deepest sympathy to Emil on the occasion of the death of his oldest sister and please convey this also to her remaining relatives. For this woman plagued by an incurable disease this was surely a relief. I hope that Regine is completely well again and please giver her and Dora our best regards. Also to Helly and Heinrich. We are happy if we can repay here even a fraction of the kindness that Helly extends to you. How are matters concerning Lisbon and with the consulate in general? Is everything all right in the matter of the crates? In any case Heinrich should not lose touch with Merzario via his Vienna shipping agent and if necessary always refer them to me.

Again all my thanks to you mother for your loving lines. I am glad that you spent the holy days in good spirits and accompanied Marie on some walks. Just keep on doing that. Whatever you and Marie and all of you are doing for your health you're also doing it for us.

Last Sunday Hansi visited the World's Fair and was enthusiastic about it when she came home. One of our American acquaintances, a "sucker" treated her. As the fair will close its gates forever next Sunday I shall try and visit it on Sunday. Hansi says this is something one should not miss and Herbert agrees.

Otto gave me his letter already yesterday for transmittal to you, so there isn't anything in it about your latest letter. He will refer to it the next time he writes to you.

I am really concerned about Olly. Her next letter should tell us already more about her date of departure. I shall send you immediately a telegram as soon as she arrives. The affidavit for mother will most likely be mailed next week and Marie/Emil's will follow shortly.

We already received an invitation from the people in Jersey for a big "party" on December 22nd. Herman's daughter Beatrice will be 17 years old and consequently ready to enter social life. Last night was a "small" party at Safirsteins's to which my former "boss" in Vienna, Mrs. Epstein had also been invited—here she has reverted to her maiden name, Ranschburg. She really appreciates Hannah who succeeded in obtaining such a favorable result in her accident case. And so I keep informing you about all kinds of important and less important events in the knowledge that as I write this you actually live closer to us.

For this time I kiss and embrace you all one after the other, leaving the best to the last, you my dearest mother, Your Emil

---

#29

New York, October 29th, 1940

My dearest, good mother,

All you my dear ones in Taborstrasse & Lessinggasse!

It is almost one year to the day that I bade you a very sad farewell, my dearest mother, and I relive these hours in my mind. We're thinking about this endlessly and we talk about it continuously. Our longing for you is stronger than ever but what is the use of it all! The only thing that remains is to be patient and never giving up hope! Nevertheless we do not want to be ungrateful and are glad that we can be in touch with you and know that all of you are in good health. For you too, my dearest Marie, it is our most fervent wish that you might soon be relieved of your afflictions! In your last letters you did not mention anything about them and we take this as a good sign!

Just today we learned that Greece too has now entered the war and our memory conjures up that beautiful city of Patras as it was spread out peacefully before our admiring eyes from our ship, the *Saturnia* as it entered the harbor. Expectantly we kept a look out for our very best friend Mela Roth who had promised to be there and oh, the joy when we actually espied her!

Today we read that planes as well have bombed not only Patras but Athens. There now remains hardly a corner on this earth that has not been touched by this war. The only exception is this continent to which heavenly providence and luck had driven us. But who know for how long this will last! Here too much has changed in the year since our arrival. How far away we thought Europe was then with its war noises and now look how close it all seems.

In the last few weeks there was introduced the military draft something heretofore unknown in the history of America, not even during the world war. We Europeans who for the most part have lived in countries in which military service was by and large one's first and most honorable duty, cannot fully understand why Americans get so excited about this. An American tried to explain this to me not too long ago. It isn't that the American doesn't want to defend his country with a weapon in his hands, but that he would as a matter of course, voluntarily follow the call to the colors, while now it has been imposed upon him as a duty. In the coming weeks we shall have Presidential elections and the possibility that a president could be elected to a third term is also something that heretofore has never occurred in the history of America and contributes to heating up emotions to the boiling point. "No Third Term" is the campaign slogan of the opposition, but even among his own party the slogan reads "For the Democratic Party but against a Third Term." Nevertheless everyone is pretty much convinced that he'll be re-elected. In any case the coming Tuesday will mark the end of an extraordinarily heated campaign and I am very curious to see who shall be the winner.

Last Sunday I put aside war, draft, and election campaign and visited the World's Fair for the first and undoubtedly the last time, because it's gates will close on October 27th, having been kept open for two years, in itself a never before occurrence. I hesitated for a long time before I made the decision to visit because the price of admission was too high, but eventually I did get a free ticket. Last not least I was glad I could go and still report to you my dearest ones my impressions. But you'll have to forgive me that I won't be able to do that after all: it is simply too much! I came early in the morning and stayed till 11PM, actually tried to see everything on this one day something for which others needed at least a dozen visits. The impression that remained with me can be reproduced only with the same hackneyed phrases I have used so often before: gigantic, colossal, grandiose, overpowering, in one word—American! Maybe I'll come back to a few details as I keep writing to you. For example: What can you do when you're too tired to keep on walking? Why, nothing simpler—you just step on an electrical device and within a few seconds you step off it fully refreshed and relaxed. Or you ride around in a small car on the grounds of the Ford exhibition—a small city by itself within the Fair and as you drive past certain exhibits a little radio in the car explains everything to you. And much, much more.

Dearest Mama and Ella, a few days ago I got a letter from Dr. Weil with the news that he passed the English-Language exam. Even more pleasing was the fact that he is over his depressions and he is now ready to begin preparations for his medical exams. I think it'll be best if I enclose his letter for you. As you can see I am here as once in Vienna, the source of mental nourishment for my friends. And there is something else I want to tell you, which will gladden your hearts: We had heard that Willy had received a letter from you while we on the other hand, came away empty handed. So they invited us to read the letter together with them. Last evening we stayed there a really long time, reading your letter, talking about you. It was already 1AM when we finally got up to leave. They are all doing well and Ada said she wrote you an airmail letter only a few days ago.

October 30th

Again we didn't have to wait in vain for mail from you. Many thanks, dearest, good Marie for your news and to you my sweet mother and Emil for the lines you added. It gives me at least some small comfort when I hear that you were able to spend the holy days in a humane and dignified manner. Also that you all support each other so that you do not suffer from loneliness, keep up with each other, don't lose touch with Regine/Dora, Mama/Ella and that Helly, wonderful person she is, does not forget about you. Neither do we forget anyone, our letters to you are also meant for them; we cannot write to them because we're simply ashamed that all we can offer are mere words of comfort. If only we could help at least once concretely without words—it would be better than always trying to comfort! Still, I can only repeat what I've already said so often to you my dearest ones, and that goes also for Regine/Dora and Heinrich/Helly, please do not lose courage! I do not mean this to be an empty phrase, in our hearts there is a rock hard, indestructible hope that we shall see all of you again happy and healthy. And that is why I am urging you not to let yourself go and put your trust in our confident feelings! Dear Marie, today we sent via the same route an amount like the last one, by telegram and we hope that this time it won't take so long.. There will be about RM115.00 of which 100.00 are for you and the balance for a sister of Helen Bohrer's husband (Grünberger). Bohrer asked me to make the transfer for him as well because he can save on fees. His sister will come and pick it up from you. She will bring along a note written by me which I gave to Bohrer and which he in turn sent to his sister. Please acknowledge the amount as soon as it arrives. We shall try to send an amount more often during the winter so that you can buy some more fuel for heating purposes. Otherwise all of you should not begrudge yourself a few of the things you like. For you mother something sweet, if you can get it, and you too, Marie do something for your health and Emil you should drink to your and all our health with a little wine.

Now I must again close: I kiss and embrace you my dearest, beloved mother and all of you most fervently and remain with many heartfelt regards to you and all our friends, your EMIL

#30

New York, November 4th, 1940

My dearest, good mother, All my dear ones in Taborstrasse & Lessinggasse!

I am only just starting this letter but will not finish it today. We're still awaiting mail from you, having been advised of the arrival today of a Transatlantic Clipper. I also want to tell you the results of the Presidential election that will take place tomorrow, *Election Day*. This is a big holiday not only because of the quadrennial election of a president but because it was on this day ca. 150 years ago, that George Washington, America's first president was elected to that office. It is tradition on this day to choose not only the president but also all other popularly chosen representatives: senators, Congressmen, governors, mayors etc. Consequently on the 5th of November there is always something going on in America; especially today when America chooses its president while the rest of the world appears to be in flames and so much will depend on this president, specifically whether or not America will be drawn into the war. Add to this the never heretofore election of a president to a third term and you can see why tempers run high and even experienced, older Americans who have witnessed 10–15 such elections maintain the election fever has reached an intensity unknown at any previous time. Most of us including myself have been caught up in the excitement of the campaign even though we cannot actively participate this time. However, I still cannot see any significant difference between the two opposing candidates. Their speeches, which are broadcast day and night, are very much alike. Each one says the same, makes the same promises, and blames the other one for wanting to draw America into the war. Each one addresses all nationalities, German-, Anglo-, and Italian-Americans, all races, all religions, always promising the blue from the sky. So where is the real difference between these two parties? Well, this is what an educated American has told me: Not the candidates make the difference, both are wonderful persons, untouchable, pure, idealistic, but the men who stand behind them are the real leaders who use these two candidates, pure as apostles, as a front to gain the support of the populace. Well, tomorrow evening we'll know more! But what we newcomers can see and learn from this occasion is once again: "America!" This country lives up to its reputation as the Land of Unlimited Opportunities when it concerns splashy displays, tempting advertisements, or just plain propaganda. Not in all areas is it possible to talk about unlimited opportunities the way we used to visualize it over there. In many respects, where I expected much more I have been disappointed.

A year ago today my dearest ones, we were steaming from Patras to Naples. Gliding over a wonderful, still peaceful Mediterranean Sea, luxuriating in sunshine from an improbably azure blue sky, looking out on a postcard like blue, smooth Ocean. The passengers on the *Saturnia* sunbathed on the various open decks of the ship, which at that time was not at all crowded. Only after departing Genoa where those refugees who had left Vienna after we did came on board, as well as other émigrés from Berlin, Switzerland, Italy, even France the ship became awfully crowded much to our annoyance. I still remember this crowding even though at that time there weren't more passengers aboard than the ship could hold. Now when we hear the stories of refugees who recently came from England or Lisbon, I realize how comfortable we had been on that crossing. Not to mention that every square foot in these ships is occupied, in the dining rooms, the areas normally reserved for socializing, even on the closed and open decks people slept on straw mattresses, they also had to keep on their clothes and over them the life-preservers for the length of the crossing. Nevertheless even those who had to endure this arrived here in good spirits, happy and full of energy. They even told of having fun with the lifeboat drills that were held several time daily. I just wish that Olly were already here. I haven't heard from her during the last few weeks and hope that the next news from her will already announce details concerning her trip here. A Mrs. Kupfermann called me recently; Olly worked in her household until Mrs. K sailed over here. She told me many nice things about Olly and is equally impatient to hear about her safe arrival here. Haven't heard from her sister Elly in some time. Does she at least write you? Did she acknowledge my money transfer? As Otto and I already wrote in our last letter we've telegraphed to you via the bank the amount of ca. RM150.00. When you get this letter you may not yet have the money but at least a notification from Berlin. Of this amount RM100.00 are for you and RM15.00 for Bohrer's sister. B. did this through me in order to save the fees for such a relatively small amount. Should you receive less than RM115.00, please turn over only whatever is over RM100.00. Inform me about the exact amount, I'll settle it later with Bohrer. My dear, good Ella, as usual I have a small task for you. My friend Robert has checked in once again in writing after a long silence. Please Ella tell this to Hansi and Emma I do not have their new address. I am sure you know where they live; at least Vally Nagler will know, for sure. Give them all my best regards. How is your weather, my dear ones? Last year around this time it was already quite cold over there. I recall that on the Semmering and further up on the Brenner one could see deep snow from the train. I am certain that you will receive some fuel and I know that I can depend on Emil and his cleverness to forage it even as far as Floridsdorf. It is a piece of luck that you need not anticipate another move. In these small quarters in the Taborstrasse & Lessinggasse you ought to be able to keep quite warm.

And you my dear mother: how are you? How do you feel? When we reach this season I am truly sorry that last year I kept postponing going shopping with you for a pair of snowshoes until it was too late. You see I want that you, even in the colder season, should not just sit at home but go out weather permitting for a walk and some exercise.

The three of us here continue to be doing well, we all have our jobs to do, but there is only one thought that pervades us and that is about you! We suffer from our great longing for you and in our hearts we carry the rock hard and indestructible hope that we shall be able to embrace each one of you in the not all too distant future. So now it is farewell again, my dear ones. You my good mother, and you others, Mama and Marie, Ella and Emil I embrace and greet you again most fervently, your EMIL

#31

New York, November 17th 1940

My dearest, good mother!

This time I am writing separately to our friends Heinrich and Helly and since our weekly report will be mailed later I just want to celebrate this day, the first anniversary of our arrival in America, by sending you our most heartfelt greetings and best wishes. A whole long year has passed since we touched this soil. Then I was full of hope that we shall see you and all our loved ones again within a year at the latest. This is still not the case and our patience is put to a hard test. Still, I am glad that we've already come this far. Every day that I am here brings me closer to the goal which occupies all our thoughts, to be reunited with you my good mother and all our other loved ones. So you too, mother, have patience, don't be unhappy over our long separation instead, think that every day brings us closer to the hour in which you will be reunited with all those you love.

Now comes winter and with it those bad times, doubly bad under the current circumstances; it is for that reason that I am turning to you with this heartfelt request to please, take good care of yourself. Fix up your modest quarters as comfortably and warm as you possibly can and if you somehow can improve on the food that is available to you, please do so. Once you acknowledge receiving the last money transfer we shall again send you some more. Maybe, mother, you can go once again to Dr. Schnardt and let me know everything he says. Actually you haven't written me anything about your health for quite some time, and I too have wanted to ask you about it for a long time already. How is your nose injury that you received shortly before our departure?

All the others about whom I think with the same love and longing, should not think any less of me because I am writing only to you this time. It's been a real need for me for a long time already to talk only to you and tell you on the occasion of this anniversary, how I think back of the wonderful and brave way you said good bye to us on that difficult day. The memory of that helps me to keep going when on occasion I feel like giving up.

On this anniversary of our landing in New York all of us (including Otto and Stella who are a little "older" Americans than we are) are invited to the Safirstein-Handels. We have some small tokens of our appreciation prepared for these people who were the first ones to meet us on this strange continent on whose soil we entered with great trepidation and heavy, bitter hearts. Their loving care for each one of us has not diminished in the least and this warmth contributed a lot to make it possible for us to bear the difficult times of our first year, succeeded in holding on and eventually asserting ourselves. They continue to be concerned about our lives here and enjoy any one of our small successes—which they are always the first to hear about—at least as much as we do. *[End of this letter]*

#36

New York, 00 December 1940

My dear, good mother,

All my dear ones in Taborstrasse & Lessinggasse! The news from you arrives a bit more infrequently now; your last letters of 28 and 23rd October I acknowledged already last week. In the meantime we've written you a lot of letters that have all remained unanswered. At least 5 letters in which among other matters we also advised you of another money transfer in progress. Did you receive it in the meantime or at least a notification from Berlin? We also inquired from you, and that applies equally to Mama Schab and Ella whether we should send food parcels. Allegedly there is a possible way. There are ca. 4–5 kinds of shipments. The contents are according to one's wishes, fat coffee, tea butter etc. Meat or sausage is not permitted. The prices, including duties, are extremely high but that wouldn't matter very much. We just would like to know whether, if we send you money instead of food items, you could obtain these yourself. In any case we shall make another attempt this week and you'll tell us whether you're satisfied. Then we shall regularize this. We shall also send a shipment to Helly and Regine. I am making every effort to explore every possibility for that purpose. I had an acquaintance of mine write to Lisbon who knows some one there. I gave him your address and also that of Regine and Helly. I need to pay only after I had an acknowledgment of their arrival. I am very unhappy to have had no success with this, except for the two shipments you received from Victor.

My dearest ones, we are now in the depth of winter And it came almost overnight. Snowfall and icy cold. All that happens so suddenly here. Until a week ago one would have thought it was summer or at least fall and now it is winter and Christmas is almost here. One is reminded of that by the business transactions, the department stores with their giant Xmas trees inside and in their display windows, the Xmas parades held by all these stores are mindful of carnival parades. We too are very busy in our shop but that is not so much because of the season.

There was so much typing to do I was able to hire an acquaintance of mine, an unemployed refugee who thereby was able to earn a few dollars. Last Sunday I had to spend all day at the office because my "boss" departed late at night for Chicago, etc. as far as San Francisco. So now I am again alone in the office making me boss, general manager and delivery boy all in one. Maybe some time in the future I will also travel into that distant, large America. Even though I've been her now for over a year I have not really left New York farther than one travels with the subway. I have never sat in a real American railroad carriage, or ridden in one of those luxurious, comfortable, giant long distance buses, which are even more popular, than the railroads. These Buses travel as far as the West Coast, San Francisco, and Los Angeles in ca. 5 days. But that is the least of my worries, I just thought I'd mention it. The trip Vienna–New York is sufficient for all my needs as a world traveler—unless I could take this trip in the opposite direction in order to pick up you my loved ones and we could return here together. My God wouldn't that be wonderful! I often dream of that, not only when I am awake but also when I am asleep.

Recently I dreamt that you my dearest mother really scolded me because I went out without a scarf. It was indeed bitter cold in the morning and I retraced my steps to get my scarf, which was still among my summer stuff. When I finally sat down in the subway I asked you whether you're satisfied with me! I believe I actually said it out loud because the people around me looked at me rather peculiarly, so I quickly opened my large newspaper and started reading about the heroic struggle of the Greeks! Oh, it is very bitter that longing for ones loved ones; sometimes it is strong at other times less so—but it is there all the time. But what I am telling you here you know yourselves, made worse by the misery, mental and physical you have to experience and which we don't even know about.

While I am writing this the radio is playing the "Mikado" and that puts me into a very special mood, more nostalgic even than the most genuine Viennese music which one hears here quite frequently, in fact sometimes too much from morning 'til night. Sullivan's music is not rare here, and especially the "Mikado." "So kehr' ich den Humor…" and the "Bachstelzelein" is sung quite passably in English by Hansi. This reminds me of the musical evenings in the Schab Household in past and better times, always introduced by and then ended with the beautiful melodies of the "Mikado." That was the beloved "house musical" for all of you. When you get here Ella, you'll surely sing on the radio on a certain New York station.

That is easily arranged without any great formalities. That is how people will hear you and then your success is assured!

Last Thursday Otto and Stella came to visit in the evening and we had a nice time. Of course always only one thought and one topic of conversation. Last Sunday the Safirsteins had a small party, Dr. Borrak et al. I arrived late in the evening having had to work late at the office. At that party too, only one subject: how can we help you, especially Regine-Dora-Frieda who had written a letter that Hannah passed around for us to read. She also had received a letter from Herman Handel in Sofia with lots of lamentation. He asked to have his affidavit renewed, which had expired. He also asked whether any of Auntie Feige's children are in America. I couldn't help myself and wrote few lines in the letter to him chastising him and his wife that it had never occurred to them to ask directly in Vienna how we or you are doing, and specifically whether Auntie Feige was all right. When they wanted to have favors done for them, no matter how difficult, unpleasant and time consuming, or to prepare Mrs. Diamant for a trip to Sofia, advance some money and help out Klara's brother, they knew only too well where to reach us. You know I give no quarter in things like that and nothing offends me more than behavior of that sort. It is almost superfluous to mention that it took only one phone call to Herman (the one in Jersey) and Isidor to have them agree to the renewal. Hannah, the indefatigable one then took care of getting the process started.

Last week I also received news from Grete's husband that he finally succeeded in having a meeting with Mrs. Redlich and she agreed to a supplementary affidavit for Heinrich/Helly guaranteed by herself and her brother. Next Sunday we are invited to Mama Beck. The other day I wrote Heinrich/Helly a few lines, too. Hopefully it won't be long now before we can embrace them here. Did you receive our letters of last week? The ones with the affidavit? How are you doing otherwise? Please save your strength in this rough season. You my dearest Marie take special care of yourself and do not fail to try anything that may help you to get rid of the Rheumatism. And the two Grandmothers should take a walk whenever weather permits that, but they should be dressed warmly. Is Emil's short jacket still wearable? Now please give my best regards to all my friends and acquaintances, your housemates, Mama Neumann, the Tragholz family, the Pr. family.

You too, my loved ones, I greet and embrace you, your Emil

#33

New York, December 15th, 1940

[Excerpts]

...Last week I received a detailed report from Victor, dated October 23rd and November 4th. He also sent me a wonderful poem, typed, so that your copy, dear Mama, is doubly appreciated since it enables us to keep it for ourselves while the other one makes the rounds among friends and relatives. The poem is really excellent and without hesitation or the slightest jealousy I herewith relinquish my heretofore-held role as House and Family poet in favor of Victor. He is a terrific guy whose every thought and wish is aimed to cover up his certainly unenviable situation and encourage others to be brave and not give up hope. His situation makes us also sad because we cannot do anything to help and it is unfortunate that he thought so late to have himself registered at the U.S. consulate in Riga.

I am very busy these days hardly ever come home before 10P but that really makes me very happy. We are just about to publish our first catalogue to which I was able to contribute a great deal. My office has been wonderfully furnished as a studio and a picture of it decorates the first inside page of the catalogue. I shall mail you one soon. Everything depends on this catalogue and we can only hope for its success. Hansi continues to be very hard at work which mans she is never "off," i.e. without work, even though, you can believe me, it is no longer absolutely necessary for her to earn money as far as it affects the personal, modest needs of the three of us. On the other hand much of our income goes for other purposes, apart from our voluntary and obvious obligations without which our life here would indeed be joyless. The mail alone is a steady item in our budget and could easily serve one person to make ends meet provided he lives very economically! But that is simply something we could not do without, as others appear to be able to. Now just before Christmas everyone makes gifts to every one else, especially among colleagues in a work place such as Hansi's, next week there is a big party in Jersey in honor of Beatrice, Herman Handel's daughter who'll be 17, complete with artists, singers, etc. Though the brothers lately always complain about business, for one's children everyone is willing to court bankruptcy—when the little daughter orders her Daddy to stand on his head then he'll do that too! In short one needs a lot and we thank God that we can afford at least some of it. Fortunately, as far as my own personal needs are concerned I need almost nothing since I came over here very well equipped, and am very protective of all my clothes. Unfortunately, my toiletries I had brought over are slowly shrinking and with every disappearing remnant of shaving soap there goes a piece of my heart not just because of reverence but also because these things are really good, much better than anything you can get here. You may not want to believe it but America is not first in all those areas the way the advertisements want us to see it.

Last week I received letters from Heinrich, Mrs. Vally Nagler and also from Hansi Lakner, which made us as usual very happy. Mrs. Nagler sent us recently an undeliverable letter addressed to our old address on 174th Street. Even though we told the Postal service of our changed address I found out much to my regret that this does not work all the time. That is one of the disadvantages of living in a country without mandatory registration laws. I therefore ask you to continue writing to our address c/o Handel. I have mailed every letter to Hansi Nagler from his mother, approximately 4 or 5, and the last one included a few tough English phrases by Herbert telling him to be a good boy and not to forget his mummy! That boy seems to be having such a good time there he forgets everyone and everything! As soon as we get news from him again I shall mail it on.

We were also very happy over Hansi Lakner's lines especially that she has learned to accept her situation and is not even very unhappy a about it. Last week I visited with her relatives George and Marianne Bachner and George promised me, that after the January 1st tax dead line he will send a supplementary affidavit for Hansi; he is now a jewelry designer and works independently in his own office on Eighth Avenue. I am also enclosing a letter from Robert Lakner who... *[Letter ends here]*

#34

New York December 27th, 1940

My dear sweet mother, dearest Marie and Emil,

Dearest Mama and Ella!

I've waited in vain now for a long time for some news from you—I had to decide to write this letter right now without any news from you even though I long especially this time to hear from you hoping to learn how you my dearest mother are doing. I console myself with the thought that there hasn't been any mail at all from abroad; so there may be many letters from you under way, I am sure, which will bring us good news about your health as well as that of all others.

We are moving into a bad time of the year, weather wise as well as in other respects and I think back of the past year when your letters reached us only very irregularly and you didn't get any mail from us at all from January 1st till the end of March. But I believe it won't be that bad this year—air mail especially with Europe is far better than last year and the delays are caused most likely by climatic conditions prevailing over the ocean at this time of the year.

In New York, however the weather is more beautiful than anyone can imagine. Yesterday, Christmas day saw a clear blue sky with radiant sunshine. Temperature was almost 20° (70°F), people strolled along without their over coats and on upper B'way where we live one could believe it was like the Easter parade. Last year it was so cold we froze our ears off. I must repeat it: the climate here is most peculiar and there is hardly another country where one can find such contrasts: tropical, polar, oceanic, dry as the desert or humid, whatever you wish! I must again admonish you watch your health and especially mother and Mama should take their walks only when the weather is clear and dry. You all have to remain healthy not only for yourselves but also for us.

Last week we visited once again in Jersey at the previously announced family party. There were a lot of people, I estimated ca. 60 persons, and that is quite a crowd for American flats even if they are proudly called 6–8 rooms "apartments." These kind of 8-rooms would fit comfortably into your corner room in the Vereinsgasse! Still it was very nice and they showed us off to their other guests; yesterday we as well as Otto received a thank you note in which they wrote that we "brightened" their gathering—they wrote this literally—asking us to visit more often and not to stand on ceremony by waiting for a big invitation. Fact is, they live very far; the roundtrip takes at least 3 hours, not to mention the expense. But time is something we simply do not have enough of, even less than money. If there is a free moment we use it to write letters. Both of us, Otto and myself brought some nice presents. They asked about each one of you, especially about Regine/Dora and they never fail to inquire whether there isn't anything else that could be done to expedite their coming over here. Unfortunately that question taxes also our wisdom and all we can do is to provide comfort and counsel courage. For everyone there it will be his hour of success, only you yourselves must not give up, either. Even Jonas, that modest, withdrawn man was there with his wife and of course Hannah with her husband. They sent special greetings for you dearest mother and they hope that you're well again.

Here is another joyful piece of news: after a long interval during which I worried considerably I received a letter from Olly in which she writes that she is well and healthy but most importantly she is now the proud possessor of an American visa! Unfortunately she must continue to be patient since the ship transport with U.S.A. is very rare and berths on ships are given out on a first come basis. You can imagine we are very happy and hope that Olly with her cleverness will surely succeed in grabbing at least a small space in some corner of the ship's dining room! This week I shall meet again with a sister of Epstein's in Riga who only recently arrived here from Italy. She came to visit me not too long ago but I was not at home so she just left a message saying she had an affidavit for her brother. Now I shall learn how much truth there is to that. My real hope is Olly who, once she is here will be able to do something not only for her parents but most likely also for her sister Elly.

Once again I am alone in my office since the boss went on a trip shortly before Christmas and won't be back until after New Year's. He is traveling with his wife this time (they are after all only recently married), partly for relaxation and partly on business. On the occasion of the holidays he remembered me rather generously, which made me quite happy since it came unexpectedly. In addition to a few small token gifts, such as cigarettes in luxurious wrappings, there was also a wallet with a ten-dollar banknote. Herbert was particularly taken with the wallet, because it is very "American," a so-called "billfold" of the type every American carries with him. You see, Herbert was always annoyed that every time I took out my European wallet it became immediately clear to any one watching that I was a refugee. Herbert of course attaches great importance to hiding his European origins, in whatever way possible and that certainly extends toward outward appearances. But I will tell you that I continue to carry my good old wallet precisely because it is large and has a lot of room in which to store all mementos of you, your photos, your letters in contrast to the "billfold" which is designed only for checks and dollar bills from $1 to $100—the latter I am sorry to say still not being part of my daily possessions. By the way, Herbert too received a similar "billfold" from a girlfriend in which she included a very nice rhyming verse, half English half German, on the occasion of Chanukah. Hansi received a giant box of candies plus a day's full wages. Maybe this will strike you somewhat suspicious as seen in the light of our European experiences and especially when you recall the times of the collective bargaining agreements of blessed memory. But these do not exist here and so it depends all on the free will of the entrepreneur. On the other hand here almost every one has the opportunity for employment, while over there only salaried personnel received Christmas bonuses and of course the millions of unemployed got nothing.

Here is something else: Fritz Neumark—he is the blond one of the

Neumark boys—came to visit me and afterwards we went to a Café. He has been here for nearly 8 months and finally managed to get my address. He had only sad news from Belgium among them that his father had died. When I listen to such news I thank the good Lord that as long as you cannot be here with us you are at least not in B. or France or England. It is terrible what people there had to go through and still are going through. You my dearest ones you must have patience, for you too a good hour will come, just do not lose your courage.

Last evening Grete Brainin and husband came to see us. We invited them on account of Heinrich/Helly since we wanted to know how matters stand with respect to the supplementary affidavit that was to have been guaranteed through Mrs. Redlich by her brother. That matter is now delayed since now is the time when most people are in Florida on vacation. Please give them our best regards and they must not lose courage. If only a way would open up from Vienna! May the New Year bring them as well as all of you the fulfillment of all your wishes! Herbert finally received a letter from Hansl Nagler, which I shall forward directly to Vally. Please, dearest Ella, do me the favor and alert her in case that letter to her arrives later. I am looking forward with great longing to you next letter, and if such arrives I shall immediately write you again. In the meantime my beloved mother, Marie, Emil, Mama and Ella I remain with kisses and embraces as ever your Emil.

[End of Letters from New York, 1940]

Vienna Letters, 1940

Vienna, January 1, 1940

This is first of all for you, my dearest Otto: we acknowledge your letter of December 16 that actually came two days earlier than Emil's. I immediately answered it with a postcard. I am happy to learn that thank God, you are both doing well and that you're already earning enough money to enable you to live decently and, if necessary, even buy some things that you're absolutely in need of. Obviously all that requires a great deal of drudgery and it occurred to me how wonderful it would be if mother Bock or myself could be with you and run your household while you're working—but, unfortunately nothing like that is going to happen very soon.

And now to you my dearest brother—I can read between the lines how unhappy you are, being still without a "job" *[uses English term]*. You mustn't feel like that under any circumstances. Eventually with the Lord's help you will find something that suits you. Just be patient and recall what it was like here. And you are also hurt because of the matter of the ship tickets, aren't you? When Willy doesn't want to contribute anything then that's just the way it is. I recall how I used to chastise you when you said Willy was not a good person. Now I can see that this is really so, just as you always said. Mama Schab is very hurt that he doesn't write at least a few lines, not even from the children and that is really the least you can ask of one's children in times like this, when letters are our only joy!

You dearest Hansi, seem to have more luck, your flower manufacture has proven itself most reliable, but then you are also very skilled; and it pays well too, with $12.00 a week. But isn't it also too demanding for you? It'll be better once Emil finds some employment, and it'll come, you'll see!

Today Donath left; he'll board the *Vulcania* in Triest on January 3rd. I have given him your address. We rented the room he had lived in: it's in the Lessinggasse 15, not too far from here. The Tragholz's too, have found lodging there, and moved in today—we'll follow them probably Thursday or Friday. It has gotten very cold now and we have lots of snow; there we shall have an iron, wood-burning stove with which to heat our place; oil is scarce and very hard to get. During this whole bothersome move mother will be staying at Mama Schab's. Just now Ella came to visit. I sold the writing desk and the cupboard where I used to "hide" our cash. It is so difficult to sell anything—they all want it for nothing. Just now one of the movers was here—he asks RM35.00 for the move plus tip; that's plenty!

1 am responsible for cleaning-up the flat we're moving to—because right now it is a pigsty. But what can we do? As matters stand we are lucky: I've got the kitchen almost for myself alone, and it is close by; the room itself is separate, and the W.C. is in the anteroom. Hopefully it won't be long before we can leave, too. My dearest Emil, you're really wonderful! All the messages and numerous other requests entrusted you by all the people here you have delivered, forgetting absolutely nobody. The good Lord will surely reward you! Mr. Streit really appreciated the postcard that you got from his nephew and he is very curious what you two talked about. Well, "chapter Hans" *[Hans Samec, Olly's fiancé who had left Vienna on a Shanghai visa]* is also complete since he's gone now for almost three weeks.

So now you must think only of yourself, Emil. We were happy to hear about our Herbertl. Thank God he is doing well. How did you spend the holidays? Nothing was going on here—it was just sad for us. Last week we had mail from dear Irma. She wants us to come there *[Palestine]* illegally. She suffers greatly not being able to help us in any way. From Mama Bock we received recently a small package of butter. They are not permitted to send anything else from Switzerland, I believe. That is really too bad because we can use everything here....

I embrace all of you my dearest one, and I kiss you one after another, I'm always thinking of you, your Mom, sister, sister-in-law and aunt Marie

Many, many kisses from Grandmother and from father a Very Happy New Year! A better and happier one than the last two. Also many heartfelt greetings to all the dear relatives there, especially to Hannah and Husband.

#40

Vienna January 24th, 1940

My dearest, beloved ones,

We shall have to get used to the fact that the mail is no longer as punctual as we expect it to be, now, during this extraordinary cold spell, which creates all kinds of additional problems, especially for airmail! Consequently you all need not worry right away should there be a delay in postal delivery. In your last letter, dear Emil, you were concerned about the housing situation as it affects your dear ones. You will be glad to know that I can tell you that the move transpired without any problems, and that everything went quite smoothly. Even though their new quarters are considerably smaller, I can reassure you that especially your mother adapted quickly and well to the new situation; in fact, as she mentioned herself, she feels even better there because, unlike in the Vereinsgasse she is almost never alone. In the new place she has quickly made contact with the people who share their quarters, and has found them agreeable and friendly. The couple that has lived there originally is really quite nice; particularly the woman is very obliging. So when Marie and your brother-in-law are not at home, well then, Mother Secher spends her time with the dear neighbors, something she really likes; I recall from her three day visit with us, that she loves to talk, is indeed quite a little chatterbox, so now there is more opportunity for such exchanges. By the way, great-grandmother Secher never fails to mention how happy she was at our place, being in my care etc., she really just liked being with us. In the morning—she slept next to Great-grandmother Schab, she too, being served breakfast-in-bed, we lit the fire a little earlier than usual, and only about 10AM did one of these Great-grandmothers finally drag herself out from under the covers, with the warm water, of course, already waiting, while the other great-grandmother enjoyed just a few more winks. They kept endlessly gossiping throughout all this and at night there was of course the warm water bottle already waiting in the bed; even the meals were very much to her liking as I told her I cooked only with margarine— and she chose to believe me! Brother-in-law Emil appears to be somewhat of a fatalist, and he too, is satisfied with their new quarters, especially since he has found there a new chaver with whom he can schmooze to his hearts content, as well as share a little Schnapps. Even Marie who at first was very anxious and quite unhappy during the first few days—I'm sure you recall how scrupulously clean she kept her own flat—is now reconciled to the situation and very glad that it is behind her. I am going into such detail just for you my dear Emil, because from your letters and many questions I can see that you want to be informed about every little detail—that, if truth be told, you'd prefer to experience everything together with them, no matter how bitter that experience would be for you. Your running into Annie Kohn for whom you always had a liking, is really wonderful. When she visits again, please give her our best regards. We also really enjoyed the letter from Hannah—it is very moving to see how much kindness exudes from it. We thank her for her good letter and ask you to convey all your relatives our most heartfelt greetings. We were shocked to read the news about the auto accident, but hope it turned out not to be too serious—that must have been quite a shock for all of you there. Please write us about the condition of that poor lady and give her our best wishes for a speedy recovery.

And now it is your turn my dearest Hansi! I hope your feelings are not as easily hurt as those of our mother, because I addressed myself first to Emil. It just happened this way. I shall attend to all your requests and hopefully Helly will soon be able to take them along. Are you again working in the factory, or are you working at home? Unfortunately I still miss some news either by or about Herbert. You can't imagine how anxious I still feel about him—he did after all do much of his growing up in my presence and so I feel especially close to him. Yesterday came a lovely letter from Friedl but no one else had added to it. It came via regular, not airmail and was dated 25. XII. I am very grateful for your efforts on behalf of our affidavits. Victor especially will be pleased. My joy, of course is only a very mixed one! I don't want to burden you too much, but please could you possibly think about the Braun sisters and whether some of the many committees there could do something for them. These women have absolutely no other prospects. The most difficult aspect of such an undertaking is undoubtedly the fact that these three insist on not being separated. There is nothing new from here. Mama was examined by a public health official and our request for an extension to the eviction from the apartment was endorsed. Until now there hasn't been any final decision, but I hope it will be favorable for now.

Dearest Hansi, Mama won't write today because she is still offended and her feelings are hurt, because until now you have not written once to her personally. I try to dissuade her from that attitude but she won't listen. This is all based, I am sure, on a certain jealousy because Emil, in every one of his letters directs so many affectionate words to his mother, while nothing comes from you. That makes her feel slighted and even humiliated in the eyes of others. Of course I am not supposed to tell you this and should just send you her best regards. That Herbert doesn't write to her personally also weighs heavily on her mind. Her attitude makes it

also difficult for me, having to concern myself in these difficult times
with such personal vanities. Let's
hope you haven't forgotten her birthday! Did you also have such bitterly
cold weather? We've had 10–15
degree Celsius for weeks. Today the
temperature actually fell to -3C.
Where Victor is they actually have
30C and even less! That surely has
got to be terrible if you are not used
to it! Heini has made up with Tanya
again and Willy Neumann is still
here. ... *[illegible]* were also forced to
vacate their apartment and now they
share one room. My dearest Herbert,
your not writing makes me very sad.
Nevertheless I am embracing you as
well as your Mammy and Daddy, as
ever your Ella

Ella Schab, sister of Hansi Secher (née
Schab) (1890–1942?). She was killed in
KZ Auschwitz.

#37

Vienna, February 9th, 1940

On the 8th of this month your dear letter of 5 January finally arrived
but I believe that there is still another one outstanding from you, approximately end of December, in which you would acknowledge my letter of
26 November; you ought to have all my letters by now, I think. The news
from here is not exactly pleasant, but what am I to do? What else can I
write you my dearest ones? We would be satisfied, if things remain as they
are as long as it doesn't get worse, but it is generally known that we shall
have to get out *[Ed.: M. uses the word* umsiedeln, *which can be variously
translated as resettlement, relocate or just plain moving].*

From Willy's family we received four letters in fairly short intervals:
Ada, Friedl and Franzi, and all of them were three to four months en route.
Even though they were completely out of date, we certainly enjoyed reading them; especially that Franzi has become such a clever girl! We have
every reason to feel proud of our nieces and nephews, they are doing well
thanks to their good upbringing as well as their natural talents—and that

is especially true of our youngest ones: Herbert and Friedl who moreover will have the advantage, once they are grown up, of being complete Americans. We learned from Victor that Herbert's picture was in a newspaper, in connection with his swimming; but there were no details.

Please give our best regards to all your dear relatives, also to Willy's family, I embrace you tightly, with kisses as ever your Ella.

Most likely we shall have to move from here in May—Mama wrote a card to you and Poldi a few days ago.

#38

Vienna, March 12th, 1940

My dearest, beloved children,

Thanks to a misunderstanding our letter, which was supposed to be sent together with sister Marie's mail, was left behind and that is why you're hearing from us separately. It's been a long time since we last had news from you directly; that is why our longing for you is so great, why we think of you even more than usual. By way of your nephew Otto we learned that you, dear Emil have already found employment, and the same is true of you, Hansi; but there were no details in his very short report. How are you my dearest ones and what is little Herbert doing? Did he get my letter to him in English? And did he laugh a lot about it? Well that is exactly what I wanted! I cannot possibly tell you how much I miss that boy! How do you get along with Willy's family? Did you already meet Dr. Weil? Are you getting together with the Becks and the Bohrers? Have you got any news from all the other children? We hear that all of them are doing quite well—Ernst seems to have really hit it off with his enterprise, and for that I thank the good Lord most fervently. Would God that you too are doing so well! Unfortunately we are again restricted to the minimum of news from our loved ones. That makes our loneliness even harder to bear. Otto's report to his mother-in-law arrived rather quickly. We're all healthy at this time but our lives are monotonous and triste; when you were so used to crowded togetherness as we were, you feel this loneliness even more and that saddens you much. Victor in Riga too, writes less often. What else can we do but try to be patient and hope that it'll get better in time. Ella as always is wonderful, continuously busy and ever so patient—may the good Lord reward her a thousand fold! I kiss and embrace you a thousand times, as ever your faithful mother and Omi.

How are your dear relatives to whom I also send my heartfelt greetings? What about starting your household again? Are you still living as guests of your relatives?

Probable date: March/April 1940

A single page headed III in Omi Schab's handwriting.

...would be unscathed past that. When you get this letter the worst should be behind us, or at the very least we'll know in what place we shall get some rest. Yesterday sister Marie came again with a long letter from you and we all sat around the table listening carefully to her reading the letter since she cannot leave it here and will take it along immediately. Mother Secher doesn't like to part with them for very long she guards them as the apple of her eye! Your lines and reports, dear Emil are always so interesting you are a real model letter writer. Your questions will be answered very thoroughly by your sister and mother. Much you already know. Mother Neuman has given me a request for you, which she asks that you carry out for her: Mrs. Neumann's father Philipp Löwy, born in Czernowitz, near Tabor, Czechoslovakia, had three brothers who allegedly emigrated to the U.S. in 1848 and there changed their name to Louis *[Ed.: more likely "Lewis"]* also a sister, married name Brandeis and they all settled in Milwaukee (Wiscotin) [*sic*], so there must be children and grandchildren around today. Maybe you could find out who of their descendants is still alive—they were all born in Czernowitz (Bohemia). Please dear Emil, do her the favor and write to those people. They are reportedly very well to do and highly respected. It's quite possible that may lead to an affidavit, maybe for Heini and Willy N. You dearest Hansi, much thanks for your very long letter—I am now well satisfied and wish that from now on you need not write so much as you are so busy with your job. I simply couldn't explain it to myself why you hadn't written, especially in the beginning soon after your arrival that you should've so little to say to your mother. But now I learn that you had indeed written, already in November and December, as evidenced by those letters that arrived only a short while ago! You must know my dear child, that this is my only pleasure to hear from you my beloved ones! Have you heard from the children, from Ernst, from Rudi, from Victor? What do you say to Felix's letter?! Isn't he a sweet and good person? Be sure that Willy, too, gets to read the letter, he feels quite close to Felix and will surely be happy to read it.

My dearest sweetest Herbert, many heartfelt thanks for your dear letter. Partly I have already answered it and the next time I'll write him more. Today I just have to acknowledge all the greetings that were sent to us and return them, from Mama Neumann, Frau Dr. Warenreich, Berta, Rosa, Mimi et. etc. You my dearest ones I embrace most fervently, and greet and kiss you 1000x, faithfully yours in love and all my thoughts, as ever your Mother and Omi.

#40

Vienna March 18th, 1940

My Dearest, my beloved ones,

As you can see from the attached letter we wrote you already last week—we held it back because we hoped fervently to receive some news from you, and that actually came in the form of the Radiogram, for which we give a 1000 thanks, and which made us immensely happy! But that must have cost you a pretty penny! Due to the short report written by your dear nephew Otto to his parents, we weren't particularly worried about the state of your health, but we just would have preferred to hear it from you directly. Thank God, Emil has found employment; he must be patient, in time he too will find something more suitable, befitting his expertise and talents. My dear ones! That was a marvelous idea to send us that Radiogram. The two old ladies were beside themselves with happiness—grandmother Secher embraced me and just kept kissing me! Maybe I shouldn't have mentioned it—it'll make Emil jealous. We are happy, dearest Emil, that you've already found employment, and would just loved to know what kind of job it really is. We hope that all the mail will not have gotten lost and that in time it'll arrive in one piece. It would just be too horrible to contemplate if it had really gotten lost! From the other children we've received twice reports in great detail. They are doing real well with the coffeehouse—Ernst has again proven his ability; and the young pair with their little sunshine is doing ok, too. They appear to be very, very happy. Mümmel earns good money and has proven to be a very mature and intelligent person despite his great youth.

With Ernst's family they are getting along real well. They are especially fond of Ernst who assists them with friendly, fatherly advise. Ernst is sorry not to have more news from you, he has written you already two times. From Felix we had a very kind, sensitive beautiful letter. Didn't think he had it in him to write with such style and feeling! Having read his letter, I can now face the future bravely and without worry, because he promises me that he will work only for me and has already begun to save money, so that I would not have to work anymore. Well, that isn't really something I want—if that were the case I'd be better off than all the others who have to slave away! I am really longing for some useful work. Not that I am sitting here, resting my hands in my lap—yet the only satisfaction I get is the knowledge that I am helping our beloved mother. Keeping house under the prevailing conditions is not something to be enjoyed; and especially not now when we are technically in the process of dissolving this household. In May it will be serious and I would love to know where and how we are going to find shelter. I do not want to ask for another extension, since even if the court grants that, it is nevertheless quite possible that we would have to leave the flat at a moment's notice and this is an intolerable situation which has not let me rest for nearly 7 months—and I'd rather have this behind me! It is possible, of course that I may be sorry later for having held this point of view—but there's something we've all figured out around here: however it's done, it'll be done wrong! Becks really have a lot of misery. The German quota has been closed until July and that just exactly one day before their registration. Helly had already adapted to the idea of leaving her mother—and now nothing moves forward. Wally Nagler sends her best regards; her son, Hansl, is doing very well. She showed me a letter from him in English— he is already having difficulties with German; also a photo of him high on a horse! I embrace all of you and kiss you, as ever your Ella

---

#41

Vienna, March 28th, 1940.

To all my dear ones, Emil, Otto, Hansi, Stelli, and Herbertl!

This week was a good week since we finally received your dear letters of 25/II, 28/I and 14/I—that is the order in which they came, and today one from Mama Bock with your note of 8/III added, my dearest Otto. The letter of 14/I arrived this week on the 24th. You can imagine very well how overjoyed we were and now we really feel informed and are able to visualize your life there. We're happy to learn that you, Emil, already found some employment—in time, I'm sure you'll be able to find something more suitable. Now as to the contents of your letter: the Affidavit for Family Streit has not yet arrived, but in any case he thanks you most profusely for your efforts on their behalf. My sweet Otto, your mother-in-law in Switzerland writes that you sent her money so she can mail us some care packages—but that practice has been stopped and I am really sorry about that—Epstein in Riga, also writes that they can no longer send anything from there, which saddens him greatly—you can see, all the sources are drying up! It is a great pity, because that could improve our diet, but the good Lord will help. Dear Emil, Epstein also asks whether you couldn't aid him in obtaining an affidavit, since all emigrants are permitted to stay there only until May. He also writes that Hans has written to Olly, he could obtain her permission to come to Manila within 3 months. There is nothing special to report from here, thanks God we're all healthy, except for my legs, mother has recovered very nicely, she bothers me continually about writing, sits behind me and "dictates" to me, just as she did long ago with you: "schreibup." Today was the first warm and beautiful day! But what good does it do us? How did you spend the Easter Holidays? How was Purim? We couldn't even afford a dinner. Sunday Regine visited with us and Monday I went to see Mama Schab, at which time she gave me your letter of 14/I. My one and only Otto, you write that you go to see a movie, all decked out, aufgestronzt in your best, all the while thinking of me here. My dearest child I am just so happy when I hear that you all are doing so well and are satisfied; on the contrary, it gives me more joy and we do not begrudge you a thing. Only Stelli and Hansi I feel sorry for, they have to work so hard, hustle all the time. What I would not give to be able to help you all! Dearest Emil, Sundays mother and I always feel so wistful, that's when we recall how you and Herbertl came all decked out, aufgestronzt to our house that was our best time!!! This week we received a care package from Mama Schab—she had received it from Güns your old friend, Emil, now in a refugee camp in Belgium. He had addressed it for Family Secher; there was a little tea. I cannot describe how glad we were to receive this, since tea is always our evening meal. Please, dear Emil, thank him for us. My dearest Herbert, I thank you for your lovely lines, Omi Secher and I are so happy to know that you are doing well and can get an education; today Otto wrote that your report card was very good, that makes us even happier, be sure to study well and that will give us and your parents lots of naches. Uncle Emil sits home now most of the time, he reads and helps me a great deal. A *Tchoch* [coffeehouse] doesn't exist any more for Jews. Dear Otto, did Adler visit with you? Dear Stella didn't write this time—but I know she has a lot of work to do. Mama Bock is very good—this week alone we had four letters from her. Irma, Benno and Heinzerl too, have written us very detailed letters. So now I am satisfied, we should only get to hear good and beautiful news from all of you! Now I need to close, I kiss and embrace you all one by one and am as ever your mother, Sister, sister-in-law and aunt Marie.

My dearest Emil, I have great joy that you visit w. Fanni and H. and that they're doing well. And that Herbert is also doing very well, thank God—otherwise nothing special, With Kisses and greetings from you mother and Grandmother Secher, Fanni. *[Written in very difficult to read script, which actually looks like Yiddish. Grandmother Secher is obviously trying very hard to write in German—Ed.].*

[The next paragraph is written in Gothic script by Uncle Emil; a very precise, clear and educated handwriting—Ed.]

My dear ones,

First of all I should like to tell you that this week was a very happy one since we got letters from everyone, as of course dear mother has also told you; of course you know, dear Emil, that I have a lot of patience and do not give up easily, but you can imagine, how both your dear sister and dear mother carry on when there is no news from you for any length of time! My dear brother-in-law as far as your dear mother is concerned, I get along with her very well, trying to fulfill her every wish—you know how much she likes to be warm and so I always try to have some material to use for heating, once I even went as far as Floridsdorf for some coal, in the last three days it has got a little warmer.

I've lit the Petrol stove, so she can wash her hair and dry it. Now I will tell Otto and Stelli about myself; I am doing fine as far as it goes, I even earned RM30.00 last month, helping Streits and aunt Zillie to move—they are so clumsy, those two; then I got ... *[illegible]* RM15.00, so I don't have to ask mother for pocket money, and I can even contribute something to the household. Otherwise my dear ones, I kiss and embrace you all as ever thinking of you, your father.

#42

Vienna, April 1st, 1940

[Excerpt]

In 3–4 weeks we shall have to get out of our home and we still do not know where to, nor do we have any idea how it'll all work out. For us it will be an enormous step whose impact at this time is still difficult for us to figure in all its manifestations; all we seem to realize, Ella and I, is that we are just not up to it. But I keep thinking, no matter how it will turn out we shall have to learn to accept it.

Heinrich and Helly are still here and waiting for the invitation to their examination by the U.S. Consulate. But that too will work out. I'd be happier myself if they were already over there with you, then you Hansi, would have someone you can understand and who could listen to your worries. They come to visit every now and then and said they'll write to you soon. Imagine, about a week ago we received at our address a small package with tea for the Secher family from Family G. I am sure that is something Emil arranged; it was 8dkg and we immediately took it over to sister Marie who was very happy with it. Have you been together with Willy's family? And have you seen or spoken with our dear Dr. Weil? How is he doing and how is Willy's family? Do you have any news from the children? I have quite a bit of trouble with our dear Ella; she is so terribly nervous, this continued search for a place to live has absolutely worn her out. I am going to be very happy when this matter has been settled and we are past it. In any case from now on you must write to sister Marie's address until you learn our new address. We think a lot about you, my dearest ones, and I wait in vain that after a noisy ringing of the doorbell your laughing face appears in the doorway, or that of Herbert or of Emil! I have to give you also the most heartfelt regards from all our friends and relatives here, from the sisters Braun, from Frieda, from Frau Dr. Warenreich, from Bertha, Rosa and naturally also from Mama Neuman. All enjoy hearing from and about you. Have you in the meantime heard anything from Dr. Lakner?

I kiss and embrace all of you, your ever so loving your Mother and "Omi"

#43

Vienna, April 15th 1940

[Excerpt] ...I am almost numb from all these letters, can't recall whether I've acknowledged them all and replied to all your questions. Now let me turn to your last letter: I am glad that Frau Ringel has kept her promise and phoned you, and most likely told you everything worth knowing. For you, Emil, to soothe your anxiety about mother, how healthy she is and that she really is doing very well. Today, for the first time since we've moved here we went for a walk together, mother and I, because, as she says, if we are going to leave from here, she'll have to get used to the outdoors and today was really the first warm, beautiful day.

We had a fire going in the oven until yesterday. Yesterday we also had a visit from Frau Helli Beck—she brought mother an orange, an apple and a piece of chocolate; these things are rarities and it is really good of her to bring them. They've had bad luck—all those who registered until 10 September 1938 at the American consulate received invitations to the medical exams—and they registered on 12 September 1938! Also, the German quota at the U.S. Consulate is now closed until ca. July 1st. Of course, partly she is glad because of her mother whom she would have to leave behind. Please tell Hannah that all of us but especially mother are enjoying her lines and we thank her from the bottom of our hearts for all the good things she has done for you—but I also see that she is doing that not only for you but also for strangers! May the good Lord bless and reward her! Since it is already so late and also because of the pains in my feet, I shall go see Dora and Regine tomorrow and tell them about the boxes and they will be very happy about that. This afternoon Emil and I visited them because you have to register with the Jüdische Kultusgemeinde if you want Matzoth, and so we registered them, too—you get 2kl per person for RM2.00 per Kilo—well we have Matzoth, everything else is left to your imagination! But what's important is that you have everything you need. Dearest Emil, Helli also said she would give me money, but for now I do not need any. Also we really do not want to be a burden to you. Just stay healthy and save your money—later, I'm sure we're going to need some. when she does leave she will probably give us some and then you can reimburse her later. We visit Mama Schab and Ella daily. I feel so sorry for them and would only be too happy if their housing problem would be nearer a solution. Emil was with me and if they need anything done he is always ready for them. Dear Emil, I wrote you we received from Güns some tea and we were very happy about that because right now we aren't getting anything from anyone. Bread with some butter and tea is our dinner now. Maybe you can ask him to send another package. *[Page ends here]*

#44

Vienna, May 6th, 1940

[No salutation]

Today we received your letter of 4/21, which brought us much joy. Last week we also got a card from my dearest Otto, 1/19 and a letter dated 2/8, also an airmail letter dated 3/10; you can see from that how variable the time is for the arrival of these letters, but airmail is certainly the fastest. Much thanks to you my dearest brother for your detailed reports, mother especially enjoys them and I do as well. They are my only points of light right now. We've heard nothing from dear Irma since 3/16. Today I received a card from Mama Beck in Switzerland in which she advised us that she had forwarded two cards from Irma but I didn't receive any so far and that depresses me greatly. There are quite a number of letters that haven't reached us from them, including one that you Otto, supposedly forwarded at one time. Well the weather report for this week is bad, nothing but cold and rain. Last Friday was the funeral of Sigmund H. Emil and I went to the cemetery—I had a very hard time. His wife Irma has, I believe, an affidavit from Mendel—you know who I mean, Otto, he owned at one time the Sporting Good store Marathon. By the way, his mother was called twice for the medical exam to the U.S. consulate and each time did not pass, allegedly because of her eyes. Mama Schab has also moved, finally, it was a difficult job and Emil helped a lot—those two old ladies and even Ella did their best but they are not as agile as you, Hansi! But now everything is in order and actually they didn't do so badly. I am curious whether Ella will give something to Emil; she is quite economical. But I do believe there is no reason for that. Please do not mention this to her. May the good Lord only let us stay in our flats until we leave the country. Thus the Streit family had to move again this week, though they stayed in the same house, only now live in a small cabinet w. a kitchen that faces the hallway of the house. M. and Olga Last had to move last Saturday, they moved to the Balls, where already the Boyniters, the mother-in-law and sister-in-law of Poldi as well as a strange woman live. You can picture what that means, in view of Ball's great nervousness! Of course Emil has to help. It's not easy to do such heavy work when there is so little food. I don't have the strength either any more. Now, as for you my beloved, dearest Hansi you added lines made me very happy and I admire you. So now you are among the big-time money earners, and you've saved a lot already, haven't you? You're writing about the many things you are buying, things we only know by name and have forgotten what they looked like, and you are getting all that without ration cards! We don't even get the milk for the coffee. I get up in the morning and don't even know what to cook, if anything! So despite the fact that you work so hard, I do envy you. And now my dearest, good sister-in-law I wish you on your birthday everything good and beautiful, your husband should only earn enough so that you no longer have to pitch in, and we should all be reunited with all our loved ones. Amen to that! We're also very happy that Herbert has turned into such a model student, we're proud of him! Dearest Otto, dearest Emil you're writing about the money that Heinrich will give us. I do believe that if you write to them, they'll do this. Helly told already at one time that if I need some, she'll give it to me, and

Regine's sister, Ms. W. offered to give me money if I need it, but at the moment I do not want to go into debt. We're quite upset that dear Jonas is not very healthy; he must stay on his diet—such good and worthy people must stay healthy, My dearest ones, Emil, Otto, Hansi and Stelli, there is so much I need to write you, if only I could! Dr. Pollatchek and his wife who lived around the corner on Heinestrasse committed suicide.

Our dear mother keeps all your letters, and she makes such a to do if I want to have one to give it to someone to read, she will not let them out of her sight! My dear ones to day is Pentecost and a so a Jahr auf ihm *[Ed.: German/Yiddish dialect, meaning he should have as bad a year as we did]* cold and very sad, nothing to eat, but we trust in God, maybe the next year will be better. My walks are mainly to Mama Schab and Regine. Is it as cold where you are? It just will not get warm this year although I'd rather have it cool than hot, heat makes you feel weak, on the other hand its better for my rheumatism. My dearest Hansi, I read between the lines that you are not too happy, and yet I envy you—you too have already forgotten! Mostly we're happy about our American Herbert, I can't understand how he suddenly became such a model student. Just keep on studying, so that we can be proud of you! Dearest Otto dearest Stelli, I'd like to have a good picture of you both, please send us one. Did, you Emil receive the pix of the relatives, which I sent you earlier and which I know your collection is lacking. Father is here at the Tragholzs they are playing cards; H. Adler is there too. Other than that I don't know of anything I can write you. I embrace all of you and kiss you I always think of you, as ever your sister, sister-in-law, mother and aunt,

Greetings for all the relatives, mother still wants to add some lines.
MARIE

#45

Vienna, September 27th, 1940

My dearest Hansi, as well as all my other beloved ones!

So you roused yourself again for a long letter, as long as you could still spare the time. You can imagine how much we enjoy, in fact go crazy over it, when one of those letters arrives from far, far away enabling us to sit down for a spell and chat with you. Of course, every one wants to read the reports by himself. What you write about Herbert makes me swell with pride. Why shouldn't he be cheerful and happy? His greatest treasure is with him, his wonderful parents, and socially as well as academically he is quite successful. Again and again I thank the good Lord who let it happen this way—that you didn't have to abandon your one and only child to strangers somewhere. The good Lord should only continue to protect you and avert all unhappiness from you. I repeat my best wishes for the year about to end, for your good relatives who have done so much for you and others for which the Almighty will repay them a thousand fold. Give them our very best for having stood by you and others in such an admirable manner. Wish them a good Yonteff and also a good Taines. Please pray for something good. Best wishes also to your nephew Otto and his darling wife. This month there were also sad anniversaries and memories—it was this month two years ago that Ernst, Willy together with their families left us, two long years of vain hopes for a Wiedersehen and on the 25th of this month the anniversary of the death of our dear son of blessed memory, Friedl, and whatever else has happened in these two years. With the exception of our good Ella, they've all gone, gone to far away places—only we have to be patient—waiting and enduring, helped only by the still hope that sometime it will change, we'll just have to be there when it happens! Next week are the Holy Days. The first ones that we shall experience all alone. News from Victor in Riga is becoming less frequent, although he wrote a congratulatory letter for Grandmother Neumann's birthday (23 September) as well as a telegram. She also got additional congratulations from her loved ones in Berlin and in Meran and everything arrived punctually on the scheduled day. Of course, there was great joy, suddenly a ray of light and hope! Your lines, my dear Emil, I only got to read yesterday—as always they were very interesting, I can only continue to admire him on account of his writing ability with which he is so blessed. You have to give him an extra kiss, Hansi, from this distance he won't be able to tell that it came originally from an elderly lady! His personal affairs surely have no end, his indefatigable efforts to obtain sponsors for friends and acquaintances; but those people for whom he works with such dedication will be forever grateful to him, I'm sure. If you get together with the Beck family, please convey to them our best wishes for the (Jewish) New Year. The little Hansl boy, Herbert's one time pupil, will be very happy to read his mother's letter I read his letter as well as that from Emil. For today, my dearest ones, I shall have to close, I've already used up my allotted space. I hope at the time of this writing you are all in good health, as are we right now. I kiss you all a 1000x, it embraces you your ever lovingly faithful Mother.

#46

Vienna, September 30th, 1940

For all my beloved ones!

Thursday, 26.IX we received your dear letter of 8.IX and we thank you so much for being so considerate and writing us so regularly, it is our only diversion during these sad times, and we wait all week long and live off it as long as we can. Thank God that everything is OK with you, that at least you, my dear ones are healthy and satisfied. There is nothing special to report from here, it is quite cool here already. This week is Jonteff, but very sad, there is nothing we can give ourselves, mainly because we do not have anything. Nevertheless we are satisfied when we think of you, our loved ones, in the knowledge that you are at least fairly well off. Ottole, my dear one, I am happy when I hear that you can afford to buy something, both of you work very hard and you shouldn't deny yourself anything. Last week we received a letter from Harry in Belgrade, written for his mother, but without his address. He and Ellen [*brother & sister of Stella*] are happily married, but she is quite sick with a lung disease, something she probably caught as a child and which now reappeared; apparently she is well taken care of by the KG there. He doesn't seem to be doing so well (financially). Of course I didn't write this to Mama Bock. That poor woman already has enough ... Also do not mention this to Stella, she would be very hurt. Saturday we also received a card from Heinrich about Irma. Thank God they are all healthy and are doing well. I am very curious what they telegraphed back to you. I thank you especially, my dear children that you keep writing in so much detail and never forget anyone. Only dear Hansi is so very unhappy according to her last letter, and she has the least reason to be that! She is lucky enough to be together with her husband and child, when so many families have been torn apart from each other; her relatives on the different continents are doing well, thanks the Lord, and Mama Schab and Ella aren't doing so badly either, they are not suffering, thanks to Victor who is still able to send care packages from Riga. If she would see Helly or Dora she would thank the good Lord and be content with her fate! I can understand that she is anxious about her loved ones here and longs for them. But please, Hansi, do not be mad at me that I am writing this—there has been a great misfortune for all mankind, and we have to bear it patiently. Dearest Emil, what you write about your boss makes us very happy—maybe that will have some effect on your salary and let us hope to the Lord that you and Otto will soon be able to earn enough so that the women no longer will have to work. But in the meantime you must also thank the Lord that you're no longer in Europe. Our greatest happiness we experience over Herbert, he is, thank God, the happiest, and let the Lord continue to watch over him with plenty of Masl. Also that he is now such a good and loving son, makes us happy, he is a smart boy and he knows what his parents, and especially you are now doing for him. Well, that is all for today. All our best wishes for the New Year to you and all our co-religionists, from the bottom of my heart, as ever your mother and sister Marie.

#47

Vienna, October 1940 *[no specific date]*

My dearest beloved!

   This time two letters came from you—14th & 18th August. Thus even greater happiness. I can read Marie's face as soon a she enters whether or not there's been mail. If there is, her whole face beams! So now, dearest Hansi, you've left the artificial flower trade and have picked up again with tailoring which you've hated all along. Well, when it pays better, one can tolerate it more easily. I admire your ability to use the language much more easily now, in view of your well-known lack of talent in that respect! Again and again I resolve to take some English lessons, but I cannot find the necessary peace of mind and the time, in general; something is always happening that doesn't let you relax and, on the contrary, puts your nerves under even greater stress. Just to take part in the lessons without being able to prepare for them adequately, serves no purpose. The Becks had to move again, now they are living in Dornbach quite nicely, but much to Hellie's chagrin, lonely, isolated, very cold in the winter, and far from all those other things, such as shopping etc., so everything will be more complicated. *[The situation of the Becks is curious when compared to others who had been left behind. Heinrich, who had been the General Manager of a large concern, often traveled abroad and frequently had the use of a company car. Hellie and mother were best friends; Heinrich and father were on good terms. I cannot remember anything about their family, other than that there were no children. How they managed to end up in that rather well to do suburb and without, it appears, having to share their residences was never explained. They had fairly close relatives in New York and they relied completely on my father to establish contact with them and persuade them and act as their sponsors. That became one of the major tasks to which my father dedicated his time and effort, alas without success.—Ed.]*

   [Ella continues]: They are very bitter about their relatives in NY, and

feel that they neither care nor want to do anything to help. That seems to be especially true of Helen and Oscar who wrote long letters to them as long as Hellie and Heinrich didn't ask them to do something; but as soon as they asked their help a great silence descended interrupted only by occasional, totally indifferent, unconcerned short messages on post-cards.

Today I am meeting with Hansi Lackner in order to give her the enclosed letters; from one of them half was missing—it was torn apart in the middle.

Dearest Hansi, Could you get in touch with that old, very rich lady who refused to do anything for the Epsteins in Riga because they were too "old," and get her interested in the Braun girls? Those women are younger and well able to support themselves with their skills: Gretl and Mimi are skilled seamstresses and Mimi can also knit and has made all kinds of sweaters, skirts, knit suits etc. Frieda is a professional cook and Mimi and Gretl are also good cooks. By the way Gretl said she'd come up with an address you can get in touch with. Dear Emil, the catalogues you requested are currently not available but I am on a list.

As far as Oscar is concerned, Hellie thinks that he must be quite well off; he has supposedly a good job and Helen also earns money with sewing of gloves; their son has a job as a tutor and that should take care of him, so, acc. to Hellie, that should enable Oscar to do something for them. About his general situation auntie Beck ought to be able to tell you something after she returns from her visit to them. Victor notified us of a package under way and possibly also of one for the Kuplers. Unfortunately, that second one, sent to the Kuplers, never arrived. That is also the first package of its kind that did not make it. All the others we got very punctually. Does the messenger boy attend school again?

Many kisses especially for him. Embraces and kisses for all of you and give our regards to your kind relatives, your Ella.

#48

Vienna, October 18th, 1940

All of you, my beloved ones!

This week I received your dear letter of September 30th from Mama Schab and I thank you ever so much. But I prefer it if you write to us directly because I notify dear Ella the very same day that we have mail from you. Father was over at Mama Schab fixing their blackout window shades, and he brought back your letter. My dearest Otto you say I'm such a good writer, but I'm not doing it because I want your praise, rather it helps to relieve my heart—when I write I feel so close to you—even though I cannot write about everything I would like to. This week we had no mail at all neither from Mama Bock nor from Heinrich, Benno's brother; he too is a poor soul to be pitied. Thus I have no news from Irma, either. Well, you get used to everything, the good as well as the bad. So I am dependent only on you for news about my dearest Irma. Again another week has passed. Today is Sukkos—but we do not have holidays anymore, only when we receive mail from you, that's our holiday. Now we have quite agreeable, cool weather, but we have already prepared our little oven, because if it stays like that we shall have to get some heat for mother who feels cold easily.

My dearest Emil, Yesterday it was exactly a year that you went to the American Consulate for your examination and on the 30th it will be a year since you left us. We had only one wish, and that was for you, Hansi and Herbert to cross the border without problems. When you had gone we suddenly realized how sad it has gotten around here; nevertheless I am so glad that you were able to leave at the right time. If only there would be for us at least a glimmer of hope! Lord knows how long this will take and whether we'll still be alive then! We are glad to learn that Olly has already got her papers, Lord willing she'll be happily over there very soon. My dearest Stelli, I thank you for your lines—I know the women over there have a hard time and frequently work harder than the men! To have an occupation during the day and then come home at night and still do the housework—must be exhausting. Oh, if I could only be of some help to you now! I hardly do anything now—I go to bed at 8P—but I can't sleep.

21st October.

My dear ones—yesterday came your dear letter of October 5th, wasn't that wonderfully fast? If only it stayed like that. So you had a pleasant time for the Holy Days and when I read your letter, Emil, detailed as usual, I immediately thought back on past times—will they ever come again for us? Dearest, sweetest Hansi you say that Ella should find out from the U.S. consulate what registration date is now being processed and how far into 1939 they are: I can tell you that, too, since it interests me just as much as Ella: they have now reached October 1938! Those on the Czech or Polish quota, like mother, and us don't have a chance unless a miracle happens. But even if it were our turn, we couldn't go because right now no visas are being issued.

You see, we shall have to be patient—but that is difficult when I think how long it'll be until we can embrace you all again. But we are satisfied if the mail continues to run regularly and brings us good news from you. Dearest Otto, on the 14th October I received a card from Heinrich about Irma. He writes they are in good health and earn enough to satisfy their needs. Zwi(ckerle) *[New Hebrew name for Grandson Heinzi]* has really shot up in height, they sent pictures of him. I would like very much to have pictures of you, real good ones; please send me some. Dearest Emil, you're really wonderful and don't forget anyone. Just now Erdheim is here and he sends his best regards. Frau Uhrmacher I see rarely—she doesn't get any news from her children and husband. Her father has died.

Fr. Prdszly. continues to be very good to us. Mama Schab will write to you about all the others you mention. She will also send you a poem written by Victor on the occasion of his grandchild's first birthday! It is very sweet and moving. They are also getting a care package, but unfortunately there is none for us. I could go on, but Grandmother is waiting to write a few words. I heat since yesterday but in the rooms it is still unpleasant. So long, dear ones I embrace and kiss you. Always thinking of you, your mother, sister, sister-in-law and aunt Marie

Thank you for the postal coupons. Father too, sends his regards.

Grandmother Secher writes: *[Ed.: barely legible in Yiddish-German script]* My dearest Emil, The good Lord will reward you for what you're doing for poor Olly—she has no mother and no father now. I have sleepless nights. What else should I write? My heartfelt greetings and kisses to all my dear relatives from mother and grandmother und aunt. Now comes the 30th of October and for me that is a big holiday! As ever your Secher.

#49

Vienna, November 1940

[No Salutations]

Though I usually write Sunday or Monday, I've been waiting for your mail so that I can acknowledge it, but nothing has come so far. Writing is much easier for me if I have some news from you. This week there isn't really anything of importance to report. On the 30th of October we remembered that we said farewell to each other, sad memories and of course tears, the longer it takes the more hopeless it seems to us that we shall experience once again embracing all of you, my dear ones! It is sad here, the days are so short, the evenings long and so terribly dark, that gives us so much time to think and that is really not good. Father was over at Helly's during the week, he did some errand for them and Heinrich gave him 5 pair of socks! You, my dear Emil will understand what that means in these times when there is no way one can afford to purchase anything. Today we received a small package of butter, ca. 40gram, from Victor in Riga that made us very happy. Tea or cacao would have been even better since I can use it for our mother; today I bought her a small bottle of cognac. Yesterday I went to see the doctor again on account of my pains; he prescribed Diathermi—we'll see whether it helps. My dear ones what's new with you? This week must be quite exciting for you because of the Presidential election. It should only be good for us J. Sunday I was at Mama Schab's and everything is OK there—and yesterday Ella came over to us. Regine and Dora have also recovered and with their aunt everything is the way it has always been, please give Hannah again regards from her. From Irmi we unfortunately still have no news and you my dearest Otto will know how that affects me—to have absolutely no contact with her. It is terrible. 6.XI. My dear one, I have not closed this letter, because I awaited some news from you—but there wasn't anything. Dearest Emil, mother will add a few lines the next time as I want to carry this letter to the post office before it gets too dark. Now I am going to close; please excuse the bad writing, I am almost groggy. Dearest Otto, is the address on your letter your home address? Farewell, you all my loved ones, you are being fervently embraced and kissed by your grandmother, father and your always of you thinking mother and sister, sister-in-law and aunt Marie

---

#50

Vienna, December 2nd, 1940

All my dearly beloved!

Finally, after a fourteen-day interval, did receive your dear letter of 15 November—arrived on 30.11 (Saturday)—and today your letter of 30.October. From this you can see that the letter mailed later arrived earlier. Thank God, we are so happy to have again news from you, and hopefully, you've also received the letters, which I regularly mail to you every week. Only it hurts me to admit that we cannot give you any pleasure with our current mail. We did receive the money and I acknowledge that in my last letter. After all the letters arrived I saw that RM15.00 were intended for Bohrer's sister, and I sent the money to them with Rosa. Mother is, thank God, well again, and we're quite satisfied with that. Only we have other worries. In my last letter I wrote that Mama Schab had to move out. My dear Emil, what we went through in the last few days on account of Ella and Mama Schab I cannot possibly describe for you. Please do not mention anything about that to our Hansi, she would be so hurt by it—but just imagine this: on 30 November was their original deadline to relinquish the apartment but only today were they able to find something, and that only a small cabinet (room)—poor Ella and my Emil ran around like crazy, but absolutely nothing could be found! And they still have so much junk; she even had ordered several bags of coal, also some groceries only where can you put them?! Well, what my Emil all did for them ... since 20 November he was at their house daily, helping to pack until very late at night; Mama Schab is only too pleased and begged him to come because poor Ella is totally down and out. It is terrible, they wanted to move into a Pension, but that wouldn't work and besides means for that are insufficient. Please notify Willy he must send them money. But Mama Neuman cannot live with them now. She would like to live with us, but we too, unfortunately lack space—you know we have a small room with one window and we are already three people. Nor do we know what's going to happen tomorrow. We shall try, that maybe she can sleep in Tragholz' room and can eat with us and keep us company. And still, my dearest ones, I'd be happy if everything with us remains as it is. My dearest, good Otto you write that it is possible to send 4kg packages via Holland. I really appreciate that but I'd prefer if you would send money, because $10.00 is a lot of money and here we get RM50.00 for it. We won't starve and are satisfied with anything, if only we know that my dear ones are healthy and doing well in other ways. Yes, we're willing to suffer through anything as long as we know that our loved ones in distant lands are ok! There is so much more I could write but I simply cannot anymore. Forgive me, if I do not reply to everything you want to know, but you my dearest brother, please continue to write so lovingly and so detailed, we live only through your lives. *[Page ends here]*

#51

Vienna, December 5th, 1940

[No salutations]

We shall be only too willing to bear whatever comes our way, provided that we know you are all right and doing well. And you my dearest Emil, please don't lose your courage, if everything doesn't go the way you want it right away, it'll happen, you'll see if only you have patience! Our dear mother is already worried that you may want to move away from New York; I too, would like it if you stayed together with Otto, you two understand each other well, he looks up to you as an older brother. We don't want to be ungrateful, the good Lord who has helped us until now will continue to be at our side. Well, I want to write about our housing problem. We got an extension until the end of December to stay in our old flat. We knew of an empty flat in the Glockengasse, in a J. house, which we wanted to rent together with the Tragholz family. So, father stood in line all day Thursday, from 8AM till 4PM at the housing bureau; but J's do not get empty flats, only one room with sharing of kitchen. Father, therefore asked to be assigned a room at Olga Last's place—she still has two rooms of which one is already rented. She was supposed to leave today for Belgium, so we might have had the room with use of the kitchen and father actually got permission for us when it turned out that another person had also received permission for that very same room and he got there half a day earlier. And Olga, on Saturday received a telegram, urging her not to leave! The poor soul had already shipped all her luggage! Now she has ship tickets and not even a place to sleep. Oh dear, do we have misery and pain here! Mr. Streit is happy that you haven't forgotten him, he asks you to get in touch with his sister and nephew and present his situation to them. Enough for today. Why doesn't Herbert write? What are you doing my dearest Stelli? And you, Hansi? Farewell all of you who are so dear to me, I kiss you all, your, mother, sister, sister-in-law and aunt Marie. Many kisses from grandmother and father.

I received a letter from Epstein in which he informs us that all emigrants must now leave the city of Riga and are being moved into the hinterland.

Do not forget to give my regards to the relatives. Dearest Otto—Today 5/12 came two letters from Mama Bock: one from M. to his parents, and one from Irma dated 19 November. He asks about you, he is doing all right, he plays in a Cabaret and earns a little money that way—Wand is also there. Kisses, your mother.

#52

[This letter was written by Ella to her brother Victor and his wife Hedi]
Vienna, December 19th, 1940
My dearest Vikerl and Hedi!

I am terribly sorry that we have not written to you in such a long time and consequently contributed to your worries about us. Unfortunately it isn't possible to reply to your telegram, which arrived today, in the same manner, and so I am hurrying to provide you with some news from us via airmail. God knows, we've been through some very disagreeable experiences, preventing any one of us three to reach for pen and paper, even though we often talk about the fact that our silence must cause you considerable worry. We had to vacate the apartment again, this time within ten days. That's bad enough for two old ladies each of whom is over 80 yrs old; but it wouldn't be the worst thing provided one could at least find something suitable that would match our already very modest needs. I cannot possibly describe for you everything in detail, but I must say that these have been the most stressful days of my life—and the same goes for the two poor old ladies! For 14 days I ran around like crazy from early morning to late evening, searching for something that could also accommodate great-grandmother Neuman, so she can be again with us. Every evening I returned without success, and with every day the situation seemed to become more hopeless and I became more desperate. At home everything was helter-skelter, there was no time for shopping or cooking, and if it hadn't been for dear Mimi we would most surely have starved! We had to vacate by 30 November but were able to remain until 4 December—and when we still had no place to go by that time, mother and I moved in with Kuplers, who only have one room for themselves, and Mama Neuman moved in with Hugo. Since we couldn't possibly stay with Kuplers for any length of time, mother and I decided to move into a very small cabinet, while Mama Neuman remains at Hugo's. We stored the greater part of our furniture and goods, since other than two beds for sleeping and one washstand plus a little cupboard there was no room for anything. The cabinet is connected to two rooms that can be reached only via the cabinet so that this becomes an almost continuous through passage, which is nearly unbearable for our mother who had already suffered immensely during the moving process at which time she also caught a bad cold. She coughed for at least one week and there recurred a bladder infection, which thanks to careful nursing through many week, we had almost managed to control. The two moves in such a short time and in this cold are of course responsible that it has grown worse. To this you must add her exhaustion and general weakness that for her as well as for myself means added burdens and suffering. Since we moved in here—12 days ago—mother has not left her bed. As far as I am concerned I have lost so much weight I look again like a skeleton; and I am also in a desolate mood from which it is hard to recover in this environment. I can wash myself only in the morning prior to 7AM or sometime late at night, when the traffic through the room has ended. In the next room lives a woman with a 20-year-old son who is paralyzed, a terrible misfortune, and in the second room... *[Page ends here]*

#53

Vienna, December 30th, 1940

All my loved ones!

Since 15 November we are without news from you—you can imagine our mood—still, we know that you are not to blame. The letters are somewhere, if only I could find out whether you're getting my letters. This condition of being cut off from you, all my dear ones, is awful—everything can be borne much more easily if we get good news from you. In any case I am writing without let up every week. So, we are all of us, thank God, healthy and only wish to hear the same from you. The notice from the Deutsche Bank about the RM100.00 being under way, I acknowledged already in my last letter. I hope it gets here after New Year; again many thanks for that. The frigid cold has decreased somewhat.

The holidays were just like any other day, dreary and sad.

I spent a day with Mama Schab and Ella who have already come to terms with their housing. None of us know what will happen with us. On the second day of Christmas I went to Regine and Dora and there too, nothing has changed so far—these two women, if I wouldn't go to them, they'd never move about at all. My dearest ones, today this year 1940 reaches its end. What will the next one bring? Will it bring the longed for reunification with you? Yesterday my dearest Heinzerl had his birthday and that is already the third one without my being able to hold him in my arms and kiss him. How big my longing is for him. If we could just wait in peace and quiet until the day when we shall have the great fortune to come to you. Now farewell, all my dear ones, all the best for the New Year. etc. etc.

Also greetings from father

New York Letters, 1941

#54

New York, January 5th, 1941

My dearest mother, dearest Marie and Emil, Dearest Mama and Ella!

Finally we received mail from you for which we had been longing for so long; it was your letter Marie, dated November 26th, over a month old. You're complaining that you had not heard from us since October 24th, but in the interval I wrote at least 10 letters as you could easily calculate yourself. In many letters there were enclosures, postscripts, etc. On November 23rd I mailed an affidavit for mother. I hope that in the meantime you've received all our letters without interruption. We're approaching the bad times of the year and you will have to be patient just as we're over here. I doubt that it'll be as bad as last year, though. I am certain you will receive our mail and we yours regularly though in longer intervals. One the one hand we were very glad to receive your letter, Marie as it told us how our dear mother is doing well again, and that was also shown by her clear, lovingly written lines at the end. We were quite concerned about her, because I assumed that you, dear Marie don't always tell me everything truthfully about her. But I am much calmer now and I thank you dear Marie and Emil as well as all the others who helped you taking care of her. On the other hand your other piece of news about the renewed forced moving from certain residential areas, has again hit us hard. All of us especially Hansi are terribly sad about this, being totally powerless and thus unable to help you in any way. We've always taken comfort in the thought that despite the many difficulties you have to endure, you were at least safe under the roof, for which you had to fight so hard last year. All our sympathy and compassion is with you, dearest Mama Schab and Ella, being forced now in the depth of winter to search

157

for some modest housing. Again we're anxiously awaiting further news from you, which, hopefully, will tell us that you were able to put this too, behind you.

You looked after the three women, now including Mrs. Neumann, put them up in your place during the move and that surely helped them a great deal. We hope that everything went well and you were able to find something suitable in an area not too far from each other. This knowledge to be so far distant from you is terrible for us and we cannot avoid the feeling of having behaved like cowards when we left you behind. The only thing we can continue to do is to counsel hope, courage, and patience and that goes for everyone in our circle of friends and acquaintances over there. Don't ever give up, always believe that the time will come when you my poor, beloved will finally come over here and you will be compensated a thousand times over for all your suffering. We shall see to that. That is all we strive for, there is no "presence" for us, everything is temporary and provisional, we only work toward a common future with you all.

In this connection I want to say something that I probably shouldn't blab about as yet, at least as far as Otto is concerned. There is a chance that Otto will go into business with a small "luncheonette," the kind he worked at last summer. This is a combination of "candy store," Ice salon, Breakfast place and cigar store but which also offers other things such as toiletries for sale, and including photo equipment. These types of luncheonettes are sponsored and furnished in the most modern way by the large ice cream manufacturers who then lease them out for relatively small amounts. Otto is motivated in doing this by you and especially father who could be a big help later on; these shops are usually open almost 20 hours a day. Stella would of course continue with her profession, it would be foolish for her to give this up. The big season for these shops are summer and that is why he is already looking around for opportunities, in fact has his eye on several possibilities. His savings, added to a subsidy from his sister-in-law Hertha would be sufficient. Of course he would not give up his current job until the matter is completely negotiated. But even if nothing comes of it right now he will continue to look for something sooner or later where he is self-employed. In that kind of businesses one can easily make $35–40 a week and Emil would really enjoy doing that sort of work. Our family lawyers are also ready with all kinds of advice. Still, should it not come about now, it'll happen later and with more savings. Our only hope is that America remains that island of peace in this world in flames! The talk here is that the U.S.A. consuls do not put any obstacles in the way of granting visas if it can be shown that children are here even if these are not the actual sponsors of the affidavit. For others too, regulations should ease up a bit, it is rumored. You ladies, mother, Mama, and you two good people Ella, Marie you shall have a wonderful life here cared for by all of us; and when you become disheartened, my dear little sister, as I can tell from the last line in your letter, then just forget the present, think only of he future and us. There is little to report about us. We're all healthy and working. New Years Eve we did not want to celebrate so on January 1st we went to a movie, after a long pause and in the evening we were at the Liebermann's about whom I've written you several times. They live in a nice place in Riverdale and Mrs. Lieberman gets along real well with Hansi and they also have two daughters a little younger than Herbert. Do you want to hear something new about New York that city with which you should be quite familiar by now?

Well, the big news is the opening of a new Subway line which is designed to be another step forward in solving that biggest of all problems, the traffic problem. A few months prior to our arrival here a new line was opened as well, and I ask myself how were things before these two additional lines had been in operation? Nobody who has not experienced it himself can imagine the extent of the masses of humanity that have to be transported in the morning between 6–8 and again in the evening between 5–7. These are the terrifying "rush-hours" and in the evening I usually stay a little longer in the office in order to avoid the crowds. I don't experience it in the morning because I go to work like a diplomat at 10AM! On the average one rides the subway about 1–1½ hours a day and I am not exaggerating when I say that by the time you get to work in the morning you feel half dead from the pain inflicted on you during the "rush-hour"! Many years ago I saw a film in a movie theatre in Vienna, which showed a film about that and I thought it was posed and exaggerated. During "rush-hour" the other wise quite courteous and polite American loses all his manners and only the stronger arm or shoulder counts for anything. The new line provides special relief for Hansi, she can even sit down and arrives quite refreshed at her place of work.

Dearest Omi Schab, we assume that this letter will arrive quite some time ahead of your birthday—nevertheless please accept my good wishes now: Health, and again good health, unbroken courage and the hope of our early reunion, a "Wiedersehen" with at least a part of your children here in the U.S.A. All the other children will then have to make the pilgrimage to us in order to celebrate with you and with us a happy Wiedersehen! I wish the same to you my dearest mother, and also to the others, I am your loving, always of you thinking, embracing you, your Emil.

#55

New York, January 19th, 1941

My dearest good mother, dear Marie and Emil, Dearest Mama and Ella! Today we received both of your letters, dear Marie, one dated December 16th, and the other 23rd, they arrived at the same time. We hope that our letters, which you received since then also provided you with a little joy and encouragement, proving that you, my dearest ones, are always in our thoughts, all our aspirations and wishes are geared on only one goal and that is to bring you here in the fastest possible way. Most of all, we want you to maintain the unshakable conviction that over here, across the ocean, there are a few people whose every heart beats for you, who feel every pain that is inflicted on you, maybe even more so because we are so desperate in our total inability to lessen your pain. Not to be able to do anything for you is in some ways worse than to share the same sorrow and pain together with you. We thank you dearest Marie for your faithful and steadfast reporting; we can imagine how difficult it must be for you, given your physical condition and bad health, your heart filled to the brim with mental anguish, to sit down and write. Hansi especially thanks you for giving us some news about Mama and Ella who at present are in no condition to bring themselves to write even a few lines, also that you and Emil do not leave them to fend for themselves and visit them with some regularity. The only real happiness we experienced on receiving your letters was the news that our good mother has fully recuperated and we could tell that also from the dear lines she added which always make us happy. We beg of you, dearest mother, to continue to take care of yourself and follow bravely all instructions that concern your state of health—especially now in the cold season of the year. We know from the newspapers that it is very cold over there, even though here it is really mild, quite in contrast to last year's weather. The last 3–4 days it was quite cold, probably the coldest we've had so far, accompanied by a strong snowfall. This was followed by ice, which made every step a danger to life and limb. But today it rains cats and dogs the streets are oceans of mud giving rise to some polemics about "America." How is it possible that in "America" whose name we never pronounced without rising from our chairs and raising our hats, it is not possible to clean the streets quickly and thoroughly?! It is a good thing that we brought along our overshoes from Vienna—in this climate they're really priceless.

Your letters arrived together with one from the Streit family, which really made us very happy. As chance will have it we are in touch with the Streit's nephew, Tibor. Lately that has been more via phone and postcard since he moved to the Bronx, which is quite far from here. Earlier he had lived quite nicely together with his brother in Manhattan. However, as it sometimes happens, the wives of the two brothers did not get very well along with each other. He has a very cute child, a red haired boy who appealed especially to Hansi who loved to talk to him. A few days ago Tibor called and asked whether Hansi, in case she didn't have a job at the time, would come as a sort of "nanny" for the boy. His wife is gravely ill and the child too, had just recovered from a long illness. Obviously Hansi cannot do it since she has a job. She will however visit with them as soon as possible and use the occasion to talk with them about the Streit matter. I do not think much will come of it—he is not doing very well, in fact he moved to the Bronx, because he could, allegedly not meet the rents here. He also has to support his mother who lives somewhere outside of the city because she did not get along with either one of her daughters-in-law. But tell Mr. Streit not to lose his courage. Once they have reached a certain point something will be done for them together with all the relatives who are living here. Please give them our best regards and we thank them that they care so much for you.

We're glad that you have news from Irma. She is really wonderful and will not forget you any more than we do.

Our life follows its regular routine, we work a lot and thank God we are all healthy. All members of the Secher family get together in the evening and, not having seen each other all day we then exchange our events of the day. Hansi leaves the house already at 7AM, Herbert an hour later, and I about 9:45AM. Of course I don't get home before 7:30PM and then we share our only common meal which Hansi has prepared ahead. Just as we used to in Vienna in earlier times we now have occasionally a goose or duck, which last us for the whole week. Much to Hansi's regret the geese here do not have any liver. Generally this kind of poultry is not much in favor over here. The "Turkey" on the other hand ranks almost as a national dish. After every Sunday or holiday it is common here to ask one's friends or acquaintances the following day "How was your turkey dinner?" Well as far as I am concerned they can have their "turkey"! For me it is simply too tough. When we're invited somewhere, you can bet 100:1 they're going to serve us turkey. And while we torment ourselves with that feathered bird we are continuously asked "how do you like the turkey?" to which we as polite candidates for citizenship always answer: "Oh, we just love it!" which means variously: it tastes great, there isn't enough, I just love it and must have more. They are really quite childish sometimes, these Americans, but maybe that is exactly why they are so lovable. Every Sunday we're having dinner at Hannah's and she regrets that we cannot come more often! But we simply cannot manage it. Every evening at 9PM sharp she calls and we have to tell her exactly how we spent the day. While we're talking Safirstein usually interjects something, such as inquiring whether Hansi's boss will soon declare bankruptcy! He says that because he is happiest when Hansi is "off" from time to time so she can take a well-deserved rest. He too is anxious about his brother who together with his son is interned in some French camp far from his wife who is now in Paris.

My dearest ones I see that I have reached once again the end of the page. Farewell my beloved, dear mother, and all you other dear ones. I am always with you and I greet and kiss you all most fervently, as well as our dear friends, relatives, but especially Heinrich/Helly—how are they doing with respect to their housing, over here people are continuously at work on their problems, the same applies to Regine-Dora. As ever, your Emil.

#56

New York, January 27th 1941

My good dearest mother,

All you my loved ones, Mama-Ella, Marie Emil! Again another week without mail from you, and that means I go about the weekly letter writing with a heavy heart. One tortures ones brain, what's going on with you, how is your health, this is the worst season of the year, do you have enough to eat, enough to heat and our biggest worry are you my dear ones in the Lessinggasse still in your flat? Your last reports were full of fear that you may lose even this roof over your head. One keeps hoping for the next letter, which will put a stop to all this self-torturing, and yet we are anticipating even that news with certain Angst. What kind of news will it bring?

I can see I didn't chose a good day for writing to you, I am myself in a very depressing mood. Who or what is to blame? Is it the weather, which once again displays its most disagreeable side: bitter cold, snow, snowstorms, so-called blizzards, one can barely stay upright when walking on the street? Is it the radio, which feeds us with bad news from every corner of the world? Is it our failure until now of every, even the most intensive, effort to bring you my dear ones over here? And that goes also for Heinrich/Helly and Regine/Dora, all of which simply makes us feel even more ashamed. All those others on whose behalf we have exerted ourselves—even to the point of being able to see some success, almost reveled in our hopes to see them soon over here—well, their coming over here has been moved even farther down the road. How we worked & sweated for Olly, overjoyed to learn that after a year she finally got the U.S. visa in her passport—only to learn now that all transatlantic passenger traffic on ships has been stopped and no date has been set when it would again be reopened.

Thousands of people there have already the U.S. visa in their passports and no opportunity to make the crossing. Many of these visas have already expired. Victor and Hedy on whom we expended every possible effort, whom we eagerly looked forward to seeing soon, now write us that for the present there is no possibility to come over here. The U.S. consulate has been moved from Riga to Moscow, the HIAS has been dissolved, the closest one is in Lisbon where they now have to write in order to get any information. All these news, are they responsible for making me so miserable and sad?

Just now I received a letter from Hans Samec in Manila in which he asks to give Olly a letter. He too heard, already months ago from her that she had received the U.S. visa and naturally assumed that she must have arrived here by now.

All this is so incredibly depressing today would be especially good for me to have your comfort, my dear mother and you all. In Vienna you always were full of hope, mother, and were the one who kept me going when I seemed to have lost my courage. Then it always came the way you predicted. Dearest, good mother, write me a few words of comfort again in Marie's next letter. If you and all the others write that you're not losing hope than everything will be easier for us as well, because we know absolutely that the time will come when we shall be able to embrace you over here.

We transmitted another amount for you this week: RM115.00. I assume, dear Marie, you already know, should this letter arrive later than the money that RM15.00 are for Bohrer's sister. Bohrers write to us fairly often and they are doing all right, though they always have something to lament about.. Although they don't talk about it, we know for a fact that upon Ernst' passing they received money from his insurance, also some tangible assets, clothing, etc. They are still engaged in a search for Ernst' violin which allegedly is worth thousands of dollars. They suspect that his last landlady has kept it even though she maintains that he had moved out a long time before his death. Where he lived later they have not been able to learn, since he used to disappear for months and years without telling his relatives his whereabouts. Most likely he no longer possessed that violin for many years.

There is not much to report about us. We are healthy, thank God, if you disregard a small cold, which jumps from one to the other in the family. Right now it is my turn. The blame lies entirely with the central steam heating and the dryness caused by it. But that is the way it goes: you poor souls catch cold because you cannot get enough heat, and we malcontents complain over too much heat. We are all very busy with our work and that is our only pleasure. Last week I bought a small life insurance. You can't escape that here once you have a regular income. I resisted it as long as I could, in view on my experiences over there. But let's face it, here it is quite different, far more secure and a person without any insurance is looked down upon.

And now my dearest ones would you like to hear some real New York news? Well, last week we were reminded that in New York reality may be just like those crime stories and detective films we used to watch so eagerly over there. Around noon, on the busiest corner of New York, maybe even of the whole world, in fact that corner is called exactly that, two gangsters, each of whom was armed with three revolvers, terrorized thousands of people. They stormed through shops and department stores and left four persons dead after a wild, barely twenty-minute chase. A policeman, a cashier (Jew) whom they had robbed, a Jewish chauffeur who tried to come to the aid of a policeman and one of the gangsters. The other gangster will in a few weeks occupy he electric chair. For once another side of America which we now, too, have the privilege of knowing.

Otto just phoned to tell me he had received a letter from Hermine Gutter. But he'll surely write you about that. In any case the Palestinians will be very happy because they hadn't heard from her in months and had become very concerned. Otto's voice over the phone sounded just like my baritone, and sure enough he informed me that he too has a cold, though otherwise he feels fine. He too, is sad not to have any news from you and so we comfort each other. I hope that Mama and Ella have gotten used to their new surroundings.

I close again, my dear ones, I kiss and embrace you my dear mother most fervently, Mama and Ella as well, and you dearest, good sister, also Emil and remain with the plea to give my best greetings also to our dear friends, relatives and acquaintances; and so I remain as always, your Emil

P.S. Did you receive the food parcel? It was sent to Mama's old address, Taborstrasse 21

#57

New York, February 4th, 1941

My most beloved mother, all you dear ones, Marie, Mama-Ella, Emil!

Last week there arrived even two clippers. The first one didn't bring anything from you, though we did get a letter from Frau Lakner and her daughter Hansi. You can imagine how anxious that made us 'cause we could recognize that the mail is working but you had not written. Hansi Lakner does not mention you in her letter; she doesn't even know Mama's new address and asked me to send it to her. Only with the arrival of the second Lisbon-Clipper a few days later—a rarity at this time of the year, for two planes to follow each other in such a short interval—did we receive the so fervently expected news from you, my dearest ones. However, there was nothing from Mama Schab and Ella, although your news about them, my dear sister, has put us somewhat at ease: you write about your last visit at Christmas time with them, and we cannot repeat it often enough, my dearest, good Marie, how much we thank you for your continuous, faithful reporting, because we can understand only too well, that writing letters is difficult for you, since you intentionally do not want to let us know more about your worries and sorrows than is absolutely necessary. What saddens us, nevertheless, is that you have been for so long without news from us, even though you're all smart enough to realize that this is not our fault. You all know that we too, send news without interruption, no mater how difficult it is for us to sit down and write. This is not due to a lack of news or because we're not doing well, health wise: On the contrary! We could fill pages if we wanted to tell you about our daily life here which for us has already become gray, every day routine—but for you, who live in a different world, still offers a multitude of interesting experiences—furthermore we are well satisfied with our lot here no matter how far it is from meeting our expectations, because it still exceeds by far that of thousands of others who arrived in this country under the same circumstances and subject to the same conditions. Nor should you worry about our health, which is fine except for an occasional small cold or similar ailment—this time, it is Stella who relieved me, and took turns with Otto! Hansi and Herbert came off the best this year—and the only thing about which Hansi kvetches continuously to me and gives her much pain in that very small cubicle within her heart where alas, vanity resides, is that she imagines having gotten fat! What makes writing letters to you so difficult is that I can never sit down to this task without feeling shame. Soon it will be 1½ years since we left you behind with the solid promise not to rest or relax until we shall have brought all of you over here—and now after these one and a half years we are not any further than we were at that earlier time and for the time being all we can do is to try and comfort you! Our relatives and acquaintances however, say we are ungrateful—the very fact that almost two years have passed since your registration at the U.S. consulate, is an advantage that money can't buy. It simply cannot last much longer and you all must not lose your patience and become despondent. There is no need on your part to worry about any difficulties in connection with the affidavits, and even the question of transatlantic fares must not worry your heads. That too will taken care of, partly in cash, partly with the sale of some valuables, we're continuously calculating and know that there is no reason for anxiety and worry on your part, even though one has to figure $400.00 or more per person since the trip to the port city must be included. Here we've heard that there are now direct trains from Berlin to Lisbon, with the cost of a one-way ticket at $60.00. Also, that the U.S. consulate in Vienna is operating again is generally known here, and possibly governed by less strict regulations than before; that gives us hope with respect to Heinrich/Helly and Dora, and to be able to see them here in the not too distant future. So please my dearest ones, remain strong and keep on hoping with us!

I also hope that in the meantime you have received at least part of our much news sent to you and are in that respect reassured. Over here it has gotten really cold—we have everything that belongs to real winter weather: ice, lots of snow, but also a wonderfully azure blue sky with glorious sunshine—a ride from our house with the bus along Riverside Drive through the snowed in parks sparkling in the sunshine is truly a pleasure which I allow myself once a week. Once only because it costs twice as much as the subway (10 cents instead of 5) and it takes about an hour and a half, when the subway covers the same distance in exactly 18 minutes. Even during lunchtime I take a short walk through Central Park located close by. There are no coffeehouses here where one can drop by read leisurely the newspapers while drinking a miniscule cup of Mocca; that is simply unheard of. Of course there are literally hundreds of small eateries all around me, but as I mentioned in one of my earlier descriptions, these are merely feeding troughs where one would be regarded as plain crazy, should you remain only one minute longer than it takes you to wolf down your sandwich together with a cup of coffee. And, always around the lunch hour, when I sit in one of these coffee bars, after which I walk around a bit—provided the weather is fine—I think about how, on the other side, I use to take a quick bus or trolley ride to your place, dearest mother for a short schmus. Once you're here I'll do the very same thing, provided you'll live here in the neighborhood of the business district. But should you live farther out, where we do then you'll be able to enjoy me sooner in the evening. Farther out, specifically our Washington Heights in upper Manhattan, roughly the area from 168th to Fort Tryon Park, it is much prettier than downtown surrounded by all those skyscrapers. You all will be able to see for yourselves how comfortably one can live here and I can assure you there won't be any homesickness for you, as is the case with some idiotic Viennese emigrants.

Safirsteins managed to obtain a very good client, I believe I mentioned his name earlier—a Mr. Wien, indeed from Wien—through my intervention, and from his last business transaction they decided to buy Herbert a very nice new suit; i.e., they simply appeared at the house to pick him up and took him to the New York equivalent of the Viennese Clothes—Neumann, Howard's Men's Clothing Store, a gigantic store compared to its Viennese counterpart. They cautioned H. not to mention this to me until the suit had been delivered since he knew I would have refused this present! This was a case when you could depend on H. to keep his little secret. Fact is he does need some new clothes, has grown out of most of the stuff he brought from Vienna. So tonight he's taking out his new suit to the theatre, where he is going to see, together with his friends, a performance of Shakespeare's Twelfth Night.

Please tell Vally Nagler, that I've received her latest letters and have mailed them on to Hansl. Hopefully she's received Hans's second letter by now, again a regular Sports Report! The boy seems to be doing real well, which is why he is so forgetful concerning his correspondence with his mother. of course we always remind him in our accompanying letter quite sharply what his duties are. So there is no need for Vally to worry. Also, she doesn't need to send me any Postal coupons, since I only get a five cent stamp for them and airmail costs at least 30 cents. Instead she should pay postage for one of your letters to us occasionally. We all send her our best regards and really enjoyed her picture, which we showed to everybody here and then enclosed it in the letter to Hansl.

#58

New York, February 17, 1941

My beloved,

Something happened that hasn't occurred since my arrival here: I missed the last Clipper to Europe and consequently I am mailing you my next weekly report together with the previous one. It is not totally my fault. I had to undergo a minor "surgery" last week, that is, I had a tooth pulled that had given me a lot of pain recently. It was a wisdom tooth, in principle still healthy, but it was already loose and rattling around in a way that its root pressed strongly against my gums, which caused the pain. It could not be saved, (not even in America) and so it had to go! Looseness of such teeth is also part of the ageing process, I am told—but what's a body to do?!

I am sending you, and especially for you my dearest mother, a page from a letter by Olly that I received last week.

Isn't it awful, that girl after nearly one and a half years of waiting was able to get the U.S. visa and is still not able to make it over here. However, after a pause of three months a ship arrived from there with nearly 600 refugees on board. It is alleged that with the beginning of the warmer season ship transportation will improve and more people will be able to cross over. I wrote her that, too, and tried to comfort her. On the second (separate) page of her letter which I am not sending you in order to save postage, she writes about her dissatisfaction with her place of work, they're demanding an awful lot of her; she barely gets some sleep, mostly she spends the nights in the air raid shelters. She never forgets in any of her letters to send her regards especially to you, dearest mother and to ask about your well being. She knows, through me, that you had been very sick but by now has also learned of your recovery. I and everyone else here hope from the bottom of our hearts, my dearest, good mother, that you really feel fully recovered. Very soon now there'll be a change of season with improved weather and you won't have to freeze, being locked up in your room; hopefully, you too Mama are well again and we beg of you and Ella, to write us a few lines again, however short. Your silence is very depressing for us. Hansi feels not only hurt by it, but she is also very anxious.

Last Friday we had a great deal of excitement. Hannah called me in the morning and said a telegram had arrived from Dora, drafted by Hapag the German transatlantic shipping line. If only we can do it right—we do not want to repeat the mistakes we made when a similar telegram arrived about half a year ago. Hannah immediately telegraphed to the U.S. consulate and sent a negative cable to Dora. Hopefully, they understood it correctly and construed its wording the way it was meant and not how it was formulated. Of course, we shall do everything in our power so as not to delay their departure. We are really curious to read the letter, which Dora surely mailed at the same time she sent the telegram. Does she already have the necessary documentary substantiation: the notification from the consulate and, something we are most anxious to know does that include Frieda? Are they going to be here very soon, so that we can have direct news about you? And if they're actually coming, then your chances, my dear ones, must improve measurably. The affidavits for Marie and Emil are already in preparation and supportive documents will be added from very substantial people, this will be done also for mother, just in case.* And how are things with Heinrich and Helly? We shall not forget them but their relatives are unfortunately difficult people whose emotional sympathies and attention to this matter is severely lacking. We know that an affidavit from Irene, as sister, as well as from Oscar, as brother, carries a great deal of weight, regardless of how well it is funded. They actually are fully aware of this—and still they delay to get the process under way. Hansi is furious and threatens to lose her temper with them any time soon—but what can that help?! They will do it eventually, and I am sure they're having problems of their own—but we just won't accept that. In case another clipper arrives today, I'll add a few more lines. But for now I embrace you my dearest mother, Mama-Ella, Marie and Emil, many, many times and greet you in love, as ever your Emil

[Ed.: The reference to the telegram from Hapag and what follows in relation to it must be assumed to refer to the booking of passage on the ocean liners for which payment had to be made in advance, yet acceptance of it also depended on how close the prospective passenger was to the issuance of the U.S. Visa. The term "negative cable" probably depends on how the original telegram had been phrased; but it is also possible that this telegram inquired as to whether payment would come from private sources or from institutional ones such as the Joint, Hias or through the local Viennese Jewish community organization. In which case Hannah would say "no" (negative) to private sources in order to engage the institutional ones—at least that would be the official line! But if those failed the family here would naturally come up with the required amounts as undoubtedly was made clear to Dora in the personal letters. In any case, all that turned out to be a false alarm and neither Dora, nor Frieda, ever made it to the U.S. and disappeared.]

#63

New York,* February 22nd, 1941

My dearest, good mother, all my dear Ones!

This time, my dearest Marie I can acknowledge your dear letter of January 26, together with the long and loving lines added by mother,

*Dated mistakenly by father as: *Wien* [sic] *22. Feber 1941*

which made all of us very happy. But we're still missing a few lines by Ella and Mama. You do mention Ella's visit at your place, but in view of a report from Heinrich/Helly we are a little concerned over Mama. He says that Mama is confined to her bed and that she has an inflamed bladder, though that is slowly receding—on the other hand, you know we're always afraid we're not being told everything, as much as we want to believe that there is improvement, as Helly indicates. But we hope from the bottom of our heart that Mama is ok again and that the next clipper will again bring us a few lines from her. Helly writes that the doctor comes almost daily and we can imagine that this is a considerable burden on your budget. I have therefore arranged with Willy to remit the amount of RM150.00 especially since Marie already wrote on January 20th that you had received the RM250.00. As we wrote to you earlier we remitted at the start of this month RM100.00 (actually RM115.00 but 15.00 belonged to Bohrer's sister).

As soon as you acknowledge we shall send you some again. We are just so sorry that the food parcels have not yet arrived. In view of the fact that even in your letter of January 26th you still had no notice of the arrival of that parcel, we have complained over here and hope to get back the money, minus the amount for telegram costs, although that won't happen very soon.

This was sort of an experiment for us and if it had worked we would have made this a regular shipment for you and occasionally also for our friends.

It appears that you haven't received anything from Lisbon either—even though I gave them not only your address but also Regine's and Heinrich's address. In the latter case I have not yet paid anything, it is due only upon receipt of a statement that it has been mailed. Until now I have not heard from them and obviously neither have you, otherwise you would have let me know. From here to Lisbon mail takes only one day. If a letter is mailed just when a clipper is due to leave, it is possible to get an answer within 3 days since the very same clipper brings the mail on its return flight. And from Lisbon to Vienna by air cannot take more than 8–10 hours. It is with a great deal of regret that I see how fast we could correspond with each other were these normal times! But of course in normal times you, my dearest ones, would be sitting right here and there would be no need to write letters.

My dearest sweet Marie, as I already mentioned in my last letter, I am still missing two letters between your letters of January 6 and 20th—so far they have not arrived. We're still hoping that they'll be late.

I am really happy to hear that our friends come to visit you frequently and you help each other to brighten up your existence and make it more bearable. This way mother has a little company and can schmooze to her heart's content about us, which is why we have almost constantly the hiccups! How are Mr. Ball and family? Does he have news from his children? I haven't heard anything from Poldi for a long time; Richard, allegedly is coming over from England and has, I heard, the U.S. visa but like Olly, so far is waiting for transportation. Please give them our regards as well as Family Streit and all the others that come to see you and haven't forgotten us.

We are now deeply into the winter weather, snow, arctic type cold with storms one fears they'll bring down the skyscrapers. Despite the central heating it gets quite cold in our room at night. As I already told you we are living in a rather larger corner room with six windows, three on each side. In America there are no double windows that can be opened wing like, instead they are pushed up and pulled down. That means they never close very tightly and in stormy weather such as today, the curtains are always in motion despite all our efforts to make them airtight. Furthermore, central heating stops at 11 PM for the whole house—it is that way all over New York—in other words we freeze bitterly at night despite our layers of pajamas and robes, etc. and Hansi even sleeps with a wool cap. Believe me, there is nothing like a beautiful, big old-fashioned tile stove or the kind of fireplace we had in the Alserbachstrasse. But please do not think that it's all that bad: it is only for a few days that this kind of cold lasts around here. As soon as it gets a few degrees warmer, it is impossibly hot in these rooms. My dearest ones, I had to interrupt here because we just learned that a letter arrived from Mama/Ella, which Hansi hurried to pick up. To a certain extent its content have calmed us down, though it is all so sad. But everything seems to be out of date because just now the evening newspapers and the radio are bringing news that almost stopped our heart beat. We are terribly concerned about you. Isn't it possible for the Love of God that you can live in peace until such time you depart for overseas? Do you really have to be deported? Please write us immediately about that. Dearest mother, Marie and Emil, what is going to happen to you and Mama/Ella and all the others? Hansi is acting like a mad woman and we are getting headaches trying to figure out what in God's name can be done! We are all turning to you my dear Emil in the hope you can bring your calming influence to bear on the women. Helly Beck writes you are the optimist of the century! Please continue to be one. We know you will take good care of them.

Just now Otto walked in, pale and very disturbed, he had heard the same news that I did and since I started this letter yesterday before we had any idea of this entire goings on, he and Hansi will add a few lines.

Please my dearest ones do not believe that we can forget you for even one minute, and may you find at least a little comfort from that in your bitter existence. And please forgive us that we've not been able to do anything concrete for you as yet—that knowledge is already punishment for us. Write very soon, even if it's only a few lines.

We're considering sending a telegram, but we know you can't answer the same way. I've wanted to write much more, especially concerning Heinrich/Helly, but I simply cannot right now, Later, when we have better news about you. Only tell them this if, indeed you have the opportunity: I have already written to Strassman for Fred's address and will happily do anything she asks us to do in this matter. If we cannot do any more for them it should be of some comfort for them that it is possible to do a little something for her brother. That thing with Ernst in Ireland was a mistake, as we learned, too, when, together with Sigi Brainin we turned to him for help for Heinrich/Helly. Only a part of Ireland is a Free State, the northern part together with Londonderry, belongs to England.

I close for now, my dear ones, have courage, keep your chin up, think of us who are always with you in our thoughts, and your pain is strongly felt also by us. I embrace you my dearest mother, all of you my loved ones, write soon. Never before have we waited with such longing for mail from you. Thousand kisses your Emil

---

#64

New York, March 2nd, 1941

My dearest, beloved mother, All my loved ones!

For nearly two weeks we're in a state of almost indescribable excitement and anxiety. You can understand this only if you can realize even in a small way what you all mean to us and that our life here finds its meaning only in your life. Hansi is in a specially terrible state, she cannot sleep, the same goes for Otto—we call each other constantly unless we are at each other's house, we go over the news and tell each other the latest reports on the radio or in the newspapers. Our anxiety and grief, I am sure can be read from the telegrams we sent, and which you must have received already a long time ago.

The first telegram was sent to assuage our first concern whether you were still in Vienna; even though we knew you would not be able to reply, it served to quiet our anxiety when the cable itself was not returned as "undeliverable." Otto in the meantime worked feverishly on the affidavit for you and has already airmailed it to the U.S. consulate in Vienna with a return acknowledgement attached. We hope that you in the meantime have already received the notification from the consulate of its arrival there. Otto keeps blaming himself for not having it mailed sooner, but he wanted to avoid a renewal if it was sent too soon. In addition he counted on improving his position by going into business for himself, which would be looked upon more favorably by the consul. We've always figured that your turn would come approximately in the fall of this year. Who could've known what was going to happen! We always hoped that you'd be able to await your departure in peace. And now this terrible news! Otto also telegraphed you that his really good affidavit has been sent. But now we're in receipt of your cable you sent via HAPAG and our immediate reaction as one of satisfaction and joy that you were still in Vienna. Let me address myself now to the content of this HAPAG telegram.

My very dearest ones we are leaving nothing unexplored to do everything humanly possible to provide you with the opportunity to wait out your turn there until such time as we can embrace you over here. Thousands of telegrams were sent here and the whole emigrant colony is in an indescribable state of uproar, each one trembles over the fate of his relatives. We can tell from the number of telegrams that arrived here what mental and physical pains you had to endure until your turn came at the HAPAG to send a telegram. Again my dearest ones do not think for a moment that we've forgotten you, don't even think of us badly in your thoughts: we are able to raise the amount of $1,200 necessary for passage for the three of you, mother, Marie, Emil. The telegram came yesterday, Saturday morning, and we've done everything immediately, and in so far that was possible, given the fact that all offices close at 12:00 noon on Saturdays. Everywhere are immense crowds so we have to stand in line. We shall continue whatever is necessary on Monday and hope to bring it to completion that same day. So far we do not know whether we shall get the ship tickets directly from the Ship Company or via the "JOINT." In any case, just to be sure and to quiet your fears, we shall send a telegram ourselves. Everything I say also applies to Mama/Ella, of which we were able to convince Willy, with whom we're in continuous touch, personally or by phone, mainly through Hansi's efforts.

My dearest ones, I can ask of you only one thing: Do not despair, no matter what happens! Do not always assume the worst. Who knows whether all this might not actually favor our luck to see each other sooner than we expected? It is said here, and most of the American newspapers are reporting it, that there are more than sufficient quota numbers available to the U.S. consuls in Vienna and other German cities because for the most part these quotas are untouched so that even late registrants at the consulates can expect to be called provided they can show evidence that passage has been booked for them. Given this fact we are certain that the German authorities too, will let you await your exit from the country in peace. All of us ask you: Keep calm and do not lose your nerves however difficult it may be for you. We know of everything that is happening, more by instinct than through the official news organs, and every teardrop shed by you, burns us a hundred fold in our powerlessness to help you quickly. Keep yourself healthy and continue your will to live, for us! Again we beg of you to do that from the bottom of our hearts!

My dearest ones, we're also working on behalf of the Braun-girls, to get them at least an affidavit—but I can't tell you how difficult that is! All those in our circle of relatives and acquaintance are already acting repeatedly as sponsors and consequently are not in a position to sponsor new affidavits. This is the problem: many are most willing to help and have repeatedly provided affidavits, but the vast majority that is certainly able to do so, is still indifferent or just lacks the necessary compassion; only when it hurts them directly can they realize the extent of the misery. I could write volumes about my experiences here with that attitude since my arrival 16 months ago. Nevertheless, they must not lose hope. We received a postcard from Sigi Brainin in which he tells us that he mailed a very good affidavit for Helly/Heinrich. We shall call them today and ask how matters stand with respect to the tickets for passage. We think about them a lot right now even though we know that doesn't really help them. It brings one to despair how little one is able to do to help. Please tell Helly that I got Fred's address from Strassman together with $3.00. He writes that he has also turned to Richard for a contribution and that I should wait for that before I mail anything. I hope we can send $10.00 from the three of us within a few days. Strassman also says he just recently sent Fred $10.00 together with a care package.

What I wrote above applies also to Regine/Dora for whom, I hardly need to mention this, Hannah is doing everything possible.

From Irma-Benno we've received within a relatively short time (mailed 2/04, arrived here 2/27) very satisfactory and detailed news. Maybe Otto will write to you about this in more detail. The poor guy, just like Hansi cannot pull himself together for a few lines to you. He was here about a half-hour ago, tried to write you, gave it up and ran away promising me something for the next day. I have to be the hero for all of them in this respect.

Last week long delayed mail came from you, dated January 4th and 14th. I knew that these letters were missing and complained already in my last letter about their absence.

From Ella also a letter dated January 23rd preceded by a letter from Mama and her dated January 26th. We were deeply moved by its content. You are my dear good Ella a small, great heroine and we can only hope that Mama's condition has improved despite the recent excitements.

I know that you my dear mother are the greatest hero of them all, so continue to be brave and patient. Emil, my good man we ask of you that you help these women the way you always have. I hope for the best and expect that you must do the same. I am with many kisses as ever your Emil

---

#61

New York, March 7th, 1941

My dear, good mother,

All my loved ones, Marie, Emil, Mama, Ella!

By mistake Otto's letter was not enclosed in my letter of March 2nd. He must have had a case of absentmindedness since he himself took this letter to the post office, thought he enclosed something and then noticed on the following day that he still had his letter! So what did he enclose? In any case we're mailing his letter with the next clipper, so that especially you, dear Marie will not feel hurt.

This time we acknowledge your dear letter of February 2nd and a postcard addressed to Otto of February 4th. Their content reassured us up to a point with its description of your daily life, of your modest room as comfortably warm, agreeable neighbors for some social life etc. if it weren't for the fact that much of it is already out of date based on the events of the last few weeks. You could probably tell from our telegrams that we more or less knew that something was going on but it was not specific, more likely than not incorrect and based mainly on rumors. The newspapers and radio news had always been very short and mostly very matter-of-fact. The same is also true in the matter of the booking of ship tickets. They say visas will be issued not only on the basis of evidence that the tickets have been paid for, but only if the name of the ship and its exact departure are also provided. This is not quite possible since the American passenger ship companies even upon full payment will not make the exact departure date available but merely put you on a waiting list.

The local "JOINT" has now taken over this process and accepts directly the payments for booking of passage and the telegraphs the Viennese KG, which in turn informs the individuals that payment has been received for them.

However, the "JOINT" accept payments starting with $20.00, with the balance to be paid by the Committee. There are also rumors that the "Joint" may charter a ship or even several for the purpose of transporting Viennese refugees over here. They say here that the German authorities are satisfied if you have the information from the KG that somebody in the U.S. has paid your ticket either in full or has only made a payment. Is it true that the U.S. consulate issues visas also to those with late registration numbers as long as they can show paid up ship tickets? In any case, we don't know much about all this and I'd be very grateful to you, dear Marie if you can report to me exactly what you know or what people are talking about. I hope that on receipt of these lines you've already been notified by the U.S. consulate that your affidavit is on file there.

Otto sent it to them via airmail, registered and with a return answer receipt.

But let me get back to the ship tickets once again: since we were unable to learn anything from the ship companies we, like thousands of others decided to make use of the "JOINT" and have paid in for each of you $250.00, for a total of 750.00. However the full passage costs a little more than $400.00 per person. But please, don't be afraid that your departure will fail due to the still lacking $150.00. If the Committee is unable to come up with the balance than we shall of course pay immediately the missing amount for all of you. Don't worry about that for even a second. That we haven't done it so far is due to the fact that we still don't know for sure what is going on. Also everybody says and there are announcements everywhere to that effect that paying in to the JOINT is still the best and most secure way. It is a fact that many thousands have taken that route for their relatives in Vienna and when recently, last Tuesday I came to the JOINT at 6:00.AM in order to make a payment it was just like those "good(?) old" times in Vienna when we had to queue up at all the government bureaus. For many days now, people stand in line there, mainly from Vienna, and even if one has never met them, one easily recognizes them as Viennese. Everyone tries to find out something, many actually believe that the JOINT will buy tickets for those without means, but of course that is pure speculation. Each one is trying his utmost to help his relatives the best he can and often people come with their last $10.00 in the hope that the JOINT will come up with the rest. I repeat again for you not to worry about that, as soon as we know something more concrete, we shall either pay the balance to the JOINT or transfer the passage money to a ship company. For the present it is simply assumed that the route via the JOINT is the preferred one. Naturally, Willy also took the same steps for Mama & Ella. Both of us were at the JOINT on the same day and I even held a place for Willy in the queue. God willing that everything can be worked out and we surely hope that what appeared so terrible at the beginning may lead to your arrival here sooner than we dared to assume originally. Just let us know everything you can find out and we shall do everything possible for you.

Mother, thank you for your dear lines, also so detailed and I as well as all the others are grateful from the bottom of our hearts that your appetite has returned and you even eat vegetables again. Unfortunately bad times appear to be ahead again for you and we utter again our fervent wish that you keep calm, don't lose your courage and do not give up your faith in God. Everything is bound to end well and as I already remarked above, who knows maybe these events will bring us luck to be reunited much sooner than we had expected. I know you're the bravest of them all and you will help all of them, especially Marie to keep up their spirits. Continue to be just as smart and I pray daily to the good Lord he should keep you and the others in good health. I must reproach you a little, dear Marie, however, that you did not accept the assistance offered you by Regine's sister in February. Don't feel any pangs of conscience; the time will surely come when we can repay the extraordinary kindnesses of Miss Weissberg. We never fail to give her greetings to her relative Hannah. Hannah H. also writes directly to her, she told me.

Dearest Ella, as Hansi already wrote you, Willy would like a telegraphic acknowledgment, or at least something in writing in Ella's telegram about the eight ship tickets, Mama and Ella are also included. You see your names were not mentioned in that telegram, though that was quite clear for Hansi and myself. You know how suspicious he can be and furthermore he still is not as well informed as he could be, and he thinks all that is not really quite necessary. Nevertheless, we—meaning especially Hansi who went to great lengths—were able to convince W. to obtain the tickets. I am closing again for this time and embrace you my dearest good mother as well as all the others most fervently. We ask of you dear Emil, to take good care of the women but not to forget about yourself. With best regards to the dear Housemates to whom new ones have now been added, from your Emil.

#62

New York, March 14th, 1941

My dearest, sweet mother, Marie and Emil, dearest Mama and Ella!

This time we have lots of mail from you to acknowledge, all of which arrived on one day. From you, dearest sister, letters dated 9th, 13th and 17th February, all of which came with a lovely postscript from mother; from you, dearest Mama, the letter dated 1st February (mailed on 10th February), together with Ella's letter. You cannot possibly imagine how these letters moved us, especially as they are all from that very period during which we waited almost despairingly for any kind of news from you. We felt every aspect of your fears, terrors, but also your small hopes as if they were our own. We can imagine what went on with respect to the two Tragholz's, how they and you must have suffered; we know there's no end to your pain, that it continues without a break and that, consequently our own ignorance concerning your fate is not yet at an end. Still, you never once complain in your letters, on the contrary you emphasize your steadfastness, your readiness to face whatever may come—in fact, you who are so in need of comfort yourselves, are actually offering to give comfort to us, indeed praising our courage and fortitude! That really makes us feel worse since we know that it is really due to our own doing that you are still in the situation you are in. Why, in God's name didn't I go the American consulate sooner to register you there, what was it that kept me from doing just that? It would have enabled you to get out at least by June of last year when the exit through Italy had not yet been closed; and with an earlier date of registration, the process of obtaining a valid affidavit could also have been started much earlier—instead, we always thought the later that process starts, the better, since that would obviate any frequent renewals of the affidavit. But what's the use of mulling this over and over again, crying doesn't help either, it just serves to make our hearts even heavier. All of us beseech you: you must be brave, must hold out, draw on all your physical strength as you've done so far—there will be a Wiedersehen, no matter the obstacles put in your way. You're all so really wonderful—your letters make us incredibly proud—no one we know here receives such calm, loving self-assured letters! You can be certain that there must be a reward for so much courage and self-denial; we are also aware that your mood is not as cheerful as you pretend it to be—that you would feel a lot better if only you could cry on our shoulder and at least relieve your tsores in this way.

In the meantime, you Marie and you Emil should have received your notification from the consulate acknowledging there the arrival of the affidavit. Soon there will arrive additional so-called supplementary affidavits, for mother, Emil and Marie—all that, just so there won't be any unnecessary delay in case the original affidavits turn out to be insufficient. However, right now there is an approaching tax payment deadline, and once that has been met, the Handels will have these supplements notarized, so that they can show immediate proof that the taxes due this year have been duly paid up. Willy has also been asked to draw up a supplement, just in case, but again only after his taxes due now can be shown to have been paid. So please be patient for just a little while longer—we know only too well that you are not lacking in that, and anyway this is not something that requires any action on your part.

Have you received any notification from the Israelitischen Kultusgemeinde concerning the transference of money for ship tickets? Please write us about that—did it have the desired effect? Please write us about that. We are very glad that you've finally received the food packages—there is no chocolate in this combination. Our sweet little mother should mix a little cacao with sugar, that's how I always did it as a child, when I wanted Chocolate and there wasn't any in the house. Should we try another food package shipment and what would you like to have? And how are you doing money wise? Shouldn't we send some again? In any case do not refuse any assistance from Miss Weisberg when she is so kind and offers to help you out. We thank her and will show our gratitude more positively whenever we can.

What's new with Regina/Dora? Hannah has no written word from them and she is worried. For them too, everything would be almost ready including payment for tickets.

From Frau Lakner we received a desperate letter. Maybe you, Ella, could tell her that on the part of her cousin Georg Bachner everything possible has been done, tickets were paid for Hansi mainly through Dr. Wolf, affidavits are under way as well, however, again only for Hansi. We have written to Robert in Singapore together with the Bachners, since we had not received a letter from him in a long time. All possible efforts are engaged in on behalf of Mother Lakner. We are all doing everything possible but it is as if we're on an ocean liner that is shipping water and we are trying to stop the leak with one hand.

We simply cannot do more for others and have only one overarching duty and that is to concentrate on you and to do everything in our powers, even more than that for you and only for you.

Last Sunday I went to see the Brainins; at last a really excellent affidavit has been mailed off for Heinrich/Helly. However a contribution for the tickets was absolutely refused by Frau R. as well as Frau Bredh.

At least Mrs. R. could be persuaded to act as guarantor on a loan. Grete Brainin and her husband would have to pay a weekly amount of $12.½ on a loan, that is impossible for those two who, together make only $15.00 a week. We are also corresponding with Oscar who is willing to contribute a monthly amount, but even that amount is still insufficient.

Nothing can be had from Irene who lives in the direst circumstances. Her husband, Gang is very ill, probably cancer. Hopefully something more favorable develops for the two Becks during this week concerning ship tickets and I can report better news. How are they doing? We're literally ashamed not having had more success for them. I personally cannot do anything, in fact dare I not until you my loved ones are here in safety.

Not much to report from us here. Our whole life revolves around our worries about you. Hansi looks terrible again; she grieves and worries about you constantly. She even buys the Yiddish newspapers and asks others to read to her from them, just to learn something about what is going on, since the regular papers hardly ever report anything about the Jews. She can hardly sleep at night, but of what use is it to tell you that we worry—that doesn't help you any.

Stella, having worked nearly one and a half years in her profession, feels she has gained so much experience that she is no longer willing to work as an employee. So next Monday she is starting out independently, sort of, by creating her own beauty parlor for ladies in an already flourishing Gentlemen's barbershop. We're convinced that she'll be successful; she already has a large clientele that will follow her to her new establishment that is very near her old place of work. During the last few days we've had an enormous amount of snow, snow and snow again; twice as unpleasant during the thaw that started now, because New York is experiencing a strike of all bus lines! Lucky, that we also have a subway—or this strike would be a real catastrophe!

Stay well, and be brave, my dearest ones, think of us even if your hearts are heavy—I embrace, hug and kiss you my dearest sweetest mother, and all of you, as ever your Emil For you dearest Emil, special thanks for your dear lines.

#63

New York, March 23rd, 1941

My dearest, sweet mother, and all my dearest loved ones!

In my last letter I already acknowledged your, Marie's, latest news of 13, 17 & 27 February, and those from Mama-Ella for the 17th & 20th. In your latest letter of 24th February, you inform us of the telegram sent by you, which arrived here the morning of March 1st. At least now we know that this telegram was sent by you of your own free will, and not because you were in immediate danger or otherwise under duress. All of you know from my letters of March 2nd, 7th & 14th what steps have been taken from here: affidavits were mailed for you, Emil and Marie, as well as payment for ship tickets for all of you—the tickets paid by me, Otto & Willy with only a relatively small amount still outstanding. However, even the "Joint" says it is better to wait a little longer with fall payment until things have cleared up a little bit over here. Most importantly, the Viennese KG has been informed that payment for you has actually been made, and the KG informed you in turn, via telegram, so that you should have in your possession the necessary evidence for the authorities. For the rest, we know very little ourselves how the whole departure is going to be handled; negotiations are in progress, we are told, by the "Joint" and other Jewish organizations with Washington designated to use money that had already been sent to the "Joint" for the purchase of ship tickets and the leasing of ocean liners to be dispatched to Lisbon. How far these plans have gone is not yet known. You can imagine the enormous interest here among those affected by these plans. Last week, the general-secretary of the "Joint" gave a talk on this subject. A lot of opinions were heard with all kinds of possibilities mentioned, reports of negotiations allegedly under way, but unfortunately without anything real positive being developed so far. Believe me, my dear ones, were it up to us, as individuals to help you, we would gladly pay for it with our blood—years of our life we would gladly give, any material sacrifices are hardly worth mentioning. But unfortunately only the organizations in question are now able to even attempt to help and we, as individuals must simply be ready to contribute whatever they demand. We can only ask of you the same, in fact we command you: do not give up, don't despair, I implore you do not give in to any feelings of despondency.

We were glad to hear that the package we mailed almost three months ago has finally arrived. Under the prevailing troubled circumstances we shall forego any more shipments, at least for now. Maybe it'll work later more rapidly and better. But we do want to send you again some money, however little. I know you advised against it in your last letter, in fact we're not even going to wait until you receive this letter since that would take too long—and of course we shall do that jointly with Willy. Did Miss Weisberg help you out a little lately? You cannot possibly live on the little money we are sending no matter how frugal you are. If she graciously offers you something, please do not reject it. We, too, here are hoping that one day we shall have the opportunity to repay her in some way. In any case we are very grateful to her for everything she does for you and are regularly in touch with her one relative here to whom we pass on her greetings. Unfortunately she lives very far from us so we haven't been to visit her personally since January as the weather has been very bad. Your news about the Tragholz's, as well as about Mrs. Last have troubled us greatly. Has there been any news from them already? And exactly what is happening right now? Got finally some news from Regina-Dora, but that is already out-of-date as it dates from 9 February and we have here letters of 24 February. Hannah and I are not worried as much as before especially since you my dear Marie, mention them in nearly every one of your letters, which is very much appreciated by Hannah. That she has done everything possible for them is known to Regina-Dora directly from her.

Immediately after receiving Mama-Ella's letter I wrote to Mrs. Altman as well as to Mrs. Laufer at the addresses listed, about the Braungirls, and if these two women have only a spark of sympathy, they should at least answer me. I have offered my services for formulating the affidavits and any other details such as getting additionally required documents, passing them on to Vienna etc. and asked to let me know when it would be convenient to have me visit them in person. I simply cannot take the risk to visit with these two ladies without some prior arrangement. The trips to and from them take hours. I never get home before 8PM at the earliest 7:30PM including Saturdays and it is unfortunately impossible to take care of something like that during business hours. Every hour not spent at work is deducted from your wages, even though my boss quite understands these matters. I have lost several whole working days during the last few weeks because I stood in line at the "Joint" starting at 6AM. I cannot waste even one cent right now, even less so than previously, not to mention the fact that my frequent absences simply would not be very welcome. But if I can in any way be of use to some one over there, do an errand, anything which is required over on your side, I am only too happy to use all my free time beginning at 7PM and if it takes all night for that purpose. Fact is that at least once I came home at 3AM from Brooklyn in an affidavit matter for the Epsteins in Riga, without success, I am sorry

to say. I really hope that these two ladies will answer me. Mrs. Altman—
of Altman & Kühne is well known here and they could surely help. But
who knows how many relatives, friends etc. they already had to help?

Unfortunately, dear Mama, though you included all kinds of data for
the Braun girls some less important than others, you did not list their current address. This is very important for the formulation of the affidavits,
though we are still very far from that. Willy is unwilling to lend any support in this matter he is adamant and hasn't changed any in that respect
in the move from the eastern to the western hemisphere! How is it possible that making a living beyond what is necessary to support oneself,
family and maybe your next of kin can still be the all-consuming purpose
in life after all we have seen and experienced? Victor has written the most
moving letters to us and Willy during the past 1½ years in which he literally begs Willy to write him a few lines: absolutely impossible says
Willy, no time, busier than ever etc! The Braun girls however should not
despair and keep their good spirits, possibly let you have a little bit of
that, don't worry, everything will turn out for the best! Please Ella, don't
take it the wrong way when I asked you to get in touch with Mrs. Nagler
and Hansi Lakner. All I meant was that you should send a postcard telling
them to pick up their letters from you, themselves. I can very well picture that you're more than just busy with Mama's and your troubles—and
if these ladies then appear in order to fetch their news, they really delay
you, who values every second, and in these narrow and cramped quarters,
without privacy, being closed off neither to the right or the left—I know
this only all too vividly. So please Ella don't be mad at me. For me it is a
question of savings on postage, otherwise I would have written to them
directly. Our postage expenses keep growing geometrically: Victor writes
to us for his daughter, and she, Hannah, writes to us for Victor and those
are not ordinary letters but at least five pages; and the postage to Hannah—I am not exaggerating—is $1.40 which is approximately one day's
wage for a refugee working in a factory here. Mrs. Lakner writes to Robert, so does Robert when he writes to her, Mrs. Nagler writes to her son
Hansi and he in turn writes his mother, my niece Olly writes her sister
Elly in Switzerland, and E. does the same when she writes to O. Olly's
boyfriend in Manila writes her and she in turn writes him and all this
correspondence goes via America, via us, as a direct correspondence
between them is impossible and I cannot refuse any one because I can
imagine how I would feel if I were on the receiving end of such a refusal.
Nobody encloses one of those postal coupons, not that it would matter
since for one coupon I get only a five cent stamp, and airmail to Europe
alone costs at least six times as much, to South America 40 cents, to Pales-

tine, Australia as much as 70 cents. We received another request for help from Rosa. It is all so damnably difficult. If only we had a starting point, an address that we could turn to. And Rosa might not even be very difficult to place here. She could certainly find a situation in a household; domestic help is still very much in demand. The problems with the colored are immense. Typical is a newspaper ad that a group of working college students recently placed in the newspapers: Do not worry when going to the theater, the movie, have fun without having to worry constantly, we'll watch your children, we play with them, we entertain them, we guard their sleep as long as you are not at home. Then in another part of the paper is a lengthy article about that kind of enterprise complete with picture of a college-boy giving the milk bottle to a baby.—While last week we had the most terrible frigid temperatures of the year, today is a really divine spring day, we are approaching the summer with giant strides, actually I am a little afraid of it—because of the climate and otherwise. What is the summer going to bring this time? Bad things, to be sure—yet there's always a little hope—maybe something good after all, most importantly the reunion with you. I am glad for you when the summer comes because the central European summer does not hold as many dangers for your health as does the winter. In the excitement of the past few weeks we forgot about Purim, already past, and the approaching Easter holidays. Please receive our most heartfelt wishes and take comfort in the knowledge of our love and faithfulness and that our thoughts are constantly with you. Will Emil be able to obtain some work in the spring that will bring him both a diversion and a little income? Please continue to write as good and constantly as you have until now, we embrace all of you, our dear ones and especially you, my dearly beloved mother as ever your Emil.

Hansi's work is now in its peak period: not a day, Saturday included without overtime—though this will stop very suddenly at Easter, only to start again, though not as strongly as before, and will altogether stop near the end of May or beginning of June. Maybe I'll send her away then for a few days, together with Herbert—possibly to the Bohrers in Middletown—only Hansi can't quite tolerate that endless kvetching of Helen's.

#64

New York, March 29th, 1941

My dear, good mother, All you dear ones!

There is no mail for me to acknowledge this time. But we don't want to be ungrateful and consider ourselves happy if we continue to hear from you regularly as we did during the last weeks and also from the same place. It is of course possible that we shall get some mail from you before I send off this letter. The arrival of a Clipper has been announced provided the plane is not late due to the bad weather that now prevails over much of the ocean.

I would like to report briefly to you, dear Mama and Ella what we've been able to accomplish in the matter of the Braun girls. Unfortunately it is not very much, though there is reason for hope. Mrs. Altman wrote me her refusal and I shall enclose it should this letter not be too heavy. Mrs. Altman sponsored 6 affidavits for close relatives who do not reside in Vienna, has moreover received many other urgent requests from more distant relatives whom she unfortunately will not be able to consider, since that would make the other affidavits worthless.

Mrs. Regine Laufer invited us for a visit to talk about the matter which Hansi and I were glad to accept. Mrs. Laufer lives here in the poorest of circumstances, together with a stepson (son of her deceased husbands first marriage), a 45-year-old man who is, according to what she told us, more unemployed than employed. Right now he has a poorly paid job but is hospitalized to undergo a Hernia operation, a consequence of his having over exerted himself on his last job. She is completely dependent financially on this son. She is 75 years old, half-blind, lives together with her son in a two-room apartment and is forced to do all the housework including laundry all by herself. However she has a second stepson who lives in Washington and is quite well off. This son does not care about her or about his blood brother. He visits New York occasionally, even visits with them but financially is of no use whatever. Nevertheless Mrs. Laufer wants to write him—I drafted her letter in detail and told only the best about the girls, especially that they would never be a burden, that specifically Grete's skills would be very much in demand. He can be assured that none of the three would ever come to Washington and that we would help them during the difficult period after their arrival. An affidavit from him would have the great advantage of having been sponsored by a blood relative. We urged him to emphasize this without fail, also the fact of his working for the government. The latter is the only occupation in America with a secure future since there are no social institutional nets such as universal health care, Old Age Insurance etc. Mrs. Laufer appears to be a very serious and decent person, well informed about all members of the family and eager to help, if only she was able to. She told us that a few years ago shortly after her return from Vienna she actually had a good job for Grete but then Grete changed her mind about coming. Be assured I shall not forget this matter and shall continue to inquire, maybe even write to Washington myself, in case nothing is accomplished within a short time.

Our anxiety and restlessness concerning you has not declined because as far as we know, they are continuing with this policy. We can only hope that you, who are able to prove at every level that you can come over here, will be permitted to wait out, like others in similar situations, the time until your departure date is set.

My dearest mother I admire your courage and composure that you are even trying to comfort us when it is you and the others are really in need of consolation. Please continue, remain steadfast and do not despair. God is everywhere, and from all over the world it is possible to find a way over here. If only you stay healthy and are doing your utmost to remain that way. Even if it is difficult for you, don't throw in the towel, think of us and for our sake pull yourself together.

Olly's U.S. visa for which she had fought so hard expired last week since it was valid for only 4 months. We kept hoping that she would suddenly appear here on some unscheduled freighter, which occurs, in some isolated instances, but unfortunately that didn't happen. On the other hand those who arrive here in one of these often completely inadequate "row boats" tell hair raising tales of their crossing, especially under the flag of a belligerent nation, so that we're almost glad she is still where she is. We expect more news from her. Not having been able to use that visa was a big blow for her. I comfort her in any case as best I can and if the visa cannot be extended and the whole process has to start all over again, I tell her not to worry because I shall be able to fix this with the sponsor of her affidavit. But I can understand how she feels: to have an expired visa is worse than not to have had one at all! Have you heard anything from Adolf and Elly? E. has not written for quite some time. Recently I tried to persuade her to go to the Dominican republic together with her husband; especially refugees in Switzerland are frequently sent over there. Those ships sail via New York where they dock for several weeks. It is said that it is not impossible to stay here at least as a visitor for several months. The reports from the Dominican Republic are not bad at all. Recently the New York Times brought an article and picture series from there.

Victor too, hasn't written in quite some time. We are in touch with Irma, thank God, but it is via a very long route: India to San Francisco. But it works and relatively speaking doesn't even take all that long. She announced a letter from Heinzi but then didn't include it because the postage would have been too high. They promised to send it the next time. Last Wednesday Sigi and Grete Brainin visited us. An excellent affidavit was sent some time ago for Heinrich/Helly and in the matter of the ship tickets too, there is some progress. We shall meet again next week.

We already wrote you last week, my dear ones, about money. Please let us know immediately, though we probably shall not wait for that and send it now. Ella of course also needs to write with respect to that.

There is not much to tell about us. We're all healthy and we all work. Slowly one can tell that spring is on its way if only from its worst side: terrible storms and just all-around bad weather. But I believe and fear that in about four weeks the skin on ones bodies will be too much! Summer arrives here without a transition and the best season is the Fall which lasts from beginning October 'til the end of December.

Have you received notification from the KG about the payment made here? Have you heard from the U.S. consulate? I kiss and embrace you my beloved mother, and all you others, regards to all our friends and acquaintances, as ever your Emil.

#65

New York, April 6th, 1941

My much beloved mother, All you my dear ones!

This time we acknowledge Mama's and Ella's letter of March 10th, from you dearest Marie a postcard dated March 6th and your dear letter of March 12th, however without mother's usual and beloved added lines. Your letter, dearest Mama and Ella we immediately passed on to W. and arranged everything necessary for the renewal of the affidavit. We have in fact already thought about it and started on it only now we shall accelerate the process and acknowledge by telegram that the sponsor is ready to continue his commitment, announcing the arrival of the new papers by airmail. It is alleged, generally, that the U.S. consulate is not applying its regulations too rigorously once it is your turn and the expiration date is easily extended for a month or two. Concerning ship tickets, your news that it has become necessary to provide name of ship, date of departure, even cabin number, makes us despair. As I already told you once before ship lines here do not accept bookings like that even for First Class. We have always tried to do the right thing for you. We booked with the JOINT because of its direct connection with the KG, which, in turn maintains contact with you as well as with the German authorities to which it has to show proof that you have the opportunity to emigrate and consequently need not be sent away. There is an organization here which represents the interests of the immigrants and also their relatives abroad and in their latest publication one can read, literally: "In most cases cables advise American relatives to make payments to the JOINT in New York." Upon receipt of the money the office informs the applicable Jewish office in Germany (in your case the KG in Vienna) that the passage money has been paid for a specific person. The Jewish committees do the booking itself in Germany. The JOINT in Lisbon or New York makes payments on orders from these committees. The offices of the ship companies in New York do not sell any tickets for a specific departure date from Lisbon. So-called "open booking" designed to reserve space for the earliest date available in view of the current overcrowding for many months ahead, is pointless as a means to secure an American visa. Farther down in this publication it also says: "The most important task for the JOINT are now: Centralization of the whole booking process and widest dissemination of information to those willing to sacrifice their last remaining resources, initiate a form of price control, possibly by chartering their own ships, plus financing of ship tickets through loans to wage earners etc." You can see from all that everyone is trying one's utmost in every possible way but still the local authorities, aid committees etc. do not know anything certain or even positive.

There is one more thing, as far as it concerns us, about which I need to calm your anxieties. I see from your letters that you're worrying about it unnecessarily: the money we raised on your behalf was not borrowed from anyone, not from relatives or acquaintances. Not one cent. We used only what we have saved for you and you alone since our arriving in this country. If it was insufficient, Otto has tapped into an amount that administered here for his sister-in-law and with her concurrence. The relatives here are unfortunately not in a favorable position right now, especially the Jerseyites—I am satisfied that they all will pitch in for the passage money for Regine/Dora. So, please no unnecessary worries—to which I'd like to add that all our valuables here are also untouched, reserved only for you when you my dearest one will with God's help have arrived over here. Today Sam Korall (Fanny's husband) visited me in the office and invited Otto/Stella and ourselves to the Seder, next Friday, April 11th. Of course I accepted, one does appreciate these small kindnesses from people—on the other hand our hearts are so heavy now, we stay away from everything and everyone. One cannot bother people with one's own misery all the time, most of the time they are really quite nice and sympathetic—still what they cannot experience on their own bodies they can empathize with only with great difficulty. We have told the Handels very categorically not to arrange anything for us for the holidays. But with respect to Fanny we have a bad conscience. We were supposed to visit them for many months now and never got around to it. You must believe us, when I say we simply cannot spare the time. Our life here does not give us one minute of which we can say it belongs only to us. I told you once before, we have more money to spare than time. That reminds me of an aphorism I read somewhere long ago: Whoever has no money can always borrow it or receive it as a gift, but a person who has run out of time has no recourse at all.

Hannah Safirstein (née Handel) and husband, Isaac Safirstein, counselors-at-law who devoted a great deal of their time pro bono to aid in the legal ramifications of immigration sponsorships and the deposition of affidavits. My family referred to them as our "Guardian Angels."

Heinrich wrote us a dear letter concerning the crates in Rotterdam; please tell him, Ella, that we already have arranged everything. The Safirsteins have drawn up a so-called affidavit (here all kinds of documents are known as affidavits) for the consulate, which explains the whole situation. Monday Grete will go to the German consulate here to obtain the confirmation, which we shall mail to him immediately. Grete and Sigi are honestly doing everything in their power for Heinrich/Helly but they are discouraged over Helly's equally despairing letter. One tries everything here, requiring enormous efforts, but it is useless to recount every single effort if one cannot report also one that is successful. But eventually we shall have that, too.

In my last letter I already wrote you in great detail about the Braun-girls. Within a few days I shall inquire again at their aunt's here. Rosa, too wrote us a letter. They too should not despair. Unfortunately everything is so terribly difficult right now when everyone is trembling and alarmed about his relatives.

Within the next few days, by the way, we shall mail additional affidavits of support for you mother and Marie/Emil. Whatever happens we shall not have to blame ourselves for having missed out on anything once you've reached your turn and it appears that your affidavits are not sufficient. I am looking forward, mother, when I visit with Fanny, to be able to talk a lot about you, especially your courage and pluck. Marie tells me that you and Emil are the only ones who display confidence. And that makes me very happy.

The weather has turned quite spring like and we no longer wear any coats. A week from this Sunday is Easter holiday, actually not a holiday since there is no Easter Monday. On Easter Sunday there is a great Fashion parade on Fifth Avenue, all gentlemen in Top Hat and Cutaway, society ladies in the latest spring fashions. Everyone is preparing for this and the newspapers are full of stories in anticipation. As much as everything seems to turn on Europe and the war—all this is very far away for the average American. What you do not experience on your own body ... I already mentioned it above, and the fact is they experience, thank God very little of it on their own body.

[Letter ends here]

#66

New York, April 12th, 1941

My beloved little mother,

And all my loved ones Marie-Emil, Mama-Ella!

We received your dear news this week and what we felt as we read these letters I cannot even begin to tell you. After two anxiety filled months in which every day, every hour was filled with worry about you during which time we read every newspaper story, listened to every radio report with trembling and alarm, nearly two months busy with running hither and thither, from Pontius to Pilate, standing endlessly in line at the various organizations, such as HIAS and JOINT, early in the morning, among people I did not know, yet whose terrified faces were only too familiar to me still from the days in Vienna when we hurried from one meeting to another where there was much talk but no information—now finally your news!

Be assured my dearest ones, we shall do even more and leave no stone unturned to bring you all happily here. As I already mentioned in my last letter, we are preparing supplementary affidavits for you. Unfortunately the process is delayed because of certain required enclosures, such as tax receipts, etc. Similarly renewal of Mama/Ella's affidavit is under way by Hannah and I've seen to it that everything is done twice since Victor's original affidavit was issued on the same date as yours. We haven't heard from Victor in a long time and we might be worried were it not for the fact that you had heard from him during this time. I have by the way, received letters and pictures from his children to be passed on to Riga on the occasion of Victor's approaching birthday, and which I sent on with our best wishes. The pictures are very good; especially that tiny Nic David has turned into a cute little kid. Write to Victor that he should send you the pictures at least just for looking at them.

Your news, dear Ella about how Hansi L. and Emma had to leave you, really shook us. On the same day I also received a letter from Robert, in which he asks me among other matters to let him know if I knew anything about his family. But I find it difficult to give him such sad news without any details. Who told you, Ella, that they had to leave, where did you find it out, were you able to talk to them prior to their departure, or did they write to you?

We all hope that Regine/Dora's health has improved, and it is our opinion they should not leave the hospital too soon. Hannah thanks you for keeping us informed about them because both of them have written very little lately, which is understandably, though one letter of Dora's from the hospital did reach us here.

During this dead time for the production of artificial flowers Hansi usually returns to her original profession of Ladies' tailor. Only this year she has no fear about finding something. As a consequence of the large-scale economic programs initiated by the government there is a noticeable acceleration of production in all areas, which, on the other hand is used by the worker's to their advantage by—frequent striking! In any case I am glad that Hansi can stop for a while and in this way get some rest. Then we can also catch up with our social obligations, visit some people, follow invitations which during the last months for lack of time and our sinking mood we had to decline. I saw Isidor Handel's son Bernie who, by chance was there on a short leave from his military base where he is on duty as a smart looking First Lieutenant. His resemblance to Otto von Hapsburg is astonishing and in the family they keep calling him "Kaiser Otto." All send their very best regards.

Friday all of us, Otto, Stella, Herbert were at Fanny's for the Seder and what occurred there was a regular food orgy. But we experience it all with a heavy and sad heart and the memories keep coming. Whatever people serve us to help us forget a little, each of us would give years of his life if only we could taste Mutter/Marie's matzo balls and Mama's delicious "Gugelhupf" in your company.

Just now Otto called and asks me tell you to excuse him for not adding to the letter. He started his part-time job again at Easter, so now he has to go directly from his factory job to the other one and gets home very late and that keeps him from writing even a few lines. He sends through me his most fervent kisses and embraces. Of course I told him it really doesn't pay to work 2–3 days till late at night for just a few dollars—but he says now it is even more necessary than before and everything is for you. Hansi will refer to your letter in her added lines and I too will answer it in detail in my next letter to you. He also read to me mother's lines. Thank you so much for that my dearest mother and especially for your good wishes for Jonteff. *[Letter ends here]*

#67

New York, April 20th, 1941

My dear, good mother

And all you my dear loved ones!

Your dear letter of March 24th I acknowledged already briefly in my last letter to you, and not only thank you but all the others as well for your faithful and continuous reporting. Since Mama and Ella, and the same goes for Dora, do not always write regularly, Hansi and Hannah would certainly be quite worried about the fate of their respective loved ones if it weren't for you dearest Marie and your regular news about all the others, whose fate lies so close to our heart. By the way, a letter did come from Dora a few days ago, as Hannah just informed me by phone dated April 1st. In this letter Dora emphasizes that Hannah did the right thing by paying in at the JOINT for the ship tickets rather than directly at the passenger-ship line. That made Hannah very happy and us too, as we did the same thing for you and have been afraid ever since that we might not have done the right thing after all. Although we only did what thousands of others did too. Not even JOINT or HIAS could tell us that at the time they received our payment, whether we were doing the right thing. All they said was that they directly notified the KG, which in turn works closely with the German authorities and informs them of the existence of the ship tickets and that moved us to choose this way and we are happy to hear that others acknowledge it as the correct way.

No matter, we shall continue to leave no way untried to get you over here and please do not let yourself become discouraged even if the consulate at times is not in operation.

We report regularly to Irma, my dearest Marie, and have kept them informed about the last developments, just as we tell you immediately about what it is they write us. So far all her reports have been most satisfactory and hope this will continue. Otto writes you always in detail about Heinzi, anything he hears about him, especially that Irma yearns for you, always thinks of you, and always talks about you and wants to know everything about you, as you can well imagine.

The Holy Days have passed and they were again an occasion to think more of you and in our conversations talk a lot about you. Thus, mother, did you used to make the Borscht differently, not with eggs but with big potatoes making it much clearer, and the Kreplach and the Bulbenik (here it is called, Americanized, "Potatonik") and the chopped eggs and Matzo balls and many other tasty holiday dishes gave us the opportunity to think and talk of you a lot. We did not eat one piece of bread all during these eight days, not that it would even have been possible: bread is simply unavailable! The bakeries and groceries have all adapted to the occasion and most are actually closed for the whole period. Radio, posters, advertisements in the newspapers was completely dominated by offerings of the best wines, the best matzo, the best cakes, and the best cookies for Passover. In New York there is a department store, MACY'S the biggest one in New York, if not actually in the world Gerngross in Vienna is not even in the same league but even Wertheim and KdW those big stores in Berlin, are midgets by comparison. Macy had a gigantic department prior and during the holy days that sold only food for Passover under the supervision of the Rabbinate. There you could get everything from Matzoth flour to live chickens. All employees, women and men, in this department wear snow-white coats and gloves. Almost unnecessary to state that the crowds there put you in danger of your life. The profusion of food stuffs here my dear ones, is fantastic and even though I am now nearly one and one half years in this country, no longer count myself among the "greenhorns," the masses of goods that radiate at you from the shop windows continue to amaze me. Apart from the small specialty food stores you find here major enterprises, so-called Food Markets, which have hundreds of branches in New York alone and many more in all America. One of the largest enterprises is the "Atlantic & Pacific Food market," known in New York simply as the A&P. In one of those markets you can buy anything that is edible from anywhere in the World. All possible kind of meats, or poultry, fish in all shapes and forms, vegetables and fruits that grow anywhere in the world. Here the latter are not bound by the seasons, anything that grows only in the summer, one can get in the winter from the South and vice versa in this incredibly large and far reaching country. The colorfulness of these markets is practically intoxicating. The eye feasts on towering mountains of golden yellow oranges, enormous pale yellow grapefruits, green lemons, large reddish brown strawberries, wonderful red apples from the state of Washington on the Pacific coast (which is almost as far as Europe from here). There are Bananas, grapes, plums, melons etc. etc. And then the canned goods! There is absolutely nothing that cannot also be bought as canned good. From chicken soup, Borscht to hot dogs—as well as any variety of compotes, Jams, Jelly, vegetables, baked beans and the most delicious asparagus. And of course all kinds of canned fish, whether they can be found in he Pacific, or the Atlantic Ocean or populate the major rivers of America. Gigantic mountains of canned goods with their colorful vignettes can be seen towering everywhere. In fact, this massive, powerful display of all saleable products, whether in giant shop windows, or elsewhere on advertisements that grace whole skyscrapers marks the character of the sales pitch here. Shopping in one of these food markets does not take the form we are used in Central Europe. Once you enter that market you're automatically guided to a place where you pick up a small cart on rubber heels (similar to the modern serve carts we had over there called "mobile servants") and slowly walk along the many departments where you want to buy something, reaching for it from the display case and place it in your cart. Hardly anything has to be weighed since most items come already beautifully wrapped and in the desired quantity. Yes, even eggs, starting with three, are packed beautifully in unbreakable cartons. At the exit you'll be relieved of the little cart all your bought articles stowed safely in a box or paper sack, the bill is typed out and after you've paid you can be sure that once you arrive home all the packages have been delivered or simply left at the door if nobody is home.

I believe my dear ones, Europe could live on what remains here untouched and uneaten. And yet the cost of living here is not as reasonable as it was in Europe, considering the magnitude of goods that is available here. I am an old conversion man—and am teased a lot on that account by my friends—because I can show them that over there in untroubled times one could obtain everything cheaper even though a lot had to be imported.

Look after yourselves; don't give in, for our sake please! How is ...
[Letter ends here]

#68

New York, April 23rd, 1941

My dearest, good mother,

All my dear ones, Mama, Marie, Ella, Emil! Again a Clipper's arrival has been cancelled, undoubtedly still tooling along somewhere over the ocean with your mail for which we yearn so intensely—so we'll just have to be patient for one or two more days. To be sure, I write much more easily, can feel your closeness better with your dear lines in front of me— but since I had already planned to write you today, I shall do so, even if the expected letter from you has not yet arrived.... On May 2nd it'll be a year that I started on my job, a small miracle in this country where everything is so short lived. When you come here into a district where you'd last been four weeks ago you hardly recognize it again given the changes that have taken place. The stores may have changed and even the houses are different! An acquaintance of mine whom I ran into the other day and who keeps himself afloat with peddling of gloves that he and his wife produce together, replied to my question why he stood there looking almost dazed: "Day before yesterday there was here a ladies' boutique full of fashions and crowded with customers. Today when I came for a new order and payment of the old ones, I cannot find a trace of the business, the owner, stock or money!"

About Herbert we can report now that if the new bill lowering the draft age to 18 yrs becomes law we shall have in him, next year, a very smart looking soldier and the U.S.A. a defender of the fatherland! Thousands of young immigrants provided they have their first papers have already received their draft notice. I just learned recently that Helly's nephew, Bruno Löhner, has been drafted into the service. Married men are, for the time being, not yet called up. During the Easter vacation Herbert worked very hard to earn a few dollars—for which he then bought himself a pair of very elegant shoes!

April 25th.

Today your dear letters of March 31st, (addressed to Handels) and April 3rd, (addressed to Otto) arrived simultaneously much to our joy. However, nothing from Mama/Ella. We do know from your letter, dear Marie, of the happy event occasioned by the notification from the consulate. I hope that there'll be some movement soon in your matters as well, Marie. We were very touched by the passing of Mrs. Neuman. This lady who had always lived such a protected life, surrounded by all her children, at the end had no one any more and was among strangers when she had to pass away.

Dearest mother, special thanks for your dear lines and that you are so optimistic, as they all say you are. I thank you for that so much, I kiss and embrace you many times, you as well as all you my dearest loved ones, as ever your Emil.

#69

New York, May 5th, 1941

My dear, good mother, And all my dear loved ones!

Unfortunately we did not receive any mail from you in the past ten days and consequently are very sad and just a bit worried. We cannot blame the Clipper, which arrived on schedule twice during the last week, with news for many others but not for us. Still we hope that there will be news, especially this week and it will be good news.

As we—Otto and I—already wrote you in our last letter, we have again wired you RM100.00 which, I am sure must have reached you by now. Please write us immediately about that. Bohrers did not give us any instructions this time thus I did not include the RM15.00. Please do not hesitate to tell us what your money situation is, whether we should send you some again, and whether Mrs. W. is still assisting you every now and then. The same goes for Mama Schab and Ella, they too should write us whether and when they need money, since W. likes to see it black on white, how urgently you need it in which case we can turn the actual transfer directly over to him. Yesterday Otto visited us, looking a bit piqued but otherwise quite ok, and it appears that his little stomach, which was already in competition with mine, has now reverted to its original size. Every time he has this annual throat condition he swears he'll have his tonsils removed, but once its over he forgets about it. As I've written before, he is under the care of Dr. Lobert a refugee physician who is always available right away and is also very nice, but it takes an half hour on the subway to get there.

Unfortunately we have another case of illness among our relatives here and that is Safirstein. For months already he has complained about bladder irritation, which has got worse. When it became really bad the doctors ordered him into a hospital and last week he had surgery there. We get daily reports about him, he is in tolerably good condition but will have to stay another two weeks in the hospital. I visited with him shortly before his surgery and he was understandably still a little nervous. The hospital is close to us, only about a ten-minute walk. It is not just one building but a gigantic complex of skyscrapers, called "The Medical Center." It is located beautifully right on the Hudson River and from its upper floors there is a striking view not only of New York but also of the other, green side of the Hudson reminiscent of our Wachau on the Danube. About the interior of this hospital which is supported by the Vanderbilt Foundation and that I admired in my usual way with eyes and ears wide open in utter amazement I shall write you some other time. On the other hand, getting sick here is undoubtedly one of he most expensive items one has to pay. Safirstein's weekly bill is ca. $60.00 and that is the reduced price thanks to his membership in a private medical insurance—without entitling him to a private room. To this one has to add surgeons' fees, examinations, X-rays and specialist consultations. This is also an opportunity to learn how backward they are here in matters of social welfare, especially medical, old age insurance etc. It is their belief here that every one gets paid sufficiently so that in an emergency he can afford to pay for it himself, that is he should be prepared to save a certain amount every month for medical eventualities, or join a private insurance company. Physicians are very expensive here and one can consider oneself fortunate if he has a refugee doctor among his acquaintances that will treat you for free—and illegally—but grateful that he can keep in practice until such time when he will again qualify for his license. On the other hand those refugee doctors who are licensed charge even more than the native ones, with some laudable exceptions among whom must be counted our Dr. Lobert.

My dearest mother I already have the supplementary affidavit for you in my possession, given by Isidor Handel, and I lack only a minor document before I can mail it. Isidor sent it to me with a personal letter in which he writes "he is only too happy to be able to help me and especially, in every possible way." I shall mail it within a few days to the U.S. consulate in Vienna with an accompanying letter. Marie's and Emil's supplementary affidavit is issued by Morris, Hannah (Safirstein) Handel's brother, who is in a particularly good position as a government employee, to act as sponsor. It too will be mailed shortly and directly to the consulate. Have you been notified about the first affidavit? I am also writing airmail to the KG on your behalf asking them to help you in case of your departure to the U.S.A. and to tell me at least approximately when you'll be able to count on that. At the same time I ask them to make sure that your ship tickets are reserved in co-operation with Lisbon. The very same letter, in Hansi's and Willy's name is being sent to the KG on behalf of Mama Schab and Ella. After a few weeks when these affidavits have arrived at the U.S. consulate in Vienna I shall try some intervention from

Washington, D.C. Mama/Ella's renewal is already complete but we hesitate to mail it now in view of Marie's letter that said Mama/Ella have already been notified and it may no longer be necessary to do so. Why don't Mama/Ella write us about it?

Last week I celebrated my one-year anniversary as employee in the same firm and my boss treated me to a glass of whisky and a check for $10.00—I would have preferred an increase in my salary but I doubt that I can count on that before fall.

On the 8th of May we shall celebrate our 20th wedding anniversary. How we would have laughed if some one at that time would have predicted in the Patzmaniten Temple, in fact even as late as four years ago that we would celebrate this event in America. Herbert too, is reaching the "adult" stage of a young man which, he feels entitles him to smoke cigarettes—not his however, but mine, much to my chagrin. He has also added a pipe to his repertoire, he schnorred it from Otto. After a period of intense heat we're again in an agreeable weather period. How is it with you? Do you take regular walks, mother? Is there a small bench you can sit down on? How is your health? Good, I hope. Has Mama recovered completely? And you Marie, still suffering from your rheumatism? You haven't written us anything about it in the last letters, should we take this as a good sign? Give our best regards to our friends and acquaintances, I kiss and embrace you dear mother as well as all my loved ones, as ever your Emil

---

#70

New York, May 11th, 1941

My dearest lovely mother, and my other dearest beloved!

This time we are able to acknowledge quite a lot of mail, after a dry spell of nearly two weeks. From Marie we received her letters of April 9 & 16 and from Mama/Ella the detailed reports of April 9, with a separate communication concerning the matter of Mrs. Elizabeth Weiss. Let me comment right away on the Weiss matter: I shall immediately contact this Dr. B. mentioned in the letter, as he lives close by, not far from the Handels where 177th Street intersects with Haven Avenue. Maybe he can also give us some support in the matter of Mr. Werk, which, as an American citizen should not be too difficult for him. Believe me, dear Ella, you can hardly imagine how devilishly difficult all this is here: the incredibly long distances we can get used to, but the lack of time, given that we are so totally involved in our daily struggle for existence, hurts most: every minute that is not spent productively at one's work is immediately deducted; but even that we can tolerate; what is so difficult to bear is the gradual realization that we are fighting against narrow minded indifference behind which hide professional jealousy, fear of having to share eventually room and board, personal antagonisms of long standing (family feuds) or even of outright envy or other kinds of wickedness. At last I had to admit it to myself after one and one half years of doing this: I acted like one who is running Amok! Add to this the constant worry over our own, our closest relatives for whom until now one has not been able to do anything, or anyway, next to nothing, who nevertheless, require all our concentration to the highest degree in order to achieve at least something concrete for them. Anyway, we shall do everything possible in the matter of Mrs. Weiss and please do tell this your neighbors at the same time that you give them our best and most heartfelt regards. Let me mention here also that since the time we talked to Mrs. L. about the Braun girls—and about which I had written to you—we have heard absolutely nothing from that lady. Only a few days ago I wrote her another card, but so far there's been no response. In all likelihood her son refused to be involved in this matter in any way whatsoever. It is better to tell the Braun girls about this right away than to raise false hopes. Hopefully, you, my dear ones, will be able to come over here real soon—and according to your latest news that might indeed be true for you—as well as for my mother, Marie, and you, Emil—and then we, who co-sponsored your affidavits, would again be free to sponsor the Braun girls and Willy, too, I am sure, would not refuse. That is their only chance as I see it right now. Have you, Emil and Marie, already received the notification from the American Consulate? How was it with our mother? Did she obtain from them, in addition to the return receipt with which you mailed the affidavit to the consulate, also a separate, personal notification?

Please be sure to tell me that. If necessary, I can then complain via Washington. I have mulled over before just letting Washington make the inquiries directly in Vienna but would do that only after you had been in possession of the notification for a while. I already told you in my last letter that I had written to the KG literally imploring them to assist all of you in whatever way possible in your attempt to leave the country, maybe they can somehow manage to reserve the ship tickets—because only the KG can do something from there we are quite powerless here in this matter. I have no idea how useful such a reservation can be—and I know that the KG cannot really afford to make exceptions, but one can't just leave everything to chance, something has to be tried at least once. We are always thinking: what else can we do? Where else can we make inquiries? Even though much of it is of no avail, something might just, unexpectedly, bring us closer to our goal and all at once there it is—our lucky hour! We cannot, we must not give up hope—I implore you, you must look after yourselves, live and remain healthy, that is my urgent and continuous appeal to all of you, my dearest ones. And as for you my dearest Ella, I beg of you do not give up at the KG and any of those other agencies, don't let them turn you down—if they throw you out at the door, climb back in through the window—and all of us here will keep our fingers crossed!

Today they are celebrating mother's day here. For us this day is hardly different from any one of the other 364 days on which we think of you with unchanged intensity in our feelings of tenderness and affection for our beloved mother and all of you our nearest and dearest. Nevertheless, today our best wishes for you must fly across the ocean in a way that you cannot help having a feeling of our special nearness. A conspicuous way in which this day is marked is by means of all kinds of gimmickry, so that it is hard to tell what is truly genuine from what is designed as the most skillful and gigantic means of advertising for the fashion, food, luxury and entertainment industries. On the street most anyone you meet, man woman or child sports a pink carnation to show that they honor and celebrate a living mother while those honoring the memory of a deceased mother wear a demure white carnation. All of us here, of course are happily displaying the pink carnation and expect, the good Lord willing, to be able to do that for many more times on this special day. In the meantime you should already have received some time ago notification, or the amount of RM100.00 itself which we had telegraphed to you. We are grateful to Ms. Weissberg for her support and we hope that we can express our thanks to her in person in the not too distant future. Her greeting for Hannah we have of course promptly relayed. We greet her as well as Regina/Dora most cordially. The latter we wish a speedy recovery, but we urge them not to leave the hospital until they have regained their health completely. They, too, ought to be quite busy with making all arrangements for leaving the country considering that everything on this side that needs to be done has been completed.

We have no news from Victor, even though we have sent him three very detailed accounts from his children Hannah/Mümmel, plus pictures, a small lock of hair of Nicolas-David. We are not really worried about them, since we received news from Epstein some time ago in which he says that V. is doing quite well producing a line of leather goods, so he probably can't spare much time for writing.

Many thanks for your loving and heartfelt wishes on the occasion of our "May Festival Days": Hansi's and Herbert's birthday as well as our Wedding anniversary and last not least Mother's Day!

We are celebrating these festive occasions only among ourselves, keeping it in fact from the others since they have worries of their own now. Saphirstein is still in the hospital though improving steadily; Hannah has our sympathy since she now is responsible all by herself, for keeping their law practice going, spending her free time at night with S. in the hospital. His illness demands much money and she told me in confidence that they had to borrow on an insurance policy. A surprise on our 20th wedding anniversary was a card from our first landlord here in New York with whom we shared an apartment for most of our first year and who obviously must have entered that in his calendar! Herbert received a number of useful gifts from us. On the occasion of all these happy days I treated Hansi and Herbert to a meal at the Cafe Vienna where our old Viennese comedian Leopoldi now sings and plays the piano. To be sure, I am not exactly enamored of places like that exuding, as they do the odor of "Emigraton" where certain types bawl when they sing "Vienna City of My Dreams," the kind of types I avoided already in Vienna! But this time I did it as a favor to some very old friends, Hugo and Ella Deutsch. And Hansi cannot get enough of Herbert as a dancing partner; Herbert created quite a sensation, he is an expert in Wuggi-Wuggi, [*sic*] Konga and whatever the name of the latest dance craze may be. According to him dancing is a required subject in his high school and the school jazz band is really tops. During the week he runs around like a "real American schoolboy" dressed in his school jacket with the big letter W both front and back (for G.W. High School), no tie and loose sweater, pants rolled up at the ankles, but on Friday for the weekly dance he appears most elegantly spruced up, even shaves (once a week, more than that is not yet possible!). Otherwise he has really turned out to be a nice guy, actually quite serious in his behavior, is determined to go to college after graduating high school. On the occasion of "American-Day" all students in the upper terms are required to write an essay on the subject of: "Why I Am Glad To Be An American." The best work chosen from entries all over the country gets a free college education. Naturally the essay is printed and published in all major newspapers, in other words the winner will be celebrated in the whole country. Herbert wrote the best piece in his class—but since he is still a refugee and not a citizen that was as far as he could compete. However it will be printed in the next issue of the school paper, "The Cherry Tree." It is interesting to observe that the refugee children always turn in the best performances. Last year as well the best essay was also written by a refugee but could therefore not enter the competition. Herbert's essay wasn't just written in excellent English but it was obviously also thought out in English—and that is exactly where youth has the greatest advantage. We shall all speak English eventually, but hardly also think in English.

Otto has fortunately recovered from his illness and is already hard at work again.

Dearest mother I thank you especially for the loving note added to the last letter—only please do not write with pencil since that requires more exertion on your part. May the good Lord keep you healthy, as well as all the others, Marie, Mama, Ella and Emil. I embrace you and kiss you all, as ever your Emil.

#71

New York, June 28th, 1941

All my dearest ones, my beloved little mother, Marie-Emil, Mama-Ella!

Since Hansi's letter was somewhat delayed, I am enclosing it with my weekly report, and I only hope that you Marie were not too much hurt by the fact that Otto's add-on was missing in the last letter. In the meantime we have your good letter of June 2nd and just now the letters of June 7 & 9. We are so happy over all your letters and especially now that the mail is running so smoothly between you and all our friends and loved ones in all parts of the world we simply regard this as a present from heaven.

Unfortunately, the events of last week have really upset us—now we must add Victor and Adolf to our problem children. May the good Lord protect them and their families. Add to this the matter of the mutual closing of the consulates as well as the temporary impossibility of transferring any money to you. We, i.e., Otto has immediately, on my advice, made contact with Hertha in Buenos Aires so she can send you something via the Reichsbank branch there. As far as I know the relations between Argentina and Germany are normal.

In any case we do not yet know whether this will work and I want to direct our most urgent, fervent request to Frau Weissberg to continue for a while at least, as she has done so selflessly before, her support for you. Her behavior toward you deserves all our thanks, which we cannot even attempt to express in words alone. We hope determinedly that most certainly there will arise the opportunity to thank her not only with words.

The only favor we can do for her right now is that we visit her relative Frau Hannah and extend to her Frau Weissberg's greetings as often as she wishes. Please convey to her our best wishes and also to Dora and Regine. Unfortunately, your news about these two are not very encouraging and I haven't mentioned this so far to the Safirsteins. Maybe you can tell Dora to direct a few lines to Hannah who worries a lot about them. By the way: Mr. Safirstein has fully recovered and he as well as his wife are very touched by your concern for them. They are sending through me this time their best regards and as soon as possible Hannah will write personally to you and also to Ella-Mama.

There have been some changes again in the U.S. visa matter, which however must not be looked upon in any way as a further aggravation. First of all as for the new regulation of not being able to depart unless no immediate relatives are left behind: that does not concern you. We, your children are already here and other than that nobody is there anymore. Also, that this matter is now being handled directly from Washington poses no additional difficulties, not even a delay, since, if so desired the applicant can take care of it by telegraph at his cost. We are not yet fully informed about this directive as this new regulation will not be enforced until July 1st ; we are of course already very interested as certain forms are being distributed that have to be filled out here and then sent to Washington. We shall see to it that any notification for Vienna is sent by telegram. Don't worry about that aspect of these changes and under no circumstances must you lose courage. Everything will turn out well—with God's help!

This week we had again news from Ernst in Sydney after a very longish interval. Thank God he and his family are doing very well and are about to open up a second restaurant and he hopes that it will be just as successful as the first one. It is almost superfluous to mention that their entire thoughts and wishes center on you and that through us they are embracing you most fervently. Unfortunately we too can only do that via letter but maybe it won't be much longer before we can have all of you here with us.

We are currently covered by a gigantic heat wave. It started already in the middle of last week then had a short break at the beginning of this week with a drop in the temperature by 40-degree Fahrenheit. This occurred without any thunderstorm, or rain. What happened was that Sunday evening one went to sleep without cover, pillow etc. kept awake by the heat until dawn, slept a couple of hours only to awake again but this time because of the chilly air—and again experienced a highpoint in the temperature. Last night we visited with Grete Brainin in the matter of Heinrich and Helly Beck and came home half dead from the heat at ca. 1AM. When we came in the door we noticed with considerable fright that Herbert was not at home.

Fortunately we did not have to wait very long—after about half an hour the young man appeared very cheerfully in our doorframe! His office had sent him on urgent business to Philadelphia and allegedly he could not reach us by phone.

He really enthused about this beautiful city of the American Quakers fully enjoyed getting there within 2 hours in a luxury express train, all air-conditioned dining car, club car etc. Today all his friends and acquaintances received picture post cards with greetings from a "business trip!"

Dearest mother, as you can tell from my last letter there was no need to remind us: your fried chickens were not absent at my birthday dinner. As a matter of fact we had some fried chicken again a short time ago and Herbert asked astonished what was going on, "Father doesn't have a birthday!" Oh my dearest little mother, if only I could put something equally good on your table at your coming birthday. How are you? I am very happy that you are in good health and that everyone is saying so many good things about you. I kiss and embrace you fervently, and all my dear ones, as ever your Emil.

#72

New York, July 6th, 1941

My dearest, sweet little mother and all my dear and loved ones in Hochedlingerstrasse-u. Lessinggasse! I really didn't want to write you today, hoping to be able to postpone it for tomorrow, Monday, the first day of my first vacation in the U.S.A. Normally, I wouldn't have been able to do that anyway, because we were all up at 6 o'clock in the morning, busily preparing for the first Sunday at the beach. We start with arranging and artfully packing all bathing suits, terry robes, blankets, sun oils, sunglasses and dozens of other beach "necessities," of which some are always forgotten in the chaos of preparations. And the most important of course is the food supply, which has to be especially abundant; Hansi roasted a small duck, carefully carved into slices and then wrapped in wax paper—added to this must be a variety of salads in boxes, sandwiches, fruit plus a water tight box filled with ice cubes from our Frigidaire that helps keep the food fresh—a little invention of mine.

Finally at about 10AM we were ready, if also half-dead from tiredness brought on by all the preparations and the heat, to get on the subway. The crowding, the crazy heat during this one and a half hour trip at a speed of about 80km, didn't bother us this time: after all we weren't going to the factory or the dusty, hot office, but to the open beach, the ocean with its refreshingly cool waves, aromatic, salty air, in which you never felt the heat of the city, to the soft sand with its thousands of brilliant shells—here we expected to relax and restore ourselves, recuperating for a few hours from the incredible heat and humidity of last week. Relaxation and recuperation despite having to fight for every free little space on the beach, because the people, who all come there on a typical summery beach Sunday, populate the beach like the millions of pebbles on the bottom of the sea. Yet already when we got out of the subway we noticed a threatening sky, which, at its horizon, showed evidence of pitch-blackness. Not to be discouraged we took a bus and rode for another 20 minutes to the Jacob Rijs-Beach, one of the most beautiful and largest beach areas in New York, situated directly on the open ocean and not just on one of the many bays or inlets as do the others. Jacob Rijs has space for 600.000 people!

The bad weather will pass, we all comforted each other, and within a half-hour we'll be enjoying again the most beautiful sunshine. Well, my dear ones, it didn't merely pass, it came down upon us with such strength and vehemence, and of the kind you can experience only—well, only in America! Now we are sitting happily at home after some refreshing baths—and after each one of us the tub was filled with sand from the beach which we brought back in our mouth, nose, ears, eyes and of course in all our clothes and blankets. Our clothes are hanging to be dried, fortunately it wasn't much, only a pair of white pants, shirt, beach sandals etc. we all feel very refreshed after our bath, currently it pours but the air has got pleasantly cool. Our food, which we took for a walk to the beach, we ate here at home, and we are happy to be in good shape and inside our four walls. In this happy mood I am sitting down to my good old typewriter—alas, the strains suffered by it are beginning to show in the bugs it is developing—and so I shall send you my weekly report. In the coming week I shall undoubtedly have another occasion to go to the beach, together with Otto who is also on vacation, and it cannot but be better and more pleasant on a weekday than on a Sunday!

Hansi will stop working—regardless whether she wants to or not—at the end of August and take a trip somewhere. We are already saving for this purpose. By the way she is working again at her factory that produces artificial flowers—they sent a postcard urgently asking her to come back. The season keeps on going there without interruption this year. Her company has large orders from South America for their shortly beginning spring season (right now it is still winter there), so they will keep on working which so far has never occurred, or at least only rarely. I think I wrote you some time ago that in the meantime she changed over to a men's coat factory, but is glad that she can get back to work she is familiar with and where she already knows people, colleagues, and bosses very well. Also she doesn't care very much for working on sewing machines.

July 7th, 1941.

Today we received your dear letters of 16 June and 31st May, as well as one dated June 6th from Mama/Ella.

We are happy over your relatively good news, although we would have liked to have mail from Mama/Ella dated from the period when you sent your last telegram requesting the additional $100.00. In the meantime there has occurred the closing of the consulates and we want to know what effect that will have. At the same time, ships are arriving weekly from Lisbon, all with emigrants from abroad, including Vienna, much more than were the case in the last months. We are very concerned about Victor and Adolf. We comfort ourselves, regarding Victor and Adolf, with the hope that these two guys, levelheaded and competent as they are in every respect, will be able to deal with any situation and carry on safely for themselves and their families. In any case I shall immediately institute inquiries concerning them at the local Red Cross office.

I repeat, my dearest ones, do not worry about the money for the ship tickets, I only wish we had already reached that stage. That will certainly not be the reason for any failure. If you could at least be assigned to one of the ship transports organized by the KG. After all, by now the new quota numbers should already be available. If the KG cannot provide the balance of the money, despite my recent request to them, for that purpose, then we shall find it somehow over here. Didn't they at least make some promises concerning the raising of this balance when they invited you to show up at their offices, in view of the urgency of my letter? But I repeat again: if this won't work under any circumstances—this will not be a reason for failure. All you need to do is to inform us as quickly as possible, by telegram, just as Ella did for the balance of the $100.00, to take the necessary steps over here. How is it with money, anyway? Do you still get some support from Frau Weissberg? Please write us about that. As I already told you in my last letter, we have contacted Otto's sister-in-law, Hertha, in South America, and we are doing the same right now with Dr. Bloch, Willy's business friend in Switzerland. Dearest mother,

I thank you especially for your added lines. I just knew that my news about Olli would give you great pleasure. She is doing real well, just as does Elli from whom you hear directly. If only we could learn something positive from Victor and Adolf. We have no further news from Irma, but according to the general news, everything is ok there and they are out of danger. We expect to hear from them again in greater detail within the next two weeks and when we do we shall of course pass it on to you as quickly as possible.

Please, all of you, watch yourselves and remain healthy, for that we pray daily to the good Lord. Don't stint on anything, as far as this is possible, stay away from unnecessary excitements, there are plenty of necessary ones! Please Marie, see to it that Regina and Dora write a few lines to Hannah, I hope in the meantime that Dora has fully recovered. Please give her our warmest regards as well as to all our dear good friends and acquaintances. I embrace you, my dearest, courageous mother, as well as you others, my loved ones, Mama, Ella, Marie, Emil, I greet you all most fervently and kiss you, as ever your Emil

---

#73

New York, July 11th, 1941

My dear sweet mother, dear Marie and Emil, Mama and Ella!

This report is written on a not very nice day during my vacation, unsuitable for going to the beach or any other open air entertainment. So far I've used this time very well and I am well tanned, just like in the old days on the Lake Balathon in Hungary, at the Wörthersee or Gastein resort areas in Austria. This is actually the first time in three years that I could enjoy the sun, which I love so much. Since my vacation coincided with that of Otto's, we frequently lay together on the beach, on real ocean sand, swimming in the real ocean and borne aloft on real waves, sometimes as high as a house—not like in the Dianabad pool where they were artificial. This is an experience for which, on the other side, one had to pay thousands of Schilling, not to mention the days long railroad trip to the North Sea, the Baltic or the Adriatic! Here it involves a 10-cent subway fare, and a ride, roundtrip, for a total of 2–3 hours. On weekdays it is exactly the way I imagined it to be: magnificent! Still thousands of people, yet in these immensely large beaches and parks they hardly make a dent, in fact the beach almost appears empty, and contrary to Sunday the public present is far more refined. Unfortunately we lack that inner peace to really enjoy all of that. One looks at the infinite horizon of the ocean, decides in which direction lies Europe, where you are and where a world has erupted in flames, while here there is peace, gaiety, and even a little happiness—at least for the casual observer—in many ways much of Europe rubs off a great deal on America, much more than would be true the other way around,—one asks why couldn't it be that way everywhere. Many surround themselves with the same kind of people who for us are still so very far away. Just like hundreds of women who are sitting in this part of the beach, I see you Marie, dressed comfortably in your bathing suit resting on a deck chair under a giant beach umbrella, your dark framed glasses sit uncertainly on your nose, while you're busy darning socks, or mending some much damaged underpants. Ella of course is swimming far out in the ocean, and, if she swims too far, is immediately cautioned loudly via megaphone by the life guards who keep a sharp lookout with telescopes on wooden towers that are placed every 20 feet or so. The beach police even use small airplanes to check up on some cocky swimmers who venture out too far. But the two grandmothers would love it here as well, enjoying the cool breeze on the terrace of the beach cafeteria, with an occasional glance at the skyscrapers of Manhattan enveloped in the gray smog caused there by the humidity and heat nearly 30 miles distant—and they would never believe that the fiery heat there is surpassed only by that in hell! And of course, I am not forgetting you, my dear Emil, by any means: you may not want to believe it, but you of all people would really feel at home here. You would see Landsleute in such masses as you've never seen them before. The appropriate and necessary English expressions with which Yiddish is interspersed here you'll be able to learn real fast, and you can make small wagers on those thousand of racing turfs that dot the map from the East to the Westcoast, more than you ever dreamed of in the Kaffeehaus Nord! You'll be able to schmooze, talk politics and swap jokes, as you wish. One of the greatest gifts that America has given to its children is the right to free speech and everyone makes use of it to the fullest extent.

Every few steps you'll see a crowd of people—what our grandmother Secher always called a "Redel" an allusion to her old native country. One person usually leads the discussion, the others are listening and express their opinions, approvingly or disapprovingly, whether its about the war over there, the new regulations over here, the President, Congress, this or that senator, Lindbergh, about everything possible or impossible. They scold, revile, they praise, applaud depending on their views and disposition. Usually on the busiest place in New York you'll find some one standing on a small lectern, usually self made, an American flag attached to it

so that the cars can see him. and take the necessary precautions, and begins
to hold a speech. People usually pass him by without paying any attention, or they stop and listen, soon a "cop" i.e., a policeman drops by, not
necessarily to disperse the crowd but simply to listen, too; soon there
develops an animated discussion, the cop too, participates, but nobody gets
mad, or aggressive no matter how far apart are the discussants. Should
the opinions really diverge, or the discussion gets too intense, somebody
is bound to start the song "God Bless America" and everybody joins in.
Similarly things develop here on the beach. If the throats run dry from
too much talk, the matter under discussion is settled with a "let's have a
drink," and the worst opponents buy each other a drink until the matter
is solved to each one's satisfaction, which just might be that there is nothing better than the brand of liquor they are in the process of sharing.

Yesterday I joined Hannah in bringing Jonas to Jamesburg, the "summer camp" of the Handels. This gave me the opportunity to ride for the
first time in a real American railroad car. Jonas had recovered fully there
after his bout with a long illness. It is really very nice, lots of woods,
though everything is flat; they take good care of you, first class kitchen.
And again I had to think of mother and Mama. You both would love it
there. Most of the ladies and gentlemen are approximately of the same
age as theirs, they all lie comfortably in deck chairs in the wonderfully
cool shade of the giant Linden trees. Obviously this won't appeal to Hansi,
it is quite true, as Safirstein wrote earlier, there is no dancing! But even
Jonas' wife would not go out there, even though her children begged her
to go with father for two weeks: "it's too quiet there" she kept repeating
whenever the subject came up. Jonas was very happy that I came along
with him. This man with whom I've hardly exchanged 10 words I like
most of all our relatives. If we fail to visit them for any length of time,
he'll send someone to get us. His first question is always: what does Marie
write, and how is Hansi's mother and the aunt? Then he asks about Hansi's
work (of which he doesn't particularly approve), then he looks at all of us
very benevolently and urges us to take a candy or praline which he himself also favors very much. That seems to be a Handel-Secher habit,
finding candy so delectable, right, Marie?

Safirsteins have asked me to include a few lines from them in order
to express their thanks for your concern about his last illness, but from
which he now has fully recovered. Please Ella, do me the favor and inform
Emma and Hansi that we received their letter and immediately passed it
on.

Unfortunately we haven't heard from Robert since May 17. However
Ernst writes that a joint acquaintance, who used to frequent Ernst' places

in Vienna and Gastein, had some business where R. now resides and made a point of visiting him. They celebrated a very merry "Lakner-Night" together, We were also happy to learn from Hansi Lakner that she has heard now from Roths in Budapest. We were quite concerned about them and have written repeatedly to their address in Athens. Could we now have their latest address? Lakners should not be mad at us that we do not write directly to them—but our reports to you are of course meant for them as well if they are interested in them. We too, know what Hansi writes to the Bachners, just as we let the Bachners know when we get letters from her. We have, unfortunately heard nothing from Frau Eisler about sponsoring them. We would like to know soon more details about matters concerning your departure. Are quotas and visas issued? And what is the role of the KG ? Are you going there as much as you possibly can and dun them—it's the only way, you know! What are you doing for money? Is Frau Weissberg able to support you with some? Please do not despair over the money—we have already started all kind of things. I am expecting your weekly news and shall mail this letter only after it arrives. I hope you my dearest little mother are in good health, as well as all of you, I kiss and embrace you most fervently, your Emil.

#74

New York, July 19th, 1941

My dearest "birthday child"-mother and all my loved and dear ones!

My first greeting is for you, dearest mother and... *[... illegible...]* My wishes for you are no different than those for the rest of the 364 days and all climax in the one fervent, big wish that stands high above all others: Health! Then all the other wishes will be granted and you will overcome this difficult time with the help of God and, finally, together with all your loved ones you will join us here—we who are waiting for you with such great longing and you will happily experience the return of that day of welcome many, many times. Then all our worries will be past and you will only have joy with your children and those who are your children's children.

It hurts me deeply that I cannot bring you anything for your birthday, not even a flower, or something you need although I know that you can use so many things, not even a simple candy that you like so much. But all that will be made up later, once you are here, making up for all the birthdays you had to spend so far from us. Already in the morning

The family in happier times—At the table, from left to right, sitting: Melanie Schab (wife of Ernst), Wilhelm Schab, Omi Schab, Ignatz Schab, Hedwig Schab (née Neumann, wife of Victor), and Felix Schab.

Standing behind them, from left: Ernst Schab, Ada Schab (wife of Wilhelm), Schindler (a very close friend of the family), Jerta (wife of Rudolf Schab), Rudolf Schab, Hansi Secher (née Schab, wife of Emil), Emil Secher, Victor Schab (husband of Hedwig).

In front of the table, from left: Guckie Laufer, Edith Laufer (both cousins), Franzi Schab, daughter of Wilhelm and Ada, Hannah Schab, daughter of Victor and Hedwig, Lisel, daughter of Ernst and Melanie, Tante Ella Schab (sister to Hansi and all brothers), and Otto Schab, son of Rudolf and Jerta Schab.

The picture was taken on the occasion of 40th wedding anniversary of the grandparents, Regina and Ignatz Schab, in 1923, in the dining room of their home at Wien II. Taborstrasse 66.

your telephone will ring and someone shall ask for Mrs. Secher: then with your receiver at your ear a choir will sing Happy Birthday, the equivalent of our Long May She Live! song and then Western Union (the telephone company) will do you the honor of wishing you in the name of all your relatives, friends and acquaintances—all of whom are named individually—lots of luck. And the telegraph boys, in white gloves bring you a mountain of telegrams, this is the way it's done here, on birthdays. And of course there will be a birthday cake—making up in height what it lacks in width—always another stepped up layer, and then another one until finally there is a little house or sometimes a skyscraper with many, many little flowers and birdies made of marzipan, and then comes another tower and then a pillar, if that is possible. The higher the decoration the more refined the cake! And because you, dearest mother, have to forego, at least this year, all these good things, we send you instead these pictures of all of us, which we had taken especially in your honor.—They are also the reason that our wishes for you are a little late since we had to wait for them. I hope, mother that they do give you pleasure even though they are not quite first class, they are after all only amateur snapshots.

What do you think of our Herbert? He did borrow the cigarette only for the time of taking the picture, just like the car he leans against. And what about Hansi? She is getting younger all the time! With great trepidation I am looking ahead to the time when I shall have to get a baby carriage for her! You too, Ella must accept my late wishes for everything wonderful on your birthday. The lateness of my wishes is indeed your fault, rather than mine. We were determined to assume that they would no longer reach you there and so we expected to celebrate here, after your arrival. Fate has put indeed all of us to a hard test. But we shall not concede defeat and we shall not lose either our hope or our courage. It is simply a postponement and not a cancellation. Of course there appear to be all kinds of difficulties just now, a number of undeniable injustices with respect to the issuing of visas—but everyone here is up in arms over that and pulling every conceivable string to counter these incidences. We simply have to start all over again this time in Washington—all affidavits must be sent first to Washington and we shall take this route undaunted in our perseverance.

Yesterday Grete Brainin and husband visited us again, primarily on account of Heinrich/Helly; Sigi Brainin will see to it that Heinrich's sponsor now repeats the same route via Washington and that should not meet with any resistance or difficulties on his part. As soon as I had received Heinrich's letters, I immediately contacted his brother Oskar in order to persuade him in my most sincere and affectionate manner of H's need of $310.00, or at least of a part of that amount, as Sigi and I would take on the responsibility for the balance. This letter was submitted to both Hansi and the Brainins for approval for we all know what a sensitive and irritable character that Mr. Oscar really is. I did not receive an answer from him this time, too, just as he ignored my letter written soon after my arrival here. But now there came a letter by him to Grete in which he blames her as the instigator of my letter and says he does not have to be reminded by anyone of what his duties are. Fact is, I did not say one word about "duty," but, on the contrary stressed that I was familiar with his contribution to the already existing amount, and that we just want for all of us to pull together for a last ditch effort to complete the remaining balance. But his opinion of me hardly affects me, since in the end he agreed and said he would do whatever he can; he also inquired at the same time from the JOINT whether, should the required amount be deposited, Heinrich/Helly would be able to leave immediately. He then reproached us for having done everything incorrectly in dealing with JOINT, HIAS, etc. If only he had the opportunity to see to everything from here he could have achieved much more. I already wrote once before to Heinrich directly, that all those who do not actually live in New York imagine everything can be handled here according to a simple plan. One goes to the Council or J. or to the H. and just orders, as needed, 2, 3, 5 or even more ship tickets to be sent gratis to one's charges. I, on the other hand, recently wrote, in Grete's name, a very detailed letter to the Rotterdam Storage Co., enclosed a death certificate of the aunt with the observation that this ought be sufficient to prove that the owner of the stored articles had never been in enemy country, etc. In any case the company should keep the boxes in storage until everything has been settled according to the satisfaction of the agent. He must have received this letter by now and as soon as we get an answer I shall write to Heinrich. In her next letter Grete will enclose a copy of the letter to the agent.

How is Helly? Has she recovered from the infection? Please give her as well as Heinrich our warmest regards. I simply must always thank her for her attentiveness to you and I am truly sad not to have been able to do more for her.

A few days ago we received your dear postcard of 25 June, addressed to Otto, it arrived after your card of 30 June. Thank God you're all doing well. You've got incorrect information: airmail functions beautifully. In any case we shall now learn how long it will take your letter with only a regular stamp to get here. There is little to say about us my dear ones. My vacation is approaching its end—Monday I relieve my boss whose turn it will be now to start his vacation. In any case this will be a time when I am not going to work too hard. We suffer a great deal from the heat. I am certain the summer this year is much hotter and more humid than the last one. It is incredible, the amount of liquids one consumes. Everything is drunk cold or, indeed with ice. Coffee with ice is made by pouring black coffee into the ice tray in the refrigerator where it freezes into black ice cubes. These are then put into the glass and lukewarm milk is poured over them, quickly melting the cubes; all this is sweetened with powdered sugar and then slurped through a straw. Tea is drunk the same way. Really popular cold drinks are the, in Europe, little known Coca-Cola and Pepsi-Cola. Millions of bottles are sold daily of these drinks. At first I found their taste rather peculiar, but by now we've got used to it and consume them practically by the dozens. A bottle (ca. as much as one of our soft drinks in V.) costs 5 cent, but 6 bottles cost only 16 cent. As with everything else in America you are practically forced to consume *en masse*. This is no joke: you see a fur coat in the window for $500.00 but if you take two you pay only $800.00. The same with dresses or men suits, they all advertise the price for one, two or three pieces if they are bought at the same time.

Again, for you my dearest mother all kinds of good and lovely things on your birthday, a feast day for us as well and you and all our loved and dear ones are fervently embraced and kissed by your Emil.

#75

New York, 28th July 1941

My dearest sweet Mother

and all my beloveds in Lessinggasse & Hochedlingergasse!

In the meantime, I hope you've received my last letter with the enclosed Photos. I even sent it registered because I'd be very annoyed if especially my birthday wishes for you and the pictures had got lost. Once you acknowledge them I shall send a complete set of pictures for dear Mama Schab.

I hope dearest mother you spent your birthday happily and I am expecting a full report from Marie. One thing you must have surely felt, my dearest mother, that my thoughts on that day were continuously with you—and when only a small part of our wishes are fulfilled by the good Lord, we should be happy indeed.

Although we are still missing a weekly mail, which usually gets here on a Monday—we were compensated with news from Irma/Benno and also from Rudi. Otto will surely write you about Irma/Benno, possibly enclose his letter—I dare not anticipate him in this. Only to say that their letter exudes a certain satisfaction with their situation, as far as living conditions and their general progress are concerned. Only Irma's great longing for you is a sorrow that disturbs her otherwise happy existence and that is something we can understand only too well. She too, would be a lot more satisfied if she only knew you to be here with us. However I shall write even in greater detail about the contents of Rudi's letter; it is the first one in nearly a year not counting one that arrived some months ago but took almost half a year to get here because he didn't send it by airmail. In my last letter to Benno I included some very sharp lines addressed to Rudi and these obviously proved to be effective. He writes that they are doing quite well, even though it takes a lot of work—what kind of work he doesn't reveal! I assume it is what they've always done: Rudi/Jerta in a Cafe, and Otto busy with his photography. They are all, thank God, healthy and some of the anxieties of the last few months have been dissipated, so now they can breathe more freely. He is in continuous touch with Ernst, about whom he reports, what you have already learned through us that he, Ernst, as well as his family, and of course Felix, Hannah and her family are doing very well especially in the businesses. On the other hand he (Rudi) complains not having heard from Victor in a long time. In the mean time our worries about Victor have increased even more in view of the latest developments there and I ask you to let us know immediately should you hear from him, just as we shall, in case something reaches us. We assume that Victor as well as Epstein will most certainly write to us first, as we represent a solid, dependable basis. Otherwise Rudi writes a little more about the heat, especially the hot winds that take your breath away, in the months of April, May and September-October. But with their heat they can hardly impress us! The temperatures this year are much worse than the ones of last year, as far as I can recollect—as it is, a lastingly dry heat wouldn't bother us all that much—when the winds come from the center of the country toward the East coast they are very hot but still dry and continental. That means clear, sunshiny days, the nights agreeably cool the morning air invigorating and pleasant. When one rides on such a morning on the open upper deck of a city bus along the wonderful Riverside Drive it is possible to imagine, when looking across the wide river to the hilly and wooded area of the New Jersey shore, that this is one of those lakes in the Salzkammergut. But when the winds soar in from the Ocean, then all of New York is "Humidity" as this moisture-laden air is called. The whole city is shrouded in a cloud of vapor & smog, everything drips, the clothes on your body feel wet, the keys in your pocket and everything metallic in the apartment is in danger of corroding, the windows perspire, but never mind my long drawn out description. Just imagine you're sitting fully dressed in one of the steam chambers in the Römerbad; nobody can escape anywhere. Fortunately such periods of humidity do not last very long: 1–2 days and it is over for another two weeks or so. And right now one can say that, well it can't last much longer! And we know that above all: there are worse things in life. My vacation is behind me and beginning this week I am back at the office. Despite the heat there are no vacations from politics and there is always something that gets everyone's feelings all heated up, at least those for whom it is still not hot enough. This time it is a proposal submitted by the President to Congress to extend the compulsory military service program. A short walk in the evening provides one with all the information on this subject by speakers at nearly every street corner. There are those who inveigh against it and a few pace farther those who are for it.

But politics alone is not sufficient to satisfy the greedy sensationalism of the American: somewhere there has got to be also a scandal in the so-called "high society." Right now the papers are full of news about a recently deceased Millionaire who had bequeathed his dollars in four equal parts to four so-called "Show-Girls" i.e., girls who dance in musicals, while his wife and five adult children had not been remembered with one red cent! Of course, each one of those lucky four girls has to be interviewed individually, so that the front pages of the newspapers can be filled up. All four agree that the deceased had been the nicest man (*ein reizender Mensch*). This is followed by interviews with wife and children who— you guessed it—maintain the exact opposite.

When I bring you these vignettes of everyday life in America, I do this in order to show you the kind of worries that concern these lucky people, as well as free you for a few short moments from your own worries.

All you my dearest beloved ones: at this time there is a deadlock in the negotiations over the whole question of immigration, and absolutely nothing can be done about it right now. This is what we're told wherever we go for information or send our inquiries—it's always the same thing. I only hope that you receive this information with more composure and peace of mind than is the case with us here. It has to change, I insist, it must, must, must change. It cannot last forever that people and countries are totally isolated from each other. And especially you who have your closest relatives here, you cannot, you will not be denied, by anyone, here or elsewhere, your opportunity to join us. You will see, my loved ones that I am right, and soon you will be able to tell me that yourself! Everything will work out ok—the good Lord is merely testing us, long and hard.

And now my dearest ones, good-bye for just now, say hello to all our dear friends, especially Heinrich/Helly (they must carry on with stiff upper lip), Regina/Dora (what is happening with them, how is Dora), please consider yourself, all of you fervently kissed and embraced by your Emil. And how would it be if my dear brother-in-law, Emil would deign to add a few lines for his son who feels very hurt and for that matter—so do we!

#76

New York, August 2nd, 1941

My dearest, good mother, Dearest Marie and Emil, Dearest Mama and
　Ella!

Your letters, dear Marie of July 7th & 14th arrived almost simultaneously, the last one only a few hours after the first one, thus actually in
record time. In your second letter you write more fully about what Emil
is doing, so that we, and especially Otto are a little more at ease about
that. We couldn't figure out from the first letter exactly where and what
he was working at and Otto assumed it was somewhere outside of the
city. Maybe you, or, even better, Emil himself could write us a few lines
about the nature of the job, etc. It would interest us greatly and we would
like to think that it isn't too exhausting. You, however, Marie, really worry
us. Aren't there any signs of improvement after such long treatments? But
I am quite sure that you do not follow doctor's orders very carefully, nor
do you spare yourself in your efforts. Otto says you shouldn't burden yourself so much with the household chores. Once all of you are over here,
with God's help, we shall have a household ready for you, dearest Marie,
in which you can enjoy life to the fullest!

We especially loved your added lines, my dearest sweet, mother. We
were happily amused, as well as moved to tears about your concern for us
over a distance of three thousand miles! What wouldn't I give to be able
to hear you scold us again, to see your critical look with which you scru-
tinized us whenever we dropped by for a visit, whether our coats weren't
too light for the season, just because it was a little cooler outside, did we
have rubbers to protect us against a heavy rain and snowshoes if it snowed.
You just as soon would have sent us home had we come without a shawl
wrapped tightly around our neck in the manner of opera tenors afraid of
cool air prior to their stage appearance. Herbert occasionally wears here,
in the manner of other American boys an open collar shirt with a silk neck-
erchief and when I see him with it I say, disapprovingly: your grandmother Secher surely would love to see you like that—but I don't! Dearest
mother I can still hear you call out twice a day, in the morning and in the
afternoon when I went to my school in the Holzhausergasse and consequently had to cross the Kaiser-Josefstrasse as it was known then: " Emil,
watch out for the trolley cars!" But to return to your admonitions, dearest mother: do not worry! There are fewer things that can happen to you
here than over there. As it were I already wrote once that the lifeguards
on the beaches watch over you most carefully. Also on all beaches here is
the most ideal shoreline you can possibly imagine: one can walk out into

the ocean for long distances and still touch bottom. And of course we always cool off before we even step into the water! As I wrote earlier, once you and Mama Schab arrive here, with God's help, you'll both be going to the beach and then, mother, you will be able to watch over all of us!

We finally received your long expected letter, Mama/Ella and so we finally learn how close you'd been to your goal. We keep asking ourselves how that could apply to you since you had already been summoned for the 30th of June and the consulates did not close officially until July 10th. But don't be sad. You and we, both are being put to a hard test but we shall succeed with God's help, and the time will not be all too distance when we can hold you in our arms.

It saddens us, my dear Ella to learn about your illness, but we are happy to know that you have recuperated. I'm sure there isn't much that you can add to this. Who attended you? How could Mama afford this? Were the Braun girls with you? We are grateful to Frieda for not forgetting you—we speak of her often and think of her even more so. We greet her most affectionately. In any case, take good care of yourself Ella, the same way you always take care of Mama and are indefatigable in attending to her needs. What is at risk here is our reunion and that must be worth something; that I must tell all of you, Mama, mother and Marie and Emil: Don't just watch over your physical well-being but also maintain your mental balance as difficult as that might be. And please do not make life more difficult for each other than it already is. Just now I learned that assistance money remittances would shortly be approved again. As soon as it is feasible we shall again make a transfer. Please let us know, dear Marie, whether and when Ms. Weissberg is going to give you some small assistance. Even though we cannot reimburse her right now, we want at least to thank her. We never fail to visit her relation here from time to time and inquire about her health. She always sends regards to Hannah and she is truly concerned about Regina and Dora. What you're writing about Dora, dear Marie is truly discouraging and saddens us greatly. How can she be helped? Is there no opportunity for her to go somewhere for recuperation? They too must not sink into apathy, especially not now; you must mutually keep each other in a positive mood. Do they occasionally have news from Frieda? Give them all our best regards and we hope that the news we all await eagerly, but especially Hannah, will soon be on its way.

How is Helly? Has her hand healed? Can she work again at her voluntary occupation? How are Heinrich and her mother? Just do not give up now!! I thank Helly that she spoils you so and we send our greetings to her, Heinrich and her mother.

This week, after an almost eight months silence, we received a letter from Roths in Budapest which made us very glad, even though it was already two months old, having come by ordinary mail. We had been extremely worried about them and had not the slightest idea where their fate had carried them. After some very risky wanderings about they made it to Budapest with no more than the clothes on their back. Gyula couldn't find any work, became very sick (pneumonia) and they fared very poorly for a while and complained bitterly about their relatives. We hope fervently that things have improved for them, they are after all very clever people, who can deal with every situation life deals them.

There is not much to tell about us, my dear ones. The heat is difficult to bear—even though at present we're in the middle of a rainy spell—but that is even worse. We comfort ourselves, as with so many other things, that this too, shall pass! Some things take a short time, others a little longer! We're looking forward to Fall which is so wonderful here and lasts sometimes until after Christmas. Jonas is already back from his vacation, but for a while he is just staying at home. Where he works, they are doing some renovating and that may take a few more weeks. Actually quite agreeable if wages would continue to be paid, but that, unfortunately, is not the custom here.

Gradually, there is spreading a wave of price increases, in all areas but especially food prices rose quite high, so much so that the government is talking about some sort of intervention. We too feel the increase in food prices very strongly—wages of course do not keep pace. It's the same thing all over the world.

Do you too suffer from the heat? Ella writes about that, also, how she suffered from it while being so sick—and you, too, Marie mention it. How is your room? Does it have sun and when? In the morning or in the afternoon? Do you have good blinds so you can protect yourselves from the sun? Are there trees in the backyard and do you see a little green? Does the same go for Mama/Ella? How do you get along with the people who share the flat with you? Do they continue to be nice? Who took the place of the Tragholz's? Do you have any news from Tragholz? And from the others who were forced to leave?

Please write, as much as you can about yourselves, however unimportant or uninteresting it may appear to you. For us everything is important. And now I see I must close again;

I embrace you my dearest, good mother, and you Marie/Emil and Mama/Ella, I greet and kiss you many times, your Emil.

#77

New York August 9th, 1941

My dearest good mother,

and all you dear people in Hochedlinger & Lessinggasse! Your last letter, dearest Marie, in which you told us of receiving the wire transfer from Hertha via the Reichsbank was briefly acknowledged in my letter to you of last week.

We were very glad that this finally worked OK, after so many failures and disappointments in other matters, especially as they affected your coming over here to join us—we had counted so much on that, but you'll agree with me, won't you my beloved ones, we are not going to be discouraged and shall not ever give up hope for a happy and glorious wiedersehen.

That you got so much joy out of viewing those two pictures from the Photo Automat makes us very happy too, even though there really wasn't much to see on them. I hope that in the meantime, you're already in possession of the amateur snapshots we had taken on the occasion of your birthday, mother—these are all a little better and you can more or less see what the three of us look like. I am again enclosing, in this letter, a few small pictures: Hansi in the park near the Hudson River bank, just a few hundred steps from our residence, and of Herbert, the way he usually looks as a "school boy." During the winter he wears over that a so-called school jacket, with a big "W" on its front and the logo of his school, circled by its name: "Washington" on the back. Well, that surely ought to keep him from getting lost! And then there is a picture of Hansi, surrounded by youth, Herbert and his colleagues. All these pictures, which we are sending now are for Mama only, i.e., also for Ella and maybe you can exchange some of them with each other. As time passes I shall always send two of each picture so that both mother and Mama have their own picture and in that way God forbid, nobody has to fight over them! But you just must be a little patient, I cannot enclose them all at once since that would make the postage much more expensive.

To return to that matter with Hertha, my dearest Marie: please do not refuse any assistance from Frau Weisberg should she offer, in her usual kindly manner, to share with you some of her own meager resources. We can repay her goodness now only with words of thanks. But surely there'll come a time when we shall be able to do something for her as well. In the meantime please convey to her our most heartfelt greetings. We have not visited with her relative, Frau Hannah since May, but if she should ask us, through you, dear Marie, that we should look her up, we shall of

course do that. Please give our regards also to Regine and Dora; we hope
that the latter has recuperated after her stay in the hospital—and maybe
you can persuade her to write once more to her relatives here who are truly
concerned about her well being. My dearest ones, I am not even going to
mention the heat to you—it must be boring for you to keep hearing the
same lamentations. To be sure in some ways we are already used to it.
Last week we again went to the beach, together with our old friends the
Deutsch's, where it is really wonderful. One is more than willing to bear
the hardships of the trip there and back—it is no pleasure even by car,
which the Deutsch's use occasionally to drive there—because once you're
there it is marvelous and even at the height of the season when millions
of New Yorkers spend their vacation time somewhere in the country, there
is not much crowding. We also visit a beach, Jakob Riis Park, that is a
little more distant (from the end of the subway line it takes the bus about
another 20 minutes, and that adds another .20 cents for the roundtrip)
so that alone cuts down on the number of people going, as well as improving the quality of people that can be found there; unlike in that well-
known but notorious Coney Island where the most people and the biggest
bally-hoo in NY can be found (a la our old Wurstelprater in Vienna).
Personally I've so far refused to go swimming in C.I., but Hansi went once
on a Saturday (when I work till about 2PM) and she liked it pretty well,
but you know her she loves to have fun. Right now there is quite a bit of
excitement among my dear Americans. There is currently underway a
small attempt to restrict the use of motor fuel and the authorities have
ordered closing the gas stations at 7PM—normally they are open 24hrs a
day. In other words not really a direct reduction of gas consumption, since,
after all, every owner of a car could fill up just a few minutes before 7P
as much as he wanted. Nevertheless, a great deal of excitement! They'd
rather suffer rationing some important article of food, even bread, but to
be subjected to regulations restricting the driving of one's car, well that
portends the end of the world! All that is lacking would be a restriction
concerning the attendance of movies and there'd really be a revolution.
His car and the movies, these are the most important things in the life
of the average American. Happy people who knows only the term "blackout" without the real experience behind it, to stories of which they can
listen almost incredulously and with continuous amazement. In the last
few days even those beautiful women of New York had something added
to their worries as well as to their topics of conversation: silk stockings!
In view of the most recent tensions between the U.S.A. and Japan where
most of the silk imports originate, silk stockings have disappeared from
the marketplace. Whether or not that occurred deliberately is impossible

to determine; possibly local business people have already learned something from their European counterparts. At any rate thousands of New York women are lining up in front of the big department stores, such as Macy's, as well as at the smaller specialty stores. The newspapers are printing many pages of "eyewitness' reports; there are pictures, cartoons, jokes etc.

For us well-informed Europeans this really is not much "news," more a form of repetition—and that there should be such a repetition in this blessed and happy country makes us thoughtful and just a little sad. At least until similarly well-informed Americans who know their country and countrymen better, try to comfort us: there is a certain childish impulse to imitate at play here, they say.

Americans hear and read so much about Europe nowadays, they see even more in the movies, as never before pictures of war, air attacks, bombs, Tanks etc. and they eagerly absorb, with a certain childish amusement, these new terms. In the many arcades and shooting galleries which cater to the public not only in Coney Island but also in other parts of the city on its main streets and parks, one can, for a nickel, drive a tank, shoot at airplanes with anti-aircraft guns, or, conversely bomb a city to smithereens from the cockpit of an airplane, engage in see battles and, to make this all even more realistic, don a gasmask while doing all that. Whatever is happening over there—in Europe—is a sort of thrill for those over here, a stimulation of the imagination, sort of what we experienced as young boys 40 years ago on the occasion of the Russo-Japanese war or the Boer war. It makes them happy and they feel almost involved when the ladies cannot buy any silk stockings for a few days. Stella has left on vacation a few days ago, Hansi leaves next Thursday (Aug. 14) for Tannersville a place in the Catskill Mountains in the state of New York, which friends of ours recommended to us with great enthusiasm. It involves a wonderful trip of ca. 4 hrs on a river steamer up the Hudson and then by bus to T. where the resort she is staying at picks her up by car. Once she arrives there she'll write you all the details.

Again I have to close, although I could go on & on schmoozing with you. But then the letter would be too heavy. I kiss you and embrace you my dearest, good mother, and also all you others my dearest ones, and with my prayer to the Lord to keep you healthy, I close and am as ever your Emil

#78

New York, September 10/16th 1941

Dearest Mother, Beloved Marie and Emil, Beloved Mama and Ella!

This time Mama and Ella were the industrious and good ones who presented us already with two letters during the past week. From you dear Marie we received only one letter, and that of August 24th–26th in which you complain of a lack of mail. However, as Mama acknowledges two letters of mine in her letter of August 30th (posted on Sept. 1st and received here on the 13th) without mentioning their date, I assume that these letters must have reached you sometime between the 26th and 30th of August, and that must have calmed both you and mother, I'm sure.

All your letters displayed such a sorrowful undertone, that our hearts became heavy with pain upon reading them. In addition there have been reports in the newspapers, that did not serve to lift our spirits. Can you actually do all the things in that one-hour a day during which you're permitted to shop, etc.? And at the same time enjoy some fresh air?

That news was again the reason for several phone calls between Otto and myself. Last Sunday Otto and Stella joined us for lunch and we stayed together till 10 PM. After Jause—not really the custom here but occasionally we still live in the old Viennese style—we went for a walk along Riverside Drive then to a movie and we didn't part until 10 o'clock at night. We spoke only of you, encouraging each other with plans for the future all designed around your arrival here. Otto is doing real well now though his job is by no means an easy one, it is at least financially worthwhile—his weekly wage is twice what he started with. He has turned into a saver and calculator, more so than I used to be in my best times! He is full of plans for you and Irma-Benno-Heinzi. There is again talk about the Cuba-project, even though Cuba had been closed during the last few days. Unfortunately the amounts demanded for that are really incredibly high: A visa sells for $250.00 and in addition a deposit of $500.00 per person is required; that deposit is returned the moment one leaves Cuba. To that must be added a Bank guarantee of $1,500.00—although it is possible to buy such a guarantee for $150.00. And to that must be added the cost of transportation. All that brings you only to Cuba with its terrible tropical climate and still four days distant by ship from New York! Although we would be able to go there ourselves and visit with you. Then there is the trip from a Portuguese or Spanish port to Cuba on one of those rickety Spanish or Portuguese lines that last sometimes 3 to 4 weeks (though under normal conditions barely 10 days). Recently a Spanish ship arrived here the *Navemar*, which brought 1100 refugees, even though it had space for only 15 (yes, fifteen!) passengers and which was at sea for 68 days! Because of the unspeakable unsanitary conditions on that ship it was not given permission to land in New York, had to return to Cuba, but finally returned and all its passengers are now quarantined in Ellis Island. For days now the newspapers report on the indescribable lack of sanitary conditions on this "ship from hell" where passengers could not change clothes for two months were fed rotten meat and suffered from a lack of water. For that the passengers paid an average of $400 to $500.00 per person, that is the money was deposited here for some while others paid as much as $1,000.00 for the privilege of traveling on that ship. Of course there was a great public outcry here and the ship captain and his officers were threatened with arrest. So we must ask ourselves, whether we can assume responsibility, regardless of costs, to encourage you to undertake such a crossing. Hopefully we may assume that this was just a special case, which will hardly be repeated in exactly this execrable way. We are also in touch with Willy in this matter of a Cuba opportunity. I was at his office today, Monday evening, and all of us will get together on Wednesday to talk some more about this. The Cuba visa could be obtained in Berlin; but I do not know whether it would require a trip there, or whether it could be done by simply mailing a passport (registered) to the Cuban embassy in Berlin which would then return the passport with the visa, also registered, of course. The Schab family will use the occasion to visit us in our new home—even though it is still lacking many things, and it will take a long time before we have furnished everything— I am sure it will be to their liking. My dear brother-in-law and old buddy Emil! Yesterday, when Otto was here to visit we used the occasion to celebrate your birthday, each one of us raised a dram of brandy and drank to your health—unfortunately I do not have any wine in my cellar—not yet, anyway! And we talked a lot about you; you surely must have gotten the hiccups, even without the brandy. Your life has not been an easy one during the latter years—and especially not in the very last ones. But we shall hope that there won't be any lasting scars, and that you'll still be the same old dashing character I always remember, the "Gunny" with his cap askew, the many glittering medals on his chest and the Cavalry Saber tugged elegantly under your arm. Or, as during the last years in your Austrian, traditional Styrian-type garb with a chamois-buck brush sticking out of your hatband. May the good Lord continue to keep you healthy, brave and courageous as always and may you be granted to come here soon together with Marie and grandmother—who you could hardly be without—to see your children who long so much for you! By the way Hansi almost had a fight with us since she simply would not believe that this is your 64th birthday we were celebrating! All the very best to you, my dear, good Emil.

Special thanks to you, dearest mother, for your added lines. So it is no longer so hot where you are and fall is already in the air. However, around here there is no chance yet of cooler weather. Yesterday, Sunday we did have a very pleasant day and I actually wore a jacket when otherwise I only walk around in a shirt with rolled up sleeves. But today it is again horribly hot and humid and the weather bureau announce that these temperatures are most likely to last well into October. Well, if I only knew that all bad things would surely come to an end as will this summer, I'd be very happy. The synagogues announce that during the High Holidays—which we'll celebrate already next week—they will be "air-conditioned," i.e., they'll be cooled down electrically. As I already wrote you once before I'll be admitted to a very nice Temple in our neighborhood where I shall also pray for you. I frequently take out the photo album and look at the pictures of our dear departed ones and do our prayers for them. I picture how I went there with you, mother and you Marie to visit their peaceful graves. I hope dear sister, that on your last visit there you also put a little stone there in my name, and maybe a flower. Did you get upset again? Please dearest Marie, do not let mother fast, under any circumstances! But the good Lord excuses you and all the others, especially Mama, from fasting also.

We're glad that you visited with Helly and Heinrich outside the city and were able to enjoy some fresh air that way. Mother was not along? Probably it was too difficult for her? Please give my regards to both of them and also to Helly's mother. Please tell them if they could be helped with some years of life or blood from the heart, not only I but also all the others here would only be too glad to make that sacrifice. Hansi and Otto are moved beyond words over what Helly does for you! We thank you so much for the greetings of Mama's friends and return them forthwith. Give our best regards to Dora and Regine, to Miss Weissberg, and not forgetting our dear friend Frieda, the Streit family, the Balls, as well as old Erdheim, all of whom we wish everything good for the Holy Days. Special greetings to the young grandmother Mrs. Pr. and her husband who hopefully were able to relax fully during their vacation.

Last and best my dearest, good mother I hail you and Mama, Ella, Marie and Emil, as ever your Emil.

#79

New York, September 21st, 1941

My dearest, good mother, Marie, Emil, Dearest Mama, and Ella!

This time I am just a little nervous, since during the whole of past week we haven't had anything from you. But I hope that tomorrow, there will be some mail. Even though I reported my change of address to the post-office here, I still drop by at Fort Washington Ave, our previous address and inquire whether something has arrived for us, and of course I also ask over at Handels. Hopefully, none of your letters to us gets lost as a result of our move. Mail delivery here is not exactly done in the expected "American" way. When, over a year ago, we moved from 174th street, a lot of letters got lost. Not ours since you always wrote to the Handel's address. But several letters from Vally Nagler did not reach us, they were returned to her and only much later she mailed them again to me. A short time ago I received a letter from Mr. Pappenheim, a friend of the deceased Hajek, which informed me of Hajek's death. This letter was in transit for 8 months, had already been here (sent to the 174th Street address), was returned as not deliverable, after which Pappenheim sent it again to the Handels's address. I would not like a repeat of this performance. Epsteins and Victor in Riga, always wrote me to the Fort Washington Avenue address; they don't know that I've moved, and it is especially from them that I always expect some mail—consequently I'm frequently at the Post office. They already know me there, and continue to report my change of address, so that letters mailed to my old address are automatically forwarded to my new one.

Yesterday the postal clerk there told me smilingly that my name on their list of address changes is marked with a red pencil. Mail is not delivered here directly to your door; instead everyone has a small mailbox, identified by name and apartment number, in the entrance hall, and in this box the mail is delivered and then locked by the mail carrier. In the morning around 9AM the first mail arrives and the mailman then sorts it out for at least half an hour during which time the recipients sit around expectantly in the hall. Nobody is permitted to approach the mailman and he will never give the mail to anyone in person. Once he is finished everyone storms to the boxes and unlocks his own. On the other hand, everything that is connected with the mail is treated extremely confidential, because mail theft or even just negligence is punished with very high penalties. For example there are no receipts for the mailing of parcels. If you insist on one you'll have to insure it. Consequently you don't have to take parcels to the post office. Next to every mail box there is also a very large box for parcels. You must know that the mail here plays an incredibly important role in the conduct of business: if you buy something in a shop that doesn't have a delivery boy available and you do not want to carry your purchase home yourself then the sales person will make a nice package, address and stamp it and then carry it across the street to the next mail box and in the morning you'll receive it at home. You can imagine that with such an operation the parcel post boxes cannot possibly have sufficient room to accommodate all parcels. Well, then you just put it down next to the mailbox, on the sidewalk! It is true, in the beginning when I still "cruised" around "downtown" i.e., in the business quarter, it always struck me as peculiar to notice, next to the mailboxes, stacked high, all kinds of parcels which the passing mail truck simply picked up. And nothing ever gets lost! As I already mentioned once, mail theft, even if it involves only a few cents, is considered a felony and punishable with long prison sentences.

Hansi has told me that in the countryside there weren't even any mailboxes—a letter is just put next to the fence where the mailman picks it up at the same time that he leaves mail there. People won't even think of putting up their own mailbox next to the fence.

So, with these remarks, my dearest ones, I have again presented you with a lively bit of American cultural history, primarily with the idea to make you familiar with this country which already has become our home and which, I am certain will also become yours.

If, with the help of my frequent descriptions you already have acquired such familiarity, and will, with the Lords help come over here very soon, finding many things that I already told you about, then this will truly be a source of joy for me—if only it would happen real, real soon! Today is Rosh Hashanah, and that means for all of us two days of not having to work. In fact Hansi and Otto will have four consecutive days off, Saturday until all day Tuesday.

The weather is wonderful, hot but not unbearably so, blue sky with radiant sunshine, a rarity for this time and these holidays. Sine Hansi has told us so many good things about her trip on the Hudson, Otto and I received special permission from our two wives who, after all already enjoyed their beautiful vacation, to take a Sunday "vacation," by way of an excursion on a tourist ship up the Hudson to the beautiful Bear Mountains and back again.

We started at 8AM in the morning, and were back by 4P.

Anyone from Vienna will characterize this trip as none other than an American version of the "Wachau" excursion on the Danube that beautifully landscaped region of old castles and vineyards—but I can now testify that it is far surpassed by this trip! To this one must add the really luxurious excursion boat, with space for over 1000 persons, sundeck, deck chairs, concerts, a public address system used to explain every point of interest—it was just wonderful. And who doesn't know that famous house, so notorious, it turns up in almost every detective thriller playing in America, which kindled our fantasies as young boys: Sing-Sing! The "Stein" of America! So this, too, Otto and I had the opportunity to observe, fortunately only from the outside when passing by. A baseball game between two prisoner teams was just in progress and the announcer explained it in a very humorous manner.

We had hardly returned from our trip, when I already sat down at my typewriter in order to write you, because I know that a letter written by me, tomorrow, on this Jewish holiday will not please you, my dearest mother. Afterwards we'll go and visit with the Handels. Among the many good wishes from friends and relatives for the New Year I also found one from Dr. Weil. He is happy to learn that we now have our own apartment, and promises to visit us soon, since he now has more time after his examinations, though he isn't sure that he passed. However, I am certain he did well, he just doesn't want to appear over confident.

This week Otto and I wrote another detailed letter to Irma-Benno, and Rudi. Also to Olly and Elly. Will also write to Ernst soon and enclose a few lines from an old acquaintance of his and Felix's, a Mr. Kugel (an old guest at the Cafe Promenaden a well as in his Hotel in Gastein), I ran into him here by accident. As I already wrote you, Otto and I inquired at the JOINT concerning that particular deposit for the ship tickets. They answered that they had telegraphed the Jewish Community Organization in Vienna to find out how they felt about returning the money. Of course, this is exactly what we did not mean with our inquiry! I am sorry that you had to appear at the KG without knowing what it was all about, since our letter there arrived much later. Please, my dearest ones do not worry about this at all. We are not going to do any thing that makes your position uncomfortable and this amount—even a little more—stays reserved for you only, no matter what happens. After the holidays we shall again send some money. On the other hand the food package mailing from Lisbon does not seem to work. Hannah experimented with a package for Regine/Dora about a month ago. We want to wait at least until we hear that this arrived ok. Officially such a shipment is not possible but there are a few people who seem to think they can do it—unfortunately they are not very trustworthy!

I hope, dearest mother, you are all well—this is my most fervent wish! Again for all of you, including all your loved ones and friends, our best wishes and our love. Please, mother and Mama do not fast! As a matter of fact nobody should—you're doing it all year long anyway. I kiss and embrace you my dearest mother and my beloved ones, stay well for all of us and especially for your Emil.

#80

New York, September 28th, 1941

Dearest Mother and all our loved ones in Lessing-& Hochedlinger-gasse!

We ought to be quite worried, because for 14 days we've been missing your mail, dearest Marie and cannot explain the reason for it—though our overwrought imagination provides us with many reasons. Fortunately we received last week such a nice, detailed letter from Mama/Ella, already to the address of our new flat, and an equally nice letter from Helly/Heinrich—that one still to our old address but forwarded in due order to our new one. In both letters we heard only good things about you, so we've calmed down a bit. Mama tells us about her visit in the Lessinggasse which made you very happy, mother, and we too are very glad, that you, Mama, can walk so well and we hope, in fact want you mother, to reciprocate this visit very soon. Also that your injections are beginning to help, Marie, we were glad to learn from Mama's letter; we share her opinion that these injections after the prescribed pause, will begin to have a much more intensive effect. And we learned that you dear Emil, despite your heavy work are still most easily satisfied and are able to humor all the others. Helly, in turn, tells us that you all visited her and Heinrich, "in the country" and thus got some much needed fresh air. only you mother, have not yet seen fit to visit, Helly complains! She also says that you, dear sister, are suffering from a painful Arthritis and that she wants to persuade you to take some X-ray treatments, and we too urge you to try this, please. Helly will surely be able to help you with this since she works in that area.

We also want to take this opportunity to tell H & H how much we enjoyed their loving detailed letter, how much indeed, they could hardly estimate. Every line, every word that reaches us from loving people who were so close to us throughout our prior existence in our old Heimat makes us happy and the greater the distance from that life the Greater is our longing for those very people who were part of that life. That is why we maintain such a far-flung correspondence with dear ones and friends on all five continents! Helly and Heinrich were our companions along the most difficult path of our lives. That they had to continue on alone, does not cease to hurt us, even more that we've been able to do so little for them until now. But they must not give in to despair! Especially not now—it cannot possibly take as long as it did so far—until they come to join us, and I say the same to you, my dear ones! We shall write directly to Helly and Heinrich, but please do convey to them just this: I've arranged with Sigi/Grete that a residence certificate and a death certificate for Aunt Kathi is to be sent to Heinrich as well, together with a copy of the letter written by Grete to Hoogewerth. We shall continue to be always in touch with Sigi/Grete—they visit frequently with us and keep us informed about what Oscar, etc. are doing in the matter of supplying valid affidavits for H&H.

As difficult as it is for me to say this, at this time all of Germany and those areas occupied by it where no U.S. consulates are currently operating, have been completely excluded for purposes of emigration to the U.S.A. and Washington dos not even accept any applications from there. There are however, a variety of organizations here that promise all kinds of "pie in the sky": Entry from Germany via Spain or Portugal where U.S. consulates are open and working, thus one can wait in those countries until the time of notification by the consulate, even entry via Cuba may be possible. We are in touch with everyone and well informed about everything (yesterday, Saturday, I returned from one of those information tours in the evening at 9PM) but I am still very skeptical. Also please tell Helly this: Through an organization that deals in such matters, I have arranged to send a package from Lisbon with the following contents: 1 pound each of coffee, cacao, chocolate, and honey—instead of honey they promised to send sardines packed in oil; they decline to give any guarantee with respect to the nature of the contents or that the package actually arrives. The choices are very poor, since Portugal can export only those products that come directly from the colonies, and that means no condensed milk, lard or similar products.

This package costs $6.75 to which you have to add postage and cable costs. Thus the price has absolutely no relation to the value of the shipment, which would cost here approximately .80 cents! This is the cheapest package and its code name is "Anna." The most expensive shipment is "Fred" at U.S.$14.25 and I am enclosing for you the table of contents of these shipments—you can then figure out for yourselves what the real value is. The $14.25 shipment contains all the food products permitted to be shipped out. There is one other shipment for the same price, mainly designed for children, which contains cans of vegetables and Nestlé's baby food. Regardless, my dearest ones take a look at the list and if you want something please write to us. Packages addressed for Germany are accepted without any guarantee, i.e., officially they are not even supposed to be mailed. Hannah already tried a month ago to send something for Regine/Dora. Please let us know whether it arrived. The shipment for Helly's brother I sent to this address: Alfred Akselrad-Burgau 304 comp. T.E. 2a section, Langlade (Gard)

France and I only hope that this address, which I got from Mr. Strassmann is the correct one.

Yesterday I arranged with Willy for an amount to be sent for Mama/ Elia, and included in that amount are RM100.00 from me for mother/ Marie. I am not sure how much Willy will send, I suggested RM300.00 in which case it'll be a total of RM400.00. But should it be less, RMl00.00 is definitely for Marie.

We thank you and Mama/Ella for your heartfelt good wishes. We know that we spread only joy among you and at the same time make you forget a little bit of your sorrow when we let you know that from time to time how we have progressed just a little bit more. All the time we get little presents or people ask what we'd like for our new flat. Hannah surprised us with a wonderful new appliance, a "Broil king," i.e., an electrical appliance that is simply wonderful. There is nothing that cannot be prepared on it: We sometimes broil a whole chicken, we bake Schnitzel, or liver, roast sausages and potatoes, we scramble eggs or fry them, indeed we bake apples or big strawberries, and occasionally even toast bread or rolls—and nothing can burn because it shuts off automatically. This appliance stands right on the table and all that needs to done is to plug it in the wall outlet. Nothing takes more than from 2–10 minutes and we're always trying our something new. Fanny wrote and the others in Jersey ask either directly or through Hannah, what we would like.

Within the next half hour we're expecting Otto and Stella and together with them we'll ride out to Jersey in order to wish them all good things for the holidays and also because we haven't visited them for quite some time: The last time we visited was in April, and the others hadn't been there since December of last year. Tuesday is Erev Yom Kippur, which we shall celebrate at home with Otto and Stella invited for supper. After the holiday, in the evening we're all at Handels. Hansi and I have already bought the Yarzeit candles for the Maskir memorial service. Hansi will go with some very good friends and I have admission to a very nice small Temple. I hope it won't be as hot as it was for our first holidays—that was simply unbearable. You must know my dearest ones that on this occasion all our thoughts and our most fervent wishes, more than ever are with you. To you, my dearest mother I say that we celebrate this day with all the solemnity and tradition that we always enjoyed at your house and at Mama's. With our prayers to keep your health and that we may embrace each other soon, I am your as ever, Emil

---

#81

New York, October 5th, 1941

Dearest Mother, Marie, Emil, Beloved Mama, Ella!

Again another week has passed without any news from you and we more than a little anxious and worried. We haven't had such a long interval in mail from you for a long time. At the beginning of last week, your letter of August 31st, dear Marie, arrived somewhat belatedly (you had mailed it on September 1st) and during the week prior to that came Mama's letter of September 6–8th already mailed to our new address. But we're counting on getting news from you tomorrow; otherwise we are simply at our wits end what this can mean. Otto and I considered sending a telegram, but what's the use if you cannot answer it the same way! Last week I met an old acquaintance from Vienna, Dr. Stiglandt, a neighbor from our very old address on Althanplatz 8. I mention this because he was still in Vienna during September, i.e., barely four weeks ago. That is such a rarity, even the newspapers remarked on it. Some isolated ships do arrive, Spanish or Portuguese liners and they bring refugees but normally those had been residing out side Germany for some time already, usually Spain and Portugal. It is extremely difficult to get out even from unoccupied France, not to mention occupied France.

A large part of the refugees came from Casablanca (Africa) and none of them had much more than the clothes they wore! However, the local committees care for them in the most kind and generous way. Though they were quarantined on Ellis Island, that place no longer has the terrible reputation it once had in the 20s, or before that in Castle Garden, where the new emigrants were detained under very bad conditions. In fact today, many of those who are released from there, miss and praise that wonderful and well-groomed little island across the bay from Manhattan where the shelters are well equipped and comfortable, the food excellent and tennis courts, plus Golf courses help to pass the time pleasurably.

Of the 1000 refugees who arrived here a few weeks ago with that "ship from hell" *Navemare* 500 were sent to the countryside for recuperation and relaxation by the local aid institutions. This Dr. Stiglandt was especially well served: he obtained his visa exactly two days prior to the closing of the Consulate in Vienna and then was able to fly from Berlin to Lisbon by special permission. Oh, how I would have loved to hear from him that he exchanged just a few words with you shortly before his departure and could've actually told me what you all looked like!

My dearest ones, today is the 5th of October and it must appear almost improbable to you when I tell you that it is as hot today as if this were the height of summer—and this past summer was well above the average in the heat index. It is impossible to stay inside our apartments and the temperature today is 92 degrees Fahrenheit, something we see normally only during the hottest months of July and August. It hasn't rained in weeks, in the Midwest and in the West roar giant forest fires, started by the enormous heat wave. Hansi received a letter from the people at whose place she spent her vacation who write that the forests there are closed to the public due to the dangers of possible fire and will not be opened until it rains for several days.

On Yom Kippur it isn't so much the fasting that is difficult but, to keep from drinking any water. Due to the heat I've also refrained from visiting a variety of synagogues in New York, the way I did last year. I just sat in the Temple—during Maskir (Memorial Service) Hansi came and sat with me on the same bench, which struck us a little peculiar, yet here it is the custom and only in the most orthodox schuls on the lower Eastside do men and women sit in separate sections. For a short while we sat together with Safirsteins and Otto in a beautiful little park in our neighborhood and the sun burnt down on us as if it were the middle of summer. In the evening, Otto and Stella came to break-the-fast with us. It was a difficult time and my thoughts were only with you my dearest mother and all you others, my beloved ones. My memory goes back almost 40 years on this day, always celebrated with the same formal ritual that made one feel as if the Earth was indeed trembling and then its final conclusion with its feeling of enchanted relief, mentally and physically, in the reunion with ones loved ones to the festive meal, full of good wishes and hope for the coming year. And today you are so far from us, and engulfed in such misery—we cannot even enjoy our own salvation! Soon we shall have finished the second year of our separation—and I can see everything as if it happened only yesterday. Those last weeks with you, the constantly rising excitement, tensions, fears, obtaining of passports, the consulate, ship tickets, followed by the difficult, sad farewell to all of you but especially you, my dearest, beloved mother. How much I would like to be able to touch you once more, my sweet, good mother, and bend my head down to you. I cannot go on today in this sad mood. It is better I continue tomorrow when, hopefully, I shall be able to hold a letter from you in my hand.

10/06/41

[T]oday arrived simultaneously, your letters, dear Marie, of September 14th and 21st/22nd, the last one already to our new address. Marie, it hurts so much what you're writing about mother. My sweet, good Marie leave nothing undone, the doctor surely can prescribe a medicine designed to strengthen the heart for mother, even if one cannot give her anything else that she would like to have. I've had this feeling for a considerable time now that something is not working for mother. Please, dear Marie do not let her write anymore in your letters—it'll make me happy enough just to see her name, as long it is written by herself!

Later when she feels much better she may again write a few lines. Ella who has garnered a lot of experience with Mama, will be able to tell you what kind of medication is most appropriate for mother. Maybe you should consult the doctor who treated Mama, and whom she found so agreeable, rather than Dr. Sch. Never mind the costs as far as doctor and medications are concerned. We have already transferred RM 400.00. RM300.00 are for Mama/Ella, and RMl00.00 are for you for the time being. There will soon come another amount for you. In the meantime we ask uncle Streit to help you out a little, and we thank him and aunt Rosa in advance for this.

Willy and Ada visited with us on Saturday evening, also Hannah and Safirstein. Otto too, dropped by, but he had to leave soon in order to pick up Stella who works till 10PM on Saturdays. The folks from Jersey will visit sometime in the near future—in the meantime they sent us some very considerate gifts such as an electric toaster and a very decorative lamp. Ada wants to know what we need and we shall let her know in time—right now we cannot give this much of our attention.

Dearest sweetest mother, don't make any trouble and see to it that you get well and soon cut as dashing a figure as you always do. You managed to get through the last winter very well, recuperating after your illness. Be smart and sensible, stay away from any kind of excitement. Everyone so loves and is considerate to you they worry about you and write so many good things about you. You and the others must remain patient and courageous because you absolutely must join us here—we live only for you and everything we plan and do here, whatever we achieve, buy, save for, we only do with you in mind, how are you going to like it, how comfortable will it be for you. We're living here very well, but only recently we said that once you, mother get here we shall have to find another flat.

After all, as I already wrote you ours faces the backyard and I know how much, you mother, like to sit at the window and look down on all the goings-on in the street. Please, mother, do your utmost and see that you get well again and then stay that way. And I'm not just saying that to you but also to all the others, especially Marie and Mama. We are happy to hear that Mama is doing real well and... *[Letter ends here]*

#82

New York, October 14th, 1941

My dearest, sweetest mother

Beloved Marie, Emil, Mama and Ella! I hope to God that, by the time these lines arrive, you, dearest mother are again fresh as a daisy, and were able to recuperate from your illness as well as you did last winter. To be sure, Marie wrote me that you aren't really sick but suffer mainly from weakness and I can see that from your writing which appears to have become more difficult for you. Marie is very unhappy that she cannot give you something to eat that will improve your strength and when I read this it literally breaks my heart and I am desperate over my total inability to help you. I already told you in my last letter that, after a lengthy interval we received three letters from you and unfortunately in each of them Marie reports that my dearest, good mother is so weak that even adding a few lines requires a great effort. Please, my beloved mother, do not write too much, I shall be happy if I only see your name written in your own hand. I beg of you dearest Marie, get some information from Ella how to treat mother, what medication would be most useful to strengthen the heart; Ella has so much experience in treating illness, her efforts with Mama met with so much success, I am sure she'll be able to tell you what might work best with mother. Possibly you can also consult the doctor who treated Mama and with whom she was so satisfied. Dearest Mama and Ella, we thank you so much for your very sweet, detailed, and despite your sad situation, so courageous letter—we also thank you for your best wishes and we consider ourselves blessed to know how happy it makes you to hear of how well we've progressed in our new home. Unfortunately this is the only way to bring you a little happiness at least indirectly, since we seem to be unable to do anything for you directly as far as the immediate future is concerned. Just now, Otto and Stella appeared at our door hoping to hear some news about you and they are disappointed when, even as they are about to enter, I shake my head negatively. So Otto sat down next to me and wrote a few lines by hand. He too cannot get up the necessary concentration when there is no mail from you, or the news is not agreeable. I am sure you'll be able to understand this and not doubt for a second that we think of you any less. We're debating again sending a telegram, especially because of our sweet grandmother. Would that the good Lord has made her well and she is her old self again!

Last week we received a very nice letter from Victor—unfortunately it was dated June 19th, nearly four month under way. Even though everything in it is no longer pertinent or out of date as so much has changed over there and we are completely ignorant about their fate or whereabouts, we were very glad to read the letter. It is amazing how they had not the faintest notion of the events about to engulf them. On the contrary, he writes how satisfied they are with their current situation, especially because he as working again and that gave their existence more meaning, apart from the fact that he was earning quite a decent amount. He also writes good things about Epsteins and that he just sent an express package to Marie for mother and he even tells me its contents: Butter, Cheese, Coffee, Tee, Biscuits, Grits and Sugar. You did write me not too long ago, Marie, that you received something, but I believe that was much earlier and not such large quantities. Such shipments from here are officially prohibited, though certain agencies accept such order however without any guaranties. The prices are incredible. Hannah sent one such package months ago to Regina/Dora. Did it arrive, in the meantime? If yes, then we shall certainly try one, too. We sent money jointly with W. this time, a total of RM400.00. I hope that you, i.e., Ella received the notification from the Reichsbank. We are most grateful to Heinrich/Helly as well as Uncle Streit for the support they are giving Mama/Ella and you respectively, from the little they have themselves. How will we ever be able to repay them? Please tell Heinrich/Helly that we received their last letter. Last Thursday we visited with Grete and they ought to have received her letter in the meantime. Also those documents needed by Heinrich, such as the residence confirmation for Aunt Kathie. The copy of the letter to the moving company they'll send now. Also photocopies of the No 13 and now No 20 forms. With these it will be easier here to get the necessary application forms. For the time being these have not yet been distributed by Washington for Germany. Only the Council hands out trial forms, which can be filled out but are not sent on to Washington. This is done to ease the correct completion of these forms when they are distributed in the original.

Despite all that please do not lose hope or your courage. Think of us who feel with you every pain you're subjected to. You will find this letter undoubtedly much less enjoyable than any of my earlier ones—but I am possessed of such a restlessness, I am simply not capable of treating you to my observations, large and small about this country which despite our now two year residence still appears strange, if no less loving to us. This much, however I can say: I am still walking around in slacks (broadlegged summer pants, belted, which, God forbid, must not have any crease in them) short sleeve shirt and light summer jacket and of course no hat. But the heat is bearable, at least in comparison to what it was. The apartment is nice and cozy but unfortunately the target of regular pilgrimages by relatives, friends and acquaintances! As much as much we delight in that we find little time for real relaxation. On Sunday we didn't even get down to the street. Among others, we had a visit from our cousin Frances (Herman Handels wife, in Jersey) who is a really decent, lovable person. She radiated happiness when she told us—under the seal of strict confidence, of course—that her daughter Beatty (Beatrice) will soon be married. Actually, we're not as sure as she is about that wedding. Beatrice is a typical 19-yr-old American girl who's been enamored before with any number of boyfriends but then dropped them unceremoniously. This time it is however very serious, true love, he being a young man and from a very good family—in this country the boys marry usually in their early 20s—until she possibly finds another one whom she likes better! Her younger sister is a very serious and shy girl. For our Safirstein with his sarcastic lawyerly tongue this is a never-ending source for scoffing and joking. By the way Ada Schab is very taken with him and they understand each other well despite his Yiddishisms that lace his language; they are more like soul mates. You know how Ada loves to downplay herself and bemoans her insufficiency in many areas; well, that has caused Safirstein to engage in one of his Barrister like speeches which culminates in the enthusiastic exclamation: "I, Mrs. Schab, I am proud of you as woman, wife, Mother and Jewish lady!"

Dearest, good Mama Schab, you know I always write when I hear from one of your children. If I do not send their lines in the original, you must try and understand that. They are all doing real well. On the occasion of the Holy Days I wrote in detail to Ernst and Felix and gave them a good piece of my mind for not writing you more often.

I must close now and I embrace you my dearest good mother. May the good Lord make you well again and grant my wish to see you once again here with us. And all of you my beloved ones, dearest little sister Marie, my brave Emil, dearest Mama, dearest Ella, our best wishes for you, we embrace you fervently, as ever your Emil.

#83

New York, October 18th, 1941

My dearest, beloved mother,

and my loved ones in the Lessing and Hochedlingergasse! Again I've spent another week in anxious suspense, waiting from one day to another for a few lines that would relieve me from this anxiety—yet nothing came. To make it worse all planes arrived exactly on schedule during this past week, so I cannot even find comfort in the thought that there hasn't been any mail at all from abroad. What is the cause of your silence now lasting for over two weeks? Is mother not well, is, God forbid, someone else not well? There were some very alarming reports again in the newspapers in recent days that made our blood run cold.

Now that we fail to receive your dear letters that during the last few months were so comforting and calming, we can see how much happiness they had brought us—while presently there is nothing and that makes us incapable of doing anything at all.

Even more, we realize how you must suffer, in constant terror over what awful things are going to happen, how much longer are we going to have to endure these tortures?

It is getting more and more difficult for me to inspire you, from this distant vantage point, with hope and courage. Please do not think for a minute that we can ever be truly happy here. Sometimes we forget, enjoy our presence here but only because we are able to prepare the way for you, hoping to make your life here too, a happy one, but that lasts only as long as your letters keep coming and we know that you're healthy and well. Absent that we must ask ourselves whether our coming here was really worth it and whether it would not have been better for us to remain with you. We feel it would have been much easier, then, for you but also for us, to share with you in your suffering. I am very worried about mother given your last reports about her. My heart is so heavy, so very heavy, I simply had to do something to find some relief and that is why I sent you a telegram a few days ago, knowing at least that you would hold that in your hand the next day! This would bring you at least a little consolation, knowing that in our thoughts we are always with you despite the oceans and countries that separate us. That, my loved ones, should help to restore your waning courage. But then I blame myself, whether it was the right thing to send a telegram. I calculated to the minute the hour at which this telegram must be delivered to your hands, I actually saw how you Marie would take it with shaking hands from the mail carrier, could hardly find the strength to open it until you finally had read it completely and fully understood it. Were you scared and what did mother say to all that? Did you all comment on it and talk it out at length? Did you my dearest sister sit down immediately in order to write me a few lines? Were you all a little bit calmer and felt comforted? But I see that my letter sounds much too sad and is more likely to upset rather than comfort you. And so I shall pull myself together and give some happier news.

Thus, e.g. when I came home from work in the evening Hansi surprised me with having adjusted and completed the window curtains on her sewing machine and already hung them all by herself. In our bedroom now hangs the wonderful wide curtain that was so decorative already in our bedroom in the Alserbachstrasse. And in our living room one can admire those beautiful lace curtains that graced our salon in Vienna. Those familiar patterns of lace welcome me here, too, as they slowly flutter in the wind when the windows are opened. Mother dearest do you still remember how you came to visit us every Wednesday (occasionally on Thursday) that was your day? When I came home from the office you looked so good and fresh, because usually you had already taken a hot bath in our house. Only at dinner we had the usual quarrel when you didn't pay Hansi's cooking the respect she felt was owed to her, because you knew that she didn't exactly follow the required ritual laws. So then the question had to be settled how you wanted your eggs, soft or scrambled, that had to serve as substitute for the good meal enjoyed by the rest of us. But you loved the tea and the wonderful biscuits from *Aida* that went with it. When you left I usually walked with you over the Friedensbrücke to the Gausplatz since you rarely made use of the tram, being very good at walking and could compete running if necessary with the likes of Nurmi the Olympic champion.

All these memories are with me, and so many more as I look upon these curtains and cannot repress my blubbering; I can see that despite my otherwise healthy figure I am totally down with my nerves.

At last we have also found a suitable picture of Mama, that we like enough to have enlarged and framed. It is the one in the corridor of the Taborstrasse, the Orangerie with palms in the background, taken by Otto Schab shortly before his departure. There are now so many beautiful pictures of you that smile at us out of very pretty small and large frames. There is Emil as cavalry officer, and you dear Marie, as Chafez our "family photographer" portrayed you in 1938. Otto had those two pictures on display for some time already in very decorative small frames, which I liked very much so now I followed his example. By the way, according to an announcement in a newspaper, Chafez is now residing in Brooklyn, advertising himself as the "famous and distinguished photographer from

Vienna" taking flattering pictures of beautiful New Yorker ladies or at least of those who think they are beautiful.

Heinzi's picture is on Hansi's night table and everyone asks who that "darling, little guy" is! Lisl's picture, she in traditional Gastein costume smiles at us, Herbert's enlarged baby pictures taken in Mondsee, Krumpendorf etc. decorate the walls of our hall way and delight our visitors who cannot believe that this is the very same tall boy of today. Today, by the way Herbert went with Cousin Friedl and some friends to the opera to hear *Cosi fan Tutti*.

While I was writing these lines Otto dropped by for a short visit hoping to find some mail from you—in vain! Tomorrow we want to go with him and Stella to search for an apartment. They want to rent a small two rooms flat with a kitchen to which is attached a "Dinette," i.e., a small eating alcove, a hall, bathroom and all the usual conveniences. That is not an easy task since they want to live in a specific area very close to Stella's business, and these types of smaller flats are rare and consequently more expensive. But it must be small, primarily because that makes it easier to keep it clean and orderly. Over here all these chores are done by oneself, but the work involved is very small compared with that in a flat of equal size abroad. Most attractive is the washing of dishes, made easy with two built-in washbasins and warm and cold running water, dish-drying rack etc. I want to go with Otto, if time permits and look up Dolfi Ball whom I haven't seen since we arrived here. By the way, Otto received a letter, dated 30th September from his mother-in-law Frau Bock in Switzerland in which she tells us among other things, that she has had a letter from you, dear Marie, and that did calm our anxiety a bit. Now I shall close and reserve a little space for myself in case Monday a letter arrives from you or mama, something I hope for with all my heart, and I can acknowledge it immediately.

21st, October.

At last, Marie—today arrived your, by us so intensely longed for letter of September 28th which reassured me a bit at least as far as mother is concerned and for which I thank you Marie with all my heart. Already from mother's handwriting I could tell that she feels a little better, and I really beg of you not to let her write too much, I am happy if I just see her signature and greeting. As I already wrote you once, we joined with W. to transfer money to you and will again send something in about two weeks. Aunt Rosa should be so kind and help you out a little bit and we are most grateful to her for that. We are enclosing the pictures for Mama; please write again, all of you, real soon and please help mother in whatever way you can. I kiss and embrace you all a thousand times, your Emil

---

#84

New York, November 9th, 1941

My dearest, beloved mother, and all you loved ones in the Lessing & Hochedlingerstrasse!

This time we did not get your much-cherished news on Saturday, as we did last week; this news, which we always anticipate with much trembling and uneasy foreboding, we now hope will arrive tomorrow, Monday, at least a letter from you, but also from Ella and Mama. To the latter we are always willing to grant an interval of 2 to 3 weeks, since you Marie never fail to report something about them, but now there is at least some news due also from them; if tomorrow is going to be at least a half-way satisfactory day for us, it should bring reassuring news about them as well as about you. We still entertain vague hopes concerning Heinrich and Helly, as well as Mrs. Weissberg, maybe a miracle happened and they were permitted to stay! We didn't ask in our last letter how things went with Helly's mother. As far as you are concerned, my dear ones please do not neglect looking after your health and if it appears necessary do go to a hospital. Dr. Schnardt, or whoever is taking care of mother will surely be able to arrange that for you. But please do it, really, and don't just depend on God—you know God helps those who help themselves. The latest reports mention a cancellation or at least a reduction of the deportations and if that were the case then surely old people and those who are ill, as well as those who, like Emil are working in some plant would be exempted from the transports. Oh, how we long to have your next report!

We received encouraging and detailed news from Irma, Benno and Heinzi—it came like a ray of sunshine to lighten up our somber mood caused by your circumstances. We were especially pleased with what Benno and Irma wrote about Heinzi. The way he helps his parents, goes shopping, bargains with the shopkeepers at the market refuses to buy shoddy goods, how he works in Adolph's bakery, later delivers the baked goods to customers, and yet he also studies and his infectious humor and happy nature amuses all those who come in contact with him. Irma for her part describes how he enjoyed the summer, that he is an excellent swimmer, and that sausages are still his favorite meal—how she cannot serve that too often because that is too expensive, but when she does

Heinzi will not eat unless there is enough for all three of them. Which reminds me that Heinzi, already as a toddler, insisted on sharing his porridge with everyone present and would start yelling and screaming if not everyone would take a spoonful. But I don't want to interfere with Otto's task of reporting to you and he will tell you more in greater detail. They loved our pictures and those that were meant for Rudi they sent on together with the letter for him. So far there was no answer from Rudi, otherwise they would have included it in their letter to us. However, they told us about an earlier letter from Rudi in which he writes that everyone is doing well, thank God. Rudi is also in touch with Ernst and he told the Gutters about Ernst and his business, but that is news we know now directly from Ernst in his last letter to us. Maybe Rudi can pull himself together sometime and write directly to us, i.e., to you via us—I write to him directly frequently, and even those letters directed to Benno and Irma are also meant for him. I try to make every effort not to lose touch with all our loved ones who are now spread all over the world, and I like to do that, not only for the sake of reporting to you, but also because I feel so attached to all of you and writing brings you closer to me; even though it keeps me from having even one minute of actual leisure time as I spend up to ten hours on a Sunday at this typewriter, not to mention that the postage takes care of almost all my pocket money. On account of this habit I've become quite well known in our circle of acquaintances and a lady friend of Hansi's asked her the other day, whether it is true that we write to our loved ones every week, and what can we write them so frequently, and anyway, do we actually write them about our new flat and other accomplishments. She, for her part, would not think of writing that to her relatives in order not to hurt their feelings. To which Hansi replied that even though we are quite powerless here to help our loved ones over there directly we are able to bring a little joy into their dreary, sad existence by relating to them some of the good things we are experiencing and that makes them forget at least for a short time their own bitterness.

In the last few weeks a lot of interesting things were happening here although because of my depressed mood I haven't paid a lot of attention to them. After a really incredibly exciting election campaign, especially in its last phase—almost more intense and exciting than the Presidential one last year: La Guardia was re-elected for the third time and is now Mayor of the largest city in the world for another four years! Here he is tremendously popular in fact surpassed only by the President in this respect. I listened to some of his campaign speeches on the radio and was amazed to hear him talk, depending on his audience, in their native language! Obviously, in English, and in Italian since that is his mother tongue, but also Spanish, and in a really giant meeting on the East side he talked for over an hour in absolutely perfect Yiddish! Well, I am sure that at the next presidential election in 1944, and especially at the next Mayoral election in 1945 we'll be eligible to vote! In the meantime, though we cannot actively participate, our hearts and minds are passionately engaged in everything that will determine the well-being or the lack of it in this great and wonderful country.

Often when we talk among ourselves, we say it might have been better had we remained with you so that we all could look the dangers in the eye, together, without this deadly torture of ignorance and uncertainty. Your letter quiets us down only for about five minutes. Then it starts all over again: What has happened since they wrote this letter, nearly fourteen days ago, while this letter was underway? May the good Lord only protect all of you! I kiss you and embrace you innumerable times my dearest good mother, as well as you all, Mama, Ella, Marie, Emil and I remain with many of my best regards to all those very few friends and acquaintances that are still there, your Emil.

Give my best regards to Regina and Dora, tell them that our hearts beat for them but our unhappiness is immeasurable because of our powerlessness to help them.

#85

New York, November 17th, 1941

My dearest, sweet mother, all my beloved ones in Hochedlinger and Lessinggasse!

I acknowledged already, in my last letter, your dear, yet so sorrowful letters of October 20th and 21st—and very shortly afterwards came your letters of October 7th (Marie) and 8th (Mama/Ella); so, to be sure, they were already out of date. There is only one piece of news that made us happy: that there is news from Hedwig and her husband. I am hopeful that eventually there will be mail from them directly to us and we can learn more details. As a matter of course, I immediately informed Willy, whom I visited just for that purpose and wrote to Ernst and Hannah. I would also like to obtain news from Olly's and Elly's parents, in order to bring some comfort to both these girls who are very worried, not having heard anything from their parents in a long time. I am full of hope that they are well and that their silence is rather the result of plain laziness.

Looking at the date above, you can see that I am writing these lines on the second anniversary of our landing on this continent, hoping more than ever that this day will bring the much longed-for mail from you. Longed-for in both hope and in fear. Unfortunately nothing came, even though today, Monday is the usual Clipper-mail day, on which we normally get your mail; only very rarely do we get your letters with the Saturday afternoon delivery. Normally the Clipper arrives Saturday near noon, and if the postal employees are especially industrious, they'll work up the mail fast enough so that it can be delivered on the same day. Generally, however this is not the case and we can only luxuriate in the knowledge throughout Sunday, that news with your personal greetings, in your beloved hand-writing is now with us in the same city, having flown from afar over the ocean and we are full of expectations, hardly able to await Monday morning even though it is the beginning of a six day treadmill of the hardest work routine. During the last weeks our anticipation for your news has grown even more, though we are no longer cheerful but obsessed by an oppressive anxiety, which literally robs us of sleep in the night from Sunday to Monday.

This very date provides us with an agonizing glance backward—not that we are in any way ungrateful for the kind fate, which let us achieve so much in so short a time—but we are farther away than ever from attaining true happiness. Can all this here give us happiness when we know you are so far from us and engulfed in your great misery? We feel your misery, as well as our own, mixed with shame for not only having left you behind, but also for having been unable to do anything worthwhile for you! What kind of feelings must you harbor when you think of us, you who have put so much hope in our efforts. Can this be of comfort for you to know that we are completely at our wits end, nerves raw and at the breaking point, choked up with tears, and sobbing aloud whenever we think of you, without that bringing the slightest relief to our hearts rent by this searing pain and never ending woe?

Yesterday we visited Handels in order to thank them again on this 2nd anniversary of our arrival, for every act of loving kindness they have showered on us prior to and during these past two years. It was all very sad.

They belong among the very few residing in this country that suffer the same pain as their brothers and sisters abroad and are unhappy over their impotence in the face of this all-pervasive misery.

Next Thursday Herbert is invited to New Jersey for the large Turkey meal. On that Thursday the whole American nation celebrates its greatest holiday, the "Thanksgiving-Day"! The nation gives thanks for everything and has every reason to be thankful. The churches and synagogues hold masses and services in honor of this holiday. No one should be unhappy on that day, joy should be spread everywhere and it is touching how even the highest places and ranks strive to make this possible.

The focus is on that all–American deity: "the child"! Thus Herbert is their guest on this day in New Jersey, while we on the other hand, politely declined. Our pain does not belong among happy people and we can be easily unfair toward those who, the Lord be thanked, have not had to experience on their own person any of that great misery, yet at the same time we recognize shamefacedly that we ourselves were no different at one time!

We are grimly bitter—all our attempts to dig up money for Cuba visas have totally failed. U.S.$3,000.00 is necessary, not including the trip; who can afford that? Even though it is here comparatively easy to borrow money at interest, still the amounts are usually for around two or three hundred dollars, certainly not for ten times these amounts! And this is what depresses us so much; only one thing appears to be left for us and that is to pray to the good Lord, from the bottom of our hearts, to continue to protect you!

Last week we had a visitor who brought us much, much happiness, especially in view of his surprising, unannounced visit: Dr. Weil and his wife. Unfortunately, he too, had bad news from his sister and is unable to help. Otherwise he looks good and is in good shape but still has no information on whether he has passed his exams. And even assuming that he had passed it, what then? He's only a couple or so years this side of sixty and wonders whether he has the stamina to build a new practice. Otherwise, he repeated the joke all émigré physicians are familiar with, i.e., that only after coming to America did they really qualify as skilled physicians! Willingly and happily he examined all of us, especially Hansi, but of course we all know only too well the real reason for our failing nerves, our rapid heartbeats, etc. If the good Lord helps and you all are able to come over here, I guarantee we shall live to be a 100! He gave us many greetings to remit, especially for you my dearest Mama Schab, and he promised us that he would write you again very soon. He is also in touch with Ernst and has the same news from him that we do. I believe I already wrote you once that his daughter got married here. After a long search his son-in-law has finally found a good job, however it is outside of New York City and he has to leave the house daily at 5:30A in order to reach his work place by subway, train and bus somewhere in New Jersey, and of course comes home very late. But now he is also liable to be drafted, from which only an addition to the family can disqualify him. How are you, my dearest sweet mother? I haven't even asked that yet—even though I always think of your well-being and pray to the good Lord to keep you healthy! The same goes for you too, my dear Mama, about whom Marie reports only good things. How are you my dear little sister? We are anticipating the coming winter with great anxiety, knowing how poorly it can make you feel. And you sweet Ella, my dearest sister-in-law how are you doing? we think a lot about both of you, Marie and Ella, and talk about you often. We know about your superhuman efforts, especially you two, and we ask ourselves, how do you manage to keep mentally and physically afloat. And what about you my dear brother-in-law Emil? How are you managing? You too, deserved a better ... [illegible] into retirement. Do not overestimate your strength, even though you like to think of yourself as a giant and super athlete.

Believe in God and don't lose courage. It just takes a little longer for you and, as is the custom one must wait longer for the good things in life.

Grete and Sig came over last Friday. It is terrible and we cannot think of Heinrich and Helly without it tearing us apart. Have you heard anything from them? We're clutching at straws with vague hopes—please keep us informed about them. If only we had already some news from you!

Herbert is studying very hard in order to finish up and if everything goes well we can view him at his High School Graduation in February in his "Cap and Gown," those symbols of academic maturity.

Otto's place is charming and homey—I truly enjoy going there. If only you, Marie and Emil, could see this! And so I embrace you my dearest mother and all the rest of you, all of you! I kiss you a thousand times! May the good Lord protect you. Your Emil

---

#86

New York November 24th, 1941

My beloved, dearest mother,
and all you dearest, beloved Mama/Ella, Marie/Emil!

We are terribly worried. It's been some time since we've been that long without any news from you; and even when we had to wait more than one week for mail from you, it used to be different, then. Why aren't Mama/Ella writing at all? There is nothing worse than to live in ignorance of the fate of your loved ones separated from them at a distance of thousands of miles. It is more difficult to lift the pen when we do not have news from you. There is only very little we can tell you and an entertaining piece of news designed to raise your spirits is hard to come by in that mood. In general there is not much to write about that is pleasant.

The popular nervousness is again reaching the boiling point because of the strained relations with Japan, and that has an immediate effect on all areas, especially business conditions. When it appeared as if the present summer would never end, we suddenly find ourselves in a severe cold snap, much colder than last year around the same time. Though it is true that cold cannot much hurt us in this land of centrally overheated flats, offices, stores, subways, etc, it makes us remember your situation. How are you faring now in this respect, are you experiencing a bad cold spell, too? Have you been able to obtain sufficient heating material? Now, when Emil has this job and is no longer able to forage for it? Do you have enough warm clothing? Is it possible to buy some and do you have money for it? The last remittance from Willy, in which we participated, seems not to have worked. We have already communicated with Herta in Buenos Aires to send you some. In any case we are forever thankful that Uncle Streit shares some of the very little money he has with you and that Heinrich used to do the same for Mama/Ella. Grete Brainin phoned yesterday and said she has a letter from Mama/Ella but to our sorrow, everywhere the information is negative.

Very soon there is another wedding anniversary for you my dearest Marie and my dear Emil—for me too, this is a special day to remember, because at the age of seven I received my first long pants, of which I was enormously proud. With mother I always had a fight whenever I wanted to put them on—it was reserved only for special occasions. And I also remember your Silver Wedding anniversary in 1928 surrounded as you were by all your children, relatives and friends. Benno in his tuxedo gave the toast. Don't be sad—you will celebrate many more feasts here with us. Emil

---

#87

New York, December 8th, 1941

My dearest, precious mother and all my beloved ones!

Again no mail and this is now the fifth week since we last heard from you and we're really driven to despair. Our concern about you my dear ones has now reached the stage where we cannot even comfort each other. We're simply no longer able to do anything—our imagination plays tricks on us and we are subjected to thinking up the most terrible scenarios;

New York Dezember 8, 1941

Mein gutes teures Mutterl
    und alle Ihr Lieben und Teuren!

Wieder keine Post, nun schon die fünfte Woche und wir sind verzweifelt!
Die Sorge um Euch meine Teuren ist so gross, dass unser gegenseitiger
Trost kaum mehr etwas hilft. Wir sind einfach zu nichts mehr fähig, stän-
dig schwebt Ihr uns vor und schreckliche Bilder umgaukeln uns. Gebe der
liebe Gott, dass alles nur ein Ausfluss unserer seit Jahren gepeinigten,
kranken Nerven ist und Ihr Euch wohlauf befindet, dass alle unsere Befürch-
tungen grundlos sind. Wir wissen, selbst wenn alles beim alten ist, so ist
das Dasein noch lange kein Paradies für Euch und doch wären wir schon zu-
frieden, wüssten wir Euch wenigstens wie im Sommer. Aber wenn wir uns noch
so zu trösten versuchen, wir wissen, es ist leider nicht mehr so wie früher,
weder bei Euch noch bei uns hier. Ich schreibe Euch diese Zeilen und fürchte
sehr, ob sie überhaupt noch in Eure Hände gelangen. Wir haben hier in den
letzten Tagen die ernstesten Stunden Amerikas miterlebt und plötzlich stehen auch wir hier, die wir uns hier wie auf einer abgeschlossenen Insel
fern von Krieg und sonstigen unruhigen Ereignissen gewähnt haben, die wir
hier alle die kriegerischen Ereignisse der ganzen Welt nur aus der Zeitung
oder durchs Radio sensationslüstern bei einem guten Frühstück zur Kenntnis
nähmen, stehen jetzt mitten drin. Wenn ich sage wir, so meine ich nicht
mich und überhaupt uns Zugewanderte; ich meine damit in erster Linie die
Amerikaner, die nie auch nur im entferntesten daran denken wollten, dass
so etwas auch sie selbst betreffen könnte. Die immer nur Zuschauer sein
wollten, wie im Theater oder im Kino, die glaubten, dass die Ereignisse
auf der ganzen übrigen Welt nur für ihren eigenen Nervenkitzel da seien.Ich
mache es ihnen nicht zum Vorwurf. Sie sind nicht ganz kalt und gleichgültig
an den masslosen Leiden der Menschheit der übrigen Welt vorüber gegangen
haben vielleicht von allen den grössten Anteil genommen und geholfen, mehr
vielleicht, als wir drüben es im umgekehrten Falle getan hätten. Aber es
ist schon einmal so, was man nicht am eigenen Leibe spürt, kann man nur
schwer nachfühlen. Doch jetzt erwachen sie. Wenn auch noch zu langsam. Noch
scheint es ihnen nicht ganz zum Bewusstsein zu kommen, um was es geht. Aber
plötzlich gibt es hier Luftschutzübungen, Verdunkelungen, New York, bei
Nacht in seiner faenhaften Beleuchtung wie ein Märchen aus Tausend und eine
Nacht, liegt plötzlich verdunkelt da, stundenlang wird die Bevölkerung durch
Radio instruiert, wie sie sich zu verhalten hat, es schwirrt nur so von
Worten wie "Blackout" (Verdunkelung) "airraidshelter" (Luftschutzkeller)etc.
und glaubt mir, man könnte weinen darüber, wie über das letzte Stückchen
Grün, über den letzten Baum etwa, die von der Erde verschwinden würden.
Ich glaube, dass auf dieser weiten Erde wohl niemand mehr ein beschau-
liches ruhiges Leben führen kann und wollte man das, so müsste man auf
den Mond flüchten. Man weiss es nicht: werden die Clipper überhaupt
noch nach Europa verkehren? Ein Schiffsverkehr kommt ja schon gar nicht
mehr in Betracht. Sollen wir wirklich vollständig von Euch abgeschnitten
sein? Der briefliche Verkehr mit Euch ist faktisch das, was uns noch am
Dasein erhält. Wie dem auch sei, ich will nicht aufhören Euch zu schreiben
und keinen Weg unversucht lassen, Euch Nachricht zukommen zu lassen. Und
wenn es anders geht, so will ich die Briefe schreiben und sie Euch auf-
bewahren bis zu dem Zeitpunkt, da ein Weg zu Euch möglich ist, und dann sollt
Ihr sie alle auf einmal bekommen um auf diese Weise über uns und unser Leben hier informiert zu sein, denn ich weiss Ihr Lieben, wie Ihr unser Leben
mitlebt.- Von Irma=Benno-Heinzi erhielten wir wieder recht ausführliche und
gottlob erfreuliche Nachricht und was das wichtigste ist, sie sind bereits
im Besitze ihrer Staatsbürgerschaftspapiere, haben also schon das Ziel er-
reicht, das uns erst nach 5 Jahren winkt. Wie gut waere das unter anderen

Above and opposite: Date: New York, December 8, 1941. This was Emil Secher's last letter to his relatives. Unlike his other letters this is not a carbon copy of the original but the original: it had never been mailed.

hopefully this is merely the result of our nerves and of having witnessed at one time for ourselves what previously we would never have imagined— God willing, you are well and all of our fears baseless. We realize that even if the conditions under which you exist remain the same, your life is no bed of roses—and yet we would be satisfied with knowing that you

Umständen für Euch Marie-Emil gewesen. Mit Leichtigkeit hätten sie Euch an-
fordern können. Mit Rudi sind sie in ständigem brieflichem Kontakt und er-
warten sogar seinen persönlichen Besuch, den er ihnen angekündigt hat im
Zusammenhang mit einer leitenden Stellung, die er in einem Unternehmen über-
nommen hat. Irma schreibt selbst, dass Rudi über sie Stellung nichts näheres
schreibt und freuen sie sich sehr auf seinen Besuch, der ihnen mehr Auf-
schluss geben soll und vor allem weil sie wieder einen lieben Menschen von
drüben sehen und sprechen können. Nach all den Schilderungen, die Otto
Euch ausführlich wiedergeben wird, geht es ihnen als auch Familie Rudi un-
berufen recht gut.- Ueber Drängen von Safirstein und Hannah mussten wir,
d.h. Hansi und ich sowie Otto und Stella vergangenen Samstag an einem gros-
sen Dinner teilnehmen, das der Verein der Bolechower, deren Altersprasident
Safirstein ist, anlässlich seines 25-jährigen Bestandes gab. Schon vor vielen Wochen hatten sie uns dazu eingeladen und jetzt wollte ich mein Mitkom-
men davon abhängig machen, dass Post von Euch kommt. Leider ist Eure Post
ausgeblieben doch konnten wir das diesen wunderbaren Menschen nicht antun,
auszubleiben. Hannah hat Hansi ein wunderschönes schwarzes Samtabendkleid
zu diesem Anlass geschenkt da Hansi weisses Abendkleid für diesen Zweck
nicht recht passte. Stella hatte übrigens ganz desselbe Kleid und sehen sie
wie Schwestern aus. Ich glaube Mutterle, Du hättest in diesen smarten, be-
frackten und besmokingten Gentlemen aller Altersklassen sowie in ihren
Damen in grosser Abendtoilette kaum die Kinder deines kleinen wenn auch
nicht minder berühmten Geburtsstädtchens Bolechow erkannt und wenn ich nicht
nie und da ein Wörtchen in heimatlichem yiddisch gehört hätte, hätte ich mir
eingebildet, zu einem Staatsessen im Weissen Haus in Washington unter Teil-
nahme aller Senatoren eingeladen zu sein. Das Dinner fand in einem der fein-
sten Hotels der Eastside statt, und nahmen über 300 Personen daran teil. Wenn
ich Euch sage, das Essen bestand aus über 20 Gängen, so besagt das gar nicht
aber eine Vorstellung könnt Ihr Euch darüber machen wenn ich Euch erzähle,
das Essen dauerte von 1/2 12 Uhr nachts bis 4 Uhr früh. Zwischen jedem Gang
gab es Darbietungen, eine erstklassige Musikkapelle spielte, resp. es wur-
den Reden gehalten und hatten wir dabei Gelegenheit, unseren Safirstein,
den ich als Redner, egal ob deutsch, englisch oder yiddisch, schon längst
kannte, nunmehr auch als guten öffentlichen Redner bewundern zu können. Ich
kann solche Veranstaltungen nicht mit vollkommen reiner Freude geniessen u.
drängen sich mir allerhand Gedanken auf und insbesondere Vergleiche. Ich
hatte Gelegenheit, das grosse Elend unserer Brüder und Schwestern drüben zu
sehen und hier im krassen Gegensatz Wohlstand, Freude und vor allem Genuss-
sucht. Nun, diese Vereine und Vereinigungen dienen alle wohltätigen Zwecken
hunderttausende von Dollars strömen jährlich aus diesen Vereinen zu den di-
versen Institutionen wie Joint, Hias, etc. und natürlich auch nach Europa
und ist jene natürliche Interesse, dass man nur schwer von jemanden für wohltä-
tige Zwecke auch nur einen Dollar herauskriegen kann, wenn man aber seiner
Eitelkeit schmeichelt, ihm Gelegenheit gibt, sich öffentlich mit seiner Frau
im Frack und Abendkleid zu zeigen, er ohne weiters für diesen Zweck 10 $
für eine Eintrittskarte und ebensoviel für ein Dinnergedeck zahlt, wenn
auch das Essen höchstens 3 $ wert ist. Die Damen erhielten auch schöne
Spenden. - 10. Dezember. Meine Teuren, soeben langten Eure Brief ein und
zwar von Mama-Ella vom 26. Okt. (bendet am 1. Nov.) und von Marie 3 Briefe
vom 26. Okt., 2. Nov. und 9. Nov. (beendet am 11. Nov.). Ihr könnt Euch
unsere Aufregung vorstellen! Freude über Eure Lebenszeichen und doch so
grosse Traurigkeit wieder über Eure Leiden. Dass nur Mutterl wieder halb-
wegs wohlauf ist! Vielen Dank Dir, liebe gute Marie dafür und auch allen
anderen und insbesondere Herrn Dr. Schmardt, dem ich Euch bitte, meine herz-
lichsten Grüsse zu bestellen. Du, liebe gute Mama bist fabelhaft unterrufen,
was Du alles im Stande bist herzustellen! Wir zeigen stolz Deinen Brief.
heute bin ich zu Willy damit gelaufen, doch hat auch er Nachricht von Euch
erhalten. Habe sie über noch gesprochen, da sie bei Ada zu Hause ist.
Hat versprochen sie uns zu schicken. Wir sind glücklich über die Nachricht
bezüglich Helly-Heinrich und Frau W.Wir geben die Hoffnung nicht auf! Ich
komme noch ausführlich auf Eure Briefe zurück. Gebe Gott, dass der Verkehr
mit Euch aufrecht bleibt, aber wenn nicht, was Gott verhüten möge, seid
ohne Sorge um uns. Ich küsse und umarme Dich gutes teures Mutterl und Euch
Euch alle Mama. Marie, Ella mur   Emi Emi

are getting along at least as well as last summer. No matter how we find
some solace, we know that nothing is any longer the way it used to be—
not with you and not with us here. As I write theses lines there is the pal-
pable fear that they might never reach you. During the last few days we
have lived through the most serious and critical hours of America; suddenly, we who thought ourselves well protected from the conflicts of this
world on our relatively isolated "island continent," find ourselves in the
midst of it. Until now the trial and tribulations of the "outside" world

reached us only via the news on the radio and the sensationalistic reporting of the newspapers which we imbibed, Epicurean-like, with our breakfast coffee.

When I say "we" I don't just mean people like myself and other newcomers; I refer especially to those Americans who never seemed to consider that they too, would one day be enveloped by this international upheaval. They preferred to think of themselves as unwilling spectators of world events played out as a stage play or cinema designed to provide for their titillating amusement. But I don't mean to sound too reproachful: they were not cold and callous in the presence of the enormous pain inflicted on the world by irresponsible, power-hungry individuals; as a people they have indeed shown more concern and given more help directly than any of the others and if the shoe had been on the other foot, I am not at all sure that we would have reacted with the same humanitarian instincts. It must be admitted, sadly to be sure, that what you don't experience on your own body is hard to sympathize with. But now they are really awake! Though still at a slow pace. It hasn't yet quite penetrated their consciousness what the stakes are in this encounter with the "old" world. Now suddenly there are air-raid warnings linked with practice alarms, blackout regulations. New York, which glows like magic as if out of Thousand and One Nights, has turned an unfamiliar dark these winter evenings. Radio almost continuously broadcast instructions on how to conduct oneself during a blackout, how to reach the nearest air raid shelter etc.—all new words that have entered everyday language here. One fears that the last place of green, the last tree is in danger of being removed from the Earth, and that there is no longer anywhere a place where one can lead an undisturbed life—unless one could escape to the moon!

We don't know whether the Clippers are going to continue their flights to Europe. I doubt that there'll be any significant ocean traffic. Are we really going to be totally cut off from you?! It is our contact by mail that more than anything else keeps us alive these days. No matter what the obstacles I shall not cease writing to you and will not leave any means unexplored to stay in communication with you. And if everything fails, I still shall continue to write and safe keep these letters till I find a way to get them to you; even if you receive them all at once—it'll show you how we are going about our lives here—because I know how much you, if only vicariously, like to experience our lives here with us. From Irma/Benno/ Heinzi we received more goods and plentiful news: they got their citizenship and thus reached that goal from which we are still three years distant. How advantageous this could have been for you, Marie and Emil, had different circumstances prevailed—they could have easily arranged your joining them. They are in touch with Rudi who said he will visit them soon and that he is about to start a managerial position with some enterprise. Irma writes that he provided no other details and they are really looking forward to his visit—especially to see a familiar, beloved face again and the opportunity to talk about how the rest of the family is faring. So according to all accounts they, as well as Rudi are doing OK, and Otto in his post-script will write to you more about that, I'm sure.

Last week, Hannah and husband prevailed upon us, also Otto and Stella to attend with them a gala dinner given by the Bolechover "Landtsman" Society whose membership consists of those Jewish families who could trace their origins back to our Galician shtetl of Bolechov in honor of Safirstein on the occasion of the 25th anniversary of its founding. Even though they had alerted us already weeks ago to this occasion I thought we might get out of it since the lack of mail from you had not put us in the right mood for such a diversion. But that proved almost impossible given how much we owe these two people—in fact, our being here in the first place—and in view of their unceasing kindness towards us. Hannah had made Hansi a gift of a beautiful black velvet evening gown—Hansi's several-year-old white evening gown from Vienna had seen better days and did not quite fit the occasion. Stella had a similar gown and they both looked very glamorous and almost like sisters. My dearest mother, I doubt you would've recognized in these smartly turned-out gentleman in their black ties or tails with their glamorized, décolletage ladies, the children and grandchildren of your contemporaries with whom you grew up in that "famous" shtetl Bolechov. Had I not picked up here and there a few heimish Yiddish phrases, one would have believed this was some very formal state dinner at the White House with senators and diplomats in attendance. The dinner took place in one of the most elegant hotels on the upper Eastside and over 300 guest turned up. If I told you that the dinner consisted of twenty courses it wouldn't mean much to you but maybe you can imagine what it was like if I tell you that it lasted from 10:30PM to 4:00AM!! During dinner a first class orchestra, well known show people, and dancing, entertained us. Of course, there were also all kinds of speeches, including one by Safirstein: I already knew that he skillfully conversed in German, English, Yiddish and even a little French, but this was the first time that I could also admire his skill as a public speaker. Nevertheless, I cannot enjoy such occasions with unadorned pleasures and some gloomy thoughts descend on me that lead inevitably to some comparisons and explanations. After all, I had the opportunity to observe on the other side the miserable existence of our brothers and sisters, while over here in crass contrast stands immense wealth, intense pleasure-seeking and the race for a carefree existence. Well, we need to remember that from just such organizations, clubs, etc. flow hundreds of thousands of dollars annually for charitable purposes, to institutions such as the HIAS, the JOINT, etc. as well as to their European equivalents, and it is an irrefutable fact that it is very difficult to squeeze out even a only a dollar from someone for charity but if you flatter his vanity, give him the opportunity to show himself in public with his bejeweled wife, he in impeccable tails, he'll be only too happy to pay $10.00 admission plus an equal amount for a dinner that is worth $3.00! In our case the ladies were presented also with nice little door prizes.

December 10th.

My dearest ones, this very minute the mailman brought your letters; from Mama/Ella, October 26th (finished on November 1st) and three letters from Marie: October 26th, November 2nd, and November 9th finished on November 11th). You can imagine our excitement and joy to hear from again and our great sadness over your latest trials. But at least mother seems to be well again! For that much thanks goes to you dearest Marie, as well as to all the others and especially Dr. Schnardt, to whom you must convey my deeply felt regards. And you, dearest Mama, are really something—the things you are capable of putting together. We are proudly showing off your letter, Mama, to everyone. I already ran over to Willy's office with it but he had also just now received news from you; those letters are still at his home with Ada so I haven't been able to read them yet. He promised to send them over to us. I am happy to learn about Helli/Heinich as well as about Mrs. Weissberg. We shall not give up hope! I will later respond in greater detail to your latest letters. Praise the Lord that the connection with you will be maintained and not interrupted—but if it is, DO NOT WORRY ABOUT US! May the good Lord protect you, I kiss you and embrace you, my dearest mother and all you others, as ever

   Your Emil

*[*This letter was never mailed and is the only original copy among the nearly 200 carbons.]*

Vienna Letters, 1941

88

Vienna, 26th, January 1941

My much beloved ones!

Continuing my letter of 23rd, I am now able to tell you that mother's bladder pains have greatly decreased; only her general condition leaves a lot to be desired. Because of the intense pain her nerves are very frail and of course all that excitement, plus having to lie down for weeks, combined with the meager nutrition, have just weakened her. Hopefully she'll soon be able to recover. Dear Mimi has helped us bravely with the moving and looked out for our well-being. We most likely would have starved since I could not make time for shopping or cooking. Did you get in touch with those addresses that concern these three women? I would be so happy if something could be done for them—they have nobody who cares about them. Grete is still very busy, working for a big export business, Mimi helps her diligently, and they work day and night in order to support themselves. My dearest ones—in my post card sent in the middle of December, which I hope you've received in the meantime, I wrote that our means are nearing exhaustion. The move brought with it exorbitant expenses, and Mama's illness, with doctor and medication also used up most of the money and it continues to flow out.

I must ask you therefore to care for us on a continuous, regular basis. The money, which was announced by the Bank in Berlin to be in transit, will probably take another two to three weeks before it gets here. Our cousin Henry wrote to me that he would help us if it becomes necessary but I refrain from doing that because of his business relationship with Willy, and in any case would not proceed with that unless Willy agreed beforehand. Please get in touch with him there and then write me the result. Under no circumstances do I want Willy to bear this burden all by himself, maybe you can come to an agreement doing it alternately, one month you, that is Willy could send something and another month, Henry. The best thing would be always the same amount so that we can plan accordingly. Helly and her husband are really very nice and compassionate. Her husband comes every week to see how Mama is doing. Helly has less time since she works more at *[illegible]*—my dearest little sister! You're really working very hard and I admire all you are doing. That you're gaining some weight pleases me, because that is a sign of good health and internal satisfaction. Just stay well. Herbert should write once again to Omi, and the same goes for Franzi and Friedl. I embrace you all and kiss you as ever your Ella. Dear Emil! After a long interval I went to see your mother and was happy to see how fresh and lively she is. If only my mother had reached that stage.

30.1.

Waited until today before mailing this, because mother absolutely wanted to write, i.e., continue this letter. Her bladder is better but her general condition is not good. You, dear Hansi will be able to remember what all my nerves have to endure! The complaints change every hour, the way it has always been with Mama. If it isn't pains in the bladder, it is palpitations of the heart, or stomach troubles, or again abdominal pains, then headaches, or dizziness etc. etc. all that accompanied by her peculiar lamentations. When I go out—which I do during the last 5 months only when absolutely necessary, and for a very short time...

[Letter ends here]

#89

Vienna, February 1st, 1941 (mailed on 2.10.41)

My dearest ones! Since I happened to have a rather good day, I shall try to keep our correspondence going again, Lord willing to progress with my improvement. Of course there isn't much detailed information I can offer you. But foremost I want to thank you with all my heart for your Congratulations by Radiogram, as well as for your letters of December 4th which arrived here exactly on my birthday on 30.1.41! Your dear lines my dearest Hansi gave me much pleasure—they were just right, just like you! one could apply to you Goethe's much quoted words with only slight changes: "From mother I have my figure,(only a little larger), life's serious demeanor, from daddy my merry nature and my tendency to spin a good yarn"—that's the way it goes, doesn't it? I always look forward to your reports. And are you still so busy? Elva visits us frequently, and sends her best regards—the same from Fray Bartha. But the rummy card groups will have to wait a while, I am still very weak, physically as well as mentally, even though I have lots and lots to think about. Only those matters that happened during the last weeks I'd rather forget. Winter has made himself very much at home here—nothing but snow and more snow. But we manage to keep it quite warm, since a hole like this, hardly as big as Felix' chamber is easy to heat. Also, the oven is quite efficient. Less pleasurable is the atmosphere that we are forced to inhale. Better to keep silent about that. I thank the good Lord that I am out of the bed, even if its only few hours every day, and that I can stand on my own two feet again! I went through a lot, physically as well as psychologically.

7.2.41

Your dear letter of 4.12.40 took a good while to get here. We were already quite impatient that we received so little news from you—even though we were certain that Emil, our faithful reporter was sure to have written. We are so happy with his letters and thank him ever so much. Please let me acknowledge again with heartfelt thanks your radiogram as well as the Bank transfer. Today we received your letter of 15.12.40, which made us very happy. In the meantime you surely have also received our report about my condition, which, thank the Lord has also improved. I am happy to learn that all of you are in good health and would only hope that this continues. Good health is truly a valuable commodity that cannot be over estimated—but which is done nevertheless, when you are healthy. It is also good news that grandmother Secher is again in good shape.

[Letter written by Mama Schab ends here]

#90

Vienna, February 7th, 1941

After nearly three months this is the first time that I can actually sit down and attend to my correspondence, since our dearest, good "complainer"—the Lord be praised—is finally improving in her health. Let us hope that her recovery continues apace now. Just so we don't get too cocky, we now have new worries added to the old ones. That's just the way it goes.

8.II.41

This is as far as I got yesterday when Frau Stern came to visit, making it absolutely impossible to even gather one's thoughts in that narrow space we have for our use—for table and sitting down ca. 1 square meter—which is made even worse and made to appear even more crowded when Aunt Irene asks at least 50 questions during the first minute—all of which she then repeats at least 70 more times in the course of the afternoon!! Given my exclusive relationship with only old women—those two, actually Rosa, Frau Stern etc. all Great Grandmothers, I'm beginning to feel almost senile myself! I had resolved to answer your letters, dear Emil, in much greater detail, but that is almost impossible since Marie brings your letters only for us to read and then immediately takes them back home again. But yesterday Rosa came in the morning with your next to the last letter of 15.XII.40, and I thought that for once I'd have it just for myself, when that above mentioned disturbance occurred and today Marie brought your letter of 5.I. and right away took everything back with her! It is so good and wonderful of you that you write so regularly and with so much detail, and that Hansi, too, always contributes to it. Our beloved Frieda, too, is always happy when she sees one of your letters and frequently I can see a tear roll down from her eyes. She is so concerned with everything that affects our family. And she never fails to send her best regards. What luck, my dearest Emil, that you were able to find such a good and personally satisfying job. We were also happy to see the added lines from Robert and little Hans. Our dear mother is doing much better and as you can see she has taken pen in hand again. It's been a long, difficult time, but we managed to live through it. If only there weren't new worries that we must face. But now, let me turn to you my dearest little sister... *[This page ends here]*

#91

Vienna, February 17th, 1941

My dearest beloved! As you can see, mother has again taken up her correspondence, and that is the best proof that she is again doing fairly well. The pains in her bladder stopped altogether, so we can surely assume that it was not some serious urogenital ailment. If she hadn't been so much without appetite she would surely have been able to recover generally and acquire more strength; but in these difficult times it is hard to maintain your equanimity, they influence and determine your mood and subjective condition. As things are I must be satisfied that mother managed to recuperate as much as she did.—My very dear ones! Via Marie you must already have heard about us, here, and a telegram should have been sent to you from Mimi. I won't see her until tomorrow and only then will learn whether she actually sent it. Its wording is as follows: "Request Joint affidavits for us three, also for Kupler; expedite Mama, Mother, Ella, Mimi." I am certain that you, dearest Emil, understand this telegram correctly and have turned your untiring efforts toward fulfilling our wishes, if that is at all possible. Mimi has been told that it will be possible to obtain valid affidavits through the currently active aid committees, though it will be necessary to be extraordinarily persistent and tenacious, which means it will require an inordinate investment of time—of which unfortunately—I should say rather thank the Lord—you do not have enough of at present. Nevertheless I am convinced that you will not leave a stone unturned to help these especially good, decent, hard working people if it is at all possible. Grete still works for that Blouse store (really beautiful things), she has her employment record and Frieda also has her position. Whether it is really true that affidavits can be accelerated, I have no way of telling. Here they are saying it is so. In this matter I depend solely on you and I am sure you will do what is possible. *[Letter ends here]*

#92

Vienna, March 19th, 1941

[Ed.: continuation of a letter begun by Omi Schab]

My dear ones! So now we thought that we're already a few steps farther along—when the announcement came that for the long term there would not be any bookings for places on ships. What can we say? Keep on waiting and be patient.

Maybe the improved weather may make it easier to bear this bad news. Unfortunately Hansi and Emma have also left us. Robert will undoubtedly be very hurt by this. It is terrible to be even lonelier than before. I too am shook up by all this. Mama Neuman has a bad case of influenza and I visit her daily at the Home. So there is always something to keep you busy and in a state of agitation. Helly feels completely hopeless, since there is absolutely no progress in the matter of her ship tickets. What's happening in the matter of the Braun girls? You must give

some kind of answer—they are such dear, good and helpful people. Please
you must write at least a few lines to Rosa, saying you are really trying to
obtain something, so that she at least has some peace of mind and/or
leaves me in peace! She has become totally unbearable. Lord, the things
I have to suffer through on behalf of my charges, each one in a different
way! After a long pause we again received a care package from Victor.
Please Emil, don't be mad at me if I don't get to see your mother as often
as before. First it was Mama's long illness that prevented me from going,
and after that there was so much else I had to catch up on—now it is again
Mama Neuman's illness, in between there is always something, some
excitement that paralyses one's will power on which to act. When you
write again to the children please tell them how happy we are to hear about
them and that they are doing well. Mama was overjoyed to learn that
Ernst and Felix are getting along so well with each other. I too, am happy
over that! Please give them our heartiest,

And give best regards. We don't hear from Rudi anything at all. Be
embraced, hugged and kissed from your Ella

#93

Vienna, April 7th, 1941.

My dearest beloved! Your still missing news I am expecting with
much anxiety since I can almost imagine how all of you will be full of
worries and sorrow. You my dearest, good little sister appear to be in an
especially heightened state of alarm and I only hope that my last two letters contributed to assuaging some of your worries. This is how matters
stand as of now; We, i.e., mother and I need ship tickets that are already
booked, in which case we would be permitted to appear for the examination at the U.S. embassy. In both my last letters I urged you to do something about that, assuming that this can be done much easier from your
side of the ocean. But now I learn again from various sources, that the
news from your side is precisely that the Ship lines there no longer accept
bookings, because the ships are fully booked months in advance, most
likely till the end of the year. Since, in the meantime, I learned from an
absolutely trustworthy source that the JKG does have occasionally ship
tickets for distribution, I turned to them for help. A very good acquaintance who knows more about this than I do, took me to the proper department there, where I was told that considering that the amount (for the
tickets] was fully paid for I should start filing for our passports. Once we

were in possession of the passports we would then qualify for bookings on a ship—always depending on how many such bookings were available at the time. So, now I have started this ordeal and I shall pretend, hopefully, that we are well on our way of reaching our goal. If only the departures from Lisbon continue to remain open. This is the real question these days, since I've just been told by one of our neighbors in this flat, that her uncle has been waiting in Lisbon for three weeks for the departure of his ship to Buenos Aires. But he didn't write how this affects the Lines to the U.S.A. Should you be able to get some results concerning the ship tickets, on your side, I assume you will telegraph immediately. In any case I hope that I shall get something in writing from you soon. In the meantime, another sad event has occurred here. Mama Neuman passed away on 24 March, the result of pneumonia. She was well liked in the Home and all the doctors and nurses really tried to get her well again. *[Letter ends here]*

#94

Vienna, April 10th, 1941

My dear Emil! Please don't be mad at me for burdening you today with another mission, anyway, a request. You are after all the only one who can be expected to carry out such a request conscientiously, and I too, couldn't refuse a favor to the people asking for it. The person in question is one of our neighboring roomers, a very nice, obliging woman, whose husband is already working for the past two years as a conscripted laborer. They have a son ca. 20 years old, who is ill, paralyzed. Herr Alexander Weisz and his wife Elizabeth received already an affidavit last January, from their cousin: Julius Werk, Head of Colcombet (sp?) Werk, Inc. Novelty Silks and Velvets, NY, NY, 58 West 40th St. For the son, who only needs a supplementary affidavit, such a document was not issued, because Herr Werk, who knows the family from an earlier visit in Vienna some years ago, was then of the opinion that the youth, as a consequence of his illness would not pass the medical exam given by the U.S. consulate. But recently this matter was reopened by another cousin there, also an emigrant, name of Gesund who has already succeeded that a communication was sent from Washington to the U.S. consulate here, stating that an entry permit would be approved for the son, provided the parents were ready for their visa and both the original and the supplementary affidavit were found to be in order. Now, in the meantime, the original affidavits having expired, Frau Weisz has repeatedly written to Mr. Werk urging the renewal of the original as well as supplementary affidavit, in fact has also sent telegrams to this effect, without receiving any kind of acknowledgment. However, since it is well known that Julius Werk is a very decent, good and charitable individual (and also very wealthy), Frau Weisz, together with all her relatives here believe that a cousin by marriage who works as a secretary to J.W. intercepts all their mail. That cousin is also an emigrant with relatives here whom he tries to get out with Werk's help and consequently has not the least interest to bring their mail to Werk's attention. Frau Weisz' request is that you, my dearest Emil, just once take the time and make the effort to call on Mr. Werk and present their problem to him. Under no circumstances should you mention her suspicion, precisely because it is only a conjecture. Just tell him that she has written him repeatedly, has sent two telegrams and now assumes that, for whatever reason, the mail has been lost, and that is why she has asked you to follow up on this matter. It probably wouldn't hurt anyway to make the acquaintance of this man (American, allegedly a multi-millionaire). It is known that he is already responsible for issuing 46 affidavits, of which 6–8 have not yet been used. That man has also paid for some ship tickets. *[End]*

#95

Vienna, April 21st, 1941.

My dearest Emil and my sweet, good little sister!

I continue to admire it and we are simply immensely grateful to you who keeps writing us every week with such regularity. Unfortunately the letters from Victor have also become fewer and take from 3–4 weeks to reach us now that airmail has been discontinued. The greater is our thirst for news. Your last letters project a grievous air—but what could we do, we couldn't just keep it secret to spare you the pain. Hopefully, you have calmed down by now, especially you my dearest Hansi. You do know also from previous letters, that we've started the task of sorting and completing our necessary papers. I believe that everything will be ready for submission—the rest is up to fate. Maybe it will be a well-meaning fate and help to reunite us healthy and happily. For the time being everything appears to me as if in a dream. Also, there are, as you well know, "two souls in my breast" and it is certainly not easy for me to hold my ground in the face of everything that confronts me. I avoid thinking about many things—I let matters approach me and let myself be carried along by a destiny that is beyond my control. I have too many inhibitions to do anything different. On 12th Mai is scheduled another transport to Lisbon; of course we won't be part of it. Yet there is still the possibility that, once we are in possession of our passports, the KG will provide ship tickets for us given that the two most important preconditions will have been met: notification from the U.S. consulate and a fully paid-up amount on deposit for the tickets. My dearest little rabbit! When I imagine that maybe I shall see you again soon, my heart beats faster! I have such great longing for all you children in whose raising I played such a great part. In any case, there is a great deal of work for me still ahead. Emil Kupler is so helpful to me, especially going on errands, which is so helpful for me since I have to keep the household going. If you have any news from Rudy be sure to send it to us, because unfortunately we can no longer count on Edith. Only Viktor is also corresponding with him, and so we hear, now and then, how things are going with him and his family. Willy's family continues to shroud itself in silence. Only Ada remains faithful and writes now and then otherwise we wouldn't hear anything from them; and even Frederick manages to squeeze off a line or two—but Frances already follows completely her father's example! Dearest Hansi, Frieda was very moved by your thinking of her and she returns all your kisses and hugs with equal fervor. She is such a wonderful, good person—but also poor because she is so unhappy. I congratulate Frau Stella to her new business and wish her much happiness and success. The same goes for Families Handel and Safirstein.

I embrace all three of you and kiss you fervently, your Ella

My dear, good people, I held back so long with answering, that today (22.IV) your letter of 27.III arrived. It is so touching the way you worry about everything and everyone! I am fully aware of the fact that you are unique in your willingness to help and sacrifice all your free time toward that end. Your sister, dear Emil, reproached me today because I burden you with too many requests. She referred of course to Brauns and Rosa. That latter matter even I do not really take seriously—I just wanted that you acknowledge Rosa's letter with a few lines to make her happy and she leaves me in peace for a while. As far as the Braun sisters are concerned, I couldn't just prohibit them from writing to you *[Letter ends here]*

96

[Ed.: The following is an undated letter from Emil Kupler, written ca. June 1941; there is not another letter of such length by EK in the correspondence.]

My much beloved children, my good Emil and Hansi,

I can tell from your latest letters that you experience much grief and worry on account of us; to be sure it didn't look too good here for a while—but I already wrote you once that we are prepared for anything, even though I was of the opinion, not everyone would be affected. And so, thank God it appears I've guessed right—though, I can tell you my dearest Emil, that our dear grandmother shared these very same views and was completely unmoved. *[These are obvious references to deportations to Poland.]* She had always said: I ain't gonna go to P.—I'm gonna go to America! Neither did I want to send you a telegram concerning the ship tickets—I did it only for mother's sake since I knew, first of all it would cost a lot of money and secondly, that it wouldn't be of any use; I was at the KG (Jewish Community Organization) and there they told me that, it would be useless given that we didn't have an affidavit and, in general it isn't even our quota's turn. In any case I beg of you, my dearest ones, not to worry about us, luck has been with us so far, we've never had any run-ins to give us trouble—let's hope the good Lord will continue to protect us and give us the opportunity to meet again, besides, now there is peace and quiet—we're doing ok and as far as the food situation is concerned one can get almost everything. Of course, our dear grandmother is still fussy with respect to food—she meticulously observes all the ritual laws—plus her old, well-known whims—but don't worry dear Emil, I always let her have her way! So now I've written to you about most everything, the rest mother has already mentioned.

My dear Otto, now I will write to you about myself, though there isn't much to say—I'm still the old phlegmatic type, actually I've remained a lazy bones; during the winter I've done some snow shoveling for a few days and after Easter I'll look again for work. I am still a big smoker and every now and then a glass of wine. Also there is frequently.... *[illegible]* and I cannot say no—also those who have to go to P. and are known to me, I had to give a little something. I have to tell you, my dear Otto, that since Emil's departure, I have spent only from what I make here and there, occasionally I borrow from mother and sometimes I forget to repay her. Well, this is all for today—greetings and kisses for all of you, also for my dear Stella, I remain your, always of you thinking father—greetings and kisses also for Emil, Hansi & Herbert, as well as to all the relatives.

#97

Vienna, June 2nd, 1941

For all my loved ones, my dearest ones, my good ones!

We received your dear letter of May 31st and are most grateful for it. I am overjoyed that my Otto is well again, I thank you, dearest Emil for your carefully detailed reports—in those moments when we hold your lines in our hands we are alive again and can forget for a while the great distance between us.

Today is the Whitsuntide holiday and the weather is beautiful, my thoughts are with you my dearest ones: is it also getting so warm where you are, can you already go to the beach? Please take good care of yourselves, don't drink too many cold drinks, guard your health it is the most precious possession we have. How is our dear Mr. Safirstein? I hope he is well again. That poor, dear Hannah is also going through a lot! Last year it was Jonas her father who got so sick and now its her husband. Yes, life can be difficult. We were happy to know that Herbert is so good at his studies and really takes it seriously. Because of that you should really let him have his little pleasures, such as dancing and smoking—he should enjoy his youth. That's why I still blame myself today if I denied my children something. Saturday Helly came to visit us. She is very bitter that her relatives let their luggage go to waste. They no longer think in terms of leaving here since they have absolutely nobody who can help them pay for the ship tickets.

My dearest ones, last week we had a note from the KG about our departure. I thought right away that you must have written to them about us. They said that at the moment they could not help us, only those who are already in possession of all the papers—or if our quota numbers were released for the specific country under which immigrants could enter the U.S., then they might possibly be able to help. So we just have to be patient. There is already very little to *acheln [Ed.: Yiddish for eating]* but we are satisfied and happy if only we get good news from you. Mother is sleeping now, Father has gone to play cards with friends, and I write so that my thoughts are with you. We still have some of the good things you have sent us; tea, coffee and cacao are really good, I often make us a cup of cacao and then we think of you. Haven't heard from Mama Bock in a long while. Do you have any mail from our loved ones in P.? I'd like to know some more again about them.

June 3rd

I interrupted this letter yesterday and went for a walk; on the Praterstern I sat on a chair but believe me I was plenty scared. But where can one go? Besides I am very weak on my feet. Today I received a letter from Victor in Riga specifically for Ella in which he writes of Ernst and his wife poor Mela about whom Mama Schab does not know yet. V. writes that he also includes a letter from Ernst but the censor has confiscated that letter. He also writes that he has news from you and from his children...

[Page ends here]

#98

Vienna, June 8th, 1941

All my dearest, loved ones!

On Friday the sixth of this month I received your letter of May 16 with postal return coupons, and I really thank you for that. I thank the Lord that you're all in good health and that my Otto is back to his old self again, because you have been through a lot, you poor boy. I also want to thank you my dearest brother, as well as you dearest Hansi, for your birthday wishes—and I wish to God that he will soon help to fulfill them! Now to my weekly report: to be sure there isn't much to tell, always the same hope, waiting for an early release and salvation. Yesterday I dropped by at Mama Schab's, Ella as usual was not at home. They already have their passports and today Ella is again due at the KG *[Jewish Community Organization]*. You, my dear ones, may think that our hearts ache, seeing them already so much farther into their preparations for leaving. But the truth is we do not begrudge them or anyone their good fortune in the least. We would be happy if we had the assurance that Mama Schab and Ella had already successfully completed their trip—it is after all an exhausting journey, especially after all we've been made to go through here—and they could bring you greetings from us. Oh, if only the Becks, as well as Dora & Regina had reached that stage. Yesterday Helly came to visit and brought us new potatoes and radishes, the very first of this season; I almost don't really want her to do that, because we have nothing with which we can return her favors. She has absolutely not a chance to come over there and she is very hurt by the fact that her relatives didn't even care enough to write to the shipping agent in... *[?]* They just received another notice from that agent to do something about those stored items or they will be seized. Regina is home again but Dora is still in the hospital—she is not doing well at all, and is mostly still feverish. Dearest Emil, Victor is wrong when he says he sent us 3 packages—we only received two. You also ask whether other than the postal receipt for mother's affidavit, we have also received a notification from the U.S. consulate. I wrote you already at the time that we got a notification. Also, I thank all our relatives for their efforts in obtaining the necessary supplementary papers for our affidavits, and especially dear Hannah who took care of everything. How is her husband, I hope and wish that he is well. Here we now have the most beautiful weather, but I think all the time how you must be suffering in your heat.

So please, do relax and take a little vacation. How are my beloved ones in P.? I would so much like to have some news from them again. This week we again got a card from Benno's brother Heinrich, he is still in... [?], he is ok and he also has mail from his wife. He would like to have food parcels sent to his sisters in Tarnov, [Poland], can that maybe done from Hungary, he asks me; I don't believe so. He wants to know about Benno via Otto. June 6th / today we got ... she is not badly off. Also, she has heard from Olli and Elli.... [Page ends here; there are ragged edges on several pages]

#99

Vienna, June 16th, 1941

All, my most beloved!

Again another week has passed—I've mailed you two letters last week—have enclosed another little picture, hope it arrives—got your letter of May 26th with Hansi's added writing, and I thank you so much. Now the mail is running real smooth, would the Lord it stays like that! Mama Schab and Ella are vigorously preparing for their departure, they already have their passports and will now be assigned to one of the transports that are to depart from here to Lisbon via Italy in about 3–4 weeks. Do not think for a minute that we begrudge them that they already have reached this stage, even though we do, of course have a little heartache over it. Yet we also take pleasure in the thought that they, who have suffered through so much, may soon send us a telegram of their happy arrival in NY. We just have to be patient—Even if the Czech and Polish quotas are now opened up, they will give out only very few numbers, so that the chances of our turn coming soon are negligible; besides a ship ticket now costs $500.00, where would you get that kind of money? It is already enough what you have done for us until now. We are not going to ask that of you my dearest ones, don't feel hurt over it, we shall carry

on. June 17th. I did not finish this letter yesterday, instead went over to
Mama Schab. They've got so much work right now; I wanted to help a
little bit and came just at the right time. The feathers had just come back
from the cleaners and had to be put back between the covers, after which
the openings needed to be sewed shut. Ella is now making a list of everything of their property that is going along with them and Mama Schab
helps a lot; they have so many things and can't leave behind even the
smallest object!

Emil went there Saturday and brought suitcases and boxes from the
W. [?] Until you actually enter upon shipboard, one really is kept very
busy! Yesterday afternoon, a package arrived from Victor in Riga. It contained: 1kg butter, 1kg sugar crystals, ½ kg coffee, a little package of tea,
½ kg grits, cheese and a box of crackers. I am so happy with that and I
thank you my dearest ones so much! Haven't heard anything from my
Irma for the longest time—have you had any mail? If one has regular mail
from one's loved ones, everything can be borne much more easily. How is
Mr. Safirstein? I don't see much of Regina, since she is with Dora at the
hospital most of the time. Otto, I have once again a request for you—you
know how it is, one cannot say no. Our principal tenant here, from whom
we sublet, Herr Hacker asks you should write a card to his son Erwin
Hacker, NY East 390 10th St. asking him why doesn't he write to his father
or to his sister; he is really worried about him. My dearest, beloved brother,
tomorrow is your birthday—mother and I are with you in spirit and only
hope that all your wishes be granted—may the good Lord be merciful and
grant us the opportunity to see each other again, in good health and with
happy spirits. So now I close my letter, farewell to you all my beloved ones,
I embrace and kiss you all, as ever your Mother, Sister, sister-in-law Marie.

#100

Vienna, June 22nd, 1941

All you my beloved!! Also Irma, Benno and Heinzi!!

After I mailed my letter to you last week, yours arrived, dated June 2nd.
My dearest ones, we are constantly trembling in anticipation of mail from
you—though right now there is really no cause for complaint, as the mail
functions perfectly—I just pray to God it stays that way. Only from Irma
and her loved ones I haven't had any news for quite some time; I know it
can't reach us right now, and I have adjusted to that, but I do want to know
that they are healthy and happy and must not worry about us. Further-

more, all you my dearest ones, I ask you do not worry about us, no matter what may happen *[Ed.: sentence underlined]*. We shall carry on as long as we know that you are well and everything is ok. Mama Schab's and Ella's departure has been postponed indefinitely, that is, at least until the situation changes—they are resigned to that.

Last week, my dearest ones I wrote of receiving a care package from Victor, which I have acknowledged to him. Today we got a postcard from him; we were very glad to receive those things. Dearest Emil, mother was overjoyed to read Olly's lines and learn that she is doing well and is satisfied with her work. My dear Otto, I've sent you again a small picture and would have liked to send one for Emil's album, but I don't think that will be possible as I do not have another picture of mother. Her nose has not gotten any worse, she puts on a small compress of camilophil tea every day, together with an ointment that Dr. Schnardt prescribes for her; he also said the medical exam at the U.S. consulate is not as careful or tough for aged persons.

Today is a beautiful, hot summer day, tomorrow is my birthday and I feel rather nostalgic in my heart.

Dearest little Herbert, I thank you so much for your Birthday wishes, it made me very happy when we receive some lines from you. Make sure you stay healthy and bring all of us much happiness, so we can be proud of you. I think a lot about all of you—now is the time when you'll begin suffering from the heat. Do you go often to the beach? I too, would like to lie somewhere in the sun, but where?! There is hardly any mail from Mama Bock. Does she write to you? Does Stella hear from her other loved ones?

June 23rd

This morning, when your birthday telegram arrived, I was still in bed. My dearest ones, why do you spend so much money?—Even without telegrams and letters I know that you think of me. Don't see much of Regina—she is mostly with Dora at the hospital. She was supposed to come home today, but her fever is still high. I shall close for now, what do you think of Vonje? I embrace you and kiss you, all my loved ones, your mother, and sister, sister-in-law and aunt Marie

Father too, sends his best regards. Many thanks for the postal reply coupons.

#101

Vienna, July 1941 (no exact date)

My fervently beloveds!

For the third time I am starting this letter to you, every time I have to interrupt it, every time there are incidents that make the previous letter out-of-date. If there were at least pleasant news to report but mostly it is the opposite. This new regulation concerning emigration to the U.S.A, with which you must be acquainted, has made all this effort and sacrifice come to naught—it appears that one has to start all over again, a new procedure that will cost more time and sacrifices and the possibility of a Wiedersehen has moved even farther away. Again we can see the truth in the old saying: Erstens kommt es anders, Und zweitens als man denkt *[Ed.: almost untranslatable as is; "you may think one way, but it'll happen the other way"]*! Ella continues: My dearest ones! I shall continue here, since mother is not very well informed on this matter. According to the latest announcements from the KG, a new regulation was issued effective July 1st, which in effect changes the immigration law. I am aware that you over there have much more exact information than we do, especially since all initiatives must be taken on your side and there is nothing that we can start from here. I am fully convinced that you are already dealing energetically and urgently with the new situation created by the changes in the law, assuming that something can still be done for us. In any case, I shall have a copy made of the announcement sent us by the Consulate concerning their approval of the Affidavit and mail it to you as soon as possible, because it shows that we were ready to be asked to come for the medical examination, which in turn proves how close we were to departure. The provision concerning close relatives left behind in European countries presents a very aggravating factor; only some very few will be exempt from this provision. See e.g. Emil K., Heinrich and his wife, Helli, Olly, Dora. Could we not also make a request concerning Victor? We worry a lot about him. If only we had some news from him. The summer this year has been quite bearable until now; lots of thunderstorms which is quite agreeable for us since our room, in which we sit around most of the time, remains that much cooler.

Herbert, my dear, congratulations on your "business trip"! That you were picked for it is certainly proof of confidence in you. Did you also manage to make a little money on it? My dearest sister, hopefully you'll be able to enjoy a little rest, and the same goes for you, Emil. You both work hard enough to deserve it. I congratulate Ernst & Felix to the branching out in their business. Please hug and kiss them many times from us. Our poor little Hannah will be quite sad and worried by now. Frieda returns your many greetings. Many, many fervent kisses, I am your Ella.

#102

[Continuation of a letter from Omi, probably from an earlier date, but included here.] We haven't had any news from Victor since March 24th, even though he has received several letters from us during this time. It appears that in that region the mail has been closed down, which is truly regrettable for us. Our last letter to Hedy contained the sad news of the passing of our dear Mama Neumann who left us much too quickly. We as well as the doctors treating her had hopes that she would recover. But within 12 days it was all over and you can imagine what we had to contend with next to all our other worries and fears; especially our good Ella who stayed with her until she drew her last breath—and while she was ill went there twice daily, bringing her everything she needed. But she passed away quickly and only the good Lord knows why that was the case, how much sorrow and pain were kept from her that way. Hedi will have a hard time believing it and even I cannot adjust to the thought that this poor woman who otherwise was so agile and robust, is no longer among us. "What is man: a breath of air, and nothing more!" May it please God to give her eternal peace.

What did the children in S. write to you? There must have been quite lot in such a long letter. *[A page is missing]*

Left: **Hedwig (Hedi) Schab (wife of Victor) b. 1896, Vienna; she was murdered in Riga in July of 1941(?).** *Right:* **Victor Schab b. 1889, Vienna; murdered in Riga in July of 1941(?).**

One hears a lot about instances where total strangers have helped people to meet the costs of the ocean crossing. The Braun girls are such poor darlings. Please continue to write so often and well—my special thanks to Emil, when we do not get anything from Victor—then you are the only ones left. For all of you fervent kisses and embraces from your faithful mother and Omi.

#103

Vienna, July 7th, 1941

My dearest ones!

No news from you for nearly a fortnight. The last mail dates from June 8th with notes from Irma, Benno and a few lines from little Heinzi. I was so happy to receive this. My dearest ones, I wonder whether you received my postcards that I wrote last week and again two weeks ago. I sure hope you did! It is so terribly sad to be cut off like that from those you love. I know you feel the same way we do. But what can you do? We can only beg the good Lord to put an end to this misfortune that has come over mankind. But everything is getting to be more complicated. Don't worry about us we are healthy. Father is working as of today—he likes it, it is so much better than doing nothing, which he is not used to. But I do miss him, because I am greatly disabled because of my pains, but we'll make it somehow. Please my dearest ones, you must not worry about us under any circumstances, even grandmother feels fine these days and only the lack of mail from you makes her unhappy. But one gets used to anything, unfortunately. We no longer correspond with either Victor or Epstein. Ella, too, is doing all right again, after her intestinal flu. They are not even all that unhappy at not being able to leave just now. I know I would have been absolutely desperate, to be so close to your goal and then—nothing! My beloved ones, all of you, how are things with you? Are you suffering under the heat? You, dear brother are now enjoying your vacation—just be sure to really make good use of it. And you dearest Otto and you sweet Stelli, I am sure you're toiling away—if only I could be of some help to you, how happy that would make me! Last week, after a long silence I had another good letter from Mama Bock that pleased me greatly. Sunday Hellie visited us, she remains the only one who doesn't forget us—and she never arrives empty handed: this time some new potatoes and even two peaches for mother; and they hardly get enough for themselves. And now my dearest ones, I must close; if only I were sure that you get my mail real soon. Stay well, all, of you and be happy, I kiss you a thousand times, and of course you must pass them on to Irma, Benno and Heinzi!

As ever your mother, sister, sister-in-law and aunt Marie. Father also sends greetings. And here are a few words from grandmother: Best regards from your mother and grandmother, thousands of kisses, also greetings to our dear relatives, I embrace all of you in my heart, SECHER

#104

Vienna, 21st, July 1941

My dearest, beloved,

This time I can acknowledge 2 letters, one of 22nd June from you my dearest Emil, with two Photos but without Otto's added lines, and today I received your dear letters of 6/28 with postal coupon and the remittance of the Deutsche Bank for RM255.00 from Herta in Buenos Aires. I cannot praise you enough for these wonderful letters, they are such a comfort in these sad times; and that you care about us in such a paternal way, for that the Almighty will surely reward you. Now to answer your letters: we loved the pictures, Hansi looks especially good, knock-on-wood, very youthful and pretty. You however, my dear brother seem to have aged a bit. Well, its no surprise, you take everything so seriously. I also thank you for your dear birthday wishes. I only missed the lines from my sweet Otto, but today I got compensated for that: your flattering remarks! One really enjoys that once in a while—when one sometimes loses all lust for life, then I think of you and am determined to hold on. Please don't be mad at father, he really doesn't have much time, now that he has work. He leaves the house at 6:30AM and never comes home before 5:30PM, very tired he has breakfast and only eats again when he comes home. But he is content, has a good appetite—if only I could give him more. I worry—what's it going to be like later! I have always hoped that we would still be able to come to you during this year of '41—but now it appears that we shall have to wait until the war is over—provided we'll be around then. I did not go to Frau Weissberg for some assistance since May, just now I wanted to ask her again for a small sum—but with the money you have sent, this won't be necessary. As it is, she has to support Dora who is still lying in bed. It would be nice if only she could go somewhere for recuperation, but where? One cannot even walk in a public garden. Frau Helly is especially good to us. She never comes with empty hands; whatever she can get, she brings to us! But now things will change. Frau Pr. will have much less time, now that she has become a grandmother: Mitzi had a little girl. Life becomes daily more difficult. Only the hope to see you, my dear ones, once more keeps us going. I am glad my dearest Otto that you can take a little rest, I'm sure it won't hurt you, after what you had to suffer through in the spring. I feel so sorry for our little Stella, if only I could help and ease your burden a bit. Our grandmother, thank God, is doing well, every day before noon she walks around a little bit in the streets of the neighborhood... *[Letter ends here]*

#105

Vienna, July 27th, 1941

All of you, my dearest, most precious ones!

I am writing you already today, because I have this urge to talk to you, sort of pour out my heart, 'cause usually, I have hardly mailed a letter to you when I remember all kinds of things that I had forgotten to mention. Well, Friday before noon as I was returning from the hospital where I get my injections twice a week, grandmother practically ran to meet me, her face radiant with happiness, waving your letter of 8th July. Last week we actually had twice mail from you—you can imagine how happy we are with your dear letters. And we even had another pleasant surprise: we received a ring of sausage; I have no idea from whom since the sender's name is unknown to us. What's more it is not from abroad. I think the good Lord sent it, the sausage is very tasty and I gave Emil some of it a few times to take along to work, mostly he only takes a thermos of black coffee and some bread. My dearest ones, with respect to leaving here, the news is again that everything has to be initiated now from abroad, also that no relatives must be left behind here. Of course that doesn't apply to us—other than some relatives of father's there's no one here. Also, you my dear Emil write that the KG should contribute to the ship tickets, but they are so poor—they don't even have enough for welfare assistance. So my dear ones, we no longer count on being able to come to you before the war ends, after all from where should you get all this money to bring us over there? It's true we are facing difficult times and would like to get away from here, but God willing, we managed to hold out until now, and we shall continue to do so, especially for your sake!

Money is tight, since everything has gotten dearer. It is lucky that father earns something; but we'll manage somehow. Once the money arrives here I shall acknowledge it immediately.

Dora has been home again for several weeks, but she is still in bed. I visit them often. My dear Emil, I can write that to you: Dora is very sick. Regina cries constantly and doesn't she have enough cause for crying? One has only one child and has to watch how it is wasting away. And nothing can be done to save it. What she needs is simply not available. One has to recognize that mankind has met with a catastrophic misfortune and the fate of solitary individuals hardly matters. Dora asked me to write you that you should ask Hannah to inquire again at the shipping company concerning her crates.

Yesterday Helly came to visit again. Such a sweet, good person she is and yet so miserable. She offered us money, but I refused, on account of you, we'll just wait—let's hope it comes soon. My dearest ones we were especially glad to receive Otto's little picture of all of you, Stella is really cute and her business partner also looks very pretty and sweet. Uncle Streit was very happy with your kind words for him, and he is most grateful for all your efforts, Emil and would like to have the new address of his son. July 28th, now I shall have to close... *[Letter ends here].*

#106

Vienna, August 3rd, 1941

My dearest beloved!

This time I can acknowledge two letters from you: one of July 14th and the other one is Hansi's letter for Mama Schab that came to our address but unfortunately is still here. Your letter my dearest Emil is so sweet and nice it is a pleasure to read. It makes one think of a country of luxury in comparison to what we have here. Thank dear Hannah for her good lines, and we are glad to learn that Mr. Safirstein has completely recuperated. On the same day your letters arrived I was visiting with Regine and Dora and read your letter to them. Dora said that Hannah should have received her letter by now. She is still not doing very well and has high fever that keeps her in bed. It is a great misfortune to be sick in these times. Yesterday I was over at Mama Schab's and gave her your letter with two pictures. You all look really good—especially Herbert looks like he's all grown up, Hansi is pretty and sweet and I hope we will get more such photos for ourselves soon. Today is Tischa Bov and mother's birthday according to the Jewish calendar. Mrs. Pr. has brought

Above and opposite: Date: Vienna, July 28, 1941; written by Omi Schab at age 81. She was deported to Theresienstadt almost exactly a year later and died there on July 27, 1942, within two weeks of her arrival. Pencil marks were made by the censor.

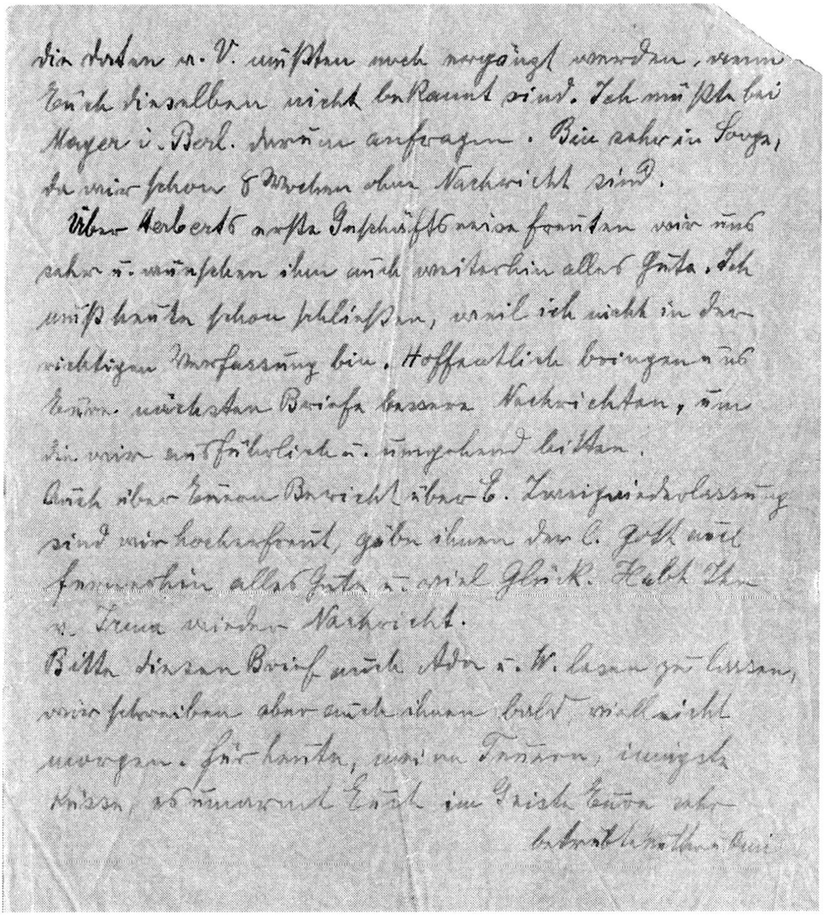

die Daten u. V. müssten noch [illegible] werden, wenn
Euch dieselben nicht bekannt sind. Ich müsste bei
Mayer i. Berl. darum anfragen. Bin sehr in Sorge,
da wir schon 8 Wochen ohne Nachricht sind.
Über Herberts erste Geschäftsreise freuten wir uns
sehr u. wünschen ihm auch weiterhin alles Gute. Ich
muss heute schon schließen, weil ich nicht in der
richtigen Verfassung bin. Hoffentlich bringen uns
Euere nächsten Briefe bessere Nachrichten, um
die wir [illegible] bitten.
Auch über Eueren Bericht über E. Zweigniederlassung
sind wir hocherfreut, geben ihnen der l. Gott auch
fernerhin alles Gute u. viel Glück. Habt Ihr
v. [illegible] wieder Nachricht.
Bitte diesen Brief auch Ada u. W. lesen zu lassen,
wir schreiben aber auch ihnen bald, vielleicht
morgen. Für heute, meine Teuren, innigste
Küsse, es umarmt Euch im Geiste Eure sehr
betrübte [illegible]

four apricots and I made mother compote she likes that so much. We've had to unlearn our "noshing" habits. Father too, had to give up smoking. But that is not the worst; he works hard but is quite content. It's hard for me when I go shopping because I have to stand a lot and that is hard on my feet. My dear Otto, at the same time as your letter there came an air-mail letter for Mr. Hacker from his son. He sends you many thanks. Mr. Ruf is still here with his child. His wife divorced him. She was not a good wife and had a very bad reputation. My dear child this week it is 3 years that you and Stella left us. It writes so easily but what haven't we been through in these three years. How many tears I've shed. And who knows how much longer it will take until I see you all again! Will I still be around, I wonder. We're living literally on the edge with our nerves—every day brings something else. I have no news from my dear Irma since May.

Please, Otto when you write congratulate Benno to his birthday, which is on August 22nd. The money from Herta has not yet arrived. I shall acknowledge it as soon as it arrives. I am not taking anything from Mrs. W. anymore; she has helped us for exactly a year. August 4th. Yesterday Helli came to visit, she apologizes that she hasn't yet answered your letter, Emil, she is waiting for Hansi's letter so she can answer both at the same time. She is such a wonderful person, she wears herself out coming to us and bringing as much as she can carry. Yesterday she brought us 2kg Potatoes, and other fresh vegetables also some fruit—and she doesn't want to take any money! And for mother a few flowers because of her birthday. If you only knew how difficult it is to obtain these things you can imagine how we appreciate this! Today came the money, RM255.00 for which we are most grateful. If only we could buy something! If only I could write you about everything!! I'll close for today; mother wants to write a few lines. *[Letter ends here]*

#107

Vienna, August 4th, 1941

I'm writing to your home address—is that ok?

My dearest beloved! I can't really tell whether I owe you more thanks for all the effort you expend on our behalf or for your regular and punctual letters. Without exception you all deserve our most fervent thanks for your good and encouraging words. And especially those photos, they made us so happy; I can't look at them enough. You my dear Hansi, are looking really fantastic: our Ada is quite right when she writes "our Hansi remains as always young and beautiful"! How do you do that? But so do dear Emil and our sweet Herbert, they look really great. In fact Emil looks very cheerful and Herbert seems to have outgrown both of you—at least physically! Your letters, dearest Emil, are always so interesting. I read them 2 or 3 times. I admire your patience and no less your distinct and detailed manner of narration. Of course, I would prefer to hear all that from you orally! Will that happen once more?? Does the good Lord know what is still ahead of us! Now you have to start all over again in your struggle for us! Do you know already the exact, official wording of the new regulation? Here in the KG nothing definite is known, and if *[illegible]* … in the Jewish News Bulletin had been official I would have copied it for you.

As I can see you stayed at home for your vacation. That was not right! A few weeks of clear air are not to be dismissed lightly. Hopefully, Hansi has allowed herself some rest and relaxation. The fact that you, dearest Hansi visit frequently with Ada, tells me that you are all getting along fine, which makes me very happy. You should always live in peace and harmony with each other that is my most fervent wish! You already wrote me two times that you had news from Ernst; but how can I learn more details, who wrote and what—couldn't you send on their letter? No, that is not necessary! You can imagine that everything is of interest to me and I am most anxious to hear everything directly and personally!

And, Herbert, my hat is off to you! You've really grown up—is Frederick still taller than you? Where is your next business trip going to lead you? I gave your picture many, many kisses because you are looking so cute! Write again some time, please. You know, not too long ago I ran across some of the essays you wrote in school and read them over again. Gradually I'd like to mail them to you, maybe you can submit them to a newspaper and you could even make a few dollars that way, right? Did Helen B. receive my letter of July 9th? How is ... *[illegible]* and Dr. Weil? Do you all of you get together occasionally. Extra greetings to the Handels and Safirsteins. Everyone admires your pictures and says: who is that trio of two brothers and their sister? *[Ed.: Picture of Mother, Father and Son] [Letter ends here].*

#108

Vienna, August 11th, 1941.

All my dearly beloved!!!

Last week right on time for August 5th, your letter arrived with birthday wishes, 4 pictures and 3 return postal coupons. You can imagine how overjoyed grandmother was especially over the pictures! You all look perfect on the pictures and Hansi is especially pretty, and Herbert looks great, too. Otto's added lines also made her very happy and she thanks you for all the good wishes which, Lord willing, should all be fulfilled very soon! There is nothing-special going on here and yet—every day brings something else! Father works, I have to go shopping for food and that is real torture. The weather is pleasant, more cool than hot. The money, which you had transferred through Herta, arrived last week and I thank you so much; for now I am not taking anything from Mrs. W. anymore.

Yesterday I went to see Frau Helli in Dornbach they are still living in relatively nice quarters there, but this too, will not last much longer, because everyone must move into our District. Nevertheless I feel sorry for her she is such a good person. I brought some small potatoes home from her—hereabouts you cannot get anything like that. She is very brave. I am very glad, dearest Emil that you are looking out for her interests by doing some favors for her she really deserves this. She also received the letter from Hansi, which made her very happy.

My dearest Otto, my beloved Stella, yesterday on August 10th I thought of you so much, it was exactly three years ago that you went away. Who would have thought then that it would take so long until we see each other again, and who knows how much longer it will take still. Sometimes I think, I won't be here when that happens and that makes me very sad. It is very difficult sometimes to carry on!

Nothing has reached us from Irma, either, since May. Here it is beginning to look like fall, and thinking of winter makes me very anxious. Only your wonderful, sweet letters help to make our load here lighter.

Now my dearest ones I should like to ask you for a favor, if it is possible. It is rumored here that it is possible to send small packages over Lisbon, Portugal. Please find out about that. The coffee and cacao that you sent quite some time ago is running low, though I still have tea. Maybe you could send us cacao, condensed milk and oil; of course it shouldn't cost too much otherwise it's not worth it. Please don't be mad at me that I bother you again this way. My dearest ones, I almost forgot to acknowledge the telegram, which arrived the evening of 5th August; why are you spending so much money? But mother did enjoy it very much. How is your weather these days? I do hope the big heat is past for you. Well, enough for today, just stay healthy and well, I embrace and kiss you all many times, your always thinking of you mother, sister, sister-in-law and aunt Marie. Best regards also from father.

#109

Vienna, August 24th, 1941

All my beloved!

Your dear letter of August 4th I already acknowledged in my last letter, and now we're waiting again for your mail which means so much to us. Our whole life now consists only of waiting, waiting, waiting for better times! Again another week has passed in pain and tzures. Father works hard, but he is content even when it gets more difficult, he doesn't care;

he likes to work if only the food were accordingly. My pains are not getting any better, even though so far I've received 15 injections—but what's a body to do, one is satisfied if it doesn't get any worse.

This week news came from Benno's brother Heinrich, he is still where he had been before, but he no longer gets any mail from his wife. He asks you, my dearest Otto, to tell Benno that the parents of Zeev are well, the sister of Zeev has gone to Zeev, but so far there has been no mail from her. Yesterday Helly came to visit us again. She really carried a lot of stuff: all for mother, whatever she can get: a little fruit, potatoes. I wish Mrs. Prdsly our old neighbor would be back from her vacation already.

August 26th

My dearest ones, I waited for mail from you and therefore did not mail this letter, but it was in vain! Well, Sunday I visited again with Regine-Dora. Unfortunately, Dora isn't any better she still has fever. It is a big misfortune, and really beyond any help.

Whenever I come away from them I am so depressed. Her husband writes regularly.

Otto, my dearest one, I must ask you to give my best wishes to Irma for her birthday, and wish all of them a happy new year. I cannot always find the right words, she knows and feels, how it goes with us, how heavy my heart is and send little Heinzi innumerable kisses. My daily prayer is to the Almighty to keep you my dearest children well—and as far as we ourselves are concerned, He should only give us the strength to live through all this!!

There is a lot more to tell, but I just cannot anymore. Farewell for this time, I embrace you and kiss you your always thinking of you mother, sister, sister-in-law and aunt Marie

[Three lines written by Grandmother Secher follow:] Best regards and 1000s of kisses from your mother and grandmother. Also for my dearest Herbert, as well as all the dear relatives. I embrace you in my heart, your grandmother Secher.

#110

Vienna August 30th, 1941

My dear loved ones!

I hope you're in possession of all our letters. It seems the mail is faster from you to us than from us to you. In the meantime two of your letters arrived. Our dear Emil writes so patiently and frequently his very detailed and interesting reports which we always look forward to and which our friends also read with great interest. I wish we could write you more enjoyable and interesting news—that would also provide us with more incentive to write. Our daily life runs on so drab and uniformly, it just doesn't pay to write at length about it.

We are glad to hear, my dearest Hansi that you finally decided to find some rest and relaxation. By the time you receive this letter I hope you've already rested and met your loved ones with renewed strength, and they too are healthy and well. The fact that you my dearest Hansi had written so rarely until now led me to believe you really needed your vacation. You know that the excitement and worries of these last months don't just stick to our clothes but prey on our poor, tortured nerves.

Thank the Lord, we are healthy and want to stay that way. The summer is coming to an end—it wasn't very hot this year so that now when the sun isn't shining it turns quite cool. We're looking with considerable anxiety toward the arrival of this coming winter, which allegedly will turn out to be very severe! What have you heard about the new regulations affecting immigration? Here we're given the most diverse information, so that we hardly know which one will turn out to be the correct one. And how about the money that has been deposited at the JOINT? They hoped to obtain ship tickets for Ella and myself prior to the closing of the U.S. consulate.

Do you have any news from the children? That Victor doesn't write worries me greatly and I speculate continuously where he could be and how they are getting along. I shall try to make some inquiries at Wilicek maybe he has an idea where we could write to him. The mail from you is now our only joy and relaxation. Dear Ella is always busy with the household. I pity her a great deal and think, where would she be by this time if she were not here for my sake.

She would undoubtedly have an occupation more suited to her abilities than this thankless task of running this household. How are families Handel, Safirstein and Beck? Recently we visited Heinrich—it was the first time that I dared to go such a long distance—but it was really beautiful. They too, have their worries and they send their best regards to all of you and will write soon. The rest of our relatives and friends here also send their greetings: Frau Bertha, Brauns, Frau Dr. Warenreich and Rosa. Do you know whether Dr. Weil received my letter? I already wrote you about the photos and which I would like to have; from time to time I take them out and look at them. Wouldn't it be possible to get such photos also from the family Willy Schab?

I am closing for today, my dear ones. Our sweet boy should also write again. What school is he attending now? Shall I send him his school essays, etc? I kiss and hug you all, always thinking of you, your Omi and mother.

Dearest Emil! Your observation in your last letter were again so colorful and allowed us a really in depth view of the conditions currently prevailing there. I thank you for your continuous concern and that you try to take care of everything affecting us. It is very necessary that the sending of assistance money should be permitted again, because we're already quite short. In the meantime Helli's husband helped us out, and we are most grateful for that.

Did you dear Emil, get some sunshine at the beach? How long has it been that I've had to do without that—I'd be satisfied with a beach a la Krapfenwaldl or Vöslau even the sundeck in the Dianabad, all off limits now.

That you dearest little sister granted yourself some vacation, made us very happy, we stand totally in awe over everything you are able to achieve. I hope you wrote us from there and told us what it looked like and how you relaxed, etc. Our dear mother is again in good health. She looks much better, is refreshed, and again quite agile, helping me in the kitchen, cleaning vegetables, etc, because I still have to watch my fingers, esp. in cold water, no splashing in the water if it can be avoided. Of course that cannot be completely avoided and that is why one finger after an interval of several months has again become inflamed. The damnable thing about this is the loss of time due to the care it demands: hot herb baths 2–3x a day, compresses with ointments over night; despite the smallness of the household it consumes a lot of time, and keeps me from getting other things done. Helly has it easier since she only has to do the shopping while her mother does the kitchen work all by herself. Marie also complains a lot now that Emil is working; she has to do more around the house, although there are still certain errands he can do for her.

We are very sad, that we still haven't heard from Vickerl. The news from your friend Frau Roth is also very regrettable. Who would have thought that?! And you my dear Herbert, how did you spend the summer? Did you go the beach a lot and did you work again as messenger boy? Please write again, I embrace and kiss you all, as ever your Ella.

Above and opposite: Undated; written by Ella Schab in the fall of 1941 shortly before the Jewish High Holy Days; she observes with great anguish that this is the fourth year she will recall the happier times once shared by the whole family. Pencil marks were made by the censor.

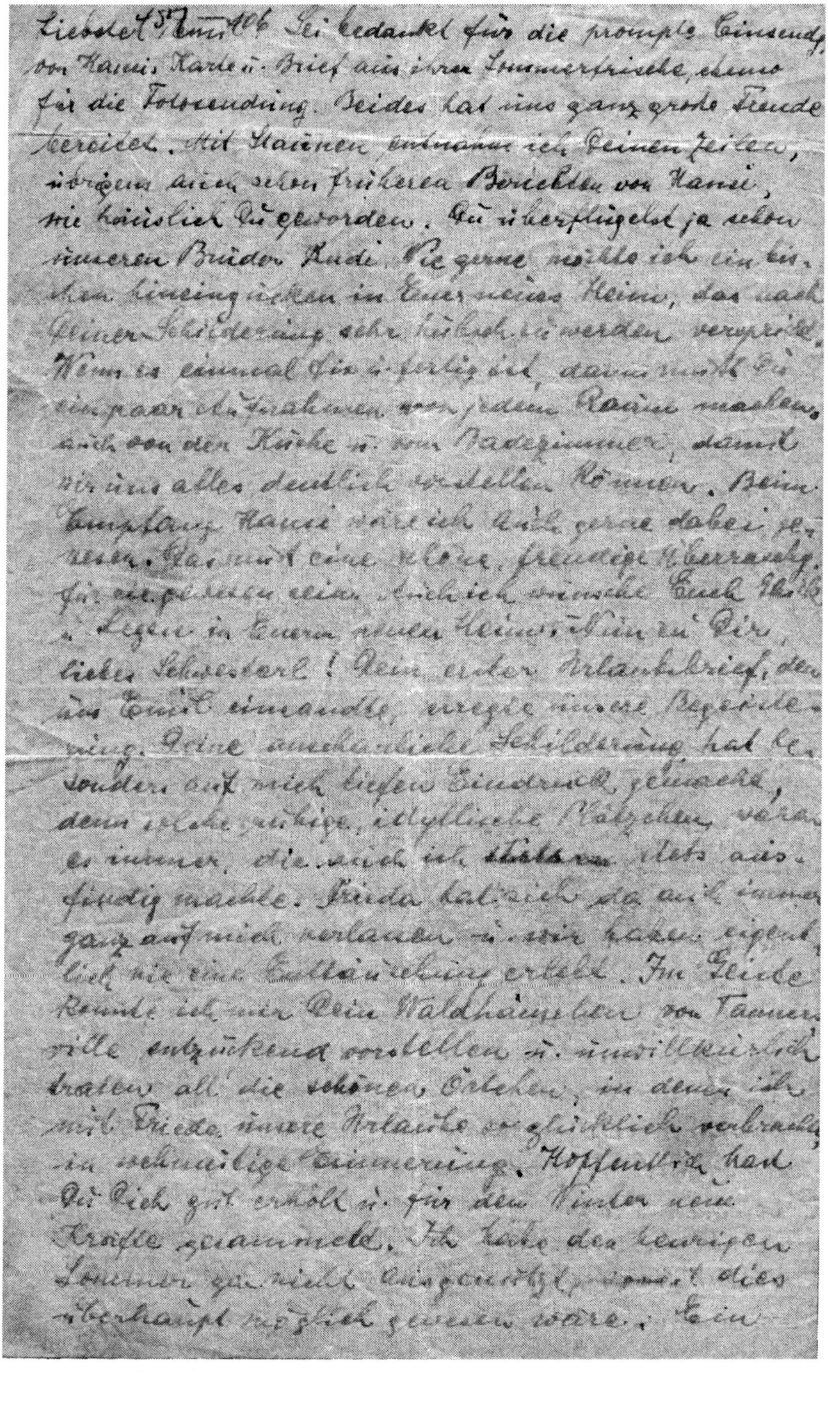

#111

Vienna, August 31st, 1941

My dearest beloved!

Last week, after mailing my letter, I received on Wednesday, the 27th, your letter of the 10th with pictures and 2 return postal coupons. The pictures are wonderful, especially Herbert is sweet and Hansi looks like his sister. We kept one picture and the other one, showing only Hansi, we gave to Mama Schab, because she already has one of H&H and his colleagues. Of course we show these pictures to everyone and enjoy that others also like them a lot. My dearest ones, by now, Stella and Hansi, too must have returned from their vacations, well rested and full of new strength ready to tackle their jobs again and you two poor grass widowers will no longer have to be alone.

There isn't much that is good to report from our side. We're worrying a great deal about the coming winter. After some very hot days it is again quite cool and raining.

This week I had mail from Mama Bock and Elli. Elli is very sad that she hasn't heard anything from Olli and their parents. Mama Bock suffers from the same pains we have except she doesn't have any worries about getting enough food. This week we had some excitement: I received a notice to appear at the Labor office and thought for sure that I'd have to accept some work. Not that I am afraid of work—but what do I do with our poor, old, sick mother? And of course I also have to take care of father who comes home from work at 6P and I have to cook *[?]* a meal *[?]*. Neither am I really all that well, health wise—but thank the Lord, nothing came of it. But grandmother was plenty worried. In my last letter I wrote that as far as our housing is concerned we don't have too much to complain about compared to others. Well, no sooner had I written that, when someone from the KG came and said that we will receive an additional tenant; not into our room but with Hackers and Adler with whom we share the flat. But what can we do, this is not the worst thing that can happen.

Went to see Regine/Dora again, unfortunately Dora's health hasn't improved a bit; she is still lying in bed. The doctor comes daily; she gets injections to bring the fever down. Maybe Hannah could send her some food packages via Lisbon, if that is possible. I am not taking any assistance from W. For the time being I don't need any. If I shall need some maybe Aunt Rosa can give us something.

My dearest ones, in three weeks we shall have our holy days again, the third time without you. You can imagine how sad that makes us. September 1st. Today I expected your weekly report but nothing came. My dear ones, I could write a whole book ... but I cannot. Fare well, you all, be sure you stay healthy, with kisses from your very sad mother, sister, sister-in-law and aunt Marie. Father sends his best regards.

#112

Vienna, September 8th, 1941

My dearest ones, so very much beloved!

Again I can acknowledge two letters that just arrived: one of 16th VIII with Photos of Herbert for Mother Secher and of 20th VIII with Hansi's so very detailed report. I don't know what gives me greater joy, Herbert's little picture with the big W on his sweater, Hansi's report about her summer vacation or Emil's detailed description of your new flat!

It's been a long time that we've had such a wonderful, happy day. The good Lord is to be thanked that He made it possible for you to settle down so quickly in your new home and feel happy and well in the process. May the good Lord continue to reward you with much happiness, health and blessings, to which I add my fervent good wishes in view of the fast approaching Holy Days, which are about the time this letter should reach you. When it arrives Hansi will already be in her new home, just the way Jerta did, who after a summer sojourn always liked to move into a newly finished flat! Hopefully, Hansi has managed to really get some good rest and relaxation. Her description of the area in which she stayed sounds like a fairy tale landscape! I hope you all moved into your new home during an hour of good fortune.

As far as the photos are concerned, I am sure I won't quarrel over them with grandmother Secher; it is after all her birthday and she has the right and privilege to keep them as her presents. But I too, would like to have these pictures, which are extraordinarily good and are admired by everyone. I therefore ask of you to send me: the picture of the three of you, an enlargement of the picture of Hansi with Herbert's three colleagues (I already have the smaller version), also Emil alone, and Herbert with the big W; I possess all the others and I enjoy them immensely when I look at them, sometimes for hours!

Was Hansi satisfied with your work in the flat and how you arranged things? And did all the crates arrive unharmed?

In our last letter we sent you photocopy of the notice from the American consulate, and their acknowledgement of our registration—did you receive this?

In your last letter you ask who took care of us during our illness? The physician was a friend of a neighbor of ours in the next room, a man in advanced years, but nice and confidence inspiring; otherwise we mutually nursed each other backs to health, as far as we were individually able to do that. In any case, Ella carried the larger burden and quite successfully, thanks the good Lord, nursed me back to health so that I have been able to go out and about already since May. Yesterday Ella and I visited grandmother Secher who was very happy over our visit. Grandmother also goes out weather permitting—that weather really changed in the last week becoming very windy, cold and wet. Today, 6th IX, it is again very sunny and a little warmer. Your dear sister Marie also feels a little better and the injections finally appear to take effect; I believe that after she's had all 20 injections, during the break, the effect will become more intensive. It will depend on that whether this treatment needs to be repeated. Your brother-in-law, Emil, carries a heavy burden, but he is the one who is most easily satisfied and he cheers up everyone else.

Please be sure to relay to family Handel/Safirstein my heartiest, most fervent blessings and good wishes for the Holy Days. The good Lord will reward them a thousand times over for all the good things they have done and continue to do for their relatives. Is Dr. Safirstein completely recovered? We greet them all.

Have you by chance any news from the children? If so please send me detailed reports. Unfortunately we have heard nothing from Vickerl. I have written to Wilicek but he doesn't know anything either. He hopes to hear from someone in the near future and will then provide us with a detailed report. Have you written to Irma?

If you meet families Bohrer and Beck, please extend to them too, our best wishes for the Holy Days. For us these are going to be very sad days. How beautiful it used to be when I was expecting you around our richly decorated table!

Nobody will come, indeed cannot come—the distance is too great. Regarding the photographed documents, please don't forget to tell us whether they arrived and whether you've been able to make use of them. Exactly what are your plans in this regard? I shall close now but not without expressing my admiration for Herbert, how well he has developed and how good he is to help his parents in every possible way. This is the way it ought to be! I kiss and hug all of you my dearest loved ones, enjoy the holidays and think of your ever loving, mother and Omi.

#113

Vienna, September 14th, 1941.

My dearest beloved!

On the 10th of this month I received your dear letter of August 25th, with two postal return coupons, in which you, my dear brother, tell us that you have rented a flat all for yourselves, and you can imagine how happy that made us, especially mother. You should live in it with plenty of Mazl! We're especially glad to learn that Otto and Herbert assisted you so well. We cried with joy! The good Lord shall only give you, my dearest ones, health and luck, and everything you undertake should be blessed! Amen! And if only Otto would have his own home soon, I'd be happy, especially if the good Lord would make it possible for us to come to you—in which case my embroidered bed cover, curtains, and other beautiful hand-made things, I shall save for you, Otto and Stella, provided that they let us take it along. I gave a lot away already in anticipation of the P. action, for example the rugs I knit. But in the meantime we got other worries: which means we'll walk about less. On the other hand I didn't go walking much until now either—except to Mama Schab and Regina/Dora. It is getting very cold and sad here. Mother worries me a bit and I went to see Dr. Schnardt again, but he said it isn't anything serious. If only I could give her what she likes so much; you know how little she eats but she does like to nosh. Yesterday Frau Helly dropped by with a peach, a few grapes and some vegetables. My dearest ones you cannot possibly appreciate this! And only the thought that you've been spared this, let's us bear our fate with some equanimity. Dora has not improved, has still fever, that poor Regine! Yesterday when I was there she said a letter from Hannah came who wrote that a small package is under way I am curious what she sends and when it will arrive. I still have some left from your package, a little cacao, tea; the cacao is only for mother. I was very frugal with everything but also shared much. Now we could stand having another one. I'll manage with the money for this month—everything is so expensive; if I need some aunt Rosa will help us out. Please write to uncle Streit—they frequently come to visit mother. Yesterday was Irma's birthday and exactly three years that she has left. You can imagine my mood, my thoughts were with her. I thank you my dear, good Otto that you congratulated her also in our name and sent some money. The good Lord should only repay you, my dearest child.

IX/15

Today came a letter from Benno's brother, Heinrich. He asks that you Otto should write Benno about him—he hasn't heard from his wife in months.

Today it is raining buckets—those are our tears that drop down from the sky; I'll close now, I hug and kiss you, pray only for good things for yourselves, as ever your very sad mother, sister, sister-in-law and aunt Marie.

#114

Vienna, September 15/25th, 1941

My dearest, good children

Many heartiest thanks for your detailed letter, which tells me that you're enjoying this summer vacation, and have found the best way to relaxation. I knew it right away and have told you several times that you mustn't exploit your strength in such a way especially in these difficult times of constantly unexpected excitements. I am convinced that neither of your two men wants you to exhaust yourself in that way. And how do you like the surprise both of them prepared for you?! Dearest Emil—you're surpassing even your brother-in-law Rudi in your achievement; his reputation as a model husband probably really spurred you on; I give you and Herbert my very personal thanks, and am really glad that you now again have your own home. May the good Lord provide you with good luck, blessing and health—these are my wishes too, my dearest ones, for the coming Holy Days. Spend them in happiness and we shall be with you in our thoughts! That all your things arrived in their good, original condition is really wonderful—were you able to actually stow everything away? And is Herbert satisfied with his little room? Maybe the good Lord will be kind enough to enable us to see all this with our very own eyes. I really do not have much hope—but the unexpected also happens sometimes. As long as the Almighty gives us our health, is all I ask!

When you have the time, dear Emil, please do not forget the photos, which I want so very much, they're all so very good, I really want to own them so I can show them around to all our friends and acquaintances and refresh myself on their admiration! You must also urge the Wm. Schabs to send us a few pictures.

Heinrich and Helly visit us quite frequently and they read your letters with great interest, Heinrich sometimes even copies some passages he finds particularly appealing. They are both very sad and have already got used to the idea that leaving here is no longer an option. For your dear relatives, Handels and Safirstein our best wishes for the New Year, and the same for Families Beck and Bohrer, also Dr. Weil should you get together with them.

September 25th, 1941

Well, you can tell by the date how long our letter, i.e., really my letter has been ready for mailing. Ella simply has a hard time finding an opportunity to write. She is very busy, but I suspect that the main reason is her listlessness, even aversion to writing right now. There is simply nothing enjoyable to write about, as much as we'd like to bring you a little variety.

In the meantime there arrived no less three letters from you and they made us very happy! Well, little Hansi what do you say to your model husband and model son—that goes far beyond Rudi and even beyond our long deceased house superintendent, Mr. Smutek whom our father, of blessed memory, always called the "model husband" because in his free time, especially on Sundays, he relieved his wife of all heavy labor in the house. Now everything you have must just be really beautiful! And we are enjoying it together with you! How are you, dear Hansi, going to maintain all this once you start working again? A larger flat demands more work and care, and your two men shall have to do more than their share, I am sure. I can imagine how Emil beams with pride and happiness now that he is again in his own home. It is indeed a masterpiece to achieve this in such a short time, and all of you have contributed to it. Congratulations also to Emil's raise, he certainly deserved it. Just you all stay happy and healthy in your new home.

Now I expect some answers to my questions in my last letter. I believe it'll be better if I draft a regular questionnaire, with those questions to which I must have an answer. I am glad to learn that the photocopies of our documents have finally arrived—I was afraid they'd gone lost. Furthermore I would like to know the following: 1. Have the children written and who? 2. Can I get those photos that I have designated exactly already in my last letter? Have you been together with Schabs recently? They sent us as usual a congratulatory Radiogram.

Did you do anything more about the amount of money that has been deposited at the Joint for the ship tickets? Aunt Irene Stern has upon request by the KG waived her claim to the amount; that money is well taken care of in your own accounts. I hope to learn more about all this very soon. In the meantime, my dearest ones I kiss and hug you most fervently, as ever your mother and Omi.

#115

Vienna, 21st, September 1941

All my dear loved ones!

On Friday—9/19—arrived your dear letter of 9/02 together with Irma's and Heinzi's added lines, plus two reply postal coupons. You can imagine my happiness to have again a sign of life from my loved ones in Palestine. That the boy studies well, gives me great joy and pride, he should only remain healthy and may his life be blessed with luck. But I worry about Irma, suffering so much from these boils, and financially they do not appear to do too well either—all this, I seem to read between their lines. My dear, good Otto, write them they should not save, if they need something they should sell the B. that you sent them from Büttenhart. I am really moved, Otto, by your decision to help defray any costs for the boy's higher education, you my dearest son, who has so much to think about, who has to care for us and who has to work so hard, to make it all possible. The Almighty should bless you and reward you with health and wealth. Did Stella recover completely? Now lets turn to you my dearest brother. That you've been able to rent your own flat pleases us greatly, especially mother. If only we could personally experience wishing you much luck! So now Herbert has his own sleeping space—the poor boy really had to work hard on this. And how did Hansi like it?

Today is Erev Rosh Hashanah. It is really sad here, with us. Last year I thought it couldn't get any worse and still it got worse. I think often of you Otto, how you said in past years when I complained, you know our life was never a bed of roses, "Don't worry, Mama, it'll get worse yet!" Only hope helps me to keep my sanity. Father will have to work on the Holy Days. We received a postcard from the KG this week—it's about the ship tickets, I believe. We shall have to sign here so that you can get your money back there. It is a pity that this money should lie around at the JOINT when we cannot leave right now. I get often mail from Benno's brother and sister; they are so grateful that I write them about their loved ones—I am the only one who writes to them. Only his brother Heinrich wants to know more about Benno—he should write to him directly.

Dearest Emil, do you remember, this used to be mother's best-loved Holy Day; she got dressed up and went to the Temple. Right now she is being very good; but she is so weak, because I cannot give her what she would like so much. You write that Fall arrives in your city with a cornucopia of different fruits—does that really still exist? To me it is like a fairy tale! We're looking forward to the care package, let's hope it'll arrive soon.

Today is again a beautiful day. I shall have to heat, nevertheless, because grandmother is already cold. Father has put up the little stove—if only we can get enough coal.

09/22

Yesterday I dropped by at Mama Schab and Ella. Mama Schab is in good health, but our mother worries me. It's not that she is really sick—but her heart is no longer functioning the way it should; but I hope she'll recover again.

Today I'll drop by at Regina/Dora. It is such a wonderfully beautiful day today. The rest of the New Year should only stay like that! My dearest ones, I wish you from the bottom of my heart that you should be able to pray for only the best things in your life, and remain your deeply saddened mother, sister, sister-in-law and aunt Marie.

Father, too sends his best wishes for this coming year.

I am short of money again and will borrow from aunt Rosa.

#116

Vienna, September 28th, 1941

My loved ones, my dearest!

My dearest brother we have only one subject of conversation right now: your new, beautiful flat! The good Lord should only be merciful to make it possible for us to be with you and see everything with our own eyes. Unfortunately mother isn't doing too well but there is no cause for alarm. She's just very weak. Dr. Schnardt comes quite frequently. This week is Yom Kippur and that makes me especially sad. That's when I have to think of you and all my loved ones. Still, I shall not quarrel with our fate, because you my beloved have been spared a lot and for that I shall be forever grateful to the Lord! I wrote you in my last letter that we received a postcard from the KG concerning the ship tickets and of course we signed. Why should that money stay dead at the Joint? We know very well that when our time comes we shall be able to leave you will again provide that money.

I am so glad that Hansi likes everything the way you dear Emil, had arranged it. And we're especially glad about your raise. The good Lord should only continue to bless and keep you healthy. How is dear Stella? Has she gotten over her cold? How is her business doing? And you my dear Otto are working a lot of overtime. Please take good are of yourself so that your throat doesn't become irritated again. Today is father's birthday—I wanted to prepare something better for his meal—but it just is not possible. Right now he is at another family's house playing cards; grandmother sleeps and I am writing—my thoughts are with you and without even trying my eyes are getting moist.

We've had a few nice days—but now it is cool again. I have to heat a little bit to take the chill off—Father brings some wood and that is what I use for heating. Yesterday I visited with Ella and Mama Schab. They've both recovered pretty good. Mama Schab actually wanted to walk alone to our place yesterday! I am really glad over that—last winter she suffered a great deal. That poor Dora cannot get well—always fever, it is terrible! I am going to her today for a little while. I cannot go out very often either because I cannot leave grandmother alone. The Streits and Bojnitzer come visit us very often. Can you remit something to us again? Or should I borrow some money from aunt Rosa Streit? But now I want to close; just you stay well and pray for something good for yourselves and for us! I kiss you all, your mother and sister, sister-in-law and aunt Marie. Rest regards also from father. 100,000 kisses from your grandmother, also for all the dear relatives.

For all our relatives there: All the best in the New Year.

#117

Vienna, 15 October 1941.

All my dearest loved ones!

I waited expectantly for your weekly report but so far there is nothing, other than the Radiogram which arrived promptly today. Well, mother is doing much better again; she actually walks about in our room and takes part in our doings. Dr. Schnardt comes once a week to give her an injection. But we also had other tsores. It's that P. *[Poland]* Action again. You can imagine our anxiety and fear every morning when we await the mail—and what a sigh of relief when it does not bring us that dreaded order. Rumor is that there is a pause for now. Would God it only were true! But my dearest ones, whatever happens, do not worry about us, we are prepared for anything, the Lord is everywhere. No matter, we shall continue to hope that we'll be spared. A large number of our friends and acquaintances have already been affected. Even Mrs. Weissberg has to go on the 28th of this month. And believe me what really hurt: Rosa came to us to return your letter that I brought to Mama Schab last week and she said the Becks *[Heinrich & Helly]* also received their orders. I am devastated; I'll go over to Ella even now to find out any details. Doesn't the Lord have any pity with us people?! Please do not send us any money now. I borrowed from Uncle Str. as well as from Herta RM 55.00. Send him the money when it is convenient for you. My dearest, my good people, do not worry about us whatever may happen. Father is working and content. Today we also received a response from Elli to our letter, which I sent her for the Holy Days. She knows nothing about their parents *[last in Riga, Latvia]* and Olly *[England]* also has no news. Otto, my dearest son, do not write Irma anything about our troubles, why worry them when there is nothing they can do to help. Now I shall close for today. Farewell, all my dearest, beloved ones, I embrace you, and kiss you a thousand times, your very downcast mother, sister, sister-in-law and aunt Marie. Father also sends his warmest regards. Postscript from Grandmother Secher: Best regards from mother and Grandmother; a 1000 kisses to all our dear relatives. For you my dearest H. special greetings and kisses. I embrace you, Secher.

#118

Vienna, October 25th, 1941

All my dear and beloved ones!

Your letter took a little longer this time but we're happy that everyone is in good health and that everything else is all right, too. A letter like that from you, in these sad and bleak times brings us the only moment of light. Hopefully you've received all my letters by now—Mother is feeling a little better again. Until now we've been spared having to depart this country, hopefully this stays that way! But many of our acquaintances have had to leave. Becks and Ms. Weissberg are still here. It is already very cold and we have to heat. Dearest Emil, it is now two years that you are gone from us. How much everything has changed. Oh, how happy we are that you are there—can work and live in peace. You write we should not be offended that you withdrew again the ship ticket money from the JOINT. We're glad you did that, we know, if there is a possibility you're going to use that money again for us. Also, my dear ones, you need not send any money right now. But when Ms. Weisberg gets to Poland, please assist her, she is such a poor soul! The food packages for Regine did arrive but it took so long! My dearest ones, if we only knew that we'd remain here, we would have you send some. If only we had this winter behind us and could remain in good health.

Now I'd rather hear more good things about you. That you my dearest Otto have been able to improve your position in the factory is good to hear, only now you'll have to work even harder in order to make more money. Got a very nice letter from Mama Bock, she writes that she is in touch with all her loved ones, even Harry, which makes me very happy. Well my dearest, good Emil, your flat is almost completely furnished and decorated, how I'd love to see this with my own eyes—are we ever going to be able to see this? Your letters are so sweet and interesting, also those from our dear Herbert. Please forgive me if I do not write you more often, what I want to tell you I cannot—I am simply not in a condition to write a great deal. But the most important thing is that we have good news from you. My dearest sweet Otto, take good care of yourself, protect your throat, you know how sensitive you are and how you suffered in the spring. I would like to hear again something about Irma. October 27th—Thought there might be some mail from you—but I was wrong! I am closing for now, fare well all of you—I embrace you and kiss you as ever your mother, sister, sister-in-law and aunt Marie

Regards from father and greetings from grandmother: "1000s of kisses, hugs, etc."

#119

Vienna, November 9th, 1941

My dearest ones,

Some mail from you ought to be due again, and we're waiting anxiously for it to arrive. I have acknowledged your letters of Sept. 30th and also of October 6th. This past Friday, November 7th, I received a Red Cross letter from Irma that had been mailed on May 29th, of course it is out of date, thanks to your letters that have kept us in formed about events there, nevertheless, I filled out the reply form of the Red Cross letter. Mother is feeling fairly well, she is getting her injections now only once every two weeks. She is in good spirits and even Dr. Schnardt is satisfied with her condition. If only there wouldn't be the nagging fear that we shall

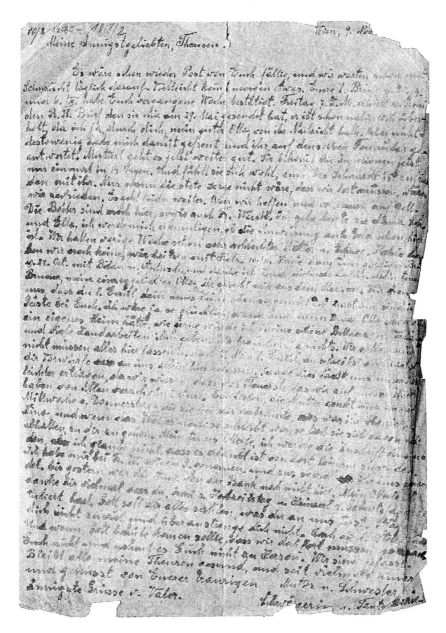

Date: Vienna, 9 November 1941; Marie Kupler writes "And if, God forbid, we shall indeed be forced to leave, please do not worry about us and let it depress you. We are calm and prepared to face the worst."

be sent away; unfortunately that continues. But we are keeping up our hopes and continue to trust in God. The Beck family is still here, as is Ms. Weissberg. I'll drop by at Mama Schab and Ella today to find out whether the money from the bank has arrived. The weather has worsened considerably and we now have snow. We no longer can get coal and have to burn wood.

November 11th

Today came your wonderful, lovely letter of October 22nd with pictures and return postage coupons for which I am ever so grateful. Emil, my dearest brother, Otto, my beloved son, you are speaking to me from the depth of my heart. We are so happy that you, Emil, have been able to furnish your new abode comfortably and we are with you in spirit. I would be ever so happy if my beloved Otto too, would soon be settled in his own flat. Only too gladly would I give him my beautiful bedspread, the curtains and much other hand-made embroidery. We certainly don't use and need them anymore. We just don't want to leave it all here for others if we are sent away. My dearest Emil, you continue to blame yourself—for leaving us here all by ourselves. But it is precisely that decision which now enables us to bear our fate more easily, knowing that the most precious people we have in this world, have been spared all this. My dearest Emil, it is still mother's greatest pleasure to think back on those weekly Wednesdays or Thursdays she spent at your home—that was her greatest joy, her amusement, it took the place of theater, movies; no matter how bad the weather she could not be discouraged from making this trip via trolley or considerable walking. I have again borrowed some money from Ms. Weissberg but only the exact same amount you are sending us; until today the transfer from the bank has not arrived. Dearest Otto, thank you for sending congratulations also in our name for Irma's wedding anniversary and Heinzi's birthday. May God reward you for everything you're doing for us. Do not work too hard, do not over extend yourself and endanger your health—the same goes for Stella. And if, God forbid, we shall indeed be forced to leave, do not worry about us and let it depress you. We are calm and prepared to face the worst. Please, my dearest ones, take good care of yourselves, watch your health, we hug and kiss you many, many times, as ever your sorrowful mother, sister, sister-in-law and aunt Marie.

[The correspondence from Vienna ends here.]

Chronology of Nazi Persecution of Jews 1938–1945, with References to the Schab and Secher Families

1938

March 12/13, 1938—Nazi troops enter Austria, a country of ca. 7 million inhabitants, of whom less than 200,000 are Jewish, most of whom live in Vienna. Hitler arrives in Vienna declaring the Anschluss completed and Austria part of the Greater German Reich, renamed Ostmark. Almost overnight Nazis impose the full range of anti–Semitic laws developed over the past five years in Germany proper. Jews technically become outcasts who can no longer appeal to the police for protection against the taunting and harassment by their neighbors or the uniformed troops of the SA, SS and HJ. Austrian Jews are immediately made aware that their existence in Nazi Germany is no longer feasible and everyone looks for a way out.

Irma Gutter (née Kupler) and her husband Benno board a raft on the Danube in Vienna floating down to the Black Sea. There they board an illegal transport that takes them and son Heinzi to Palestine.

April 22, 1938—The Nazi authorities, in order to impress upon the Jews that their presence is no longer desired, establish the Office for Jewish Emigration.

Rudi Schab, together with his wife Jerta and son Otto, also takes the dangerous way out by floating down the Danube on a raft and boarding a leaky steamer that illegally delivers them to the coast of Palestine.

April 26, 1938—The decree on the reporting of Jewish assets is enacted into law.

Willy Schab, his wife Ada and children Frances and Frederick decide to escape quickly to Switzerland, leaving all of their property and personal belongings behind. Although the parents had to separate from the children to pursue separate routes, they successfully cross the border and hope that they will now be able to await the quota number assignment required by the U.S. immigration process.

June 14, 1938—Nazis order Jewish businesses to register prior to turning them over to Aryan claimants.

July 6, 1938—Nazis prohibit Jews from trading and engaging in a variety of specified commercial services. Vienna's Jews begin to queue up by the thousands at the U.S. Consulate with the intent of obtaining registration numbers, the first step toward qualifying for U.S. visas. They learn that it will take from 12 to 18 months for their turn on the German quota.
Otto Kupler and bride Stella escape into Switzerland, where they are interned awaiting quota assignment toward immigration to the U.S.

July 22/September 30, 1938—All Jews over 15 must carry identity cards to be shown on demand to any police officer. Jewish physicians lose their license to practice on anyone except Jewish patients. All streets named after Jews are renamed. All Jewish women must add "Sara," and Jewish men "Israel" on all legal documents.

September 29/30, 1938—At a conference in Munich, Prime Minister Chamberlain and Premier Daladier of France agree to let Hitler annex the Sudetenland portion of Czechoslovakia in order to protect ethnic Germans residing in that region; this will bring "peace in our time," explains Chamberlain.

October 5, 1938—All passports owned by Jews must be stamped with a large letter "J" in red ink.

October 28, 1938—Ca. 17,000 Jews born in Poland but residing in Germany are deported to the frontiers town of Zbaszyn, where they are denied entry. Unfed and unsheltered they languish in the no-man's-land between the two borders. In the group are the parents of one Herschel Grynspan, then living in Paris.

November 7, 1938—Hershel Grynspan enters the grounds of the German Embassy in Paris and assassinates the first and only official he encounters, Ernst von Rath, a Third Consular Secretary.

November 9/10, 1938—Kristallnacht—The Night of Broken Glass. Organized, uniformed troops of the SA and HJ are commanded to attack thousands of Jewish-owned businesses, homes and synagogues; they are looted and destroyed at will with at least 90 deaths and many injuries among the Jewish population across Germany. This action was presented as "the voluntary and spontaneous outpouring of public indignation" over the Jewish intrigues that led to the murder of von Rath. Over 26,000 Jews were arrested and sent to the KZ (concentration camps) at Dachau, Buchenwald and Sachsenhausen, with their release contingent upon the surrender of all property and wealth prior to immediate emigration.

November 12/28, 1938—In the wake of the November pogrom known as Kristallnacht, a variety of decrees and laws went into effect for the express purpose of the total Aryanization of the German economy; all were designed to remove Jews from commercial and industrial enterprises, making it impossible for them to maintain a social existence and forcing them to emigrate. The question was where. An international conference had taken place in the summer of that year in Evian, France, for the purpose of finding a solution to the Jewish immigration problem. No country was willing to take the first step, including the U.S., which was represented by President Roosevelt. Each nation wanted the other ones to take on the burden. The conference ended with no plan and thus no hope having emerged for the Jews of Europe under Nazi domination. Among the measures put into force in Germany under penalty of the law were the following:
Surrender of all precious metals to the government.
Reduction and/or elimination of all civil & military pensions to Jews.
All intangible properties, including art, could be sold only to the government.
Jews must live in segregated residential areas.
Jews could no longer keep or obtain driver's licenses.
All radios owned by Jews were to be confiscated.
Tenant protection laws no longer applied to Jews.

December 3, 1938—*Law for the Compulsory Aryanization of All Jewish Businesses* was passed. These businesses could either be shut down or signed over to Aryan (German) citizens. The former owners received little or no compensation—if the former, hardly a fraction of the asset's real worth. Any Jewish employees were simply fired.

December 8, 1938—All Jews were formally expelled from German universities.

December 14, 1938—Herman Göring takes charge of resolving the "Jewish problem."

1939

January 30, 1939—Hitler, in his anniversary speech marking his accession to chancellor in 1933, threatens the annihilation of the Jews in the event of war.
Willy Schab, wife Ada with children Frances and Frederick relocate from Switzerland to England, still waiting for their U.S. visas.

February 21, 1939—Nazis force Jews to hand over all gold and silver.
Hannah Witton (née Schab), completes immigration to Sydney, Australia, where husband Emil (Mümmel) has already preceded her. Her parents Victor and Hedwig Schab decide to relocate to Riga, Latvia, where they would wait out their turn

on the immigration quota to the U.S. Later that spring Felix Schab, youngest of
the Schab siblings, escapes to Belgium, then France, where he joins his brother
Ernst, Ernst's wife Melanie, and their daughter Lisl. Ernst and Felix start plan-
ning for their immigration to Australia.

March 15, 1939—Hitler's military completes the occupation of Czechoslovakia
and creates the "Protectorate of Bohemia and Moravia."

April 30, 1939—The removal of Jewish families into Jewish apartment houses,
where they must share limited space with other Jewish families, begins.

August 12, 1939—Hitler and Stalin sign non-aggression treaty, leaving Hitler
with a free hand in Eastern Europe.

September 1, 1939—Nazis invade Poland on the pretext of alleged mistreatment
of ethnic Germans by Poles. This was revealed later as a monumental, carefully
prepared hoax by the Nazis.
  Emil Secher and family receive notification from U.S. Consulate to appear on
  October 10 for medical examination and subsequent issuance of immigration visas.

September 3, 1939—Great Britain and France declare war on Germany.
  Willy Schab and family find themselves on the high seas just as the war begins,
  on their way to America. Shortly thereafter Ernst Schab with family and brother
  Felix embark for Australia from a French seaport.

September 17, 1939—As part of a secret protocol on signing the non-aggression pact, the Soviet Army invades and occupies the eastern part of adjoining
Poland as the Polish army collapses.

September 23, 1939—Jews in Germany are forbidden to own radios.

September 27, 1939—Warsaw surrenders to German armed forces.

October 6, 1939—Proclamation by Hitler on isolating Jews and their eventual
resettlement in designated areas in Poland.

October 10, 1939—Establishment of the Government General in the eastern
portion of Nazi occupied Poland and the annexation to Germany of its western
half (formerly Silesia).
  The Secher family appear at the U.S. Consulate and after successfully passing the
  medical exam are issued American immigration visas. They now begin their search
  for financing of the passage via an Italian line.

October 12, 1939—Concrete plans are initiated to begin the deportation of Jews
from Vienna, ostensibly in order to "resettle" them in certain designated areas of

the Government General in Poland. An SS officer by the name of Eichmann is put in charge of this project.

Emil Secher almost immediately receives instructions to report with his wife and son and a minimum of luggage at the Northern RR Terminal for resettlement in the East. Only the U.S. immigration visas already stamped in their passports saves them from having to follow this order.

They are able to satisfy the financial requirements necessary for the ocean passage thanks to aid from their relatives in the U.S. (both Willy Schab, Hansi's brother, and Herman Handel, a second cousin of Emil in New Jersey). They are scheduled to embark on November 1 from the Italian port Triest on the cruise liner SS *Saturnia. They arrive in New York on November 17.*

November 14, 1939 — New curfew restriction prohibit Jews in Vienna from using streets after 4:00PM.

November 23, 1939 — In Poland all Jews over the age of 10 are required to wear a yellow Star of David.

1940

January 25, 1940 — The town of Oswiecim (Auschwitz) in Poland, not far from Cracow, is selected as the site of a new concentration camp.

Emil and Marie Kupler, together with Grandmother Secher, are evicted from their comfortable home in the Vereinsgasse, Vienna II and move to one room in an apartment house in the Lessinggasse, also Vienna II. During the move Grandmother Secher stays with Omi Schab and Ella.

February 12, 1940 — Deportation of German Jews into already established ghettos in Polish cities begins.

April 9, 1940 — Nazis invade Denmark and Norway, and in the same month Greece and Yugoslavia.

May 10, 1940 — Nazis invade France, Belgium, Holland and Luxembourg.

During this month, Ella Schab and her mother are evicted from their comfortable quarters in the Taborstrasse and move in with a Jewish lady somewhere on the same street.

June 22, 1940 — France signs armistice with Hitler; Paris falls and becomes part of occupied France. Non-occupied France retains Vichy as its capital with General Petain as head of government. Italy now enters the war on Hitler's side.

July 17, 1940 — The first anti-Jewish measures are taken in Vichy France, including denial of citizenship to naturalized Jewish French citizens.

For Ella and her mother, Regina Schab, now hopefully close to being granted

American visas, these events foreclose departure through either Atlantic or Mediterranean ports assuming a visa is actually forthcoming. The closure of the U.S. consulates for weeks, allegedly to catch up with the "backlog" of immigration business, makes this a very doubtful expectation.

September 27, 1940—The Tri-partite (Axis) Pact is signed by Germany, Italy and Japan.

October 3, 1940—Vichy France passes its own version of the anti–Jewish Nuremberg Laws.

In November 1940, Ella and her mother are required to leave the quarters they had moved to earlier that year because that street was no longer part of the Jewish section reserved for Jews only. After an exhausting search in the depths of winter they finally settle in a tiny room in the Hochedlingerstrasse—the room serves also as a passageway for others who share that apartment.

1941

Throughout this year in Germany various repressive measures with criminal penalties against Jews take effect, e.g.: Using public transportation; keeping pets; using barber/beauty shop services; owning typewriters; owning electric appliances; keeping fur coats and woolen clothing.

March 7, 1941—German Jews become part of the local and national forced labor pool.

Emil Kupler starts work, not further identified, somewhere in Vienna; his wife Marie fears that she too may be called up and would have to leave Grandmother Secher alone; fortunately this fear never materializes.

May 15, 1941—French Jews are sent to "labor camps" by the Vichy government.

June 13, 1941—Vichy government alleges Jewish interference with Franco-German relations and deports 13,000 Jews to concentration camps.

June 22, 1941—Germany invades the Soviet Union.

U.S. State Department issues revised rules for immigration relevant to European Jews only, effective July 1. Their significance lies in the nullification of all applications for immigration, requiring anew the filling out of lengthy and complicated visa immigration forms. This applies immediately to Ella Schab and her mother Regina Schab. It postpones immigration indefinitely, aggravated by the lack of feasible exit ports from Europe.

July 1941—During this month the German armies advance toward Moscow. The SS *Einsatztruppen* follow in their wake and conduct mass murder of Jews, aided enthusiastically by citizens in the Ukraine and the Baltic countries.

September 1, 1941—Jews in Germany are ordered to wear the yellow star at all times.

September 3, 1941—Experiments are conducted by the SS with Zyklon-B gas on 850 prisoners at the KZ Auschwitz. Approximately 600 are reported to be Russian prisoners of war. The experiment is judged a success.

September 6, 1941—As of this date all Jews over the age of 6 must wear a yellow star on which is superscribed the word "Jew" (*Jude*). Also, Jews will no longer be able to wander out of their immediate residential area without permission by the police.

September 17, 1941—Progress is reported of general deportation of Jews to the ghettos of the occupied areas of Poland.

September 23, 1941—More experiments with Zyklon-B gas are conducted on Jews at Auschwitz.

October 14, 1941—Direct deportation of Jews to specific concentration camps as laborers begins in Germany.

October 23, 1941—Emigration of Jews from the Greater German Reich is now prohibited.
> *November 9, 1941—In Vienna Marie Kupler mails the last letter to reach her brother Emil in New York.*

November 24, 1941—The so-called model ghetto at Theresienstadt (Terezin) is established in Czechoslovakia; chiefly older people are transported there and its existence is used for propaganda purposes when the Red Cross visits.

November 30, 1941—Continuing mass executions in Riga, Latvia, of Latvian and German Jews carried out by the SS *Einsatztruppen* and the members of the Latvian *Ordnungspolizei*. Between 25,000 and 27,000 Jews are murdered in one day.
> *Among those killed are Victor and Hedwig Schab, as well as Adolph and Malvine Epstein, parents of Ollie Epstein (later Donat), Emil Secher's niece, whom he was able to welcome from England upon her arrival in New York after the war.*

December 7, 1941—Japanese attack the United States at Pearl Harbor. The following day the U.S. and Great Britain declare war on Japan.

December 8, 1941—Continued "*Aktion*" at or near Riga, Latvia, resulting in the shooting death of thousands more Jews. A small Jewish contingent remaining in the original Riga ghetto apparently is not included in this operation.

December 11, 1941—Hitler declares war on the U.S. which in turn does so on Germany. This ends the uneasy neutrality of the U.S. government vis-à-vis the Hitler government. All mail or telegraph contact with Germany stops.
Emil Secher's last letter to his loved ones in Vienna remains unmailed—they have truly been left behind.

1942

January 11, 1942—Wannsee Conference determines the "Final Solution" to the "Jewish problem," which at this stage means primarily the continued overcrowding in the ghettos in Poland and other areas in Germany proper, mainly cities, including Vienna. Very soon after that conference, mass killings of Jews begin in Auschwitz-Birkenau using the now perfected method of gassing with Zyklon-B. Himmler later orders the exhumation of bodies from mass graves and their cremation in open pits in order to conceal the evidence of this mass murder.

April 20, 1942—German Jews are banned from using public transportation, most likely as a gesture to make the Führer feel good on this day, his birthday.

June 1942—More gas vans are brought to Riga to accelerate the pace of mass murder.

July 2, 1942—Jews from Berlin and Vienna are transported to KZ Theresienstadt.
Among these Jews is Regina "Omi" Schab who arrives there on July 11, 1942. She dies on July 26 at age 82. Nothing is known of the fate of Ella Schab, who presumably was deported directly to Auschwitz and killed there.

September 18, 1942—Further reduction in food rations for Jews remaining in Germany.

September 26, 1942—Any valuables found in the possession of Jews deported to Auschwitz or Majdanek are collected and turned into cash by the SS. German banknotes are sent to the Reichsbank. Diamonds, jewelry and other valuables are sent to the SS Headquarters of the Economic Administration. Watches, clothes and pens are distributed to troops at the front. Clothing is distributed to German families. By February 1943, over 800 boxcars of confiscated goods will have left Auschwitz.

October 5, 1942—Himmler orders all Jews in KZs located within Germany proper to be sent to Auschwitz and Majdanek.

October 28, 1942—The first transport of Jews, mostly old and handicapped, is sent from Theresienstadt to Auschwitz for "disposal."

December 10, 1942—The first transport of Jews from Germany arrives directly at Auschwitz.

1943

May 19, 1943—Nazis declare Berlin to be cleansed of all Jews: *Berlin ist judenrein.*

September 11, 1943—Beginning of entire families being transported together from Theresienstadt to Auschwitz.

November 1943—The Riga ghetto is finally liquidated. Whoever did not perish in the previous *Aktions* certainly did not survive this one, and among the victims are Victor and Hedwig Schab. No trace or record of their final demise has ever been located.

December 2, 1943—The first direct transport of Jews from Vienna to Auschwitz arrives there.
> *Should Ella Schab, Emil and Marie Kupler have survived till this date, having avoided death from illness, maltreatment, starvation and/or violence, then on this date their fate was sealed. From then on any remaining Jews in Vienna were transported directly to Auschwitz-Birkenau where few, poor or no records were kept of these arrivals. Only Regina Schab's deportation to Theresienstadt is recorded with her arrival and death dates. Post-war contacts with others, non–Jews living in Vienna, confirmed these deportations for "special treatment." Thus the precise dates of death, or their immediate causes remain forever unknown—what is known is that they did not survive.*

1944

June 6, 1944—Allies land at Normandy. During this month a Red Cross delegation visits Theresienstadt after the Nazis have carefully prepared the camp and its remaining Jewish inmates; the expected result is a favorable report.

October 28, 1944—The last transport of Jews to be gassed arrives at Auschwitz—2000 are from Theresienstadt.

October 30, 1944—The gas chambers are used for the last time: Himmler orders their destruction and that of the crematoria.

1945

January, 1945—Soviet forces liberate Auschwitz-KZ

May 2, 1945—Theresienstadt is taken over by the Red Cross.

May 7, 1945—Unconditional German surrender marks the end of the war in Europe.

June 15, 1945—H. Pierre Secher becomes a U.S. citizen in Madison, Wisconsin. His parents, Emil and Jean (Hansi) Secher were sworn in as U.S. citizens in New York earlier, in March 1945.

Index

Page numbers in *italics* have photographs.